THE COMPLETE BOOK OF SPELLS, CURSES, AND MAGICAL RECIPES

SOME OF THE OTHER BOOKS BY LEONARD R. N. ASHLEY

The Complete Book of the Devil's Disciples
The Complete Book of Devils and Demons
The Complete Book of Magic and Witchcraft
The Complete Book of Superstition, Prophecy, and Luck
What's in a Name?
Elizabethan Popular Culture
Colley Cibber
George Peele: The Man and His Work
Ripley's "Believe It Or Not" Book of The Military
Authorship and Evidence in Renaissance Drama
The Air Defence of North America (NORAD)
Nineteenth-Century British Drama
Mirrors for Man: 26 Plays of World Drama
The History of the Short Story
Other People's Lives
Tales of Mystery and Melodrama

editor

Phantasms of the Living
Reliques of Irish Poetry
The Ballad Poetry of Ireland
Shakespeare's Jest Book
Soohrab and Rustum
A Narrative of the Life of Mrs. Charlotte Charke

co-editor

British Short Stories: Classics and Criticism
Geolinguistic Perspectives
Language in Contemporary Society
Constructed Languages and Language Construction
Geolinguistics 1997

THE COMPLETE BOOK OF
SPELLS, CURSES, AND
MAGICAL RECIPES

DR. LEONARD R. N. ASHLEY

SKYHORSE PUBLISHING

Skyhorse Publishing books may be purchased in bulk at special discounts for sales promotion, corporate gifts, fund-raising, or educational purposes. Special editions can also be created to specifications. For details, contact the Special Sales Department, Skyhorse Publishing, 307 West 36th Street, 11th Floor, New York, NY 10018 or info@skyhorsepublishing.com.

Skyhorse® and Skyhorse Publishing® are registered trademarks of Skyhorse Publishing, Inc.®, a Delaware corporation.

Visit our website at www.skyhorsepublishing.com.

10 9 8 7 6 5 4

Library of Congress Cataloging-in-Publication Data

Ashley, Leonard R. N.
  The complete book of spells, curses, and magical recipes / Leonard R.N. Ashley.
      p. cm.
  ISBN 978-1-61608-098-3 (pbk. : alk. paper)
  1. Incantations. 2. Blessing and cursing. 3. Recipes. 4. Magic. I. Title.
  BF1558.A74 2010
  133.4'4--dc22

                              2010018377

Printed in the United States of America

FOR MARK

How blessed are we to live in a more charitable and
enlightened age, to enjoy the comforts and and conveniences
of modern times, and to realize that the world is continually
growing wiser and better.—Phineas T. Barnum (1810–1891)

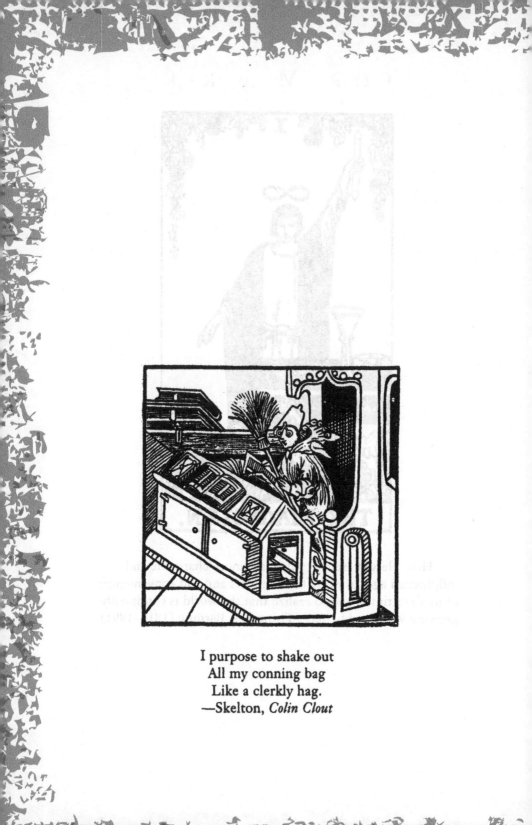

I purpose to shake out
All my conning bag
Like a clerkly hag.
—Skelton, *Colin Clout*

Table of Contents

READ THIS FIRST...9

CHAPTER ONE
SPELLS AND CHARMS 13

CHAPTER TWO
CURSES AND ILL INTENT 63

CHAPTER THREE
PROTECTIONS AND CURES..109

CHAPTER FOUR
MORE WONDERFUL THINGS...167

CHAPTER FIVE
MORE MAGICAL RECIPES...209

CHAPTER SIX
RITUALS AND CEREMONIES..239

CHAPTER SEVEN
LITERATURE AND FOLKLORE 319

Necromancy. Edward Kelley and (probably) Paul Waring stand in a magic circle and raise a spirit from the tomb at Walton Le Dale (Lancs.).

Read This First

Although I know that it is received opinion that readers seldom or never read the author's preface to a book, I want to begin with an introduction. It can position *The Complete Book of Spells, Curses, and Magical Recipes*. It can put it in context. I am told that the books that constitute the series of which the present volume is the latest sell themselves because the curious person, picking up the paperback because of the title, dips in at random and within a page or two is able to find a brief piece which, complete in itself, both stimulates and rewards attention. Enjoying a first taste, the browser may flip to one or more other pages. If those pages prove equally interesting, she or he may think, "This is the kind of book I'll find entertaining and informative, and I want to take it home and curl up with it. I want to read more and think more about what I read."

I invite you to dip into the rest of this book more or less at random and see if the reader-friendly, generally undogmatic, rather undemanding style appeals to you. I invite you to see if you agree with me the complex concepts can be broken up into assimilable bytes. But please, don't do that yet, now that you have glanced here first. Hear me out. I promise that this introduction will be short and worth your time.

Here I can take a moment to explain what the series as a whole means to do and how it is structured. It began it with my book reprinted under the title *The Complete Book of Superstition, Prophecy, and Luck*. That book presented a variety of illustrations, in lively words and pictures, of the persistence of folk belief regarding the supernatural. It made the point that the superstitions of the modern age are clearly the inheritance of an age-old "religion of the ignorant." It stressed the fact that the human mind has a penchant, if not a capacity, for making sense of the puzzling; that it prefers patterns; that, confronted by the baffling, it makes up an explanation if it cannot discern one. Voltaire, the book notes, denounced superstition as a monster that Enlightenment ought to crush. His more practical friend, Frederick the Great, assured Voltaire that superstition was as old as mankind, and just as unlikely to be demolished.

Those who believe in superstition and marvel at fancies are one group. Those who take the bull by the horns and determine to do something about

9

it are another. They are the subject of the second book in the series, reprinted under the title *The Complete Book of Magic and Witchcraft*. Witchcraft boldly—if dangerously—undertakes by force of will to bend even the supernatural to people's own ends. "Do what you will, as long as you harm none." That's their motto. The motley crew attracted to the black arts constitutes a fascinating collection.

In the third book—and each volume can be read as a single entity, though they add up to something more than the sum of the parts—I deal with the problem of evil. *The Complete Book of Devils and Demons* gets more psychological—or theological—and with (it is hoped) more clarity than is usual in these areas of discussion it attempts to explain precisely how in the Judeo-Christian culture and in all other cultures around the world, in the past and in the present, mankind has personified The Adversary and attributed to forces outside of humanity all the evil everywhere apparent in the world, all destruction, disease, and death. This book is more philosophical and more erudite than the others in the series. It is packed with sensational history and rich in bibliographical resources for students who wish to delve deeper into the history of demonology and the demonizing of individuals.

In the next volume in the series, *The Complete Book of The Devil's Disciples*, we go into greater depth about the dark motives and vengeful persecution of those who are thought to be servants and dupes of the Enemy of Mankind, those rebellious outsiders who strive to manipulate evil forces for their private ends: the witches, the magicians, the sorcerers, the necromancers, the Satanists. There is something, of course, about white witches, but all witches have traditionally been regarded as beyond the pale, frightening, and have been hunted down and destroyed if possible. The history of the Devil's disciples is written in blood and fire. Once again the subject is gripping, and there are numerous guides to further investigation of the subjects in life and literature.

In the present volume, *The Complete Book of Spells, Curses, and Magical Recipes*, we arrive at what some have been seeking all along: the answer to "Exactly what do they do?" or even "Precisely what can I do?" Now there are still numerous colorful characters and startling histories but one no longer has to search widely in *grimoires*—books of magic. I have done that for you. Here are the DIY (Do It Yourself) instructions. The directions given, you proceed at your own risk, because now we are more than ever in what a student of Madame Blavatsky succinctly ticked off as "the neurotic, the hysterical, the destructive, and the downright mad." However, you are not compelled to risk your sanity or your soul. You can just read about magic. I do not advise you to try it.

If readers enjoy this book as much as they have enjoyed the others, I may write more, but this is the end of my original plan. We have moved from the vague recognition of the possible existence of a realm above and beyond the normal, but interpenetrating quotidian life, to the history and philosophy of demonology, to the exercise of magic. Not the magic of stage conjurers, not sleight of hand, but the metamorphosis of reality (or the connection to a higher level of reality, or an alternate reality) by what Aleister Crowley liked to call *Magick*, with a *k*, to distinguish it from mere trickery. We are talking about fact beyond fancy, the application of the human mind to the alteration of the universe and the command of fate.

Once again, though this time opinions and larger contexts (and therefore bibliographical references) are less important, there are guides to future study. However, this time the emphasis is on actual practice. Though this book is no less thoroughly researched and authoritative, we need not so often cite authorities. This is a sort of magical cookbook. Follow the recipes carefully, if you dare. I guarantee nothing except that the book will hold you fascinated.

In attempting that difficult task I have had much assistance from scholars and practitioners too numerous to mention. I thank them all, but I will not trouble you with footnotes. I simply want to express my gratitude to the many authorities I have consulted, and to the many librarians (at Brooklyn College and numerous libraries elsewhere) who have helped me do my research. Once again I express my thanks to my patient editor, Ellen Brand, and my publishers.

If you like my book, tell your friends. If you do not—or if you care to encourage me or correct an error of fact or emphasis—you can write to me in care of those publishers. As ever, I cannot undertake to answer all the letters that I receive, but I assure you I read them all, I appreciate them all, and slips can be corrected in future editions, if any.

Now read on, and God Bless You and Blessed Be.

Dæmon mutus 1997

Witches cast a spell and make rain. From Ulrich Molitor's
De Lamiis et phitonicis mulieribus (1489), the first book to have
a woodcut of witches flying.

1
Spells and Charms

WHY?

Why do people turn to magic? All the usual reasons for human excess: the desire for dominance, wealth, love, fame, the cancer of malice and revenge, self-assertion and self-discovery and self-validation and self-destruction. Magicians black or white seek to be different, even outlaws. They are obsessive about thrills, contemptuous of the bonds of rationality. They court tragedy. They are reckless but prepared well, not dissimilar from modern mountaineers, who these days reach the top of Everest in packs of more than thirty, with satellite phones and Internet-connected computers, and who have ghostwriters, agents, editors, and public relations hacks. That is, magicians use everything they can lay their hands on to get to their goals. They are embodied willpower, and that in our lackadaisical world may look totally crazy. Consider, though, what Francis Parkman (1823–1893), a great American historian (though not of magic and witchcraft), wrote:

> He who would do some great things in this short life must apply
> himself to work with such a concentration of force as, to idle spec-
> tators who live only to amuse themselves, looks like insanity.

To some The Work (as magicians call it) looks crazy. So does mountain climbing.

Bruce Barcott of Seattle has taken on a mountain of books about mountain climbing and in "Cliffhangers" (*Harper's* for August 1996, 64–69) he has produced more than the review of a clutch of books, more than a history of masochistic mountaineering. He gets to the very heart of a puritanical (allegedly anti-puritanical) and daring (actually semi-suicidal) sport in which the ultimate is to suffer damage or to die. He penetrates the minds and motives of climbers. I am struck by the fact that climbers seem very like would-be magicians. They have the urge to explore the unknown, to get to perilous places, to stand where humans have never stood before or to get "highs" by ridiculous routes never before attempted, to attain the sublime and maybe survive and write a book and make a lot of money. Theirs is not merely the famous excuse for attempting Everest: "It was there." "The Devil drives"; the motives of many, from love of danger to hope of reward. Climbers closely resemble those who take on the mysteries and the risky business of magic. Climbers, frighteningly like those who conjure, are brave and stupid and often irrational. They boldly seek both power and punishment.

Barcott writes:

> They climb to discover the "new frontiers" of the human mind, to test the limits of the body's endurance, to peer into the dark crevasse of death, but succeed only in performing a parody of discovery....Mountains are the site of these staged showdowns because they're the place where civilization cannot hold sway....The mountain doesn't play games. It sits there, unmoved.

Magicians have always believed that with their arcane knowledge and adamant wills the world itself, by spells and incantations and command of the supernatural, *can* be conquered. From cave paintings of prehistory, from the magic discussed in books such as Jacques Gafferell's *Forgotten Curiosities of the Persian Talismanic Art*, from the life of Apollonius of Tyana as recorded by Philostratus, from writings ancient and modern, from all the literature and history of magic, one thing stands out: Will. "So mote it be!"

It is in this outrageous rejection of humility that magicians stand in opposition to the Judeo-Christian tradition of our western civilization. They fundamentally agree with the leading scholar of the Dead Sea Scrolls, who went wild and denounced Judaism as "a gutter religion." They agree with Friedrich Nietzsche that Christianity preaches a "slave mentality." They stand against our God; they stand with Satan, the Adversary. Or they ignore the millennia of Judeo-Christian dominance and utterly reject the God of Judeo-Christian tradition and of Islam and say their religion is older, better, and truer.

To support them there is the foolishness of the masses. "We are all," wrote Pliny of the Romans with their dreads and amulets and superstitions, "afraid of being transfixed by curses and spells."

HUNTING MAGIC

Primitive man painted magic pictures of game on the walls of caves. American Indians had magic to bring the buffalo, and so do the Inuit today to bring fish and seals. Sir James Frazer in *The Golden Bough* (1890) writes of many examples of hunting magic. Here is some of what he records in this particular:

> The islanders of Torres straits use models of dugong and turtle to their destruction. The Torajades of Central Celebes...hang up the jawbones of deer and wild pigs in their houses, in order that the spirits which animate these bones may draw the living creatures of the same kind into the path of the hunter. In the island of Nias, when a wild pig has fallen into the pit prepared for it, the animal is taken out and its back is rubbed with nine fallen leaves, in the belief that this will make nine more wild pigs fall into the pit, just as the nine leaves fell from the tree...When a Cambodian hunter has set his nets and taken nothing, he strips himself naked, goes some way off, then strolls up to the net as if he did not see it, lets himself be caught in it, and cries, "Hillo! what's this? I'm afraid I'm caught." After that the net is sure to catch game. A pantomime of the same sort has been acted within living memory in our Scottish Highlands....

FROM THE BABYLONIAN TALMUD

"Thy mother hath well warned thee and said, 'Beware of *Shabriri, Briri, Riri, Iri, Ri, I.*' As the demon's name was shortened, so he was supposed to dwindle in power."

UNDOING PUNISHMENT FOR BREAKING A TABOO

It is not unknown for societies who wish something to be avoided to call it taboo and to say that divine retribution will descend on those who violate the taboo. This can add the power of fear of the gods to common sense or even to foolish rules.

In ancient Sumeria, there were various taboos, and anyone who broke the rule had to take an onion, a date, a piece of woven matting, and a handful of wool and reduce each thing to small pieces, reciting for each item:

> Like this thing which I dismember and throw into the fire...so may oath, curse...pain, weariness, guilt, sin, wickedness, transgression, the pain which is in my body, my flesh, my sinews. [disappear]....

FROM THE LAWS OF THE ROMAN EMPIRE

> Whosoever performs or commissions nocturnal rites in order to cast a spell, to curse or to bind someone, shall be crucified or thrown to the beasts....

Paulus in *Sentences*, a third-century compendium of Roman laws, comments:

> It is the prevailing legal opinion that participation in the magical art should be subject to the extreme punishment, that is, thrown to the beasts or crucified. But the magicians themselves should be burned alive. It is not permitted for anyone to have in his possession books of the magical art. If they are found in anyone's possession, after his property has been expropriated and the books burned publicly, he is to be deported to an island, or, if of the lower class, beheaded. Not only the practice of this art but even knowledge of it is prohibited.

PYGMY SPELL
TO PROTECT AGAINST A FALLEN ELEPHANT

From the earliest human societies, the pardon of the slaughtered animal was sought. The pygmies chant to the dead elephant even today:

> Do not let us feel your wrath!
> Henceforward, your life will be better!
> You go to the country of the spirits.
> Our forefathers are there to cement the alliance.
> Henceforward, your life will be better!
> Do not let us feel your wrath!

MAKING PASSES

Casting a spell or otherwise doing magic often requires gestures. Think of the gestures of blessing in Roman Catholic and other religions; there are gestures of anathema also. Many magical gestures involve making the passes that seem to massage the aura of a person, that direct magnetism to their eyes, that implore and draw, that push away and wipe away. Some of the gestures and stances can be seen in drawings as old as the Egyptian dynasties: the arms reaching upward, thrown out to the sides, hands clasped and raised to heaven, head bowed and arms thrown down and back, and so on.

Everyone knows the power of a human touch, how babies need to be fondled (and grownup ones, too), how touch and massage helps, how the hand has healed in every civilization from ancient Israel and before to the Inupiat and Indian in our time, how the laying on of hands is supposed to transfer the power of the spirit. Some research needs to be done to investigate with scientific rigor the clear-cut benefits of "magical" passes with the hands. There is something more here than a symbolic gesture. "I'm gonna wash that man right outta my hair...."

You'll read more about this (uncanonical) Roman Catholic St. Expédite to whom New Orleans voodoo worshippers pray to hurry up results. Presto! say magicians. "Quickly, quickly!" say some of the oldest spiels of which we have record. Those who cast spells are so impatient for results!

The magic wand is also used, one might say to direct spirits the way the conductor directs the orchestra.

In the Lesser Ritual of the Pentagram in the ceremonies of the Golden Dawn, instead of the Sign of the Cross you are supposed to make a five-pointed star.

With a steel dagger in hand and facing East, you draw an imagined five-pointed star on your body. You touch the forehead with *Ateh* (Thou Art), the breast with *Malkuth* (The Kingdom), the right shoulder with *ve Geburah* (and The Power) and the right one with *ve Gedulah* (and The

Glory), clasp the hands on the chest with *le olam* (forever), and then with the dagger held in the hands and pointing upwards *Amen*. Then you bring the dagger to the "centre of the Pentagram" and say *Tetragrammaton*. You repeat this procedure facing South, West, and North, ending respectively with *Adonai*, *Eheieh*, and *Agla*. You conclude with the center of the penta-gram and "Before me Raphael, behind me Gabriel, at my right hand Michael, at my left hand Auriel."

As with so much of this stuff, we must ask: Where did you get this? With what authority is it used? What does it mean and, most importantly, how do you explain how it works? The Sign of the Cross is usually sim-ple piety, but these are supposed to be effective magical gestures. Are they? Is the Sign of the Cross magical in any way? How does it work when it is used—so very often—in Christian ceremonies, particularly of blessing and exorcism? Is its use superstitious?

Asians and many others honor the aged, and claim that the powers to bless and curse increase with age. A blessing or curse from a father or grand-father is supposed to be especially effective. The blessing often involves placing hands on the head of the one to be blessed.

POINTING THE FINGER

The two so-called sacred fingers are the first and second fingers of the right hand; they are used in blessings. The forefinger, wet with saliva, is some-times used to curse, pointed at the victim. It is also believed, claims Ben-jamin Walker in his *Encyclopedia of Esoteric Man* (1977), that "a poppet stroked with a saliva-moistened finger will increase the pain of the victim."

AND THE WORD BECOMES PHYSICAL

A spell can be more than words. If you write it on rice paper, you can dis-solve the paper in water and the spell goes into the liquid, which can be applied, sprinkled around, or drunk.

TO CAST A SPELL ON A SUITOR

Or rather to cast a spell on whomever happens to come along, if you are that desperate to get married. What you do is, if you find nine peas in a pod, place one of them on the lintel of the door. The first single man to come through the door will marry you.

Most spells have a more specific intention, though not necessarily as serious an intention as this one. Some are simpler: if you want a man, put bacon in your shoe and after three days cook it and put it in his food: the way to his heart is through his stomach, indeed. If you want a woman, they say in old Scandinavian folklore, put a piece of honey cake in a sweaty armpit for days. Then get her to eat the cake.

AN INCANTATION RECORDED AT NINEVEH

Two millennia before Christ the following was written on clay tablets at Nineveh:

> He who makes the image, he who casts the spell,
> The spiteful face, the evil eye,
> The mischievous mouth, the mischievous tongue,
> The mischievous lips, the mischievous words,
> Spirit of the Sky, remember! Spirit of the Earth, remember!

ANCIENT INCANTATIONS

There may even have been earlier incantations—the Latinate word recalls that they were chanted, and enchanted—but the earliest written records of them are found among the literary legacies of the Babylonians and Assyrians. At that time some basic aspects, including rhyming, that were to be handed down to the Judeo-Christian world were in evidence. The words worked magic, as in the Cabala or the Mass. The deity was petitioned for the basics of life ("Give us this day our daily bread"), good weather and good crops and sufficient food, the protection of cattle and people, prosperity in peace and victory in war. Naturally, bad things could be asked for in connection with one's enemies. Today prayers and magic-working incantations (*Hoc est corpus meum*, "This is My body," derided by some as *hocus-pocus)* continue in all the leading religions. New Age people still purchase *mantras* from gurus. The repetition of *mantras* is supposed to effect magical change.

In some religions you can get time off (from Purgatory and so on) for the good behavior of repeating prayers. You can use more than 100 beads on a rosary to help you count the formulae, or fondle so-called "worry beads" (the rosary's origin), or simply put your hands together in a sacred gesture of supplication. You can kneel by your bed or in church. You can stand up and keep nodding your head as you intone the syllables. You can prostrate yourself or touch your forehead to the ground. You can "talk to

God" in your own words, though many people believe He pays more attention to traditional formulae. Or you can pray as you work—or offer up your
work as a form of prayer.

Felix E. Planer discusses all this as mere *Superstition* (1988) and says
on p. 179:

> Among the most ancient incantations, the following extract is a typ-
> ical example. It served as a charm against the demons and sickness
> sent by an angered god or goddess:
>
> > May the sickness in my body,
> > in my flesh and in my limbs,
> > peel away as does this onion.
> > Let it burn this very day
> > in the flames of scorching fire
> > Let the burden be removed,
> > May I see again the light.

The opposite position, struggling to accept, being humble and undemanding and learning not to be driven by desires, is the Buddhist faith,
or philosophy. In Buddhism three drives (existence, pleasure, power) are
said to stand in the way of perfection and The Devil is called *Varsavati*,
which can be translated "He Who Fulfills Desires."

PRAYERS

The onion used with the words above is a clue to the magical aspect: it is
a spell more than a prayer, though prayers must be reckoned to be a kind
of magical utterance, too. Often it is difficult to distinguish between an
imploring and an invoking, between a prayer and a spell. In the mid-
nineties, a poll showed that sixty–five percent of all Americans believe that
prayer gets results. I would have thought that number would have been
higher. The latest version of The Bible in English translation asks us to
pray to "Our Father-Mother" (along with sitting Christ no longer on "the
right hand of God" lest the left-handed among us object!) but many also
pray for the intercession of The Blessed Virgin and various saints, those
on whose feast day they were born or whose name they were given in baptism, or patron saints of various activities and professions, among whom
you may wish to know about St. Genesius (actors), St. Bernadine of Siena
(advertising), St. Vitus (comedians—I think that ought to be dancers), St.

Martin of Porres (hairdressers), St. Teresa of Ávila (migraine sufferers), St. Gabriel (postal workers), St. Crispin (shoemakers), St. Clare of Assisi (television workers), and St. Nicholas, Bishop of Myra, otherwise known as Santa Claus, the patron saint of brewers.

Some religions think that God regards us (as one African tribe says) as of no more importance than we regard little black ants. Adherents of such religions seldom bother to pray to divinities and expect the worst. Others live in great fear of gods and devils and pray and sacrifice to placate them. Some religions have benign supernatural figures to whom one can appeal. French tradition says that if a saint doesn't respond as desired, you can punish her or him by turning her or his statue to the wall, throwing it into water, or (in extreme cases) burning it or sawing it in half. This was common among the peasantry of Britanny, Normandy, etc., up to the last century and may still persist. Northern French peasants also had some strange saints, too, including a St.-Mauvais (St. Bad) to whom you could pray for evil purposes!

If saints are not enough, you could move up the hierarchy. There are magical formulae for addressing Thrones, Dominions, Principalities, and such. If you'd like to talk to archangels, may I suggest you forget about Metatron, who some authorities say only archangels can distinguish from God Himself, and apply to Raphael by burning an orange and a black candle together and praying fervently. Raphael is said to give the fastest results of all archangels—and he offers Wednesday matinees.

You might like to dip into some of the many books on angels, who (as you see here) have been in the news for a century or more and also are "hot" these days with many new and old dictionaries and encyclopedias of angels, such as

Hania Gzajkowski, *Playing with Angels* (1997)
Alma Daniel, *Ask Your Angels* (1996)
David Goddard, *The Sacred Magic of the Angels* (1996)
C. W. Leadbetter, *Invisible Messengers* (1896)

THE OLDEST PRAYER IN THE WORLD

An inscription of Egyptian heart-scarabs may be the oldest record of a prayer-spell we have from any civilization:

This was placed with the heart of the mummified corpse and somehow connected to the *ka* (double) of the individual. Sir E. A. Wallis Budge gives a translation:

> Heart of my mother! Heart of my mother! Heart of my being!
> Oppose me not in my evidence (or testimony). Thrust me not
> aside before the Judges [of the dead]. Fall not away from me

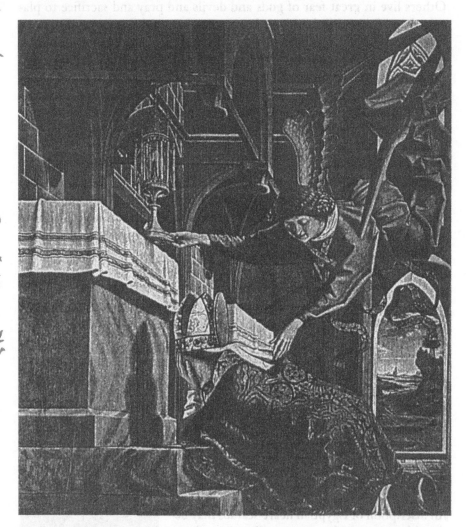

St. Wolfgang's prayers cause an angel to bring a miracle. One wing of an altarpiece of the Four Fathers of the Church in the *Alte Pinakoteck* (Old Painting Gallery), Munich.

before the Guardian of the Balance [who weighs the soul against a feather]. Thou art my KA in my body, Khnemu making sound my members. Come thou forth to the place of happiness (or felicity) whither we would go. Make not my name to stink with the Assessors, who make men, during my existence. Make good a good bearing with joy of heart at the weighing of words and deeds. Utter no falsehood concerning me in the presence of the Great God.

Assuredly thou shalt be distinguished rising up as a speaker of the truth. These amulets appeared on Egyptian corpses for more than 3000 years and the text still strikes our hearts with feelings for those who sincerely believed that judgment came at the end of life and that there were recording angels, such as also were spoken of by Christians and followers of Islam.

The devout Egyptian read in *The Book of the Dead*, or was told by the priests who could read the hieroglyphics and therefore control the society, that daily spells were required to preserve him or her in safety in a world full of dangers. "Whosoever readeth the spells over himself daily is whole upon the earth and escapes death and never doth anything evil ever touch him." Egyptians of old also tried to get information in dreams by saying before they went to sleep:

Tharthar, thamara, thatha, mommon, thanabotha, oprana, brokhrex, abranazukhel.

I have no idea of what language that is in (if any), or what it might mean. I mention it as an historical fact and also to underline the point that spells do not require you to understand the words, just to get them exactly right and say them at the appropriate times.

HOW CHRISTIANS ARE TO PRAY

Jesus Himself instructed Christians what to say, beginning with "Our Father"—which feminists now are objecting to vehemently and in some quarters have altered! The traditional "Our Father" (in Latin *"Pater Noster"*) has been minutely examined by a modern committee who are concerned about what Jesus did say and what is fathered on Him by tradition. Most of the traditional "Our Father" is a later addition; but He did at least start with "Our Father." As He was dying and felt God the Father had forsaken Him, Christ began His prayer "My God, my God."

WHAT THE FLYING WITCHES SAID

High on aconite, henbane, belladonna, hemlock, and other hallucinogens mixed into a salve, the witches flew—or thought they did—and cried as they went:

Thout, tout a tout, tout, throughout and about!

The cry of the Celtic celebrants was *Oiv! Oiv! Oiv!* (pronounced something like *Hum, Hum, Hum*, someone suggests).

THE MAGICAL ENVIRONMENT

This is the title of a section in Part IV of The Story of Civilization, *The Age of Faith* (1950). Here is a typically concise summary paragraph from Will Durant's book on the West from the Emperor Constantine to Dante:

> Belief in witchcraft was next to universal. The Penentential Book of the bishop of Exeter condemned women "who profess to be able to change men's minds by sorcery and enchantments, as from hate to love or from love to hate, or to bewitch or steal men's goods," or who "profess to ride on certain nights and on certain beasts with a host of demons in women's shape, and to be enrolled in the company of such"—the "Witches' Sabbath" that became notorious in the fourteenth century. A simple witchery consisted in making a wax model of an intended victim, piercing it with needles, and pronouncing formulas of cursing; a minister of Philip IV was accused of hiring a witch to do this to an image of the King. Some women were believed able to kill by a look of their "evil eye." Berthold of Regensburg thought that more women than men would go to hell because so many women practiced witchcraft—"spells for getting a husband, spells for the marriage, spells before the child is born, spells before the christening...it is a practice on them." Visigothic law accused witches of invoking demons, sacrificing to devils, causing storms, etc., and ordered that those convicted of such offenses should have their heads shaved and receive two hundred stripes. The laws of C[a]nut[e] in England recognized the possibility of slaying a person by magic means. The Church was at first lenient with these popular beliefs, looking upon them as pagan survivals that would die out; on the contrary they grew and spread; and in

1298 the Inquisition began its campaign to suppress witchcraft by burning women at the stake. Many theologians sincerely believed that certain women were in league with demons, and that the faithful must be protected from their spells. Caesarius of Heisterbach assures us that in his time many men entered into pacts with devils; and it is alleged that such practitioners of black magic so disdained the Church that they travestied her rites by worshipping Satan in a Black Mass. Thousands of sick or timid people believed themselves to be possessed by devils. The prayers, formulas, and ceremonies of exorcism used by the Church may have been intended as psychological medicine to calm superstitious minds.

CANDLES AND PRAYERS AND SPELLS

Religious people benefit from the psychological powers of sacred places, objects, and rituals. They use votive lights and candles to mark their prayer. Magicians use candles to cast spells. For spell casting, you really ought to make your own candles and "charge" them with visualization. Colors are dictated by tradition: pink for love, red for lust, green for money, white for "centering," and black for protection and more nefarious intentions. Traditionalists prefer beeswax to paraffin candles, but they are more expensive. Many spells call for candles to be burned for a long time; remember that it is always dangerous to leave a lighted candle unattended, so extinguish candles when you go out. Some spells ask you to burn a candle in seven steps; you have to watch each one. Some call for more than one candle at a time: for success in the job or better working conditions, for instance, you burn red, orange, and brown candles (all three at once) or red, orange, and pink.

Skip the tall, cheap pillar candles in glass (often with prayers to saints on the glass container). If they worked, *bodegas* would be in wealthier neighborhoods. They don't work—maybe because people expect them to do something without their full participation. There is seldom an effective fast-food approach to the banquet of magical delights.

CAST A SPELL ON YOURSELF

By concentration, or by submitting the body to a regime of deprivation or pain, you can manipulate your mind wonderfully. Anchorites and hermits subjected themselves to many tortures. Nuns scourged sex out of themselves. St. Thomas More wore a hair shirt under his robes as Lord

Chancellor. Some other saints castrated or starved or otherwise "mortified the flesh." Or you can just sit down, according to Marsilio Ficino (1433–1499), and think your way to harmony of mind and body. In his *Libri de vita* (Books of Life, 1489) he recommends you visualize a beautiful young woman carrying flowers and fruit.

BENT OUT OF SHAPE

Old spells and charms sometimes survive in strange and mangled forms. Take, for example, the chant of the children at Douglas on The Isle of Man on Hollantide (12 November). Carrying jack-o'-lanterns made not from pumpkins (like our Halloween ones) but from turnips, the children go about a sort of trick-or-treat procedure and chant:

> Jinny the witch
> Goes over the house
> To fetch a switch
> To lather the mouse.
> Hop-tu-naa.

Quentin Cooper & Paul Sullivan in *Maypoles, Martyrs & Mayhem* (1994) give a version of these rhymes almost identical with that quoted and add: "This is the last remnant of old anti-witch charms."

I'M PRAYING OVER A FOUR LEAF CLOVER

The traditional spell to say to turn your four-leaf clover into a magic charm to bring luck (especially at gambling and love) is:

> *Christus factus est obediens usque ad mortem, mortem autem crucis,*
> *Propter quod Deus exaltavit Jeschue.*

Point: you must pick your four-leaf clover at the hour of Jupiter, before sunrise, on the first Tuesday of a new moon.

INTO EACH LIFE A LITTLE RAIN MUST FALL

To make the rain go away so that they can go out an play, Spanish children say:

La cueva, la cueva, la Virgén de la cueva....

What the connection of The Blessed Virgin with caves, or rain, is, I don't know.

FOR A GOOD MARRIAGE

No wonder most marriages in the United States today end in divorce (and many others are rocky) if we forget (as we do) the last line of the poem that advises the bride how to cast the right spell:

> Something old, something new,
> Something borrowed, something blue,
> *And a sprig of furze!*

MEDIEVAL SPELL AGAINST THE EVIL EYE

Three biters hast thou bitten,
The hart, the ill eye, the ill tongue.

Three biters shall be thy boote,
Father, Sonne and Holy Ghost or God's Name,
In worship of the five wounds of our Lorde.

Father, Son, and Holy Ghost, The Blessed Virgin, and various saints and angels and archangels appear, surprisingly, in spells of pagan origin adapted to Christian use and in black magic conducted in open defiance of the church.

THREE OLD IRISH SPELLS FOR WOUNDS

The briar that spread, the thorn that grows,
The sharp spike that pierced the brow of Christ,
Give you power to draw this thorn from the flesh,
Or let it perish inside,
In the name of The Trinity. Amen.

A child was baptized in the River Jordan;
And the water was dark, but the child was pure and beautiful.
In the name of God [the Father] and of the Lord Christ,
Let the blood be stanched.

The poison of a serpent, the venom of the dog, the sharpness of the spear, doth not well in man. The blood of one dog, the blood of many dogs, the blood of the hound of Fliethas—these I invoke. It is not a wart to which my spittle is applied. I strike disease; I strike wounds. I strike the disease of the dog that bites, of the thorn that wounds, of the iron that strikes. I invoke the three daughters of Fleithas against the serpent. Benediction on this body to be healed; benediction on the spittle; benediction on him who casts out the disease. In the name of God. Amen.

IRISH SPELL TO DRIVE AWAY FEVER

"God save thee, Michael, Archangel, God save thee!
"What aileth thee, O Man?"
"A headache and a sickness and a weakness of the heart. O Michael, Archangel, canst thou cure me, O Angel of the Lord?"
"May three things cure thee, O Man. May the shadow of Christ fall upon thee!

May the garment of Christ cover thee! May the breath of Christ breathe on thee!

And when I come again thou shalt be healed."

For this spell the patient is standing, arms out to the sides as at The Crucifixion, and water is sprinkled on his head as the words are repeated.

IRISH CURE FOR MADNESS

From Sheila Anne Barry's *Irish Cures, Mystic Charms & Superstitions* (1990), a compilation of two books by Lady Wilde (1826–1896), *Ancient Legends, Mystics Charms, and Superstitions of Ireland* and *Ancient Cures, Charms, and Usages of Ireland:*

> Madness is ...cured by giving the person three substances not procured by human means, and not made by the hand of man. These are honey, milk, and salt, and they are to be given him to drink [here comes the magic part] before sunrise in a sea-shell. Madness and the falling-sickness (convulsions, epilepsy) are both considered hereditary, and caused by demoniacal possession.

A LITTLE COLLECTION OF SPELLS FROM THE NORWEGIAN PEASANTRY OF YORE

When a troll has taken possession of your horse, spit on your hands and run them over the animal from head to tail as you recite three times:

Du troll skal ikkje meira/ merri rida.	You, troll, shall no more ride the
Du skal ta pada til est og ormen skal	horse/mare. You shall take the
du leggia på til beisl og du skal ljota	toad for mount and put a halter on
rida til svartaste helvite og der	that and you shall grimly ride to
skal du sitja til domedag	the darkest hell and there you
	shall stay until doomsday.

You finish by giving the steed a good kick. Norwegian farmers in Surnadal attributed horses and mares getting all swollen up from eating frozen grass to the ill will of trolls.

Norwegian farmers also thought white bubbles on standing water or hoar frost on the grass was white spittle of trolls or witches and they employed this spell to ward off evil:

Hr. Braa spurte han Ra	Mr. Brå asked Ra what he could do
om ham kunde, gjera aat for	against the Brå disease
Braasotten "Salt i Næve, Spyt i	"Salt in the fist, spit in the mouth,
Mund, Gud gje det maatte baat	God may [arrange] that it will be
aa i samme Stund."	cured at the same instant."

This was to be followed by "In the Name of the Father, of The Son, and of The Holy Spirit. Amen."

Trolls (especially when manipulated by those nefarious Finns, masters of evil magic!) might fire poisoned, magical darts or "shots" at people, and to protect themselves people said (with the same "Three Names" tag):

I Jesu Navn gjør je aat for alle Slags	In Jesus' name I take remedy
onde Fin-Skud:	against all kinds of evil Finn shots:
For Hær -Skud, for Jord-Skud,	Against army shot, against earth
for Lunge-Skud, for Lever-Skud,	shot, against lung shot, against
for Galde-Skud, for alle Slags Skud	liver shot, against magic and all
som svæver imellem Himmel og Jord	sorts of shots, which fly between
	Heaven and Earth.

THROWING THE BOOK AT THEM

The Bible, once just about the only book that people were likely to have in the house, has been used for many purposes over the centuries besides pious reading. The Bible has been a place to record births, marriages, and deaths and a place to get (sticking your finger in at random) names for children or news about the future. It has also been used for nefarious purposes. An old superstition says that you can curse anyone by reading any verse of The Bible three times in a row and mentioning the victim's name each time. This might as well be noted under "Curses," but I put it here because lately this method appears to be in use in order to cast spells rather than curse. It is blasphemous.

SEPHIROTH

Jewish tradition says that miracles were wrought by the nine names of God in the *Sephiroth*. In my opinion, they will not work because they are not, in fact, the sacred names but substitutes for (or titles instead of) the great names, or secret names (some of many well-guarded syllables). But here are the nine names, if you want them:

EHIEH or EMET   IOD
TETRAGRAMMATON ELOHI   EL
ELOHIM GEBOR   ELOAH VA-DAATH
EL ADONAI TZABAOTH   ELOHIM TZABAOTH
SHADDAI or EL CHAI

Hebrew *El* is "God"; *Elohim* is plural! "The God of the Sabbath" is not a name. Neither is "Tertragrammaton, " which is nothing but the four consonants—Hebrew does not write the vowel—of what we call *Jehovah*. But *Jehovah*, God's reply to Moses, who dared to ask His Name, translates simply "I AM." That is all God wanted you to know of Him. *Tzabaoth* (variously spelled) is the "name" Moses is said to have used to turn the rivers of Egypt to blood. Aaron used *Anephenton*. *Agla* occurs often in Jewish-derived magic as a name of God. *Schemes-Amathia* is said to be the name by which Joshua made the sun stand still in the heavens (though it is always still—it is the earth that moves, God knows). Jesus was the *Emmanuel*, the *Alpha* and *Omega* (from the Greek letters beginning and ending their alphabet).

The story is told of how *Emet* was written and placed in a golem—or constructed monster—along the lines of Victor Frankenstein's but supernatural. The rabbi who made the golem with this name brought it to life. Instead of the science which brought to life Frankenstein's monster (with a bolt of lightning to furnish electricity) it was religion that vivified the golem (with a symbol of faith). When the golem threatened to destroy him, the learned rabbi erased the first letter of *Emet*, and, because *met* means "death" in Hebrew, the monster instantly perished. So powerful is the word.

"In the beginning was The Word, and The Word was with God, and The Word was God."

In the ritual magic ceremonies fathered on Pope Honorius III (reigned 1216– 1227)—also falsely attributed by some to Pope Honorius II—there is mention of

the great Names of the God of gods and Lord of lords, ADONAY, TETRAGRAMMATON, JEHOVA, TETRAGRAMMATON ADONAY, JEHOVA, OTHEOS, ATHANATOS, ISCHYROS, AGLA, PENTAGRAMMATON, SADAY, SADAY, SADAY, JEHOVA, OTHEOS, ATHANATOS, á *Liciat TETRAGRAM-MATON, ADONAY, ISCHROS, ATHANTOS, SADAY, SADAY, SADAY, CADOS, CADOS, CADOS, ELOY, AGLA, AGLA, AGLA,*

ADONAY, ADONAY, by the ineffable names of God, to wit, Gog and Magog, which I am unworthy to pronounce....

Athanatos is basically the Greek for Hebrew *Emet*. I believe that all these names have little effect except perhaps on the celebrant of the rites, because I place immense faith in the power of auto-suggestion. Tantric Buddhism teaches that illusions persist even after death and only by freeing ourselves from all the levels of illusion can we be free to enjoy *nirvana*; some magicians work themselves into "higher states" right here by self-conviction and the emotional power of incantations and rituals. Éliphas Lévi says in his *Transcendental Magic* (translated by A. E. Waite, n.d.) that such procedure "in Black Magic is to disturb reason and produce the feverish excitement which emboldens great crimes."

The 10 stages or centers of the *Sephiroth* are numbered from the top down and from right to left in each row. The diagram attempts to illustrate very complex thinking and in it are four levels or dimensions, four worlds, and much more, but if you will look at the illustration, I shall at least translate the Hebrew words for you, as follows:

1. *Kether* Supreme Crown

3. *Binah* Understanding   2. *Hokhmah* Wisdom

5. *Din* Power   4. *Hesed* Love

6. *Tiffereth* Beauty

8. *Hod* Majesty   7. *Netsah* Endurance

9. *Yesod* Foundation

10. *Malkuth* Kingdom

By the way, it is *Din* (Power) that magic always seeks the most, although with *Kether* (variously read, but I say "Supreme Crown") one attains the highest level of mastery and the Philosopher's Stone which transmutes everything into perfection. In alchemy this meant the power to transmute lead or other base metal into gold, in ethics total purity, in theology the godhead, and in demonology the dominion over devils and demons.

WITCHCRAFT SPELL OF HATRED

Elbeee Wright in his *Book of Legendary Spells* (1968) repeats many items from old books. Here is what he calls a "spell of hatred" which came to light as a result of a trial by the Holy Inquisition in Toledo—long a cen-

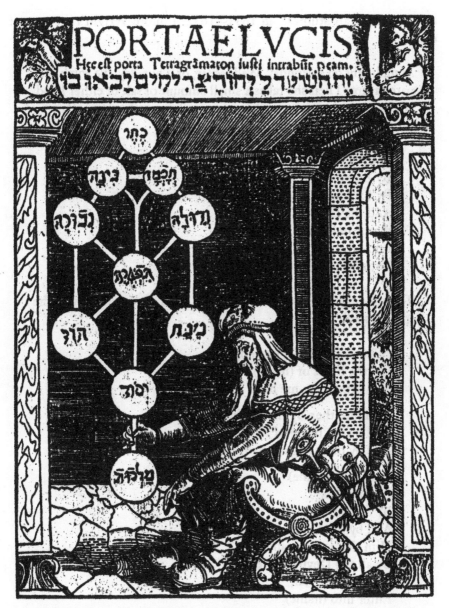

Ten *Sephiroth* (Emanations) add up to the *Pleronia* (Life Divine) in the system of Jewish mysticism call The Cabala. In *Portae Lucis* (Gates of Life) of 1516 we see a fine example of how a *converso*, Paul Ricci, brought cabalistic learning with him into Christianity. The Tree of Life, shown here held by a magician, was taken up by wizards, alchemists, philosophers (such as Pico della Mirandola), and others in the hermetic world of The Renaissance.

ter for witchcraft studies—in 1631– 1632. I quote Wright's account of it in full:

At midnight on a Monday, Wednesday, or Thursday, the witch prepares a fire. Then she takes a small amount of salt in either hand, adds a bit of coriander herb, and a small piece of sardine. Passing this from hand to hand, she says:

"I conjure thee, salt and coriander,
By Barrabas,
By Satanas,
And the Devil; I conjure thee
that is most able,
I do not conjure thee as salt and coriander,
But as the heart of (name),"

Then she throws the mixture into the fire and continues with the spoken spell:

"Thus, as thou art burning,
Let the heart of (name) burn,
And bring it to me here.

I conjure thee by the Sardine Queen,
And by the name of Hell,
And by the navigators who sail the sea.

I call thee (name)
By Barrabas,
By Satanas,
And by the Devil, I conjure thee,
Him that is most able
By all the Devils in Hell,
Devil of the Star,
Enter into (name),
And bring him to me here
Quickly.

Devils of the abattoir,
Guide him here to me;
Devils of the Cocodover,
Bring him to me as dast [fast!] as you can.

> With more messages I send to call thee,
> By the Saracen Queen,
> By the Queen of King Faraon,
> Who walks by day in the fields,
> At night by the Crossroads,
> Catching wars and battles,
> I join all of you, and go,
> And into (name) I enter,
> And from there bring me
> Diligently; well seized.
>
> Seizing his side,
> His lung,
> And the strings of his heart."

The above spell was to be repeated three times. Repetition was just as important as sound in the chanting of spells and the number of repetitions, like all numbers to the superstitious, was of crucial significance.

HATEFUL SPELL AGAINST A FAITHLESS LOVER

Pierce the shoulder blade taken from a sheep with a sharp knife and say:

> It's not this bone I wish to stick.
> But the heart of N I wish to prick.
> Be he asleep or wide awake
> I'd have him come to me and speak.

A SPELL EASILY DONE

Simply lie down on your face with your arms and legs stretched out and quote The Bible: "In the midst of life we are in death." If nothing else, those who are being opposed will have the trouble of dragging you off the way police do protesters at a rally.

TO INVOKE A DEMON

Just say *Bagahi laca bachabe*. That's it.

FOR LOVE

Just say, while kissing passionately, *"Anck thazi n epibatha cheouch cha anok!"*

SPELLS EVERYWHERE

Every society deals in enchantments. See various studies such as:

Gagin, Bernard D. "Some Wogeo Songs and Spells," *Oceania* 12 (1972), 198–204.
Rosaldo, Michelle Zimbalist." "It's All Uphill." pp. 177–203 in *Sociocultural Dimensions of Language Use* (ed. Mary Sanches et. al., 1975) [Ilongot, Western Indonesia]
Sinnet, A. P. *The Occult World* (1884)
Skelton, Robin. *Spellcraft...Binding and Bidding* (1979).

ELVES

The land of Elfin is one of the most—well, charming in our literature in English. The Scandinavians have their trolls and the natives of China and India an uncountable (but not unaccountable) host of minor spirits. English elves are in a class by themselves. The superstitions that surround them, as I say elsewhere, take us back to the very first even partly civilized people encountering the most primitive. Elves belong to the earliest memories of our race. When Christianity came as another civilizing force, the folk beliefs were too deeply imbedded to be eradicated. The Christianizing of the folk beliefs of a thousand years ago simply meant that Roman Catholic views had to be modified and Roman Catholic rituals devised for dealing with the elves.

A fascinating book is Karen Louise Jolly's erudite study of *Popular Religion in Late Saxon England* (1996). It has some wonderful elf charms in it.

Of course in modern times, J. R. R. Tolkein's writings have brought dwarfs and elves and such to the attention of millions.

TO MAKE BUTTER

When ordinary folk did their own dairying, they worried a lot not only about mischievous elves but also about witches making their cattle barren, riding them to exhaustion by night, drying up their milk . Witches were said to be able to milk an ax handle. They were believed to sour milk.

They could keep butter from forming in the churn. In another book I mention the habit of putting a silver coin in the churn to foil witches in this, but one of the witches who was tried before King James himself is said to have revealed the charm to make butter come:

> Come, butter, come!
> Come, butter, come!
> Peter stands at the gate,
> Waiting for the buttered cate.
> Come, butter, come!

Cate is an old word for "cake." Who Peter is supposed to be, I don't know. The dasher (handle) of the churn must go up and down with the rhythm of the verse. I wonder if there is anything sexual in all this. I mentioned this charm in another book and I add more here. I'm still working on it.

By the way, butter is used to "christen" magical poppets and in various spells. Wrap a stick of butter in a paper in which you have written your wish or spell, tie it with a red ribbon, and concentrate on your desires as you throw the package into the fire.

THE HORSE WHISPERER

An Irish way to tame a horse: whisper the Apostle's Creed in his right ear on a Friday and in his left ear on a Wednesday, weekly until he is tamed.

TO MAKE LOVE

In an old French magical manual of the eighteenth century (which may contain materials of a much older origin) called *Opération des sept esprits des planètes* (Operation of the Seven Spirits of the Planets), you are advised to cast a potential lover's horoscope and while speaking of the date of marriage you gaze soulfully into the person's eyes and repeat the formula

> *KAFÉ , KASIRA NON KAFELA ET PUBLIA FILII*
> *OMNIBUS SUIS.*

That done, "you may command the female and she will obey you in all that you desire." The book also recommends touching her hand gently and saying

BESTABERTO CORRUMPIT EJUIS MULIERIS.

This will be noted, of course, because it is difficult indeed to imagine slipping these sentences unnoticed into ordinary conversation. But you must not repeat nor explain the sentences. At that point, pounce. This sort of thing is not for the modern, civilized, politically correct lover, nor are some other old American love charms contained in B. A. Botkin's "regional miscellany" *Folk-Say* (1930), well worth seeking out. There are many books in print on sex magic (Amand, Crowley, Wrede, etc.); they form a significant part of the collection in any occult bookshop.

However, many people who use sex magic never read a book. They picked up hints from the oral tradition. Sampson snakeroot will "soften hearts" and harden a man's member. Watch out for women charming you by putting things in your drink such as menstrual blood, blood from beef kept under her armpit for days, etc. Men can use many attractions: an odd one (from Oklahoma folklore) is a wasp's nest carried in a breast pocket to "make the girls fall." To hold onto a woman you have, one so-called authority says, "make a toby of one of her menstrual bandages, then wear it sewed into the waistband of your trousers." You may not find that sort of thing in your *Book of Enchantments* or *Spinning Spells* or *Dagger Magic* or *Astrological Magic* or even *The Magical Diaries of Aleister Crowley* (reprinted 1996).

In addition, superstition widely followed in America—I mean astrology, which presents itself as nothing less than applied science and is in practically every daily newspaper as well as in special journals, a stack of books, etc.—dictates that you marry with horoscopes in mind. A friend went to a Chinese astrologer. The Chinese have twelve different signs of the Zodiac, such as Dragon, Boar, Dog, Snake, etc. She was told "Don't marry a Dog." That seems like excellent advice for us all, whatever our horoscopes.

To cast a love spell without worrying about horoscopes, simply tie five chestnuts together with red string, three knots between each nut, and as you tie each knot recite:

> I tie this knot to snare the heart of N.
> Let her [or him] neither sleep nor rest
> Until she [or he] turns to me.

ANCIENT LOVE SPELL OF ATTRACTION

This one is touted as an excellent divination by fire, "than which none is greater." It attracts (heterosexual) partners "and makes virgins rush out of their homes." You write on a piece of pure papyrus, the Egyptian equivalent of paper, with the blood of an ass, these names and the picture we illustrate below and you stick up the papyrus with "vinegar gum" on the dry roof of a public bath's vapor room, but "watch yourself that you are not struck." Marvels are promised if you adopt this method.

Translation (by E. N. O'Neil): "Come Typhon, who sit on top of the gate, IO ERBETH IO PAKERBETH IO BALCHOSETH IO APOMPS IO BIMAT IAKOUMBIAI ABERRAMENTHO/ THEXANAX ETHRELUOÓ TH TOPU SETH, as you are in flames and on fire, so also [be] the soul, the heart of her, NN, whom NN bore, until she comes loving me, NN, and glues her female pudenda to my male one, immediately, immediately; quickly, quickly."

Titania Hardie in *Hocus Pocus* (1996) offers a lot of what she considers to be spells, but putting red carnation petals and borage flowers and leaves to steep in a bottle of champagne is, in my view, preparing not a spell but just refreshment. Still, "liquor is quicker...."

CELTIC LOVE SPELL

String six horse chestnuts on a red cord, with three knots between each one. When the moon is full, burn a red candle and say (thrice):

O Diana, goddess of love and of the hunt,
I pray to thee!
I pray these knots will tie up the heart of N.

> May she neither rest nor sleep
> Until she sleeps with me!
> Until she submits to my will, my love.
> O Diana, bring about our love, and bless it!

Then throw the charm into a blazing fire. She will come to you, one book assures, "before the embers grow cold!"

Or you could powder ten hemlock leaves and keep putting the powder in her food. Or hold hands with the desired person for ten minutes while keeping a sprig of mint in your hand. If someone is willing to hold hands with you for ten minutes, however, you may not need the mint.

ONCE YOU HAVE FOUND HER, NEVER LET HER GO

When your spells of attraction have succeeded and you are *in flagrante* with her, you can try on your woman a sex spell from the *Brihadaranyaka Upanishad*. Indians, under the misconception that semen is "from the heart," like to use it as an aphrodisiac in food and in sexual congress. Inserted in and caressing and kissing your partner, say to your semen:

> You take your origin in every part.
> You're generated in the heart.
> From all internal parts compiled,
> Drive this woman's sex parts wild.
> Now strike her mad and to the marrow
> Like young doe hit with poisoned arrow.

You may wish to read more about sex and magic in the likes of:

"Brother Moloch," *Sexual Sorcery* (1997)
Lama Rechung, *Tibetan Medicine* (1972)
E. Röer, *Brihadaranyaka Upanishad* (1931)
O. A. Wall, *Sex and Sex Worship* (1919)

TO SAFEGUARD VIRILITY

Clutch your testicles. The Greeks think this is particularly necessary when encountering a Greek Orthodox priest, despite the fact that Greek Orthodox priests (unlike Roman Catholic priests) are not celibate. This may have something to do with Christianity, being an end-of-the-world religion, from its inception being anti-sex.

HOW DO YOU KNOW IF YOU ARE BEWITCHED?

If we are to believe the Renaissance encyclopedist of witchcraft, Francesco Maria Guazzo (*Compendium maleficarum*), the symptoms look like some-

From H. Burgkmair the Elder's *Weisskunig* (White King) series, a woodcut in the art museum of Basel, Switzerland, shows the young king being taught the art of black magic.

thing between CFS (Chronic Fatigue Syndrome) and AIDS (Auto-Immune Deficiency Syndrome), curses of the modern world.

Look for lassitude and a general feeling of malaise; sweating and sometimes fever; anemia and jaundice; loss of appetite—including the appetite for sex (in extreme cases the patient believes that not only his potency but actually his penis has disappeared); pains around the heart, neck, kidneys, belly, and elsewhere; short temper and hallucinations; vomiting (in extreme cases, of needles and pins, foul materials and small animals, feathers, etc.). According to Fra Guazzo:

> The sicknesses with which those who are bewitched suffer are generally a wasting or emaciation of the whole body and a loss of strength, together with a deep languor, dullness of mind, various melancholy ravings, different sorts of fever...certain convulsive movements of an epileptic appearance, a sort of rigidity of the limbs giving the appearance of a fit...such a weakness as pervades the whole body that they can hardly move at all....

Some bewitched people were reported to be wary of priests. Can you blame them? Just as physicians often believe that it's people's own fault they get sick, not taking good enough care of themselves, some priests used to think that there might be a good reason the person was possessed, or bewitched.

Today people are more likely to say they are depressed than that they are possessed, or that they are suffering from Epstein-Barr or something than that they are bewitched, but the practice of inner-city medicine (to put it politely) does suffer from the superstitious beliefs of a number of ethnic groups who still fear evil spirits and associate them with disease, and who may well attribute symptoms of anything from the common cold to cancer to curse.

TO TURN YOURSELF INTO A HARE

English witches were believed to be able to turn themselves in hares by reciting:

> I shall go into a hare, with sorrow and such and mickle care;
> And I shall go in The Devil's name, aye while I come home again.

It was said that such hares could not be shot except with a silver bullet, which gave some excuse when you fired at a hare who, missed, ran blithely off.

WALKING ON WATER

This was one of the miracles that the Gospels report of Christ. It is also attempted by spells, and during the Civil War in England in the seventeenth century a woman was put to death as a witch for "surfing" on a river, while many still try by magic to walk on water.

Ramakrishna told his disciples the story of a man who spent fourteen years learning how to perform this miracle and that he had said to the man, "My poor boy, what you have accomplished after fourteen years' arduous labour, ordinary men do by paying a penny to the boatman."

TO INJURE AN ENEMY

All the preparations having been made, the words that are recited over the image (wax figure, photograph, etc.) according to one *grimoire* are VSOR, DILAPIDATORE, TENTATORE, SOIGNATORE, DEVORATORE, CONCITORE, ET SEDUCTORE. Then the image is consecrated to evil and put away for a day perfumed with vile-smelling stuff.

Much easier to accomplish—if you should be silly enough to try such a thing remembering that "what goes around, comes around"—is to follow the advice of "Donna Rose" in her pamphlet on *The Magic of Herbs* (1978):

> TORMENTILLA ROOT...to create distress for your enemy, do the following: obtain a picture of your enemy, and sprinkle the herb on it. As long as the herb remains in position, the tension and crises will remain.

Or, from Sara Lyddon Morrison's rather camp, chatty *Modern Witch's Spellbook* (1994)—though she states frankly that "there are times when death magic can, and perhaps should, be used":

> If you have need of punishing a faithless lover, draw the curtains and at midnight light a candle. Take a needle and prick the candle many times, saying:
>
> > As I prick this candle, I prick thee,
> > Break your heart, unhappy be!

"Donna Rose" is not so bloodthirsty. She recommends that one add to all conjure bags "astrological herbs." For Gemini, for instance, she suggests "lilly of the valley" and "lavendar," among others. The spelling is hers. So, I think, is that tormentilla recipe, probably simply suggested by the existing name of the plant.

Likewise suggested chiefly by the coincidence of names are superstitions about these powers of plants (among others):

ADDER'S MOUTH will keep people from talking about you behind your back
ANGELICA will attract angels and banish devils
BLESSED THISTLE will attract good spirits
COLT'S FOOT will cause evil and illness to run away from you
COUCH GRASS will help you get someone to bed with you
CUCUMBER kept in the bedroom will promote fertility
DOCK SEED tied around the left arm will cure bareness
HEART'S EASE will make your love life more pleasant and comfortable
KNOT GRASS will assist you to untie difficulties, undo hexes
MINT tied around the left arm will settle stomach disorders
MUGWORT will protect you from being mugged
NETTLES tea will cure dropsy (but must be collected in a churchyard)
QUEEN'S ROOT will attract women and effeminate gays
SOLOMON'S SEAL will exorcise demons
WITCHES' GRASS will help witches succeed with their spells

Many have elaborate conditions attached. Take *crowsfoot*, which the Irish use for veterinary purposes. It must be just nine leaves and must be crushed against a stone that "never was moved since the world began, and never can be moved." It is mixed with human spittle and salt and applied in the appropriate dose for the animal concerned.

TO GET THAT TELEPHONE CALL

So successful was Mrs. Morrison's first *Modern Witch's Spellbook* that a second volume was called for (1995). It is padded with real and maybe imaginary characters for whom she has cast spells, but it has the advantage of being adapted to modern problems. Here is a spell to "make someone call you on the telephone, and you can (she avers) use stationery instead of bothering with parchment:

take a piece of parchment (the type used for writing expensive letters [she means the expensive paper used for writing letters] is fine) and inscribe the journalist's name in a circle twice so that the letters meet end to end. While doing this, concentrate on his face and the desire that he call. Then take a needle and put it through the paper in the center of the circle of his name....Put the charm near the telephone.

Wait. She claims, "It's infallible."

ESCAPE CLAUSE

Elizabeth Southiel (1488–*c.*1570) is remembered by her married name, Mother Shipton. Born at Knaresborough, she became one of the most famous witches of the Elizabethan period, and people flocked to the cave in which she lived to hear her prophecies. (Tourists can still visit it. Knaresborough also boasts St. Robert of Knaresborough, 1160–1218, likewise wonder-working and likewise so poor he lived in caves, although he once got a place under a church wall at Spofforth and was taken into a hermitage on another occasion.) When her prophecies were collected in 1797 and 1881 they still fascinated the public. She became a legend, and a British butterfly with a marking that resembled her face is named for her. Richard Head (1684) said she was carried off by The Devil and bore him a child. What you might be most interested in is the spell she used to escape from court in a witchcraft trial. She chanted

UPDRAXI, CALL STYGICIAN HELLUEI

and Updraxi, a winged dragon, swooped in and carried her off to the amazement of the judge and jury and all the spectators. A person like that you do not retry!

THE *SAGENSPRECHER*

Mother Shipton was much consulted by the locals who wanted their fortunes told and was looked upon as something of a local utility. Not all dabblers in the supernatural were regarded as bad by the peasantry in medieval times and even into The Reformation. In Germany, for instance, there was the *Sagensprecher* who "spoke blessings," that is, cast spells that brought people good rather than harm. Of course this was in the minds of the sophisticated mere superstition and in the minds of the clergy an unwarranted assumption by laity of powers the church considered to be reserved to her own ministers.

In a study by Alison Rowlands in of "Witchcraft and Popular Religion in Rothernburg-ob-der-Tauber in the anthology on *Popular Religion in Germany and Central Europe, 1400 - 1800* (1996, ed. Bob Scribner & Trevor Johnson) we have the cases of several people who were punished for doing good.

In 1582, for instance, George Kissling, the smith and cunning man of Ergersheim, was set in the pillory, flogged and banished for activities which included using a crystal ball to retrieve stolen goods and special herbs to protect animals from worms and witches. A year earlier, traveling quack Anna Gebhartin had also been banished after being set in the pillory and having a cross burned into her forehead and two holes burned through her cheeks. She had claimed that she could make bad marriages good, restore male potency and find hidden treasure with the help of a spirit.

BLOOD

The Jews believed that "the blood is the life," and they would not eat the blood (soul) of animals. This custom is preserved in *kosher* dietary laws. The old custom of blood brothers, each cutting his hand and shaking with the other to exchange blood and become one, is well known. It was still done when I was a boy—but that was before anyone heard of hepatitis and AIDS. Less well known, but reported in Herodotus, was the Scythian custom of making a contract by each participant cutting himself and dropping some blood into a vessel of wine. Then the wine and blood mixture was drunk by all parties.

Thus vampires seek the blood, that is the soul, of their victims. Thus pacts with The Devil were supposed to be signed in blood and several alleged pacts are still preserved in museum collections. In Marlowe's *Faustus* there is a dramatic scene in which Faustus's own body rebels against his signing in blood and coals (representing heated passions) are brought to make his blood flow well enough to be used for ink. Some witches were thought to sign pacts with The Devil in menstrual blood.

The blood of kings and commoners was shed in magical rites to give fertility to the soil. (Some pagan kings such as Halfdane the Black, and perhaps Oswald, were dismembered and the pieces buried in a number of different locations, thus spreading the fertility widely.) Soil taken from the place where King Oswald of Northumbria was struck down was said to have worked medical magic and to have made buildings fire-proof . In his ecclesiastical history of the early English, Bede reports solemnly that bits of wood from the stake on which Penda placed Oswald's bloody, decapitated head could cure the plague. With the blood of such powerful people, amazing spells could be cast as well. If you were a Viking who wanted something from Odin, a blood sacrifice was usually required. The Germanic tribes (at least so their enemies said) always sacrificed the first person they captured in a battle; then their bloodthirsty god would be well disposed to grant them a victory.

Blood is sacrificed in some Satanist rituals to the god of the witches. A drop of a witch's blood and you can reverse her magic—you cannot use her tears because witches don't cry. Blood is essential to the rites of voodoo, albeit mostly chicken blood. Isidore of Seville and other medieval encyclopedists and theologians often comment on how demons love blood and reward necromancers and others who offer it to them, and of course the pages of the history of the persecution of witches by church and state are stained with blood. Blood is demanded for the casting of certain dire spells and one's own blood or that of others may be called for in certain hellish recipes. The blood of the person to be enchanted, surreptitiously obtained, is occasionally required. Afterbirths and menstrual blood should especially be guarded.

Finally, blood sacrifices were replaced in Judaism by sacrifices of bread and wine (as in the Roman Catholic Mass) and in folk custom by sacrifices of animals and even birds. In England and Scotland old human sacrifices were recalled on St. Stephen's Day with the ritual killing of a wren, "the king of the birds," but tradition says that William Rufus, the son of William the Conqueror, was ritually murdered in the New Forest in a ceremony of "the King Must Die" to ensure the prosperity of his people. William Rufus may have been sacrificed to some Continental superstition. In Brittany until fairly modern times a thrush or blackbird was killed ritually. Elsewhere in France it might be a robin. Some spells have reduced human sacrifice to the witch producing a drop of her own blood, a bit of her own soul. Know what the symbols mean! Any magic that involves blood in any way is black magic, whatever pseudo-Wiccans tell you.

TO PREVENT FROSTBITE

The Finns have a spell to prevent freezing of the fingers. It goes:

> *Pakkenen puhurin poika*
> *Aläkylmää kynsiäin'*

Alä käsiäin pälele
Palele ves' pajuja
Kylmä koivun konkaleita

This I translate as:

Old Cold, pup of puff,
Don't you freeze my fingers up.
Don't you freeze my little hands.
Freeze the willow where it stands
By the water, please.
Freeze the clumps of white birch trees.

TO KEEP FROM BEING HYPNOTIZED OR ENCHANTED

Cross your fingers. Wear a garment inside out. Wear a cross, a scapula, an amulet (such as a tooth or coral or the first letter of the Hebrew word

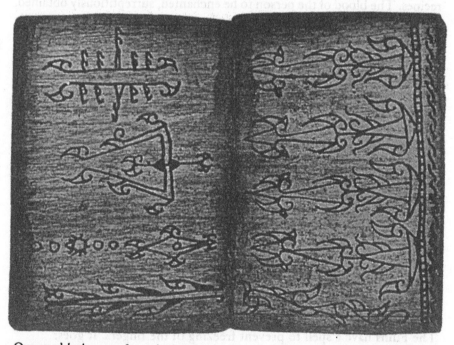

Our word *book* comes from the beech tree. Here on pages of bark is a Batak book of spells from Sumatra.

for "Life" or the Hand of Fatima) or blessed medal or a birthstone. Carry some straw or some other natural product that defeats witches. Drive a nail into your doorpost, or your fetish. Stay out of certain dangerous places where spirits are known to walk abroad. Stay in a state of grace so that your Guardian Angel—no, not the one in the red beret—can be protectively by your side.

RUSALKAS

Slavic superstition is full of malignant creatures such as *rusalkas*, who lurk in plants and deserted spots, bring bad luck, spirit away children, and cast very evil spells. There is not much you can do about them except stay out of their way, maybe keep an icon around, cross yourself frequently, and pray.

MOONLIGHT

Moonlight has traditionally been thought to help spells, and it is said that if you use a mirror to reflect moonlight into the closed eyes of a sleeper the person will be under your spell.

TABLE OF CONTENTS

Madame Blavatsky was always being asked to perform some trivial wonders, and often she did them. She would produce an oil of sandalwood from her palms whenever you wanted any, sometimes balls of light when you didn't. Kurt Vonnegut wrote irreverently of her and her Theosophists, but in *Wampeters, Foma & Granfalloons* (1976) he repeats a story he told about her in an article in *McCalls*.

> She visited some relatives in Russia...after she had learned some new tricks. Her brother was skeptical of her Marco Polo yarns; dared her to show him something he couldn't explain. She told him to lift a small chess table, which was easy to do. Then she stared at the table but didn't touch it, and she defied him to lift it again. He might as well have tried to hoist the Kremlin. Other heroes had a go at the hoodooed table, too, and they split it—but it wouldn't leave the floor. Madame Blavatsky pronounced the table as light as a feather once more, and lo, it was so. I call this hypnotism.

Or did she cast a spell on it, or them? Was the table "hoodooed," do you think?

ABSOLUTELY FORBIDDEN

Christianity, like all new religions, had great difficulty in eradicating the deeply ingrained beliefs and practices of the older religions. Inevitably, for a long time—or should I say still?—Christianity warred with paganism. No amount of the destruction of pagan temples—a practice of a great many saints and other heroes of the early Christian church—could totally obviate recourse to old spells, charms, and other superstitious practices. Though some of the old temple stones were used for new Christian churches, though some of the miraculous pagan wells were changed into wells of the saints, the old beliefs lingered. No matter how much popes and prelates thundered against the old practices, the old ways often continued—sometimes with the active cooperation of clerics and the faithful. In the *Vita Eligii episcopi Noviomagensis* (Life of Eloi, Bishop of Noyon) the very vehemence with which he rails suggests the magnitude of the problem in his time. (This saint lived 588–658 and brought Flanders to the Christian faith.)

> I hate above all and I absolutely insist that no one believe in sacriligious pagan customs. No pretext, no illness, nothing whatsoever can warrant the presumption of your approaching or questioning the casters of lots or seers or soothsayers or enchanters. Such wickedness will instantly wipe away your baptismal grace. Similarly, you may not regard signals such as sneezes to tell you what to do, nor ask answers of the cries of birds when you depart on a journey. Instead, whatever you undertake, a journey or another enterprise, cross yourself in the name of Christ, and recite the Creed or the Lord's Prayer, reverently and with trust, and then nothing can harm you....
>
> No one should consult about his own fate or fortune or suggest that it is determined at birth.... And when someone falls ill, do not resort to enchanters, or diviners, or soothsayers, or the casters of lots, or place diabolical charms in springs or at trees or crossroads.

Also noted by Valerie I. J. Flint in *The Rise of Magic in Early Medieval Europe* (1991) is St. Caesarius of Arles. I reproduce part of what she quotes from one of St. Caesarius's sermons as translated by M. M. Mueller and slightly amended by Flint. St. Caesarius was much disturbed by adherence to the cult of Diana as moon goddess and that the new Christians also turned to "drawing down the moon," witchcraft, and pagan superstitions rather than Christian prayer or even the blessed oil in which St. Eloi wanted them to place their faith. These insufficiently-converted Christians, he preached,

> do not ask for the church's medicine, or that of the author of sal-vation and the Eucharist of Christ ...or place all their hopes in God....They say to themselves: Let us consult that soothsayer, seer, oracle or witch.... Let us sacrifice a garment of the sick person, a girdle that can be seen and measured. Let us offer some magic let-ters, let us hang some charms on his neck. In all this the Devil has one aim: either cruelly to kill the children by abortion, or to heal them still more cruelly with charms.

Now, the real dangers from reliance on charms and spells, and (some would add) belief in holy oils, are in such positions you might take against sci-entific medical care and rational thinking. At the same time, practically no one is totally rational all the time and—we must admit this—the "life lies" that Ibsen fulminates against, the "pipe dreams" that cripple some of Eugene O'Neill's characters living on hope (in a bar run by Harry Hope, of course), are essential to prop up some people. Would you kick the crutch out from under a friend who broke his leg skiing, and tell him to be a man, buck up and walk on his own?

Religion and superstition can contend as much as they wish. They both work. Most people, though they might deny it, need at least a modicum of each to get along.

"If the doors of perception were cleansed," wrote William Blake, "every thing would appear to man as it is, infinite." Meanwhile both science and faith, both religion and superstition, are part of a whole and ought to be infinitely more tolerant of each other.

FORETELLING THE FUTURE

By conjurations and spells Eleanor, Duchess of Gloucester worked with Bolingbrook (a "conjuror") and John Southwell and John Hume (whom Shakespeare assumes are priests), Margery Jordan (a witch), and others to discover by magic what was going to happen next in the topsy-turvy reign of Henry VI in the fifteenth century. A spirit (Asmath) was called up and asked a list of prepared questions. But the authorities broke up the ritual because the duchess and her cohorts had been detected, and they were charged with a "pretty plot" and condemned. She was banished for life. Others died, horribly executed for treason. Shakespeare's *The First Part of the Contention betwixt the Two Famous Houses of Yorke and Lancaster* (also known as the second part of *Henry VI*):

Heer do the Ceremonies belonging [to the conjuration], *and make the circle,* [the priest] *Bolingbrook or Southwell reads,* Conjuro te, [I conjure you], *&c. It thunders and lightens terribly; then the Spirit riseth.*

SPIR. *Ad sum* [I am here].
M. JORD. *Asnath,*
    By the eternal God, whose name and power
    Thou tremblest at, answere that I shall aske:
    For till thou speak, thou shalt not passe from hence.
SPIR. Ask what thou wilt; that I had said, and done!
BOLING. First of the King: What shall of him become?
[Reading out of a paper.]
SPIR. The Duke yet lives, that Henry shall depose:
    But him out-live, and die a violent death.
[As the Spirit speaks Bolingbrook writes the answer.]
BOLING. "[Tell me] what [fate awaits] the Duke of Suffolk?"
SPIR. By water shall he die, and take his end.
BOLING. What shall [betide] the Duke of Somerset?
SPIR. Let him shun castles.
    Safer shall he be upon the sandy plains,
    Than where Castles mounted stand.
    Have done, for more I hardly can endure.
BOLING. Descend to darkness, and the burning Lake!
    False fiend, avoid!
Thunder and lightning. Exit Spirit [sinking down again].

It is worth noting that the stage directions do not bother to describe how to inscribe the magic circle nor do they give more of the incantation than the *incipit*, the first words—assuming the actors will be able to recite the whole thing!

BREAKING UP LOVERS

Take two candles of any color (some people prefer black for this nefarious act). On one write the name of one person; on the other write the name of his or her lover. Each day, light the candles, concentrate on your intention of breaking up their love, visualize it happening—and move the two candles a little farther apart. Your nasty mental state may be enhanced in this business by burning incense, oils, or herbs. Try aloe, balmoney, blueberry, buckthorn, dog grass, verbena, etc. A waning moon might help. What really works is what you are truly convinced will work.

Anna Riva's *Modern Herbal* recommends Dog Grass.

HALLOWEEN SPELLS

This end of the Old Religion's year, *Samhain*, has always been a great time for spells and incantations and trying to find out whom you will marry. Get the peel off an apple in one piece, throw the peel over your left shoulder, and it may land in a shape resembling the initial of your intended. Or you could drop hot wax (more dangerously, molten lead) into water and try to decipher the shape it makes. Or you can put your shoes on the floor in the shape of a T and say:

> Hoping this night my true love to see,
> I leave my shoes in the shape of a T.

That's an old British one (but I don't think it works). You might have better luck with giving a name to each of the apples you bob for, or the chestnuts you place at the fire to roast. The one that bursts open first, or burns first, whichever you like, will give you the name of the one bursting with love for you or all-fired ready to marry you.

On this night, light bonfires to drive away the witches. Wear masks so that the bogeymen won't recognize you. Treat those who arrive at your door for trick or treat, all disguised, as if they really were spirits you wanted to keep friendly, because you never know (as with angels) what disguise, even the disguise of a tot with anxious parent accompanying her or him, might be assumed by the Little People, a pixie, a fairy, a troll, a ghost....

And do not rely too much on spells for telling the future. Only bad horror movies about Halloween, not real life outcomes, are utterly predictable.

A sorcerer sells sailors winds magically tied up in three knots in a rope. From Olaus
Magnus' *Historia de gentibus septentrionalibus.*

WINDS IN THE KNOTS

Thomas Heywood, in *The Hierarchy of the Blessed Angells* (1635) wrote:

> The Finnes and Laplands are acquainted well
> With such-like Sp'rits, and Windes to Merchants sell,
> Making their cov'nant, when and how they please
> They may with prosp'rous weather cross the seas.
> As thus: they in an hand-kerchief fast tye
> Three knots, unloose the first, and by and by
> You find a gentle gale blow from the shore.
> Open the second, it encreaseth more,
> To fill your sailes. When you the third untye,
> Th'intemperate gusts grow vehement and hye.

CASTING SPELLS

We began executing witches pretty early in colonial America. The first condemned to death was Alice Young, on 6 May 1647. Later in the same century came the hideous stupidities of the Salem witchcraft trials. However,

casting spells went on and on and became a standard part of American folklore. The spells and incantations could be as simple as childhood's

> Rain, rain, rain, go away,
> Come again another day.

Or, for luck,

> Ladybug, ladybug, fly away home.
> Your house is afire and your children alone.

Or to banish the bogeyman in the closet or under the bed,

> Criss-cross, double cross,
> Tell the monster to get lost!

DISPELLING SPELLS

Another way to get rid of a spell easily: just blow on your fingers. Make a "fig" —an obscene Italian gesture—to ward off *malocchia*, the evil eye. Point your two first fingers at anyone trying to curse you. Or give them five fingers, "Five in the face." (equivalent to "Ashes on your head"). Cross your fingers. Make the sign of the cross. Spit. Draw a picture of a corpse in a coffin and put it under your mattress. Keep a glass of water by your sink. And carry a cinder in your hand when you walk out at night and whistle when you pass graveyards.

BLASTING CROPS

When the world was chiefly occupied with just feeding itself, agriculture was profoundly involved in magic and witchcraft. First, what is more magical than the beautiful flower, the helpful herb, the useful vegetable, or the giant, shady tree springing from a seed? Maybe a great oak growing from an acorn, which takes a very long time even to get started. What is more miraculous than nature rising from the dead every Spring? So Persephone and Dionysus and Mithras and Jesus and others who were credited with commanding nature to rejoice were resurrected in the Spring. Easter is the first Sunday after the first full moon after the vernal equinox, a date that your average modern person finds difficult to predict. In olden days, everyone knew about the equinoxes and the turns of the seasons. Additionally, they knew about witches, who carried into Christian times the Old Religion of Mother Earth, and held a big celebration each time the season turned. The greatest of their holidays we still celebrate as the Feast of All Souls. It's Halloween, and today some Americans who cannot distinguish between Wicca and wicked want to remove all that pagan nonsense. The Grinch tried to steal Christmas; these people want to destroy Halloween so that the kids can no longer masquerade (as the Grateful Dead of folklore) or make skull-like Jack-o'-Lanterns out of great big pumpkins. Charlie Brown's cheerful god, The Great Pumpkin, is threatened with extinction in the name of anti-Satanism. He is banished from the elementary schools in the name of separation of church and state. Throw away your orange Crayola! Watch out! Now there may be a razor blade in that shiny apple you put in your loot bag!

There was always the fear that the crops would fail and the people and cattle would starve. Witches might curse the land and its inhabitants; or, alternatively, good witches might be able with spells and conjurations to counter bad witches. Like lawyers, one might say, witches made business for each other. Sometimes, like doctors, the general practitioners in the church (inadequate with their blessing of the fields and the fishing waters, the wells and the harvest festival) might send you off to a specialist, a "wise woman." She could chant for you the magic words nearly as old as the magical pictures that cavemen made to bring them luck in the hunt, before mankind even settled down to agriculture.

Then also there were traditions handed down since time immemorial by word of mouth among the peasantry. These encapsulated the practical experience but also the irrational beliefs of the common folk. There were things, people heard, that the individual could do to control the occult forces. Planting by the seasons (sometimes measured from the feasts of saints) or by the phases of the moon turns out to be simply sensible. Few books are as

Isn't that a horned demon sharing an illuminated initial, in a thirteenth-century MS, with a bishop?

pragmatic as the various farmers' almanacs. They deal not in astrology but in agronomy. But there were many superstitions as well, and as the farmer sowed beans, for instance, he would mutter a recognition that not everything one plants comes up, that some sacrifices are made for the benefits obtained. His "bean counting" went:

> One for rook, and one for crow.
> One to die, and one to grow.

FOR PROTECTION BY NIGHT

You can kneel by your bed and pray:

> Now I lay me down to sleep.
> I pray The Lord my soul to keep.
> If I should die before I wake,
> I pray The Lord my soul to take.

Or

> Matthew, Martin, Luke, and John,
> Bless the bed that I lie on.

The difference between prayer and a spell is that a prayer supplicates and a spell commands. To some, particularly children, charms and chants are indistinguishable; prayers and spells and even jokes get all mixed up. Some children used to try variations such as:

> Now I lay me down to snooze.
> By the bed I leave my shoes.
> If I should die before I wake,
> Give them to my brother, Jake.

The Tex-Mex version of the pious prayer is:

> *Cuatro esquinas tiene mi casa.*
> *Cuatro angeles que la adoran:*
> *Lucas, Marcos, Juan y Mateo.*
> *Ni brujas, ni hechiceras,*
> *Ni hombre malhechor.*

This is followed by the sign of the cross with the Spanish equivalent of the standard, "In the name of The Father, The Son, and The Holy Spirit. Amen." (By the way, since ancient Jewish times *Amen* has been regarded as a little more than a clincher, more like a magic word that adds power to what has been spoken.) I translate the Spanish like this:

> My house has corners four.
> Four angels it adore.
> Luke, Mark, John, Matthew.
> No witches', no sorcerers' charm,
> No man can do me harm.

THE VOODOO PRIESTESS SUPREME

I have met a few self-appointed voodoo priestesses. (In witchcraft, as in fraternal orders, Americans like to give themselves high, astounding titles.) I would really like to have met Marie Laveau. She was the rage in nineteenth-century New Orleans. When she died her daughter quietly took over from her, placing and removing hexes, getting blacks and creoles and some whites who surreptitiously visited special favors, love, freedom from prison, etc. New Orleans people thought that Marie herself was living to a very great old age—two lifetimes. Some of Marie Laveau's spells and a lot of her reputation is still for sale in The Big Easy. Not everyone there thinks of this as simple tourist stuff.

PARACELSUS

This German scientist (and pseudo-scientist) keeps cropping up in my books, probably because I am fascinated with onomastics (the study of names) and have written *What's in a Name?* (which has a chapter on "The Names in Magic and the Magic in Names") and a great deal on all aspects of names and naming. His real name was Theophrastus Bombastus von Hohenheim, and "Paracelsus" was his characteristically boasting pseudonym: he considered himself "beyond Celsus." Celsus was the greatest of Greek physicians after Hippocrates. Paracelsus has some claim to be the father of all the modern physical sciences.

Paracelsus was obsessed not only with the physical (he made great advances in chemistry and physics) but also with the metaphysical (he discovered cobalt, named for mysterious little creatures called *Kobolds* in the mines). He was one of the forerunners of psychosomatic medicine because he knew that spells helped his prescriptions to work.

Elsewhere I write of modern "Paracelsians" in California and of the persistence of some of his kookier ideas. I resist giving some of the spells of Paracelsus for fear some people will try them and hurt themselves or others. If you are ill, see a reliable medical specialist. The white coat and the diplomas on the walls will be sufficient to help the treatments to work. You don't need spells.

SOME LADIES WITH CHARM

Needed or not, books on spells are, if not as common as cookbooks by women, perhaps nearly as popular. A list of writers of recent books on spells must include Laurie Cabot, Gerina Dunwich, Janet Farrar, "Jade," Anna Riva, Donna Rose, and many more. Many of these books are the result more of borrowing than of burrowing, but the women are certainly challenging—and may already have bested—the men such as Gerald Burns, Barry Dolnick, "Papa Jim," Ray Marlbrough, Joseph Naveh et al. The modern women are far more likely to deal in herbs and even vegetables from the supermarket in magic than to ask you, as mages of old did, for human blood and animal sacrifices. The commonest desires remain ever the same, however—love and money.

A RECIPE FOR INVISIBILITY APPEARS AGAIN

The *Grimorium vera* (True Guidebook to Magic) gives a recipe which calls for a decapitated head to be buried with nine black beans and "watered" with brandy, rather like a Christmas fruitcake is prepared.

TO BANISH ALL GHOSTS

Someone wrote the following pithy and profound verses to the *Public Advertiser* for 5 February 1762 when all London was agog because a ghost was supposed to be haunting Cock Lane:

> Should Latin, Greek, and Hebrew fail,
> I know a charm which *must* prevail:
> Take but an ounce of Common Sense,
> 'Twil scare the ghosts, and drive 'em hence.

TO DRIVE AN ENEMY AWAY

Gerina Dunwich has written several interesting books on Wicca, and in *The Wicca Spellbook* (1994) she offers a number of spells, including:

> TO MAKE AN ENEMY MOVE—When the Moon is in a waning phase, write on white parchment [she means paper] the full name of the person you want to move away from you, along with his or her complete birthdate (if know) [she means "known"]. Roll up the paper along with a photograph of the enemy (if you happen to have one handy), place them inside a bottle of vinegar, and toss it into a moving body of water as you visualize your enemy moving far away and never bothering you again. This is an ideal spell to use when all else seems to fail.

As with this and with all other spells, the rational person will want to ask: Precisely how does this *work*? Who or what is producing the desired effect and how is it accomplished? Those who give us spells to try seldom try to give us explanations.

WHITE MAGIC

I believe there is only one "color" of magic, and that a lot of people who say they only do white magic—just good—are lying. Aleister Crowley always insisted he was just performing white magic. Would you believe that? Don't declare yourself a white magician until you have read at least all of these:

Alice A. Bailey, *Treatise on White Magic* (1974)
G. Knight, *A History of White Magic* (1978)
Eric Maple, *Magic, Medicine and Quackery* (1968)
David G. Phillips, *White Magic* (1981)
Leslie Shepherd, *How to Protect Yourself against Black Magic and Witchcraft* (1978)

A LITTLE LIBRARY OF SPELLCRAFT

Daniel Cohen, *Curses, Hexes, and Spells* (1974)
M. DePascale, *The Book of Spells* (1971)
Stuart Holroyd, *Magic, Words and Numbers* (1975)

Ellen Evert Hopwood and Lawrence Bond, *People of the Earth: The New Pagans Speak Out* (1997)

William Mackenzie, ed. *Gaelic Incantations, Charms & Blessings of The Hebrides* (1895)

Eric Maple, *Incantations and Words of Power* (1974)

"Brother Moloch," *Hidden Key of the Necronomicon* (1997)

David Norris & J. Charrott-Lodwidge, *The Book of Spells* (1974)

MORE GOOD ADVICE

Max Gunther gives wisdom for the stock market—if spells were easy and effective just imagine what would happen *there!*—in the classic *Zurich Axioms*. Though directed to those who gambol (and gamble) in the financial fields, these words of wisdom are quite relevant here.

> ON RISK: Worry is not a sickness but a sign of health. If you are not worried, you are not risking enough.
> ON GREED: Always take your profit too soon.
> ON HOPE: When the ship starts to sink, don't pray. Jump.
> ON FORECASTS: Human behavior cannot be predicted. Distrust anyone who claims to know the future, however dimly.
> ON PATTERNS: Chaos is not dangerous until it begins to look orderly.
> ON MOBILITY: Avoid putting roots down; they impede motion.
> ON INTUITION: A hunch can be trusted if it can be explained.
> ON RELIGION AND THE OCCULT: It is unlikely that God's plan for the universe includes making you rich.
> ON OPTIMISM AND PESSIMISM: Optimism means expecting the best, but confidence means knowing that you will handle the worst. Never make a move if you are merely optimistic.
> ON CONSENSUS: Disregard the majority opinion. It is probably wrong.

The story of The Wandering jew is told in this picture and in this chapter. From an old French print.

2
Curses and Ill Intent

CALLING DOWN EVIL

The word for imprecations, calling for powers to bring evil upon someone, may be related to the Late Latin word *cursus*, which meant the order
of religious service or collection of prayers intended to bring good upon
people. Both involve invocation of super powers to affect change, bad or
good, and in this magical metamorphosis and religious faith are once again
found to be inextricably intertwined. Rationalists and atheists can neither
curse nor pray.

A HEART-FELT CURSE

Moving but powerless, more concerned with symbolism than action, curses
often resemble the pitiful cry of rage from a Christian stepfather of one
of the three grade-school children, stripped, mutilated, and murdered in
West Memphis (AR) in 1993. It seems no time for Christian forgive and
forget. In the documentary film by Joe Berlinger and Bruce Sinofsky (*Paradise Lost: The Child Murders at Robin Hood Hills*, 1996), the bereaved step-
parent screams revenge and curses at the absent teenagers accused of the
crime:

> I really hope y'all believe in your master, Satan, Sluice-foot, the
> Devil himself, because he's not going to help you. He's gonna laugh
> at you, mock you and torture you, because he didn't need your help.
> He's got all the devils he needs....The day you die I'm gonna praise

C	A	S	E	D
A	Z	O	T	E
B	O	R	O	S
E	T	O	S	A
D	E	B	A	C

A magic square even S.L. Macgregor Mathers said "should never be made use of." Placed where anyone can find it, it brings harm to the finder. To undo any spell it has placed on you, dear reader, snap your fingers *now*.

God. I'll make you a promise—the day you die, every year I'm gonna come to your gravesite. I'm gonna spit on you.... I'm gonna curse the day you were born. And I'm sure while I'm there I'm gonna have to have bodily functions let go upon your graves. I promise you, with God as my witness, I'll visit every one of your graves.

THE BIBLE

Religious believers, even ones like the stepfather and his wife, gleefully hateful in vengeance, bent all out of shape by miseries they cannot bear, can find in religion—if not acceptance —of the will of God then action through prayers and curses. There are some 1000 curses threatened in The Bible; look in Genesis, Judges, Job, 1Samuel, Jeremiah, Numbers.... Jeffrey Scott Anderson wrote about "The Nature and Function of Curses in the Narrative Literature of the Hebrew Bible" as a doctoral dissertation (Vanderbilt 1993), in case you want to get deeply into this. Otherwise, next time you pick up a Gideon Bible in a hotel or motel room, take a peek at the astonishing list in Deuteronomy XXVIII: 15–68. Or read in the New Testament how Jesus cursed a tree!

If you in turn curse God for your troubles, as Job's wife advised him to do (Job II: 9), you will die. The advice may have been well meant (because dying would have put Job out of the misery he was suffering) but St. Augustine denounced Job's wife as the handmaiden of The Devil (*diaboli adjutrix*) and John Calvin called her the organ of Satan (*organum Satanae*). God has a bad temper. And Jesus, who angrily drove the moneychangers out of the temple, was a chip off the old block. Don't get on the wrong side of Them.

Also, do not use Their names in vain. Cussing can bring on cursing.

ANATHEMA

It doesn't seem like Christian forgiveness, but the Roman Catholic Church (among others) reserves the right to excommunicate members formally as well as automatically when they do not follow the rules.

We exclude him from the bosom of our Holy Mother the Church, and we judge him condemned to eternal fire with Satan and his angels and all the reprobate, so long as he will not burst the fetters of the demon, do penance, and satisfy the church.

The book is closed. The bell is rung. The candle is extinguished. The wretch is cast out, deprived of the sacraments.

CURSES AS PROTECTION

Threatening a curse on anyone who disturbs your property can sometimes keep it from being tampered with. Probably the most famous such curse in the Western world is on the stone that covers the grave—or says it covers the grave—of William Shakespeare. It is a plea to be left alone—and a curse on anyone who dares to disturb the resting place. A. L. Rowse notes that "strangely enough, this wish has always been respected. "

> Good friend for Jesus sake forbeare
> To digge the dust encloasèd here!
> Bleste be the man that spares thes stones
> And curst be he that moves my bones.

Considering what it might be possible to do not too many years from now with the DNA of William Shakespeare, can this curse last another century?

AN ANCIENT CURSE

> I will bind Sôskileia and her property and general reputation and fortune and mind. Let her become hateful to friends. I will bind her under murky Tartarus.

And on the reverse of the lead tablet of the third century B.C. is this, addressed to the Furies, familiar vengeful creatures of Greek belief:

> In troublesome bonds with Hecate [Queen] of the Underworld.

There follow two names, written backwards (as is common in these magical operations and upside down), and:

> for the dizzying Furies.

This was found in a grave. Sometimes such objects were put in graves through pipes left for the purpose of adding offerings. Other lead tablets with curses have been found in excavations in London, dating to Roman times, thrown down holy wells in Wales, from medieval times, and so on. Lead is often associated with curses as well as with coffins and the like, and everyone knows that silver (not lead) bullets are supposedly required to dispatch vampires and similar horrible monsters.

THE ELIZABETHAN LAW AGAINST WITCHCRAFT

From the time of the Anglo-Saxon kings, the law in England tried to put down witchcraft and sorcery. But witch persecution really began after the passing in the fifth year of the reign of Elizabeth I of "An Act against Conjurations, Enchantments, and Witchcraft." In her long reign (1558–1603) Elizabeth saw more than 500 people indicted under this law, but only 82 executed. Her law:

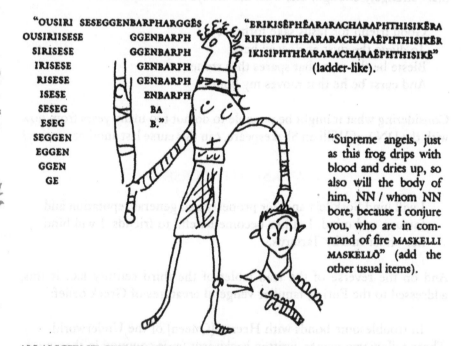

"OUSIRI SESEGGENBARPHARGGĒS
OUSIRIISESE GGENBARPH
SIRISESE   GGENBARPH
IRISESE   GENBARPH
RISESE   GENBARPH
ISESE   ENBARPH
SESEG   BA
ESEG   B."
SEGGEN
EGGEN
GGEN
GE

"ERIKISĒPHĒARARACHARAPHTHISIKĒRA
RIKISIPHTHĒARARACHARAĒPHTHISIKĒR
IKISIPHTHĒARARACHARAĒPHTHISIKĒ"
(ladder-like).

"Supreme angels, just as this frog drips with blood and dries up, so also will the body of him, NN / whom NN bore, because I conjure you, who are in command of fire MASKELLI MASKELLŌ" (add the other usual items).

AN ANCIENT CURSE: "Take a lead lamella and inscribe with a bronze stylus the following names and figures, and after smearing it with the blood of a bat, roll up the lamella in the usual fashion. Cut a frog and put it into its stomach. After stitching it up with Anubian thread and a bronze needle, hang it up on a reed from your property by means of hairs from the tip of the tail of a black ox, at the east of the property near the rising of the sun." Translated by R.F. Hook.

Where at this present, there is no ordinary or condign punishment provided against the wicked offenses of conjurations and invocations of evil spirits, and of sorceries, enchantments, charms, and witchcrafts, the which offenses by force of a statute made in the 33rd year of the late King Henry VIII were made to be a felony, and so continued until the said statute was repealed ...in the first year of the reign of the late King Edward VI; since the repeal thereof many fantastical and devilish persons have devised and practiced invocations and conjurations of evil and wicked spirits, and have used and practiced witchcrafts, enchantments, charms, and sorceries, to the destruction of the persons and goods of their neighbors and other subjects of this realm, and for other lewd intents and purposes contrary to the laws of Almighty God, to the peril of their own souls and to the great infamy and disquietness of this realm: I. For the reformation whereof, be it enacted by the Queen's majesty, with the assent of the Lords spiritual and temporal, and the Commons, in this present Parliament assembled, and by the authority of the same, that [a] if any person or persons after the first day of June next coming, use, practice, or exercise, any invocations or conjurations of evil and wicked spirits, to or for any intent or purpose, or else [b] if any person or persons...shall use, practice, or exercise any witchcraft, enchantment, charm, or sorcery, whereby any person shall happen to be killed or destroyed, that then as well as every such offender or offenders...their aiders and counselors, being of either of the said offenses lawfully convicted and attainted, shall suffer pains of death as a felon or felons, and shall lose the benefit of sanctuary or clergy....

The Act goes on to say that rights of inheritance of the goods, etc., of such convicted felons are not taken away, but that any harm to other people's property from such offenses is to be punished after the first conviction by a year in prison and appearances in the pillory. Moreover, anyone who undertook to "take upon him or them by witchcraft, enchantment, charm, or sorcery, to tell or declare in what place any treasure of gold or silver be found or had in the earth, or other secret place; or where goods, or things lost or stolen should be found or be come; or shall use or practice any sorcery, enchantment, charm or witchcraft to the intent to provoke any person to unlawful love; or to hurt or destroy any person in his or her body, member, or goods" was to be imprisoned for a year and appear in the pillory four times at market days. A second conviction for non-capital offense in such matters meant that the offender had to "forfeit unto the Queen's majesty, her heirs and successors, all his goods and chattels and suffer imprisonment for life."

A FAMOUS "CURSED" OBJECT

As an example of an object with a curse on it, take the Hope Diamond, 45.52 carats, which Harry Winston (unable to sell it?) gave to the Smithsonian (and took off his income tax?).

It takes its name from one Henry Thomas Hope, who bought it in 1830 for his wife, otherwise unknown to fame. She left him for another man. It had come from the French royal family—and you know what the French Revolution did for them. It went after the Hopes to another social climber, Mrs. Evelyn Walsh McLean, and she lost her husband, her young son, and most of her inherited fortune, which is where the "curse" reputation got its real start.

If you want an unlucky gem, you can always wear an opal. They are not as expensive as diamonds and are nobody's best friends. But no gems are cursed.

AN ECCENTRIC MAN WHO WAS SURE HE WAS CURSED

"You only live once," you hear hedonists say. Some eastern religions say that's not true, that you are doomed to keep being reincarnated until you get it right! Here's the story of an Irishman who was sure he was cursed to be reincarnated as a chicken—and whose other odd ideas make him almost incredible by anyone's standards, eastern or western.

Adolphus Cooke (1792 –1876) was the illegitimate son of an Irish landowner who had him brought up, with just a nurse to look after him, away from the Big House but in a little cottage on the ample estate at Cookesborough he was one day to inherit after his half-brothers died (one in 1811 and one in 1835). I tell his story as it appears in Peter Sommerville-Large's gripping collection of *Irish Eccentrics* (1975), where for my money Adolphus Cooke more or less "takes the cake." Of him Somerville-Large writes:

> He represented the extreme in country-house eccentrics whose wealth encouraged oddness and yet helped him to skirt the boundary of true madness.

Cooke came to believe that his father had been reincarnated as a turkey—Adolphus demanded the servants tip the hat or curtsey to the turkey—and so it seemed only natural that he would come back as a chicken. He had very odd ideas about the crows on his estate and made his servants build them nests (which the crows would not use). His strange theories extended to his horses and cattle and even his employees, whom he made toe the line in strict military style. His leading overseers—one was named Tom Cruise, modern movie buffs may be happy to hear—were also very strange.

But few men could have been stranger than Adolphus on the subject of their tomb (an odd obsession, you may think, for someone who is planning to return as a chicken). Adolphus planned a huge mausoleum, a forty-foot marble cube he hoped would shield him in death from the sounds of jackdaws. He installed a marble fireplace, library of books, chair and table. He organized a perpetual supply of pens and paper, and wanted a lamp to burn perpetually in this cozy retreat.

But he was not buried there. The local priest, who noted that Adolphus did not have a bible among his 9,000 books (and who had told the priest he preferred the Koran) saw to that. Adolphus was buried more simply, with his father and childhood nurse. The elaborate tomb never held him. And nobody can say for sure that he did not come back as a chicken or (as he later began to think he might) as a fox. He left his estate to a younger son of the then Earl of Longford, and the fellow changed his name from Pakenham to Pakenham-Cooke to get the inheritance. "After a long dispute and the bankruptcy of the estate," writes Somerville-Large, "considering that it was not worthwhile carrying out the wishes of his benefactor, [he] dropped the Cooke from his name and became plain Mr. Pakenham once more."

Had Adolphus Cooke been more prescient, he would have leveled a terrible curse on anybody who did not bury him as he had wished or tried to go back on the conditions of the inheritance he left them. A chicken has a hard time haunting people.

THE CURSED TWO-DOLLAR BILL

People say the American two-dollar bill is unlucky and some suggest this is because it looks so much like a one-dollar bill that it may in error be given for one. But American bills have always looked too much like each other; we need a color-coded system such as has been adopted by Canada and a lot of other sensible countries.

People used to tear a corner off a two-dollar bill on receiving it. This was, presumably, to distinguish it from other bills in their wallets or purses. By the time this had been done three or four times about all you could do after that was tear up the bill. Today, people save two-dollar bills as curiosities. They appear to be rare.

Claudia de Lys in *A Treasury of American Superstitions* (1948) writes:

> Among the poor whites and Negroes, the two-dollar bill superstition implies the obvious bad luck of twins in the family. Therefore, to prevent this economic burden falling on them, they, too, tear off a corner of the bill. Some persons, especially cashiers in restaurants, when they receive a two-dollar bill, make a pretense of [kissing], or actually kiss the bill. In this case the mouth is the counter-magic charm, although those who do this are not aware of the meaning of their action. Saliva, which keeps the lips moist, was believed to be a powerful transformer of evil into good. (Saliva is an enzyme and was used in primitive brewing.)

She goes on to say that two bucks used to be the price of a vote and that the receiver of a two-dollar bill for such chicanery was in haste to get rid of the evidence. In the modern world of expensive television advertising, not to mention clergymen who may or may not have been bribed to keep their New Jersey congregations out of the polling booth, the price of a vote or a nonvote is well over a couple of greenbacks.

Actually, the two-dollar bill may be the one "cursed" piece of US currency but the really hated item was the Susan B. Anthony metal dollar. The only pieces I personally know of as useful in magical rites are real silver dollars from long ago, those being (at least long ago) easily obtained pieces of the silver so frequently used in magic.

A FAMOUS CURSED PERSONAGE

Baruch Spinoza (1632–1677) combined his interest in science (especially optics) with an interest in philosophy (Cartesian) which did not appeal to his fellows in the synagogue in Amsterdam. In 1656 they excommunicated him with this curse:

> The Lord blot out his name under heaven. The Lord set him apart for destruction from all the tribes of Israel, with all the curses of the firmament which are written in the book if The Law.... No man

*"CHAÒR
CHTHÒR
CHARARBA
CHOLBAS
CHTHRYTHYR
CHORBATH
CHTHAMNÒ
CHTHODYCHRA
CHYCHCHYCH

("CHOAR"[1] to the bottom)

"I conjure you by the great names: throw Philoxenos the harpist into strife with his friend Gennadios. Throw Pelagios the elder into strife with Philoxenos the harpist."

*Tr.: R. F. Hock.

shall speak to him, no man write to him, no man show him any kindness, no man stay under the same roof with him, no man come near him.

BEATING YOUR ENEMIES BY MAGIC

What if, instead of just cursing your enemies and hoping some punishment will fall on them, you could beat your enemy yourself—from a safe distance? Here's how.

Before sunrise on a Saturday cut a hazel wand with a single stroke from a tree that has never been touched before by human hand. This is the regular procedure for getting a magic wand, but get a strong stick because this time you will be using it to beat an enemy, not simply wave in the air. As you cut it you say, "I cut you, branch grown this summer, in the name of N., whom I wish to punish."

Back home spread a woolen cloth that has never been used before on a wooden table and repeat this three times (the crosses mark the places at which you should make the sign of the cross with three fingers up—like the salute of the Boy Scouts!):

In nomine Patris † *et Filii* † *et Spiritus* † *Sancti , et in cute Droch.*
Mirroch, Esenaroth †, *Betu* †, *Baroch* †, *Maaroth* †.

You have called on Father, Son, and Holy Spirit, and some demons. Then you say:

Holy Trinity, punish him [or her] who has done evil toward me, and deliver me from this evil by Thy great justice. *Elion* †, *Elion* †, *Esmaris* †. *Amen.*

At the *Amen*—which means "so be it," by the way—bang your stick on the table as hard as you like and the victim of your curse will feel the blow! In fact, you can beat the table as hard and with as many blows as you like and the victim will feel them all—and not know you are the one causing him the pain.

Of course you must realize that you are disobeying God's instructions in taking matters into your own hands like this. He prefers to mete out justice Himself and has said so. But practitioners of black magic like this often disobey the rules, even while asking God or his angels to help them to do so—and witches are famous for malice and revenge, while good Christians are supposed to turn the other cheek, forgive others as we hope to be forgiven.

The availability of outsiders and heretics like witches and wizards who stood ready for *maleficium*, deliberately doing evil such as revenge, hurting, even killing, by magic, constituted in tightly organized societies with oppressed peasants an escape valve, a way to get around orthodoxy and authority, a power which, though condemned by church and state, could still be exercised by or for the individual, even the malicious individual. The vicious circle continued: those to whom evil is done, as the poet says, do evil in return.

Maybe if God had forgiven Satan and the other rebellious angels in the first place we wouldn't have them urging us to evil all the time. But "vengeance is mine, saith The Lord" and the battle began. Perhaps you ought to rise above the God of the Old Testament—He has a nasty temper—and reject vengeance, set Him a good example of mercy rather than justice. On the other hand, as one of the race of Cain, you may have inborn the desire to bash your brother with a rock, so it isn't easy to forswear revenge.

BREAD AND BUTTER

If you are walking with someone and pass, for instance, on either side of a tree, do you say, "Bread and butter"? If so, you are avoiding the curse of breaking a pair and just mentioning two things that go together. "Death and taxes" might do just as well.

ST. MYLOR

The relics of St. Mylor rest in Amesbury Abbey in Wiltshire in the west of England. They are extraordinary in that, while touching most holy relics is supposed to be beneficial, touching the bones of St. Mylor will kill you. They carry a curse.

Legend says that Mylor was a prince whose father was murdered by Mylor's nasty uncle, Rivoldus. Rivoldus also wanted to dispatch young Mylor but was content to have his right hand cut off (replaced by a silver one) and then his left foot cut off (replaced by a bronze one). When Mylor went off to a monastery, Rivoldus was not rid of him, because Mylor started to perform miracles: if anyone touched his metal prostheses they were instantly healed (I mean the supplicants, not the extremities). So Rivoldus figured he had better give Mylor one more chop. Mylor's head was cut off. However, as soon as Rivoldus touched it, he fell sick and died. And since that time no one wants to take the chance involved in touching the fatal relics of the sainted Mylor, who rests in peace at last.

THE WANDERING JEW

One of the most famous stories of an accursed man is that of Ahasueras, the Wandering Jew, who mocked Christ in His Passion. When Christ was struggling along with His cross to the place of crucifixion, the Jew is supposed to have struck Him and said, "Hurry along. Don't dawdle!" Christ is said to have replied, "I indeed am going, but you shall wait until I come again."

So the Jew was condemned to walk the earth with his guilt until Judgment Day. Though this may sound like a tale of the unforgiving vengeance of the wrathful God of the Old Testament, it was a tale of Christian times and the legend of the wanderer as a Jew seems to have reflected the Diaspora and have come from the anti-Semitism of thirteenth-century Britain. It is first recorded in the *Flores historiarum* (Flowers of History, 1228) of Roger of Wendover. It was elaborated in the *Chronica majora* (Major Chronicle, 1259) of Matthew Paris.

After them the legend was of a Wandering Jew, cursed with near immortality. The Jews were otherwise cursed (according to the Christians). In 1602 Franciscus of Piacenza (a Jew who had converted to Christianity) published a frightening list of afflictions laid on all the Jews as Christ-killers. They had their Temple destroyed and their people dispersed and despised, they were prone to hemorrhages and hemorrhoids—there was not much that the Christian cleric exempted them from (but he hadn't ever heard of Tay-Sachs Disease). Bigots, like Franciscus (and the many Spanish Jews who became *conversos* and contributed so much to the terrors of The Holy Inquisition), believed firmly that Jews were cursed with certain skin diseases which they tried to cure magically with Christian blood, that they killed Christian babies to get innocent blood to put into magical *matzohs*, that they were all involved in black magic (their mystical tradition was greatly misunderstood), in league with the Devil, enemies of God, calling up demons, making a *golem*, and on and on. Until fairly late in the twentieth century the Jews were described in Roman Catholic prayers as "perfidious." However, the Wandering Jew suffered the most of all. It was said he would live on and on and suffer all the while and that when he died that would mean the world was coming to an end, that the Second Coming was at hand. He was said to have appeared in Italy as Giovanni Buttadeo (John Strikegod), in Germany as Ahasuerus, in Ypres and Brussels and Paris in the seventeenth century, in Newcastle in the eighteenth century, in Salt Lake City (as a Mormon named O'Grady) in 1868.

When one Johannes Cartaphilus (Doorkeeper) died at the turn of the seventeenth century in Europe, many people thought he had been the Wandering Jew and in their millenarianism looked for The Antichrist and Armageddon.

But the world did not end with 1600 (or 1601) any more than it did with the first millennium (much feared). The Wandering Jew went on and on, as Joseph Gaer and G. K. Anderson each records in the *Legend of the Wandering Jew* (books of 1961 and 1965). The doomed Jew's story varied from one country to another. Shelley touches on it in *Queen Mab* and *St. Irvyne* and there is something of it in Matthew "Monk" Lewis's sensational gothic novel *The Monk* and in Charles Maturin's romantic tale of *Melmoth the Wanderer*, and in Caroline Sheridan's "undying one" *Morton*, and in that huge "feast of blood," *Varney the Vampire*, among others. Oliver B. Fulmer has a dissertation (Tulane) on *The Wandering Jew in English Romantic Poetry* and Werner Zirus a book on *Der ewige Jude in den Dichtung vornehmlich engliscen und deutschen* (The Wandering Jew in English and German Romantic Poetry, 1928).

One of the many Continental versions is by the "coarser Dickens" of France, Eugène Sue (1804–1857). His novel *Le Juif errant* (1844–1845) was sensational in two senses of the word. We could touch on it under "Literature," but it will fit just as well here under "Curses."

It is worth describing this once-classic, now unread book, and in fact the summary of the melodramatic plot, with its contrived but effective *fris-*

sons, may make *The Wandering Jew* of Sue look better than it is, because in summary the disadvantages inherent in the cardboard characters and the clumsy prose disappear while Sue's concern with the health (he was trained as a doctor) and social conditions (he was always a polemicist for reform) of the time pop up even in a bare outline.

Here is the story. It begins with an old man named Samuel trudging downhill in Poland on his long journey to Paris. He has to be there for 13 February 1832, when the descendants of Marius de Rennepont, Blanche and Rose Simon (twin daughters of a Napoleonic marshal and his Polish wife, who was exiled to Siberia long ago), are to collect the legacy that results from Samuel having been given 150,000 francs by his friend Rennepont to invest. That was all that Rennepont could salvage from rapacious Jesuits. The Jew was asked to guard it for the descendants. Thanks to the miracle of compound interest, over the many years the legacy has become millions.

François Baudoin (called Dagobert), a family friend of the Simons, brings the twin girls to Paris to get the legacy which has accumulated over well over a century. Why so long? It was under the care of the deathless Samuel, who is the Wandering Jew. Also headed for Paris is a woman in America. She is Herodias, likewise cursed down the centuries, for she demanded for her daughter Salome the head of John the Baptist. The Jesuits likewise, having taken most of Rennepont's money years ago by dastardly deviousness, now are after the rest, and they have more or less tricked Rennepont's descendant Gabriel de Rennepont into joining the Society of Jesus. Little do most people know how evil the Jesuits are and that they were the ones who had Marshal Simon and his Polish wife exiled and who have never ceased trying to get at the legacy. They are now trying their best to prevent those converging on Paris from reaching there. In the absence of these people, Gabriel de Rennepont will inherit. With his vow of poverty, all the money will go to his order, the Jesuits. That could then finance what the French have always somewhat suspected, that the Jesuits have long had a plan to seize France and run it for their own nefarious purposes. The Father General of the Jesuits is conceived of some kind of black-robed Hitler with megalomaniac plans to rule all of Europe.

Baudoin (Dagobert) and the twin girls no sooner reach Paris than a Jesuit plot imprisons them in a convent. Other Rennepont claimants have been dealt with in other ways: for instance, Ardienne de Carrdoville has been declared insane and hidden away in an asylum and Jacques de Rennepont (whose nickname is *Couche-tout-Nud*, to be translated roughly as "Sleep-in-the-Buff") has been thrown in jail for debt. Moreover, others were also rendered incapable of fighting the Jesuits' dark plan. This is a plan driven by an alleged jesuitical basic conviction that the end justifies the means. Their plan was working.

On the fateful day in February, Fr. Gabriel de Rennepont goes to claim the money at Samuel's house in Paris. The priest is made to sign it all away to the order, represented for the occasion by the Father Provincial of the Jesuits (the Abbé d'Aigrigny) and his toady secretary (Rodin). The will is read. The money has reached 212,175,000 francs! But, in the best melodramatic tradition, just as the money is being handed over to Fr. Rennepont (to be handed over to the Jesuits), in comes a mysterious woman with a codicil to the will. She is Herodias. Remember her? The codicil calls for a three-month wait before the money is distributed.

Now the Jesuits fear the complete collapse of all their plans. Adrienne de Cardoville in that amount of time could get out of the insane asylum, Jacques could borrow enough money on a bridge loan to get out of debtor's prison, the Simons could get their act together, not to mention such others as Prince Djalma (drugged, who will regain consciousness), and François Hardy (who was sent off on a fool's errand but soon will discover the ruse and return to Paris).

Rodin steps in and organizes the Jesuit response: he will turn each of the claimants against themselves, and their own actions rather than simple Jesuit violence will bring their destruction. Rodin, deceitfully pretending to have turned on his Jesuit masters, will be the kingpin of the plan.

Rodin insinuates himself into the confidence of the Simon twins by getting them released from imprisonment and of Adrienne de Cardoville by springing her from the insane asylum, though Rodin has a bad patch where a servant of Adrienne de Cardoville makes a dying confession that she was deeply implicated in a vicious Jesuit plot to destroy her mistress. The poor servant had been blackmailed into spying. Hardy's factory is burned by arsonists employed by the Jesuits, Hardy's mistress is kidnapped by them, and Hardy himself is taken off to a Jesuit retreat where the penances (and perhaps poisons) are too much for him and he dies. Jacques de Rennepont is also separated from a mistress, is inveigled into an orgy (arranged by the Jesuit plotters), and perishes. The twin girls are put into a hospital where presumably they will be safe, but the Jesuits know full well that cholera rages there and of course it does in both Blanche and Rose Simon. Prince Djalma, who came from India, seems greatly infected with French ideas and he gets the news (false) that Adrienne de Cardoville has become the mistress of Baudoin/Dagobert's son (Agricola Baudoin), so the prince kills Agricola and a woman with him whom he takes to be Adrienne. But it is not Adrienne, so he despairs and takes poison. Adrienne decides to die with him. The bodies are piling up almost as impressively as the money did.

Now Fr. Gabriel is the sole heir and the Jesuits are going to get the whole legacy but—miracle of miracles (can you imagine the *coup de théâtre* this could be on the melodrama stage?)—the money bursts into flames and the whole legacy is utterly destroyed just as Rodin was about to get his hands on it. Sensation! But—wait! Now Rodin falls to the floor. He had taken some poisoned holy water from the hand of an Indian who was working for the Jesuits but, secretly, of course, was in the employ of Prince Djalma. Rodin dies in throes of agony, howling French vowels.

Fr. Gabriel, poor but honest, goes to live with the Baudoin/Dagobert bunch and spends the rest of his life reflecting on how the love of money can be the root of all evil. In time Fr. Gabriel dies and is buried but naturally Samuel—remember him? he seems to have functioned here throughout as nothing but a deathless banker who outlives everyone—has a final scene with (who else?) Herodias at a giant cross in a romantic setting. As the morning light reveals the changes that centuries of suffering have wrought in these two doomed people, they become aware that (why, for Heaven's sake?) their long sentences are over. The Wandering Jew and the cursed Herodias find peace. Tableau. The curtain falls.

Apart from the fact that you might say the depiction of the Jesuits in this novel as plottters for world domination is as outrageous as the anti-Semitic *Protocols of Zion*, Jews in general and the Jew Samuel, wandering or not, are not really essential to the basic story. The book in its attack on the Jesuits might well have earned it a place in the Roman Catholic *Index prohibitorum*—books that attack Jesuits so fiercely as to undermine faith,

French novels such as Voltaire's *Candide* and Dumas's *The Three Muske-teers*. Did you know no Catholic can read those without special need and special permission? Now you know the whole plot and so no one need check out the big, bulky tome of *The Wandering Jew*. If you can find it, read the Irish writer George Croly's "historical" novel of *Salathiel* (1828), which gives the Jew some elements of the Byronic hero.

THE CASE OF RAYMOND LULL

The list of those who came to a bad end because they were cursed by others would be interminable. Here, as an example of those who ended badly because they cursed another, is one of the most extraordinary personages of the Middle Ages, Raymond Lull (also called Lulli or Lully). He was born about 1232 on Majorca and died on a ship just coming in sight of Majorca on 10 June, 1315.

Between those two dates he had an extraordinary career as Grand Seneschal of Spain, theologian, philosopher, writer on magic and medicine, alchemist widely believed to have turned base metals into gold—thousands of pounds of it in the Tower of London, says one story, but he may actually never have been in England at all—and opponent of Islam. Disappointed in an extramarital affair, he resigned his position at the court of Spain, and heard a voice that told him to go and convert the Mohammedans—and also die in the attempt. When a Mohammedan servant learned of this and took a dagger to him to speed up this prophecy's fulfillment, Lull fought him and won. He also could have died at the hands of Mohammedans when he was sentenced to death for preaching Christianity in Tunis in 1291, but they offered him the option of just leaving town, and he took it.

Lull traveled widely, wrote much (including the *Ars magna*, a major contribution to epistemology), and lectured at Rome, Paris, and elsewhere on alchemy and philosophy, mysticism and theology. Having already been expelled from Bougie (in Algeria) in 1305 for preaching Christianity, he boldly returned and tried it again a decade later. The second time he cursed Mohammed in public. The crowd stoned him. Half conscious, he was put on a boat for Majorca but died, as we noted, just before he got back home, the victim of his wild determination to bring the Mohammedans to Christ.

A DEMON CURSED

There are many stories of a demon—or even a human being—cursed to stay inside a bottle until released by magic or some sympathetic passerby.

Claud Golding, who told the story of Raymond Lull in one of his *Cavalcade of History* volumes, also tells the tale of how the poet Virgil (70–19 B.C.) learned necromancy. Virgil was in the Middle Ages widely believed to be not only a great epic poet but also a masterful magician. His reputation was marred by rumors he sacrificed children to learn the future and called up the dead for more information.

The story goes that one day when Virgil was a young man he chanced upon a cave and went in to explore it. A disembodied voice asked him to pull up a plank that had a magical inscription on it. The voice told him that it was that of a demon that had been driven out of someone and had been consigned to spend the rest of eternity under this plank unless he could get someone to release him. He promised Virgil wonderful books on necromancy if Virgil would pull up the plank.

"Let's see the books," was Virgil's response, and he instantly was shown them. Having examined them and considered their worth, he pulled up the plank. The demon emerged as an "eel" but rapidly grew into a giant of a man.

Virgil was amazed at this, and asked the demon if he could get small again as well as grow so big. The demon said that of course he could. Virgil bet him he could not. The demon got small again and Virgil put him back and slammed the plank on top of him. "Rest there until your appointed day." And thus the demon had to live out his curse for eternity, and Virgil walked off with a magical library of stupendous value. With it he is said to have performed various fantastic feats, such a building as bridge through the air to get to his love, the daughter of the Sultan, or founding the city of Naples on a bed of eggs.

"There is a great deal more of this fanciful stuff in the apocryphal history of Virgil, which makes amusing reading but has not a vestige of truth," comments Golding in *The Second Cavalcade of History* (n.d.).

FOR THE BIRDS

Some birds are popularly supposed to be bad omens. The raucous cry of the raven, for instance, is said to herald evil. Shakespeare refers to this superstition in "The Scottish Play." The Devil is supposed to be able to change himself into all sorts of birds, especially black ones, all but the robin redbreast, harbinger of new life in spring. The war goddesses of Ireland and other deities in other civilizations were said to be able to turn themselves into black birds. Like cats, birds seem to have some uncanny abilities.

Killing some birds is unlucky and everyone knows of Samuel Taylor Coleridge's "The Rime of the Ancient Mariner." In that long poem we learn of the terrible fate that followed a sailor's killing of an albatross at sea.

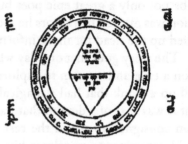

> Farewell, farewell! but this I tell
> To thee, thou Wedding-Guest!
> He prayeth well,who loveth well
> Both man and bird and beast.
>
> He prayeth best, who loveth best
> All things both great and small;
> For the dear God who loveth us,
> He made and loveth all.

Powerful protection from *The Book of Râziêl.*

ODD MAN OUT

The Swedes and Norwegians have especially colorful ways of telling, as the year ends, who is doomed to die in the next year, but my old English grandmother (born in the mid-nineteenth century) told me her infallible way of getting the bad news. It was to note if there was any local funeral between Christmas Day and Epiphany. If there was, it would mean a funeral a month in the community for the next year. At a Yuletide funeral you must be careful to walk with someone. The one who walked alone would surely be the next to go. She said she had seen some departures from the rule about one a month, true; but the one who walked alone—why would anyone do it, I wondered—was, shall we say, a dead certainty in her opinion.

THOSE BODACIOUS BODINES AND OTHER PSYCHIC SERVICES

On one of the many television shows that cater to (and increase) the interest of couch potatoes in the occult, *The Paranormal Borderline* (Jonathan Frakes, host) in 1996 introduced us to what was touted as "America's only professional psychic family," the Bodines. The Bodines live near Minneapolis. They do a brisk trade in ghost-busting and other useful lines. They charge $40–60 an hour for their ministrations and are available to deal with a purported "haunted theater" (a male ghost was "refusing to leave a balcony seat") or your personal peeves. They look like friendly people.

Anyone can set themselves up as a psychic, though few claim generations of occult abilities in their lines as the Bodines do. I used to know Sybil Leek, who claimed to come from many generations of witches stretching back to the middle ages, but (as I say in another publication) she struck me as most talented in her very twentieth-century publicity abilities. In retrospect, she looks very much better, in my view, compared to "The Witches of Salem" ("if you like talking to psychics...you'll love talking to witches"). Those so-called witches from Salem cost $3.99 a minute. That's well over $200 an hour, and for that you can get first-class psychiatric help, which is probably what you need if you like talking to psychics and witches who think they can usefully operate over the telephone.

I forbear to say whether Edgar Cayce could actually diagnose, let alone treat, illness long distance, but I feel very confident in saying that modern psychics ought to be examined and licensed before they undertake to give counseling to the confused. The recommendations of Dionne Warwick and Brigitte Nielsen and such faded show-biz personalities ought not to urge you to spend good money on long-distance readings. At the least the Bodines—or your local "psychics"—will see you in person. Or you can take in Summerhawk (Serman, New York) in season; at least you get, with Wicca, Maat, and whatall, fresh air and sunshine, and it doesn't set you back $200-plus an hour.

I confess to having encountered some "psychics" with real talent. None of them would think of "reading" on the telephone. The most amazing of them, like the traditional folk healers in Britain, refused payment. "How can you charge others for what you received as a gift?" Find one of those, or read books, or settle for feel-good Sixpack Something *ascended masters* on TV. Free (though they will try to sell you books and tapes—but doesn't everyone, even me?).

PILLOW TALK

In an important article on the superstitions of New Orleans in *Harper's* for 25 December 1886, Lafcadio Hearne discussed many beliefs—chiefly of blacks but also of creoles and whites who had black mammies from their infancy. One of the now almost forgotten items was what he called "pillow magic,"

> which is the supposed art of causing wasting sicknesses or even death by putting certain objects into the pillow of the bed in which the hated person sleeps. Feather pillows are supposed to be particularly well adapted to this kind of witchcraft. It is believed that by secret spells a "Voudoo" [*sic*] can cause some monstrous kind of bird or nondescript animal to shape itself into being out of the

pillow feathers—like the *tupilek* of the Esquimau *iliseenek* ....[which] grows very slowly, and by night only; but when [it is] completely formed, the person who has been using the pillow dies.... Some say that putting grains of corn into a child's pillow "prevents it from growing any more." Others declare that a bit of cloth in a grown person's pillow will cause wasting sickness; but different parties questioned by me gave each a different significa- tion to the use of similar charms. Putting an open pair of scissors under the pillow before going to bed is supposed to insure a pleas- ant sleep in spite of fetiches [*sic*]; but the surest way to provide against being "hoodooed," as American residents call it, is to open one's pillow from time to time....

He also mentions that "Negroes believe that in order to make an evil charm operate it is necessary *to sacrifice something*" and when he adds to the "wine and cake" —and he might have added the coin that on occasion is found with voodoo dolls—that "candies are scattered over the sidewalk" it occurs to me to see the Mardi Gras favors thrown from floats in a whole new way. Put that in your pillow and sleep on it!

HISPANIC MAGIC

Scholars—a few of them—will know the names of French-language schol- ars (such as Méry and Bougerol), who have written about curses and magic in general in Santo Domingo and Guatemala respectively. There are also many works on *Obeah*, *Santería*, and of course voodoo (sometimes called *vodun*),few examples being collected recently and reliably (as in Mary Alice Owen's *Voodoo Tales as Told among the Negroes*, 1969). Good new books—such as Suzanne Preston Blier's *African Vodun* (1996)—are too rare. There is, however, a lot of reportage of the sort that featured Sara María Aldrete-Villareal in New Mexico (1989), Rosileide dos Gracias Oliveira (Pres.Manuél Noriega of Panama's witch from Brazil) in 1990, and Mama Lola of Brooklyn (1991). Oudin (Benin) may be the voodoo capital of the world, but we have plenty of such beliefs and rites right here in the Americas.

Sound studies are lacking on the Amerind, Meso-American, and South American manifestations. It seems odd that Americans are concerning themselves professionally with Asian demonology and curses in Babylon- ian cuneiform and the heresies (from a word meaning "choices") of the

Cathars and so on down the alphabet and ignoring the Cubans in Florida, the Puerto Ricans in New York, the Chicanos in California, and so on—the whole panoply of magical beliefs and curses and cures in our very own American folklore, not to say the fascinating ancient and modern civilizations of Mexico, Peru, and more. A few *kachina* dolls, "eyes of God," and little balls of blue chalk are sold. These last Puerto Ricans buy in New York City *bodegas* to inscribe magical messages on their skins to keep vampires from bothering their sleep. These things are only the tip of the iceberg of Hispanic superstition and pagan religion operating right here in our country and in the territories of our neighbors to the north (Inuit and Iroquois magical practices are hardly known at all) and the south (there is no reliable, thorough book on Mexican magic in English and, so far as I know, only trivial pamphlets and more or less passing mentions in Mexican Spanish). Every once in a while we see that a lonely scholar such as J. Davy (*The West Indies before and after Slave Emancipation*, 1854) records crucial information about the *kembois* in St. Lucia or Jay D. Dobbin describes *The Jombee Dance of Montserrat* in the Islands (1986), or someone writes a film script about demonic possession of a Puerto Rican teenager in The Big Apple.

If you look in my local *botánicas*—and in fact in most such places anywhere, you will see only a few pamphlets among many that are not just trashy. Mostly there are merely dream books and magical herb books (one copied from another, none too accurately), and badly printed and much overpriced and underproofread publications, although on occasion a good one on Brazilian or African magical ceremonies crops up.

Santería is probably the best reported of these topics. See such studies as:

> *Santería: Vodun African Religion in The Caribbean* (1976)
> *New Religions of Africa* (1979)
> *Santería: African Religion in America* (1982)
> *Santería from Africa to the New World* (1993)
> *Santería: A Journey into the Miraculous* (1995)

For outlines of the many Hispanic cults (among others) consult the *Encyclopedic Handbook of Cults in America* (1985), the *Dictionary of Cults, Sects, Religions* (1993), etc. In South America, evangelical Christianity is making great inroads on Roman Catholicism's traditional hold on the people, but in some U.S. urban centers both are giving way to pagan cults.

A CURSED FAMILY

The royal family of France was cursed (by Jacques de Molay, the last grand master of The Templars, whom they ordered roasted over a slow fire). The present royal family of Britain seems to be having a bumpy ride. But right here in America we have legends of curses ringing down the generations. Or chasing a modern family from place to place: the Batzel Family has moved about a dozen times in the last twenty–five years and poltergeists keep following them from home to home. "Oh, my God! Not again!"

They have been studied for decades by one of Duke University's scholars of the paranormal but he has reached no conclusion except that there is allegedly "a strange energy" around wherever the Batzels go and that they are "clearly a very unusual family." Yep.

They are not unusual, however, in sharing with the rest of us the All-American "passion for publicity" that Sir Noël Coward was quick to notice

here. They may be disturbed by the knocking around the house and the flying objects, but so long as they get their names advertised without getting knocks in the press, presumably they will have some enjoyment out of their singularity.

I mention them chiefly to bring up the point that, particularly in our nation in which everyone wants their share of the "famous for fifteen minutes" that Andy Warhol promised us all, the study of people who think themselves to be cursed or possessed or otherwise distinguished by the presence of evil in their lives is complicated

by the difficulty of separating those who want cures from those who want coverage, not to say those who have real rather than trumped up problems.

TURNING LUCK WHEN TURNING BACK

When you set out on a journey—and that should never be on a Friday, a bad day for any new enterprise—you will be cursed if you turn back. Suppose you have forgotten something and must return for it. Simple: just sit down when you get back and have collected the object or objects you want and say

> If I sit
> Bad luck will flit.

Count to 10. Then set off once more and don't look back. African-American superstition says: "If you have started anywhere and turn back, to avoid bad luck make a cross on the ground and pull a hair or two from your head and throw it in the direction you were going." The same source (Dr. Roland Steiner of Georgia, 1899) says that if people are called back, they have to retrace their steps. Blacks mark a cross on the ground, and spit. If on the way they meet a stranger, they turn around, make a cross, and slightly change the direction in which they were walking. If they see an X in the road, they will walk around it the first time and thereby obviate bad luck. In future, they can safely step right over it and keep right on going.

CATS

Felines were worshipped by the Egyptians, and many are rather uppity about that. People used to say, "When you move do not take the cat with you," but the ASPCA may have other ideas. They say owning a black cat brings you lovers. There is a brisk trade still in the whiskers of black cats (useful in various charms and amulets), but people are being cheated with horsehair substitutes.

Certainly if you have ever tried to wash a cat you know they prefer to do that themselves and hate water. So if you throw a cat overboard at sea, expect a cursed bad storm to follow.

THANK GOD IT'S FRIDAY

This is the office worker's exclamation. But in magic, Friday is not good. Curses leveled on Friday stick. There is a long list of things you should never do on Friday, but I happen to be writing this sentence on a Friday and one of the *verboten* items is making lists. So instead, here's why you should not comb your hair on a Friday, according to one of Newbell Puckett's Ohio informants in 1958 (a superstition I have never seen noted anywhere else):

> According to a legend, on the Flight into Egypt, Mary asked a
> woman to hide Jesus in her long hair. The woman did not answer,
> so Mary put a curse on the comb for all Fridays.

The idea that The Blessed Virgin would curse rather than bless is highly unusual. She is often depicted standing on a snake, crushing evil. Visitations report her as a caring individual.

BLESS THIS HOUSE

To ward off evil, never sweep dirt out the front door; it might annoy the protective spirits who live around your doorstep. Check your doorstep and remove any voodoo doll or conjure bag there. Don't leave a broom outside the door (where a witch might be attracted to it as a vehicle); hang up a mop outside instead. Never rock an empty armchair (ghosts like a free ride), or carry a hoe into the house on your shoulder, or take anything at all out of the house on New Year's Day, or burn sassafras or black locust wood in your fireplace, or let a bee die on your premises (show it out courteously, and be sure to inform the bees if anyone in the family dies), or cut a loaf of bread at both ends (or serve a piece on the end of a knife or fork, or even slice it rather than tear it), or cross your silverware after the meal (which only makes people cross and argumentative). Also, don't keep a cracked mirror in the house or any one of a bunch of unlucky flowers. If a picture falls watch out (someone may die—folks say a clock may stop with the person's last heartbeat). Never have thirteen people sit down to dinner (the Last Supper would have been better off without Judas Iscariot, and there are thirteen in a witches' coven), and of course never invite a vampire to come in (he can't enter unless you invite him). Oh, and be careful what colors you paint rooms, because each color has its definite effect upon you. I used to have a dining room painted what some interior "desecrator" friend called "Venetian Red"—actually it was about the color of barn paint, but with all the gilt and mirrors of a very old house it was anything but rustic—but then I learned that the Chinese say that if you paint a room red you will promptly go crazy. Now it is *café-au-lait* (or *caffé latté*, if you are from Seattle) and I am not sure I caught the problem in time.

Legends abound about cursed families and the houses they inherit. Everyone knows about the cracked Roderick and his cracked House of Usher in Poe's creepy tale. Britain's most overemphasized disturbed house was probably Borley Rectory, though the British Isles abound in interesting houses that are cursed, haunted. Sir Noël Coward's song about "The Stately Homes of England" gets a lot of laughs out of ghosts and other attractions in the houses that are kept up "for Americans to rent."

LUCKY HORSESHOE

The fact that you have to nail up the traditional lucky horseshoe with your left hand shows there is something sinister going on. In case you are going to nail up a horseshoe anyway, I repeat here the formula you need to put up this protection against spells and curses. I like it because it manages to get into one little poem both Christian and pagan deities, so you get a kind of double protection:

> *Father, Son,* and Holy *Ghost,*
> *Nail* The Devil to the post.
> *Thrice* I smite with Holy Crook.
> With this mell I thrice do *knock*.
> One for *God,* one for *Wod*[in], one for *Lok*.

I have printed this before and received a whole lot of variations on the verses, in some of which the Scandinavian deities' names were totally mangled and nonsense syllables used. Hit the nails on the italicized words. That may, I'm told, be more than you need but "it feels very satisfying."

TO BRING EVIL UPON AN ENEMY

There are anthologies these days of "dirty tricks" you can perpetrate, but old methods are still in use. Some of these involve a photograph of the person you detest, which may be easier to get than hair or fingernail clippings. Burn the photograph with imprecations. Stick a pin through each eye of it. Drop hot wax on it as you chant a curse. Make an X or stick a pin in the photograph at the point where you want pain to strike. Bury the photograph.

A CURSE ON THE GORDONS

For some reason only New York could explain, most of the people I happen to know who are surnamed Gordon are Jewish. But there is a curse of some Scottish Gordons. The story goes that the Gordons of Strathnaver (in the Highlands) heard there was a witch who had a magic stone. They demanded it of her and she denied them. They dragged her to the loch and drowned her, but not before she tossed the precious stone into the water with the curse: "May the stone do good to everyone alive except the Gordons of Strathnaver." Then she perished, crying *manaar* (shame) in Gaelic.

To bring Astaroth, one of the most vengeful of demons.

Quentin Copper & Paul Sullivan, in their delightfully quirky book *Maypoles, Martyrs & Mayhem* (1994) write:

On the Monday of or after the 12th [of February], *Loch Manaar*[,] between Strathnaver and Strath Halladale near Betty Hill in Highland Region, is on great form for those seeking *healing*. Last century travellers from all over Scotland would make the journey. A sympathetic reporter in an 1877 edition of *The Inverness Courier* describes them as: *'the impotent, the halt, the lunatic and the tender infant.'* They would all hang about in the dark on Sunday until the stroke of midnight—the key time for the Loch's magic. Loch Manaar (also spelt Monaar or mo Naire) is equally effective on the Mondays of or after the 12th of May, August and November.

Perhaps this bit would fit as well under "Cures" as "Curses," but we began with some cursed Gordons, didn't we?

THE CURSE OF IMPOTENCE

To remove from mankind the power to follow the mandate of the God of the Old Testament to increase and multiply, or threaten the pleasures of the flesh for recreative rather than procreative purposes, is to strike at an enemy in one of the most painful ways. Small wonder that those who were infertile or impotent suspected that they were under some malevolent curse.

Impotence was superstitiously believed to be created by a number of potions (walnut, for one) and spells, but probably the most famous way of depriving a male of his virility was the simple matter of tying knots in a cord, with the appropriate curses. Kings of England and Scotland (notably James I and VI) and France, as well as The Prophet himself (the Koran condemns the practice strongly), were said to be thus hurt by witches. In order to remove the curse, one had to get the cord and untie the knots.

Some of this superstition may go all the way back into the mysterious past of Indian culture in which, from time immemorial, certain peoples believed that there was magic in knots. For instance, at marriage ceremonies all knots in the clothing of the bride and groom were untied and thereby all evil spirits loosened from them; then the couple tied the knot in marriage with a symbolic tying of one to the other. Some variation of lovers' knots and ceremonial tying together persists in a number of western religions even to this day.

In the ceremonies inducting apprentices in certain aspects of The Craft, hands are tied with special knots, then unloosed. This has nothing to do with impotence, however, but rather makes a gesture of gaining power.

THE UNINVITED

In one of his plays, Oscar Wilde has a character say that nothing annoys people quite so much as not being invited to some festivity. We see from the story of *Sleeping Beauty* that a wicked witch, not invited to the christening, put a curse on the baby, saying she would grow up to prick her thumb, go to sleep, and remain in that state until released by the kiss of Prince Charming.

In history rather than fairy tale, but still redolent of medieval superstition, is the legend of the dismal figure that appeared at the wedding feast—some say it was an uninvited witch, some say a ghost—of King Alexander III of Scotland. Alexander (who ruled Scotland from 1249 to 1286) first married Margaret, daughter of Henry III of England. She died in 1275. Later he married Yolande, daughter of Robert IV, Count of Dreux. It was at that second marriage feast that the ominous figure foretold Alexander's death within the year. He died in a hunting accident right on schedule. It was said that Nostradamus foretold the death of a French monarch in the sixteenth century, that the horoscopes of Louis XVI and Marie Antoinette foretold their gruesome deaths, and that many other important figures in history have died of curses or had their ends frighteningly foretold.

It is said that a mysterious masked man, all in black, came to Mozart to request he write a *Requiem*. Was it his father's ghost, his archenemy Salieri, one of Salieri's minions in disguise, or who? Mozart felt it portended his death, and he died soon after.

TO MAKE A WOMAN HATE A MAN

Janet H. Johnson has translated a defective little piece of papyrus which contains a spell to make a woman hate a man. The instructions are

> You bring dung, hair, and hair...which is dead, and you mix them
> with fresh blooms and you put it in a new papyrus after writing
> on the papyrus first with my ink, saying, "May [supply name], born
> of [supply name], hate [supply name], born of [supply name]. And
> you recite these true names over it seven times, and you bind the
> papyrus, and you put it in the water of...."

What are the seven true names? They are mysterious demotic Greek. The papyrus says:

Here are the true names: IAKYMBIAI IAO IOERBETH IO BOL-GHOSETH BASELE OM GITAHNAGS APSOPS O. EL.T, separate [supply name] born of [supply name], from [supply name], born of [supply name]; hurry, hurry; be quick, be quick.

For a modern voodoo curse to make two people hate each other—one way to get a rival in love out of the way—you could put something belonging or representing each of them into a jar with a magnet and vinegar, burn a candle to an evil spirit, offer him sacrifices or gifts, and strongly and persistently visualize the bad things you want to occur.

KAPU

It could be said that the promises that bad luck (or worse) would fall upon anyone violating the taboos of the Hawaiians (called *kapu*) were some sort of curses. Actually, the *kapu* were basically "keep off" signs posted by the powerful chiefs of the superstitious society. So touchy were they about their personal property that if you touched it, even if you simply stepped on their shadows, you were in big trouble. It is a sure sign of how primitive their society was that this foolishness caught hold and was, in fact, rigorously enforced.

However, as we see the all too human motives behind the alleged taboos identified by the gods it is wise to note that our supposedly advanced society also has some pretty silly taboos and that we ourselves still fear so-called cursed people, places, and things.

KARMA

Taboos are not often regarded as curses, but they involve something resembling a curse in that they promise ill. So does what is called "karmic debt" by such practitioners of occult sciences as numerology. Numerologists, working with the details of your name or birthday, undertake to predict the course of your life. They count in predicting the Life Path the debt you owe for "misapplication of energies in a past life." Hippies of the sixties (and later imitators of flower-power imitations of eastern thought) have often remarked that "what goes around, comes around," and by that they mean there is a certain justice in life so that those who commit evil deeds get their comeuppance eventually. Your missing out on that great apartment in the East Village, they would say, is directly traceable to the fact that two years ago you weaseled out of helping Staycie move.

But they are speaking of this life, and karma presupposes reincarnation, which is something most western moderns find it difficult to believe in. In addition, karmic debt is run up in past life by selfishness, which many think is perfectly OK to indulge in. We had a Me Generation after the hippie one. In this life, says Matthew Oliver Goodwin in the two volumes of his *Numerology: The Complete Guide* (1981) the karmic debt

> developed from the abuse of power in a past life....The subject may
> be completely immersed in his own concerns and may have great
> difficulty becoming aware of others' needs...[he encounters] neg-
> ative reactions to his endeavors....is unhappy with his dependent
> nature....will continue to meet with substantial difficulties unless
> (1) he can look past his own needs....OR (2) he can work toward
> independence no matter what forces are tending to keep him weak
> and dependent.

That's for a 19/1. If you are a 13/4, 14/5, 16/7, the Life Path, Soul Urge, etc., are affected somewhat differently by the bad balance you have in the karma account. Like most things in numerology, it is a complex matter—but if you were not born on the thirteenth, fourteenth, sixteenth, or nineteenth of any month, forget it! You miss *that* curse, anyway. And for the others, with a deficit to make up, take heart, for like most dire predictions in these popular prognostications you are threatened but not doomed. After all, magic is about doing something actively to change your world, so it would be out of character for it to make much of spells that cannot be broken, curses that cannot be lifted, hexes that cannot be unhexed, and so on.

Witches are like lawyers: we have noted above that they may be somewhat feared and generally despised but at least they create business for each other. Even the numerologist, who undertakes to read rather than manipulate your numbers, will tell you that once you know about your Secret Self and your Fate you can get your act together and try to change your personality and direct your luck in a more positive direction. Even astrology—where there isn't a lot you can do to counter the position of the planets at your birth and their inexorable movements now—tells us, if a little unconvincingly, that the stars impel but do not compel. Even readers of The Tarot suggest that what is clearly coming can somehow be avoided.

But if the future can be foretold can it be altered by you now? Isn't destiny fixed? In fact, isn't personality pretty hard or impossible to change after a certain age? On this, and on the age at which you become a Basically Unalterable You, psychology disagrees and pseudo-psychology is silent. Numerology, however, likes to speak of the numbers adding up to The Expression, your potential rather than your present character. So don't worry about being cursed with a bad debt. You can always straighten out and pay it. Or, maybe, declare bankruptcy.

Change even the spelling of your name and you can start over—like Dionne Warwick. That bill in the mystic mail then will be returnable as "unknown at this address."

HANDS OFF!

Curses have been written on various objects to warn people away from disturbing or stealing them. The curse on anyone who might disturb his bones on the grave of Shakespeare at Stratford-upon-Avon is probably the most famous but by no means the only departing shot of its kind. When I was in what we used to call grammar school, kids wrote terrible curses in their schoolbooks to warn "borrowers" that dreadful effects would descend upon any thief. Later I read of many such inscriptions on all sorts or articles. In their anthology of American *Folklore* (1973), Tristram Potter Coffin & Hennig Cohen tell us of the powder horn of a hunter, James Fenwick of Ogdensburg, New York, who in 1817 did "kill 30 wolf/ 10 bear; 15 deer/ and 46 partridges" and still had idle hours to inscribe that record on the horn along with this sentiment:

> The man who steals this horn
> Will go to Hell so sure he is born.

Curses have over the centuries worked well to keep the superstitious from stealing, from desecrating sacred places, even from ruining historical artifacts and documents. An Anglo-Saxon legal text says, "Whoever alters this, may God turn His face away from him on the Day of Judgment." In a lighter vein, there is flyting and "doing the dozens" and other lively wordplay in every verbal art form from epic poetry to rap.

That ill-tempered sumabitch Reinhold Aman edits a journal called *Maledicta* which has turned verbal aggression into a goddamn scholarly discipline.

TO MAKE SOMEONE'S HANDS BURN

Another "Negro superstition" collected by Newbell Puckett in Cleveland (1957) but long known in the Deep South:

If you want someone's hands to burn, put [cayenne] pepper on their hand print.

This is an unusual application of the doctrine of sympathy which is the basis for a great deal of malevolent magic of the sort of sticking pins in dolls and even white witch stuff such as *frying* someone's footprint (collect the dirt and take it to your kitchen) to make them love you. Turn someone's picture upside down and they will be discomfited. Kiss it and you send love to them.

CONJURED

To Grovetown (Columbia Co.), Georgia, for the next entry, also quoted in Coffin & Cohen, and collected from a freed slave, Braziel Robinson. He arrived at the plantation of Roland Steiner "after the war to test the question whether he was really free or not" and take a job. He could "see spirits," he said, because he was born with a caul, but, he was quick to add, "I never speak to one unless he speaks to me first." Mr. Robinson tells this story (in *Journal of American Folklore*, 1900, 227 -228):

I was conjured in May 1898, while hoeing cotton. I took off my shoes and hoed two rows, then I felt strange, my feet begun to swell, and then my legs, and then I couldn't walk. I had to stop and go home. Just as I stepped in the house, I felt the terriblest pain in my j[o]ints, I sat down and thought, and then looked in my shoes, I found some yaller dirt, and knew it was graveyard dirt, then I knew I was conjured, then I hunted about to find if there was any conjure [charm, etc.] in the house and find a bag under my door-step. I opened the bag and find some small roots about an inch long, some black hair, a piece of snake skin, and some graveyard dirt, dark-yaller, right off some coffin. I took the bag and dug a hole in the public road in front of my house, and buried it with the dirt out of my shoes, and throwed some red pepper all around the house [to drive off evil spirits]. I didn't get any better and went and saw a root-doctor [magician], who told me he could take off the conjure, he gave me a cup of tea to drink and b[o]iled up something and put it in a jug to wash my feet and legs with, but it ain't done me much good, he ain't got enough power, I am gwine [going] to see one in Augusta, who has great power, and can tell me who conjured me. They say root-doctors have power over spirits, who will tell them who does the conjuring; they ginerally uses yerbs gathered on the changes of the moon, and must be got at night. People git conjur from the root-doctors and one root-doctor often works against another, the one that has the most power does the [effective] work. People gits most conjured by giving them snake's heads, lizards, and scorpions, dried and beat up into powder and putting it into the food or water they drink, and then they gits full of the varmints; I saw a root-doctor cut out of a man's leg a lizard and a grasshopper, and then he got well. Some conjur[ing] ain't to kill, but to make a person sick or to have pain, and then conjur is put on the ground in the path where the person to be conjured goes, it is put down on a young moon, a growing moon, so the conjur will rise up and grow, so the person stepping over it will git conjured. Sometimes they roll it up into a ball and tie it to a string and hang it from a limb, so the person to be conjured, coming by, touches the ball, and the work's done, and he gits conjured in the part that strikes the ball, the ball is small and tied by a thread so a person can't see it. There are many ways to conjur, I know a man that was conjured by putting graveyard dirt under his house in small piles and it almost killed him, and his wife. The dirt made holes in the ground, for it will always go back as deep as you got it, it goes down to where it naturally belongs. Only root-doctors can git the graveyard dirt, they know what kind to git and when, the ha[u]nts won't let everybody git it, they must git it thro' some kind of spell, for the graveyard dirt works trouble 'til it gits back inter the ground, and then wears off. It must git down to the same depth it was took from, that is as deep as the coffin lid was from the surface of the ground.

As for cutting whole lizards and grasshoppers out of people after they have ingested powdered ones, I ought to add that in the middle ages and even today (in Mexico, to my personal knowledge), charlatanism may be found: the magician palms the object as he lances the victim and by sleight of hand produces from the head, or other part of the victim, to the amazement of spectators, the stone or animal alleged to have caused the suffering. Some people refer to these tricks as "psychic surgery." By the power of suggestion, though, it does effectively "remove curses" and "conjures" and produces cures of many complaints from madness to arthritis.

If, as The Bible says, faith can "move mountains" it certainly can cause and cure diseases, real and imaginary. It can produce the *stigmata* and with startling rapidity heal the wounds of mystics. It can terrify and relieve the adherents of voodoo. It can conjure and cure.

DIVINIDADE

This is Portuguese for a magical protective power which can likewise level curses against opponents. It figures more than you would think in the politics of Brazil.

"It has become a common joke in Brazil," one of the friends of the late Pedro Collor de Mello was quoted as remarking (*New York*, 13 February 1995, 29) that Pedro's brother, Fernando, "the flamboyant ex-president of Brazil," has magical powers. "You don't want to fuck with this guy Fernando," he adds, inelegantly but sincerely. The manager of The Plaza hotel is quoted as adding: "The common people of Brazil believe that Fernando has an aura—he has *divinidade*, or protection from evil spirits." And he can command them. "Anyone who goes against Fernando—bad things happen to them."

Forget "voodoo economics." Consider "voodoo presidency"—in Brazil, in Haiti, and.... I'd better not make this list longer.

ROOT WORK

You can place curses by burning appropriate candles with the victim's names scratched on them. You can try herbs. To hex people you can burn asafetida during the hour ruled by Saturn, a coconut shell stuffed with snakeroot, maiden hair fern to which a lock of the victim's hair has been added (this will cause baldness), or vervain with a lock of the victim's hair. This you burn with a piece of paper on which you have written the name of the victim and you chant nine times:

> Burn, hair, burn! Quiet, words, quiet!
> Your voice goes as your hair is consumed!

Grabbing a handful of bittersweet (in your left hand) say:

> O Lucifer, plague my enemy with your powers! Make his heart ache, his body wracked with pain, his words turn to gall, his feet turn from their intended path!

Or line a small box with mullein and Devil's shoestring, both of which draw evil. Take a potato to represent your victim and scratch his face on one side and the victim's initials or name on the other. Place the potato in the open box, face down, and drive nine pins into it. Leave it in the sun. As the potato shrivels, so the victim will decline in strength.

HOW DO CURSES WORK?

It is difficult to produce a plausible explanation of how a curse can affect the person cursed unless she or he learns of the curse. However, knowing you have been cursed can work rather like posthypnotic suggestion.

You may have seen hypnotists who can plant a suggestion in the unconscious and affect behavior of the person after the hypnotic state is ended. Five minutes after I snap my fingers and you wake up, says the hypnotist, you will jump up in the audience and shout the following sentence. Or maybe long after you are "brought back" you can be counted on to assassinate someone—that's the plot of *The Manchurian Candidate*, you may recall.

Two minutes after reading this sentence in this book you have dipped into in the bookstore, you will purchase this book or, if you have already obtained the book, you will telephone five friends and talk them into getting copies for themselves!

This may even work on the unhypnotized person, argues Felix E. Planer in the revised edition of his *Superstition* (1988), where he says that

> information registered in the subconscious, not only during hypnosis, but equally in the conscious state, by the fact alone that the material is emotionally charged or anxiety-provoking....predictions of future disaster, or curses, may exercise a powerful, subconscious influence towards fulfillment of the prophecy.

Surely this is part of the foundation of L. Ron Hubbard's *Dianetics*, because Scientology recognizes and undertakes by various methods to "clear" lurking and damaging ideas placed in the mind when we were younger and even more vulnerable. It is part of Aesthetic Realism, also.

The "talking cure" of Freudian analysis even earlier developed somewhat similar theories and methods to unearth the crippling and negative ideas, errors of perception and association, distortions of memory and damaging beliefs, to examine them, and destroy their curse.

Spirits hear what spirits tell,
'Twill make a holiday in Hell!

POWERFUL OBJECTS

Freud and other psychiatrists proved that the old saying that

> Sticks and stones can break my bones
> But words can never hurt me

was utterly wrong. But as much as the power of words and suggestions can do, the use of objects that carry or impose a curse must not be ignored. Everyone knows about the alleged curse of the Hope Diamond, or of the ill luck that attends those who steal sacred objects, the curse on Shakespeare's tomb and the alleged Mummy's Curse that protects ancient Egyptian tombs. "King Tut" is said to have used one.

Here is a story of a curse bone. Marian F. McNeill tells it, and illustrates it with a photo, in the British journal *Folk-Lore* 15 (1944). She found in the Scottish National Museum of Antiquities an old cursing bone that then had recently been acquired by the institution. It was a somewhat oval ring of bone from a deer enclosed in a ring of bog oak. It belonged to a witch who lived near the head of Glen Shira (Argyllshire) some forty years before. The Rev. J. Finlay Dawson had been one of the few, if not the only one, of the locals who dared to touch the witch's powerful tools. He gave it (not for magical purposes) to a woman who eventually placed it in the museum.

This is how the witch used this object. She would go by night to the henhouse of the person she wished to curse and steal the favorite hen of the cock (identified because it was the one that would be perched nearest him). This poor creature the witch would kill and then pour the blood through the hole in the cursing bone. There may be, with all this cock and hen business and the penetration of the oval object, some sexual significance here.

Of course the witch's incantation is now unknown—it died with her—so the cursing bone has no evil power. In its day, however, it was much feared and believed to be powerful.

It was the belief that it worked that gave it its power over the people, people who even if they were

Talismans: A (love), B (fortune), C (good luck). These are sold not only in occult stores but widely in mail-order catalogues that offer books on alien abductions, prophecies of Nostradamus, and other evidence of what one critic called the popular *Occult Explosion*.

not personally informed they were so cursed could imagine that they might be. In a similar way the dolls of the voodoo priestesses can scare the life out of believers. I have seen a staff used for cursing that when pointed at African natives by their witchdoctor caused them to fall down dead on the spot. The power of the mind over the body we still only very partially understand, and the power of suggestion of the mind is well beyond our present understanding.

THE CURSED KISS

In Joseph Glanvill's famous history of witchcraft triumphant, *Sadducismus Triumphatus* (1689), we read of the trial of an Irish woman, Florence Newton, accused and convicted of killing with a cursed kiss. History does not record what her fate was, but she was probably strangled, burned at the stake, or both, as was the custom in Ireland in the seventeenth century.

It began in Youghal, where there was a little colony of Puritans, in 1661, when the Cork Assizes heard the case of Mary Longdon against a crone called Florence Newton. Mary had known Florence for several years before she encountered her at the house of John Payn, where Mary was a servant girl. Florence arrived at Christmas and asked for some of the roast beef that was prepared for the feast. Mary refused the request, saying she could not give away her master's beef. Florence went away emptyhanded and mumbling. Was she mumbling curses? Mary was worried.

A week or so later Mary was at a well drawing water when Florence came along, seized her, forcibly kissed her, and said she wanted bygones to be bygones. "I bear you no ill will," Florence told Mary, "and I hope you bear me none."

But Mary still worried and would wake to see (or dream about?) a veiled woman standing beside her bed, accompanied by an old man dressed in fancy silk clothes. The old man drew the veil off the woman and—lo and behold!—it was Florence Newton. The old man then spoke to Mary and asked her to follow his instructions and promised that if she did he would grant her anything she desired. Mary testified under oath about this and repeated what she said was her staunch reply to this offer: that she was a good Christian and would follow only The Lord Jesus Christ.

Thereafter Mary began to have fits and four strong men could not hold her down. She was possessed, she thought. She vomited up needles and pins, wool and straw, and other objects. As she went from room to room she was pelted with small stones which vanished when they hit the floor but hurt her considerably. This was seen not only by herself but by other reliable witnesses who were certain that witchcraft was involved, and they were sure they knew who was responsible, for when pins were mysteriously stuck in Mary so deeply that others had great difficulty in drawing them out Mary screamed that Florence Newton was torturing her. Presumably the witch was in her lair sticking pins in a magical poppet made to resemble the victim. To everyone's astonishment, Mary was also subject to being levitated right out of bed and rudely transported all over the house, even winding up in a clothes press in John Payn's bedroom.

When the authorities were appealed to and brought Florence to confront Mary, Mary's fits were fierce. So Florence was put in jail in Youghal and Mary calmed down. When Florence was transferred to the jail in Cork, the persecutions of Mary grew worse, and so Florence was chained up in solitary confinement in the jail in Cork. In the middle of the night there was heard a great clanking of chains and Florence was heard to be addressing someone in her cell. She later said it was a familiar of hers that had appeared, in the form of a greyhound. She also was reported (according to evidence given at her trial by Nicholas Pyne, who had visited her in jail in the company of Joseph Thompson and Roger Hawkins, who would vouch for what Pyne said) to have confessed to "overlooking" (but not cursing) Mary and that they ought to investigate whether such other witches in the vicinity as Mistress Halfpenny or Mistress Dodd had leveled the curse which she, Florence Newton, was so unjustly suffering for. She also, it was said, made the same statement to Richard Mayre at Youghal after he had threatened her with the water test for witchcraft.

In jail in Cork she was visited by and watched by two citizens, Francis Besely and David Jones. They engaged in conversation with her, hoping to win her away from The Devil, with whom popular report had connected her. They were also curious to see if any of the strange familiars that people said she had around her would appear, and they kept looking through the grate in the jail door in hopes of seeing a black cat or some such creature with her.

David Jones talked with Florence Newton kindly and asked her to recite the Lord's Prayer. (It was commonly believed at that time that no witch could do this, being of The Devil's party.) She replied that she was an old woman, her memory was failing, and that she was not sure she could remember it all. David Jones coached her, standing at the grate, and noticed that she could not say "Forgive us our trespasses." Did this mean she really was not contrite about her evil? Apparently so, because she said she wanted to kiss David Jones's hand—and he was going greatly to regret that he put his hand through the grate.

After that Jones went home and told his wife, Eleanor, that the witch had kissed his hand. Now he had a pain which traveled up his arm and he was not afraid (as one might be today) that such a pain spreading through the left side might signal a heart attack but was convinced that it meant he was cursed.

He remained in great pain for a week as the pain reached for his heart. He died blaming Florence Newton two weeks after the fatal kiss.

The widow and Francis Besely testified before Sir William Aston (on whose legal notes Glanvill based his unquestioning account) that Florence Newton was responsible for the death of David Jones and that when Besely visited him on his deathbed Jones swore that the witch was trying to tear his arm from his body.

Many witnesses appeared against Florence Newton at her trial. The Rev. Wood and lay persons both reported strange behavior when she was in Mary Lonford's presence and when Mary was among others. The mayor of Youghal had forced a confession of witchcraft out of Florence, it was said, and the famous "stroker" and witchfinder Valentine Greatrix had tried on her a supposedly infallible method of detecting a witch. This involved making the suspect sit on a stool and having a shoemaker attempt to stick a sharp awl into the stool. In Florence's case it took three tries to do this. When they asked her to rise from the stool, she said she could not, but she explained this by saying she was very tired by the proceedings. They pulled her off the stool by main force, but they had a great difficulty trying to pull the awl out of the stool. Part of the blade broke off. But then no one could detect where the blade had been stuck in. Then they placed the awl in Mary's hand and tried to make her stick the awl into the suspected witch's hand, but it just bent and would not enter. When Florence's hand was then cut with a lancet, it would not bleed. When her other hand was lanced, both hands started to bleed.

At the trial Mary insisted that the others accused by Florence (Mistress Halfpenny and Mistress Dodds) were "honest women, but it is Mistress Newton that hurts me." Florence Newton was also accused of the deaths of three children in Youghal who died supposedly mysteriously, children of aldermen of the city.

The case brought condemnation to Florence Newton but increased interest in Valentine Greatrix (or Greatrakes or Greatorex, 1629 –1683). Where the witch's kiss could kill, it was thought, his laying on of hands could heal. In *Witchcraft in Ireland* (1967), Patrick E. Byrne summarizes the story of Florence Newton and quotes Glanvill in England on the great discourse now at the coffee houses ...about Mr. G., the famous Irish stroker. He undergoes various censures here; some take him to be a conjuror, and some an imposter; but others again adore him as an apostle. I was three weeks together with him at my Lord Conway's [Edward Conway became an English baron in 1625, an Irish viscount in 1626, an English viscount in 1627, and died in 1631], and saw him (I think) lay his hands upon a thousand persons; and really there is something in it more than ordinary; but I am convinced 'tis not miraculous. I have seen pains strangely fly before his hand, till he had chased them out of the body; dimness cleared, and deafness cured by his touch; 20 persons at several times in fits of the falling-sickness [epilepsy] were, in two or three minutes, brought to themselves, so as to tell where their pain was; and when he had pursued it, till he had driven it out at some extreme part; running sores of the King's Evil had dried up, and kernels brought to a suppuration by his hand; grievous sores of many months['s] date, in a few days healed; obstructions and stoppings [were] removed; cancerous knots in the breast dissolved, etc.

The King's Evil was a skin disease for which the monarch "touched." James I often did so. John Aubrey and others report success in this line. Of course Christ is reported to have performed miracles of curing the sick in His Father's name. Greatrakes did so in the same name.

Passes made over people are now beginning to be scientifically studied and even professionally used, but the superstitious go on being cured without resort to science. It appears that while unkind words can kill in curses, well-meant touches or passes can cure. The cure even of cases that medicine has abandoned is frequently reported from Lourdes and other sites, and healers operating through prayer or mumbo-jumbo do produce amazing results. I have seen instant cures and even, in Mexico, as noted, "psychic surgery."

The Devil Enchained. From an Anglo-Saxon manuscript.

If such things do not outrage your rationality, as the old Jewish grandmothers with chicken soup and other panaceas in Brooklyn are said to say, "Try it—it couldn't hurt." Especially in these days when we no longer strangle and burn witches and are expanding every year our parameters of alternative medicine.

REMOVING A CURSE

There are many, many ways of undoing a hex, and we shall list a lot elsewhere, but here is a quick and inexpensive and widely-used method: Sprinkle cayenne pepper or red chili powder around the house.

Often one has to find the magical work to remove the curse. For example, a simple curse is affected by dropping a lighted candle into a hole in the graveyard and quickly covering it up with dirt. Unless the candle is found, the cursed person will continue to suffer—or die.

CURSING

All kinds of vulgar expletives are commonly called cursing, but only "God damn you" and "To hell with you" and such are true curses. Swearing ("By God!" and the French mild "*Mon Dieu!*") is not cursing. A curse is a kind of spell, but always a bad one. Spells we shall deal with below.

CURSE THIS HOUSE

It brings a curse upon the house to take away fire on May Day or any churning day or to remove anything at all on New Year's Day. Never give away salt when churning is being done in the house. Do not call the name of anyone in the house from outside on All Soul's Day. Do not let a redheaded person be the first to set foot in your house on New Year's Eve or New Year's Day. Do not bring a cat from an old house to a new one, especially

BAAL

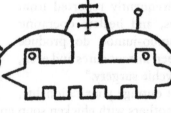

BELIAL

BERITH

a "red and white" cat and over any water, but if a black cat comes of her own accord take her in; she is a good spirit. Do not leave eggshells uncrushed in the house; fairies like to live in them. Do not sweep dust out the front door. Do not leave a broom outside the back door. Check your doorstep frequently for voodoo or other hexes placed there by enemies.

I BENANDANTI

Documents of the fifteenth and sixteenth centuries regarding rural witchcraft in Friuli were discovered among the seventeenth-century papers of the Holy Inquisition in the archives of Venice. They are presented and discussed by one of the most interesting of twentieth-century Italian scholars, Carlo Ginzburg, in his *I Benandanti: Stregonaria e culti agrari tra Cinquecento e Seicento* (1966, 1973).

The battle of the forces of light against the dark forces of evil, these Friulians believed, explained the success or failure of their agriculture. If the *Benandati* won, all was well; if the bad witches won, there would be failure and famine.

The *Benandanti* were very special. Like our modern Superman, they came from another planet. This was marked by the fact that they were born in human form with a *camisa* (shirt) of amniotic membrane. One recalls that children born with cauls have traditionally been assumed to have special occult powers. These *Benandanti* "shirts" were preserved and even sometimes worn on the person, but the identity of these special people was kept secret lest they be attacked by the populace. When the individual so blessed grew up, four times a year in sleep his spirit would leave the body to fight (with fennel stalks) the bad witches (who were armed with sorghum reeds). Because of their special powers, the Good Guys could ferret out witches in real life, too, and remove curses, break spells, free the people from evil. When they died, as a reward for their services, the *Benandanti*, largely unrewarded in life (because of the secrecy that surrounded them), went straight to heaven. Unlike witches who went to *sabbats*, they were the friends and protectors of the community, and it must have been comforting for the peasantry to have had an explanation other than meteorological why the crops succeeded or failed and an invisible if part-time army fighting evil for them each and every year.

Maybe the peasants were cursed in having to scrape a precarious living out of the earth, but they had the secret champions to defend them against the curses of witches.

NAWALES

In *Magic, Witchcraft and Curing* (1967, ed. John Middleton), there is a fascinating essay on "Witchcraft as a Social Process in a Tzeltal Community." In it, Manning Nash finds among some Meso-American people a unique link between the totemism which dates back to Paleolithic times and the witches' familiars which are so much a part of the history of witchcraft in Europe in the middle ages.

The Tzeltal people believe that some special individuals have an animal counterpart (*nawal*) and that there can be a shift back and forth between the two, giving humans some magical powers and animals some human characteristics. The persons who use *nawales* for good are the healers of the society; those who do not are the bad witches. The chief good that these specially gifted persons to do is to banish evil, counter curses, and cure disease. The main evils that they can do is to bind and blight, curse and kill.

PICO DELLA MIRANDOLA

This great Renaissance thinker may have died of a curse. He believed in astrology, as most learned men of his time did, but he believed that (as with magic) there was good astrology and evil astrology. When he attacked the latter, his opponents retaliated (or it may have been chronologically the other way around) and Bellanti of Siena cast the horoscope of Pico and announced that Pico would die young. Pico was taken aback when he read that—he threw up—and at age thirty–three he threw in the towel.

"Was this," asks Daniel Lawrence O'Keefe in his social history of magic called *Stolen Lightning* (1982), " a kind of voodoo death from suggestion?"

DECLARING WAR

A curse is an opening salvo in a war. Curses and wars come into existence by virtue of being declared. The struggle that ensues must have in the case of a curse a winner and a loser. The self can join in on either the winning or the losing side.

JANNES AND MAMBRES

You probably do not recognize these names. They are seldom mentioned, but these were the two Egyptian magicians that two more famous residents of Egypt (Moses and his brother Aaron) were able to best before the pharaoh. The two Bad Guy magicians (The Bible reports, but it may be biased, being Books of Moses at this point) were able to bring tremendous numbers of frogs upon the land—but then could not get rid of them. The point seems to be that Moses' magic is positive and the enemy's negative. Still, it was Aaron who produced swarms of mosquitoes and other pests and the god of Moses Who let go with curses on the Egyptians—plagues of frogs and locusts and worse.

BALAAM

Another story of a curse from the Old Testament is the tale of Balaam, a magician of Mesopotamia, to whom Balak, king of the Moabites, appealed to fling a terrible curse upon his greatest enemies, the Israelites. Once again the story is told from the Israelite angle, but here it is.

Balak's messengers arrived with lots of gifts to reward Balaam for his curse but he refuses to go to Balak's court. Then he is wooed by officers of greater rank and tempted with greater rewards by Balak. He is offered *carte blanche*, in fact, if he will put the Israelites under a terrible curse, for Balaam has an unfailing power: those whom he blesses stay blessed and those whom he curses are forever cursed. Balaam rather reminds us of Peter, to whom Jesus said that those whose sins he forgave were forgiven and those whose sins he would not forgive were not forgiven.

Balaam turns out to be in the employ of the enemy of the Moabites, Jehovah, Who is very sneaky around this time. (The Balaam story is thought to date from the earliest or "Jehovistic" scriptures of the Jews.) At first He will not hear of Balaam taking his magic to the land of the Moabites. Then He relents and says that is allowable if Balaam will be guided by Him and speak not a word other than He instructs. Balaam goes to the Moabite kingdom and greatly disappoints the Moabites who welcome him.

When Balaam is taken to the temple of Baal (Lord) on heights near the border of the kingdom, to which the king himself comes to greet the visitor, instead of cursing Balaam blesses the Israelites. When he is taken up to the top of Pisgah, from the mountain top he blesses the Israelites. When he is taken to the mountain top of Peor, temple of the phallic god Baal Peor (whom Christians later identified with the Roman Priapus), Balaam once again blesses the Israelites. Balak is (understandably) furious. His temples have been desecrated, his sacrifices wasted on one set of seven sacred altars after another, and over and over and over Balaam has blessed those whom Balak has hired him to curse. Worst of all, his dabbling in the entrails of sacrificial animals has only permitted Balaam to prophesy the ultimate triumph of Israel and its god.

IN OLD IRELAND

> In the case of a sudden fainting or swoon, the individual is supposed to be struck by a curse, and if he is unable to answer questions, he is tried with a grannoge, or hedgehog, and if it erects the spine it is a sure sign that the person is under the influence of the devil. Or the suspected person is wrapped in a woman's red cloak, with the hood over the head, and laid in a grave cut two feet deep. There he remains some hours covered with clay, all but the face, and if he becomes delirious and raves, then the people know that the devils are round him, and his death is considered certain.
> —Lady Wilde, in *Irish Cures, Mystic Charms, and Superstitions*.

"RIGHTEOUS HEX"

"Zsuzsanna Budapest" in The Holy Book of Women's Mysteries (1989) offers many feminist rituals, spells, etc., and "reserved for violent criminals only....*when you know, not just think*, that someone has harmed you," this vengeful operation. Ms. Budapest thinks "cupcakism, turning the other cheek is not for witches." In spades! Here is her ceremony for vengeance performed at the waning moon.

> Prepare a black altar [table with black cloth, 2 black candles, incense burner, she suggests "a shell"]. For the centerpiece, use the Goddess's hag image, Hecate, who is threefold. Decorate the altar with cones, blackthorn and mandrake. From a black cloth, cut out a doll-shaped form resembling your enemy, sew it around from east to north to west to south (widdershins), and leave only a small part open. Stuff it with boldo leaves and finish the sewing. Indicate the eyes, mouth, nose, and hair on the doll. On a piece of parchment paper, write the name of your enemy and attach it to the image. Say:
>
> *Goddess Hecate, to you I pray,*
> *With this enemy no good will ever stay.*
> *Cut the lines of his life in three,*
> *Doom him, doom him, so mote it be!*

When you pronounce this, take a mallet and break his "legs" by breaking the herb inside. Dust it with Graveyard Dust; anoint it with Double Crossing Oil, and burn your Black Arts incense. Imagine him totally miserable and with one leg broken. (It is a nice way to incapacitate rapists until they can be apprehended.) Do this three nights in a row. On the third night, burn the doll and bury it. Draw a triple cross over his grave with Dragon Blood power [she means "powder"]. Walk away without looking back.

> *Note: Dispose of hexes as far away from your house as possible. Each night you can break something else in him, or stick black-headed pins into his liver or penis. May patriarchy fail!*

Z was high priestess of the Susan B. Anthony Coven No. 1, the first feminist coven (it is claimed) in Los Angeles. Later she moved to Oakland and has been a leader in the politicized women's spirituality movement.

CURSES IN VARIOUS CULTURES

Falassi, Alessandro. "A Note on Two Tuscan Curses..." *Maledicta* 2 (1978), 175–176 [Italian]

Faron, Louis C. *The Mapuche Indians of Chile* (1972)

Laude-Certautas, Ilse. "Blessings and Curses in Kazhak and in Kirghiz," *Central Asiatic Journal* 18 (1974), 9–22 [Turkic languages]

Matisoff, James A. *Blessings, Curses, Hopes, and Fears...* (1979) [Yiddish]

A FINAL WORD—A CURSE ON GHOULS

In Richmond Lattimore's *Themes in Greek and Latin Epitaphs* (1962), a favorite subject is the curse on anyone who despoils or disrespects a grave:

> I, Idameneus, built this tomb to [my own] glory. May Zeus utterly destroy anyone who disturbs it.

A Tibetan woodblock print of a man with a padlocked mouth protects against gossip and slander.

3

Protections and Cures

WHO'S A WITCH?

One of the first things you may have to know to protect yourself is, "Who is a witch?" An ancient superstition suggests a simple method of identifying a witch: Drop a walnut in the suspect's lap. If she cannot stand up, she's a witch. This is easier than looking for "the Devil's mark" or throwing the suspect into water to see if The Devil will cause her to float. The Anglo-Saxons had another way: they made a suspect eat a mixture of oats or (likelier to cause choking) barley. If you choked, you were guilty; if you did not, you were not a witch. This was one of many trials, probably the worst of which was having to take and carry a red-hot piece of iron.

A SELECTION OF BASIC BOOKS

"Dion Fortune," *Psychic Self Defence* (1930)
Draja Mickaharic, *Spiritual Cleansing* (1982)
Marion Weinstein, *Positive Magic* (1981)
C. A. Burland, *The Magical Arts* (1966)
Christopher Neil-Smith, *The Exorcist and the Possessed* (1974)
Franz Hartmann, *Magic White and Black* (1980)
Henry Charles Lea, *Materials Towards a History of Witchcraft* (3 vols., 1957)
Wallace A. Notestein, *A History of Witchcraft in England 1558-1718* (1965)
Margaret A. Murray, *The Witch-Cult in Western Europe* (reprinted 1963)

WARDING OFF, FIXING UP

In the first book in this series, reprinted under the title *The Complete Book of Superstition, Prophecy, and Luck*, I note folk superstitions about the cures for a number of diseases (such as epilepsy and rheumatism) and minor inconveniences (such as toothache and cramp). Here, for example, is what I wrote about curing cramp:

> Wear an eelskin around the leg to relieve leg cramps. Or wear a moleskin around your left leg. Or tie a cotton string around your ankle. Or lay your shoes across the aching member. Or use cork; wear cork garters or lay pieces of cork between the sheet and the mattress of your bed. Or stand on the leg that has the cramp and recite the following:
>
>> Foot, foot, foot is fast asleep;
>> Thumb, thumb, thumb, in spittle we steep;
>> Crosses three we make to ease us;
>> Two for the thieves and one for Jesus.

This clearly recalls a number of biblical details. Christ used His spittle (part of His essence) to cure. The Sign of the Cross was believed to be powerful and is used in numerous magical as well as religious ceremonies. Christ was crucified with two thieves (tradition called them Cosmos and Damian, but The Bible left them unidentified), one on either side of Him. In incantations such as this, the fine line between religion and superstition is blurred, as it usually is. I remark elsewhere that Dr. Margaret Murray, whose works on witchcraft (though hotly debated) were considered to be of encyclopedic authority, confessed that as expert as she was, she could not clearly define the difference between religion and magic.

On the subject of cramp, I also mentioned the popular magical cramp ring of the middle ages and later. It was usually made from the nails, hinges, or handles of a coffin, but in the American West a horseshoe nail would do. Britain's King Edward the Confessor (whose epithet underlined his religious reputation) wore a cramp ring which was handed down for several generations as a powerful heirloom. Then it got lost. Early Tudor kings revived the fashion and consecrated silver and gold each Good Friday. This was then made into such rings. The custom was abandoned, as smacking of papist superstition, by the young Protestant king Edward VI, in the sixteenth century. I have seen cramp rings in use in Britain in the late twentieth century.

Wearing such rings is clear evidence of belief in magic, though people who today swear by copper bracelets to drive away pain would claim they are being scientific. You might say that the cures I note in that book for the common cold (such as eating dried rats' tails, drinking beer in which sumac leaves have been boiled, or stuffing orange rind up your nostrils— all old folk remedies) are, in fact, folk medicine and not folk superstition. Very recently, in fact, it has been discovered that in orange peel are flavanoids that have powerful medical applications. A medical school in Beijing showed that powdered orange peel after each meal counteracts the toxic substances found in some processed food and can prevent gastric cancer or relieve some of its symptoms. There is nothing but superstition, however, in the old cure for the ague, which called upon you to visit the nearest crossroads at midnight on five different occasions and bury an egg. Transferring pain or disease to another object is magic, not medicine.

It's true that Chinese folk medicine—that orange peel business— knows more than the West does about a number of useful treatments. So do so-called primitive societies everywhere. In the mountains of Chiapas, as I have said more than once already, I was fascinated by the Mexican women who crouched at the market at San Cristóbal de las Casas offering leaves, twigs, berries, and other folk remedies laid out on the ground on neatly cut pieces of newspaper. These medicines work and I would not hesitate to use them. Untold generations have relied upon them. I did balk at consulting a wise woman near Lake Chapala, however, renowned for being able to cure baldness. I said I was afraid she might, instead of replacing my thinned out hair, shrink my head to fit the hair I had left.

Folk medicines are not all superstition; they can be a kind of primitive science. There may be something in moleskin that is good for you, for all I know. But when you are told to wear it as a garter on the left leg— the sinister one, the side that belongs to The Devil—then magic is involved, just as when you are told to take this or that remedy with a prayer or incantation or at midnight at a crossroads. Or to go to a crossroads with a black rooster under your left arm to meet The Devil. Still, I am ready to believe that two grams of orange peel powder after every meal did reduce by 62 percent toxic compounds in the Chinese tummies of sufferers from gastric cancer. What I am not so ready to believe is that tying a cormorant skin around the stomach can be 100 percent effective, or that sleeping on a bearskin will help wounds heal faster. And I decline altogether to believe that a sick person is helped if you wash her or him and then throw the water over your cat. My cats resent water very much.

Still, because of magical beliefs we have been given a number of wonderful drugs, such as quinine (originally called Jesuit's Bark because those missionaries got it from South American natives) and digitalis. The first users of digitalis for heart disease chose it because of the Doctrine of Signs, a belief that nature gives us clues to the uses of plants, etc. Digitalis has heart-shaped leaves. It's the same sort of thinking that says a chameleon, with his prominent and strange eyes, is good against the evil eye.

We ought to get over our western prejudices and examine the folk medicine and even the folk magic of other cultures. There is a lot we could learn.

I would, however not recommend that you fail to bring serious symptoms early and frankly to the attention of your licensed physician, nor that you abandon all interest in standard medicine in favor of superstitious or simply alternate medicine, and especially that you do not rely on these old practices:

MEASLES—three drops of blood (cut off a cat's left ear to get them) in a wineglassful of water

COUGHS—"two or three snails" boiled in barley water and presented to the patient as ordinary water

FEVER—an agate placed on the brow will cool it

WHOOPING COUGH—a lock of the hair of a person who "never saw his father" is to be tied (according to Irish custom) in red cloth and worn around the neck

ERYSIPELAS—the blood of a black cat (just cutting off a bit of the tail will suffice, the Irish believe)

TUMORS OR WENS—the touch of a hanged man's hand

EPILEPSY—bury a black rooster alive on the spot where the sick person fell in a fit and include some of the hair or fingernail clippings of the sufferer so that the identity of the person for whom this sacrifice is made is known—or grind up nine pieces of a human skull with a "decoction of wall rue" (an Irish cure collected by Lady Wilde, who reminds you to use up all the mixture lest the dead come back looking for pieces of the skull)

WORMS—boil earthworms in water, cool, and drink the water

JAUNDICE—nine lice on a piece of bread and butter

The weirdest such cure? Maybe, just maybe, the frog-in-the-throat methods. When we say today that we have a frog in the throat we mean that we are hoarse. In times past there was a method of curing a child's croup or coughing or even whooping cough that involved inserting a live frog into the child's mouth—hold tight to the back legs of the frog! The frog was supposed to breathe in the evil, relieving the child of the symptoms. The Irish preferred a trout to a frog for this practice.

Or maybe the strangest is the old practice of curing jaundice with a fish. In Bohemia people used to tie a fish to their backs and wear it all day. As the fish died and turned yellow, it was supposed to be soaking up the jaundice. At the end of the day you threw the dead fish into a stream and away went your jaundice.

WHEN YOU MOST NEED PROTECTION

The Complete Book of Superstition, Prophecy, and Luck goes into which times are, according to various superstitions, most or least propitious, but here we can summarily note that the unlucky days are:

TUESDAY the day of Mars (violence, war, the red of blood, the iron of hard discipline) and blood (the Arabs say that on a Tuesday Cain slew Abel, Eve first menstruated, John the Baptist, Zachariah, and St. George were killed)—be wary especially from 3:00 to 4:30 P.M.

FRIDAY the day of The Crucifixion, the day of Venus (green of hope but also with envy, love, and lust), the bad taste of copper in the mouth, the beginning of the Sabbath, a bad day to commence any enterprise—especially 10:00 A.M. to noon

SATURDAY the day of Saturn (who ate his young, black of mood, black of death), a day of danger, destruction, and deceit (his brothers sold Joseph to the Ishmaelites on a Saturday, say the Arabs), a day of leaden despair—especially 9:00 to 10:00 A.M.

Get your protections and cures ready! Astrology says you also have unlucky and unlucky conjunctions of planets, favorable or unfavorable days of the month and months of the year. Magic depends upon your being convinced that you are beset and urgently need whatever help you can get. One of the cheapest protections of all is described in this Irish instruction: Take ten blades of yarrow, throw away one (a tithe to the spirits) and put nine in your stocking under your right heel. You will travel in complete safety; the Evil One cannot touch you. And, as the Irish say, may you be in Paradise long before The Devil knows you're dead!

THE TOP TEN AMULETS

A subjective call, but, in no particular order, I suggest:

> The Christian cross (worn anytime)
> Jewish phylacteries (worn at prayer)
> The Hand of Fatima (for followers of Islam)
> The caduceus of Mercury
> A winged phallus or other male genital charms
> The fleur de lys (used in Florence, France, Bosnia, etc.)
> Coral and certain other precious and semiprecious gems
> Any charm shaped like a pig or (Tibetan favorite) bolt of lightning
> Any blessed medal, medicine bag, *mojo*, or other thing recommended
by your religion
> Blue beads with an eye on them or any other protection against *malocchia*

THE TEN MOST DISGUSTING AMULETS

> A dried phallus (reproductions in silver are often worn today)
> The hand of an executed criminal (the so-called Hand of Glory)
> The skull of an enemy (also used as drinking cup or candlestick)
> The fat of an unbaptised baby (used in magical potions)
> Bits of mummies (worn, or as an ingredient in some medieval concoctions)
> Pieces of human skin (worn, used as drumheads, seats of judgment, etc.)
> Human bones (ground up for magical potions, worn, tossed to tell
fortunes)
> Menstrual blood (much feared by some, much used by others in magic)
> A human finger (carried like a rabbit's foot, for luck)
> The human heart (offered in sacrifices to gods and demons—or eaten!)

AMULETS AND TALISMANS FROM NATURE

In all societies some objects found in nature have been treasured as offering protection and power. The Chinese and (oddly) the aboriginals of Mexico thought jade had immense powers. Indeed any stone with a natural hole in it or of certain colors was eagerly collected and carried. A stone's yellow color, for instance, might associate it with the sun—or with curing jaundice. Parts of animals (fur, feathers, talons, claws, bones, and so on) were worn as charms, as were shells of all kinds. The eagle feathers, porcupine quills, bear's claws, and so on that adorned Amerind warriors, the quetzal feathers worn farther south in the Americas, or the whalebone or tooth jewelry worn in the far north—all these were far more than decorative. Anything that looked unusual, in shape or size or color or whatever or was found under unusual circumstances, might be thought to *be* unusual.

Shakespeare wrote of

> books in the running brooks,
> Sermons in stones, and good in everything.

and superstitious humanity saw the possibility of power in many aspects of nature—magic in everything. Still does!

A BABYLONIAN DEVIL TRAP

In the British Museum is a terra-cotta "devil trap" made to protect the house of Bahrran and Bathniun against Lilith (the demon first wife of Adam) and other night devils. The Hebrew letters begin in the center and spiral around, ending at the arrow on the left side. It says it is a "bill of divorce" for the demons; they must go away and never return. The object is discussed in the British *Proceedings of the Society for Biblical Archeology* for April 1890.

AN ANCIENT HEBREW AMULET

Obverse   Reverse

"The greatest of all the amulets known to the Hebrews was, and is," writes Sir E. A. Wallis Budge, "the Book of the Law." In addition to The Torah, however, Jews had and have many amulets and Sir Ernest shows this silver one in his *Amulets and Superstitions* (reprinted as *Amulets and Talismans*, 1968), with a translation of the expanded abbreviations:

OBVERSE

1. In the Name of the Lord God of Israel we shall do and prosper.
2. "I beseech thee by the power of the greatness" of God, the Lord of Hosts, the God of Israel.
3. In the names of the angels of the God (of Israel) I conjure you all
4. kinds of Lilin (i.e. night devils), male and female,
5. and Demons, male and female,
6. by the power of the holy Name.
7. "Accept the prayer of Thy people, exalt them, purify them, O Thou Who art tremendous," combined with
8. its root (i.e. source) YHWH [Yahweh, Jehovah], that they do not

REVERSE

1. enter to any
2. place where there be
3. in it "O mighty one, those who beseech Thee," nor shall touch
4. it at all, nor hurt by the power of
5. the holy Name "'Thy right hand shall loosen the bondage,"
6. "Thy single ones, like the apple of Thine eye, guard them," combined with
7. its root (i.e. source) AD[O]N[A]I, and with
8. the name of 26 (letters) (the Tetragrammaton) "Accept our entreaty, and hear our cry, Lord who knowest the hidden things."
9. "May the Lord preserve thy going out and thy coming in from now and evermore. Amen. Selah."

The quotations are from the Hebrew scriptures. The name of twenty–six letters is not the four letters of the Tetragrammaton (YHWH) but one of the more elaborate secret names of God. There is a seventy–two-letter secret name also, once known only to the High Priest of the Jews.

CURING A TOOTHACHE

Even the Stoic philosophers, an old saying used to go, could not bear a toothache patiently, and from the clay tablets of Babylon onwards there have been all sorts of magical ways of getting rid of such pains. There must be a whole book of toothache superstitions and spells to be written. Early on it was decided that the pain in teeth was caused by—worms! The plant *Hyocyamus niger* or "toothache grass" was prescribed but if that didn't work you could put a spoonful of boiling water in a spoon under the tooth and, people said, the worms would drop down into it. Or you could recite a magic formula the usual three times. Here's one that the Norwegian folklorist A. C. Bang gives. I quote it because I am amused by the apt opening line:

Jeg harm Orm i mine Tænder.	I have worms in my teeth.
Vad heller de ere røde eller hvide	Whether they are red or white or
eller graa	grey
da skal de saa visselig dø	they shall die anyway,
som Jesus er fød af en Jomfru Mø.	[as sure] as Jesus was born of the Virgin Mary.

And you add as usual: "In the Name of The Father, of The Son, and of The Holy Spirit. Amen."

In another toothache cure, you rubbed a pin on the sore tooth and then drove the pin into a tree (transferring the pain) with a formula about the sufferings of Job. The transferring of pain or evil in charms—and you can give warts away to a tree—is related to the familiar concept of the scapegoat. The oddest cure may be rubbing a wart with a piece of meat (which must be stolen) and burying the meat to rot, the wart disappearing as the buried meat disappears. The most familiar example to us of transference of evil is Christ taking on the sins of the world.

THE BEST BUDDHIST PROTECTION

Take a white thread spun by "a clever maiden." Say the AMBTA and SVAB-HAVA *mantras* over it and tie twenty–one knots in it, saying a *mantra* at each tying. Call upon Tara to "protect the bearer from the terror of thieves and beasts of prey RAKSHA RAKSHA SVAHA."

Typical of Buddhist charms, you are asked to say this "100,000 times," but if you say it fewer times it still has some value. You wear it upon your person at all times. One authority says this is "the highest of protections." In the Buddhist universe of innumerable and grotesque demons, some powerful protection is absolutely essential.

A MEDIEVAL PROTECTION

This is from Albertus Magnus (born in Germany in 1205), one of the great thinkers of the thirteenth century, sometime bishop of Regensberg (Ratisbon), scientist and occultist. I recall mentioning in a previous book that Albert the Great was always accompanied by a huge black dog; people were sure it was a demon in disguise, his familiar. He taught people to protect themselves from demons by repeating this thrice:

> You persons look upon me for a moment until I draw three drops of blood from you, which you have forfeited. The first I draw from your teeth, the second from your lungs, the third from your heart's very core; and thus I take away your powers and thus shall you remain until I shall remove from you the iron band.

"TAKE A LITTLE WINE FOR THY STOMACH'S SAKE"

That is one of my favorite biblical quotations. Wine occurs in many magical potions and is part of the transubstantiation of the Mass. A superstition in Surrey was that "an ailing or weakly child will be cured with a drop of sacramental wine," but presumably not wine that has become the blood of Christ, for children are not given the sacrament of communion.

WRITTEN PRESCRIPTIONS FOR DISEASES

It was not uncommon for people to carry upon their persons, even wear in a bag or other container around their necks, certain holy scriptures, or quotations from them. The Muslims did and still do this. The Jews have a couple of verses of *Deuteronomy* in their *mezuzahs* still but have ceased to wear bits of the Old Testament. Buddhists may wear prayers (as well as have them tossed around in prayer wheels turned by hand, by the wind, and so on). Englismen used to do so. Here is a magical document dated 1798 found on a body at Hurstpierpoint in Sussex:

> When Christ came upon the cross for the redemption of mankind, he shook and his Rood [the cross] trembled. The Chief Priest [of the Jews] said to him, "Art thou afraid or [h]as thou an ague?" He s[a]id unto them ["]I am not afraid neither have I an ague["], and whosoever believeth in these words shall not be troubled by any fever or ague. So be it unto thee.

SAGE ADVICE

The plant sage is said in superstition to absorb all evil influences around, so keep some in a bowl in your home to keep the place spiritually clean. Amerindians such as the Oglala Sioux used sage in their magical ceremonies.

There are other plants you can sleep on, eat, burn, or otherwise employ in magical ritual. Burn frankincense to give your place holiness. You can use acaccia and ginger, holy herb, hyssop, rosemary, and carry flax seeds and other plant protections against sorcery. Two licorice sticks made into a cross tied together with red thread is useful to have on you at all times, or wrap a small piece of sandalwood with red thread. Carry this with your charm bag, which (of course) contains other ingredients besides sage.

THE DEAD

The dead can be dangerous, though spiritualists and channelers and God knows who else want to talk to them. The problem is that nobody ever seems to get any really useful information. Best to leave the dear departed alone—and say nothing but good about them. People still say "bless her soul" or "may he rest in peace" and so on when mentioning the name of the dead or—in some societies other than our own—never ever speak the name of a dead person or even a word that sounds like that name.

Take the corpse out of the house feet first, head covered with a sheet, and after you bury it put a big rock—call it a headstone—on top of the grave to keep the dead from coming back up. Maybe an iron rod on the grave will help, too. The funeral procession should return from the cemetery by a different route than the one by which it reached it; we want to make it hard for the ghost to get back home. In case it should wander back, have the furniture in the room in which anyone has died immediately rearranged. The ghost won't recognize the place, or that's the thinking.

Slavs believe that the dead are likely to linger in the house for forty days after death. They keep a pitcher of water near the blessed icon and check it regularly to see if the dead have been sipping from it. Other people have various ways of checking on the presence of ghosts. Some people ban white flowers from the house because they are said to attract the dead. The dead also like orange flowers; Mexicans deck graves with these as they party on The Day of the Dead. Ghosts are supposed to come and party with the living.

At the celebrations for the dead the food may be burned so that the dead will receive it or the dead may simply and magically extract the essence from it, after which (as one Mexican lady once informed me) you can eat the food and you won't get fat no matter how much you consume because "all the good is gone out of it." This could be the basis of some new weight loss plan, I suppose.

As for feeding the dead, if you want to get details you could look up the lecture on the subject given at the University of Leipzig by Philip Röhr in 1679. It was published in Latin as *De Masticatione mortuorum*. I once gave

a lecture at the University of Leipzig (it was called Karl Marx University by that time), but it was, I confess, on nothing nearly so startling. It was about linguistics, not ghosts.

If you see a ghost, ask it what it wants. Show it a crucifix, if it's a Christian. Wear a ring of chalcedony or basalt, as the Egyptians did, and you may never see ghosts at all. Such rings are rare today, and you would be amazed at the percentage of Americans as the twentieth century concludes who are ready to swear that they have seen ghosts.

Visions of saints means seeing ghosts, but visions of The Blessed Virgin (because if the doctrine of the Assumption adopted in the nineteenth century) do not involve a ghost. The Holy Ghost is not a ghost, either.

ASSYRIAN AND BABYLONIAN RELIGION

"The only religious texts that survive from Assyria are exorcisms and omens."—Will Durant, *Our Oriental Heritage* (1954, p. 276). As for the better-documented religion of the Babylonians, Durant writes:

> Giants, dwarfs, cripples, above all, women, had sometimes the power, even with the glance of the "evil eye," to infuse such a destructive spirit into the bodies of those toward whom they were ill-disposed. Partial protection against these demons was provided by the use of magic amulets, talismans, and kindred charms; images of the gods, carried on the body, would usually suffice to frighten the devils away. Little stones strung on a thread or a chain and hung about the neck were especially effective, but care had to be taken that the stones were such that tradition had associated with good luck, and the thread had to be of black, white or red according to the purpose in view. Thread spun from [the wool of] virgin kids was particularly powerful. But in addition to such means it was wise also to exorcise the demon by fervent incantation and magic ritual—for example by sprinkling the body with water taken from the sacred streams—the Tigris or the Euphrates. Or an image of the demon could be made, placed on a boat, and sent over the water

with a proper formula; if the boat could be made to capsize, so much the better. The demon might be persuaded, by the appropriate incantation, to leave its human victim and enter an animal— a bird, a pig, most frequently a lamb.

It was from the Babylonian and Assyrian religions that the Jews and Christians got their devils and demons, their angels with wings, their Lamb of God, their blessed medals and exorcisms, and a great deal more. As for threads, our superstitions believe that black silk cords protect children, red strings prevent rheumatism, and so on.

Scapulas, little magical—or should we say religious—bags hung on strings around the neck, are worn by Roman Catholics. My Catholic mother hung one on me when as a tot I was sent off to camp. It was supposed to prevent drowning and generally work in tandem with the blessed medal my ecclesiastical cousin had gotten from the pope. I didn't know that scapulas were supposed to prevent drowning and, because it was only cloth with something that felt like paper inside it, I always carefully removed mine before going into the water.

FINGERNAILS

You will often see these mentioned in magic recipes, but did you know that the Egyptians decorated their fingernails to protect themselves from evil spirits? Or that the fingernails of a sick person must not be cut until she or he has recovered?

PROTECTION IN WAR

It was always useful for the warrior in earlier days, when (s)he was not safe in a bunker somewhere pushing buttons to dispatch missiles but had to grapple with the armed enemy face to face, to have luck as well as courage. Warpaint often was used for magical protection and not just to frighten the enemy; that is why the Picts were painted, why naked men painted blue were seen in British battles, why Amerinds and Aztecs were decked out as they were. People screamed magical words as well as giving scary howls as they dashed into battle. Their swords might have been blessed. They may have relied on consecrated shields, amulets (including parts of dead opponents), promises of invincibility from their holy men, even (as in the case, for instance, of certain Amerind warriors) shirts that were supposed to be bulletproof.

LIPSTICK

Egyptian women painted their mouths more to repel demons than to attract men.

SOME OLD IRISH CURES

FOR THE NINE-DAY FEVER:

> Write the name of Jesus nine times on a slip of paper, then cut the paper into small bits, mix the pieces with some soft food, and make the patient swallow it. So will he be cured if he trusts in the Lord.
>
> Nine handfuls of mountain moss, dried on a pan to powder. Nine pinches of it, and nine pinches of the ashes from the hearth, to be mixed in whey, taken every Tuesday and Thursday.

FOR JAUNDICE:

> Nine young shoots from the root of an ash tree that has been cut down. These are placed in a bottle, which is then buried in a secluded spot, the patient not being allowed to see it. As long as the bottle remains in the ground, he is safe from the disease; but, should it be broken, he will have a relapse and probably die from mental distress, caused by fear of the result, before many days are over.

FOR MUMPS:

> Take nine black stones gathered before sunrise , and bring the patient with a rope around his neck to a holy well—not speaking all the while. Then cast in three stones in the name of God [the Father], three in the name of Christ, and three in the name of Mary. Repeat this process for three mornings and the disease will be cured.

FOR RICKETS:

> A blacksmith, whose [fore]fathers have been smiths for three generations, must carry the child in his apron three times round the anvil for seven days in succession, repeating the Paternoster [Lord's Prayer] each time. But no money must be accepted for the cure.

THE STORY OF TWO WILD AND HOLY GUYS

In Anglesey in the sixth century there were a couple of pious lads who may have developed the kind of gay attachment that appears to have sprung up in some all-male communities. Or maybe they were just buddies, not lovers; but in any case they used to go to considerable trouble to meet every day, which required one of them (St. Seriol the Fair) to walk a considerable distance and the other (St. Cybi the Tawney—he was the one with the good tan) to walk and then boat or swim to what became known as Holy Island, their picnic spot. In time the town of Holyhead was started, and all this holiness came from these two holy friends.

From the holiness of St. Cybi, too, came a holy well at Llangybi—Welsh makes it just a little difficult still to see his name in that placename—in Gwynedd. It had eels in it, and if the eels twined around you could be sure your complaint would be cured. Today the well is used for magic of another sort. Maybe because the pair of saints was an affair, the well has the reputation for being able to tell you whether your significant other is faithful or not. Drop in your handkerchief. If it floats north there is no problem but if it floats south you'd better expect unfaithfulness—for which no cure is offered.

HAVE A SEAT WHILE WE CURE YOUR INFERTILITY

We shall sidestep a discussion of the miracles wrought or said to be wrought by the holy relics of religion; there is no need to offend anyone's faith. Instead of the religious use of (say) the head of this saint, the arm of that one, or the whole body—and the whole body of some saints is claimed to be in several different churches—let us speak of the clearly pagan superstition attached to the chair of St. Bede.

This author of an ecclesiastical history of England itself not without extraordinary stories, Bede (who died in 735) might be displeased but certainly would not be astounded to hear that his oak chair, in St. Paul's church in Yarrow, has been used to cure infertility.

It is amazing it is still around, considering how many people took splinters of the wood to put under their pillows (to dream about whom they would marry) or into their food (to alleviate labor pains). Once the church began to guard it more carefully, couples married in the church on their way out paused to sit in it to ensure fertility.

"DEMONS AND WITCHCRAFT ...AVERTED BY CERTAIN MATERIALS"

Chapter 21 of Book 5 of *De Præstigiis dæmonum* by Johann Weyer in sixteenth-century Germany, is devoted to the beliefs of the ancients and the

Amen-Ra, King of the Gods.   The God Amsu, or Menu.   Amset, or Mesthâ, or Ca'tha (son of Horus).   The Goddess Ânit.   The God Reshpu.

The Goddess Âatat.   The God Ânpu (Anubis).   The Goddess Ânqet.   The God Âsâr (Osiris).   The God Seker.

The God Âsâr (Osiris).   Âsâr-Hâp (Serapis).   The Goddess Ast (Isis).   The God Âtmu.   The God Bennu (i.e., the Soul of Osiris).   The God Mentu-Ra.

The God Bes.   Hâpi, the Nile-God.   Hâpi (son of Horus).   The God Horu (Horus).   Horus-pa-khart (Harpokrates).   The God Nefer-Tmu.

The Goddess Hathor.   The Goddess Hathor.   The Goddess Hathor.   The God Seb.   The Goddess Ketesh.   The God Ptah-Seker.

The God Khepera.   The God Khnemu.   The God Khenu.   The Goddess Mata.   The Goddess Menhet.   The God Reshpu.

Roman Catholic church in cleansing by the fumes of sulfur, and sea water, salt and holy water. Pope Alexander I, who reigned 107–116?, recommended the extensive use of holy water, still available to the public in all Roman Catholic churches and much used in ceremonies both of the church and the magicians. Weyer mentions the use of the herbs frankincense, myrrh, verbena, valerian, "Christ's palm (carried on the person)" and still distributed to the faithful on Palm Sunday (in some European countries where it was unavailable willow branches were substituted), and "antirrhinum, or dried root of bryony, the smoke of the dried birthwort root, and also *benedicta*, and garyphyllon, and quill or sea-leek hung in the entry to the house....The herb Holitha, which repels evil spirits, grows in small quantities in Moravia....the smoked bile of a black dog, or its blood smeared upon all the walls of the house, is said to be most excellent for repelling demons and witchcraft wherever found." He mocks the "mutterings" the Roman church makes over chrisms (holy oils), but these are used in various ceremonies to this day, including the coronations of British monarchs.

For the coronation of Elizabeth I, excommunicated by Rome, no holy oil could be obtained from the pope. There was a little in the bottom of the container used at the coronation of Elizabeth's predecessor on the throne, her Catholic sister, Mary. That was brought forth. "This grease smelleth ill!" remarked the outspoken Protestant queen, but she opened her dalmatic and was, like all monarchs, anointed from the throat to the belly button and from shoulder to shoulder across the chest. She was then a sacred person. Elizabeth II submitted to the same ceremony, but the bishops in their commodious copes crowded around and shielded the queen from the prying eyes of television during this embarrassing procedure.

FOR THE FAIRY-STRUCK

Children who are "fairy-struck" pine away. Give them the juice of twelve leaves of foxglove. And next time be sure rowan branches are placed above their cradles or beds to protect them. Weave a branch of rowan into the roof of your cottage and the whole house will be safe. Replace it annually. This is one of many folklore protections that need renewal each year, according to custom.

REPAIRING YOUR SOULS

The Haida of British Columbia use a soul-catching bone, carved and inset with abalone "mother of pearl" (used in various other societies' magic, too) to help the shaman draw the sick soul out of the body and repair it. The soul is then put back into the patient. Human bones are part of all shamans' equipment in Tibet. They may even wear skirts made of them.

KNOCK ON WOOD

This brings good luck. (Gods used to live in the trees of the dark forests from which the ancestors of the Anglo-Saxons came; that's why we have Christmas trees.) To avert bad luck, when you spill your wine in Spain you tap with your fingers on the table a couple of times and then on the middle of your forehead. This is more than the gesture of hitting your forehead to "wake up your brain" when your thought is confused or you recognize you have made a foolish mistake.

THE DEMONS OF DISEASE

Thanks to Ola J. Hoten, here is an old Norwegian way to cure disease. Say:

Vor Herre Jesus gik sig Veien fram!	Our Lord walked along the path.
saa mødte han den onde Røita.	There He met the evil Rot.
"Hvor skal du hen," sagde Jesus.	"Where are you going?," asked Jesus.
"Jeg skal til Nesseby at suge blod	"I'm going to Neeseby to suck blood
og røite Kjøt."	and rotten meat."
"Nei, du skal atter vige," sagde Jesus,	"No, you shall go back," said Jesus,
"til den Skog, som ingen Mand bor,	"to the wood where no man lives,
"og til den Skjø, som ingen Mand ror."	and to the lake where no man rows."

I suppose that *Nesseby* is some dialectical Norwegian attempt at *Nazareth*. In Scandinavia, the demons of disease are banished to suffer the frightful winter weather of wind and water. They are told to dwell in stones, in the Blue Mountains—anywhere but in the bodies of believing Christians. In Finland there are formulae for sending disease demons back to Satan, who sent them to plague humanity. Another formula (from the great folklorist A. C. Bang, *Norske hexenformulater og magiske opskrifter*, Norwegian Witches' Formulae and Magical Recipes, 1901–1902):

Je skal udmete og udstevne alt ondt	I shall confront and expel all evil
tur Merg og i Ben ,	out of marrow and out of bone,
tur Ben og i Kjod og Blod,	out of bone and flesh and blood,

tur Blod og i Skind ,	out of blood and out of skin,
tur Skind og i Hud,	out of [human] skin and [animal] hide,
tur Hus i Veier og Vind	out of house and into weather and wind
og aldri komme herind.	and never to come in here again.

This is followed, as so many spells, whether of pagan or Christian origin, with the Christian formula: "In the Name of The Father, The Son, and of The Holy Spirit. Amen."

One more, one of the very many formulae to stem the flow of blood. Ignoring my habit of translating as closely as possible, this time I shall strive for rhyme as well as accuracy, rhyme being regarded as magical from the very earliest times.

Blod bli staaende i aaren	In the vein stand still the blood
som Kristus paa Korset batten.	As Christ was still upon the Rood.
Blod bli hengende i vunden	Blood within the wound abide
som Kristus paa Korset bunden.	As Christ upon the Cross was tied.

Ola J. Holten (with whom I have been writing for some years a book on the folklore of the northern countries of Europe) has been of great assistance not only in researching Scandinavian examples for me but also with the meanings of words in these formulae, some very ancient and very obscure. He has brought his own meticulous scholarship to my assistance and also brought to my attention such basic references as

A. C. Bang, *Norske hexeformulater of magiske opskriter* (1901–1902) for witches' formulae and magical operations

Arthur Brox, *Folkeminne frå Ytre Senja* (1970) for the folklore of the island of Senja

H. Falk & I. Reichborn-Kjennerud, *Frosken og padden i nordisk folkmedisin* (1923) for folk medicine

Ronald Grambo, *Norske trollformler og magiske ritualer* (1984) and other books by the leading Scandianavian authority

Finn Hødnebø, *Trolldomsbøker* (1974) for troll lore

F. Ohrt, *Gamle danske folkebønner* (1928) for old Danish superstitions, by the author of many standard books

J. T. Storaker, *Sygdom og forgjørelse i den norske folketro* (1932), by the author of several good books on folk superstitions

C. H. Tillhagen, *Finnen als Zauberkundige in der skandinavischen Volsuberberlieferüng (1962)*, one of his many authoritative studies of magic

AMERINDIAN HEALING PLANTS

Not only were peyote and saguaro liquor and tobacco and other drugs used in ceremonies by Native Americans long before the European came; there was also a long tradition of herbal medicine. Cattail pollen was one of the really useful medicines. It cured diseases, promoted the fertility of both the crops and, in a multi-day ritual, of human beings. Herbs dried in sunlight, made into concoctions with the pure water of fast-flowing streams, were both medicinal and magical. In the magical bundles, called "medicine bundles," unwrapped with great care on special occasions, each tribe or nation had its religion and the health of the people and their environment all tied up. At the heart of some medicine bundles was said to be a stone in which "the heartbeat of the world" was heard.

Some of these were considered "bad medicine" and blasphemous by Christians. The religious objects were outrageously destroyed by zealots in the same deplorable spirit in which a bishop of Chiapas burned many of the priceless codices of the pre-Columbian civilization. Some such sacred objects were stolen to be placed in museums; they ought to be returned.

To early man, all healing was magical, just as words and signs were magical. There was magic in the word and in the symbol. The concepts were far from primitive.

THE SLAYER OF MONSTERS

That's the way you say *garlic* in Sanskrit, and in many languages and civilizations garlic is a ghost-buster and a spiritual cleanser as well as adding zing to food. It was used, for instance:

> IN GERMANY in the mines to protect against kobolds
> IN ENGLAND (put in your socks) to ward off whooping cough
> IN CUBA in strings of 13 cloves worn for 13 days to cure jaundice
> IN TRANSYLVANIA, as every horror movie fan knows, garlic was used to drive off vampires. In one

scene in the parody horror film (and miserable ego trip) by Mel Brooks, *Dead and Loving It*, a bedroom is lavishly festooned with braided garlands of garlic. What few seem to know is that only garlic's white *flowers* affect vampires, not the cloves of garlic.

From Anna Riva's *The Modern Herbal* (reprinted 1992):

To behold marvelous visions, mix together some beef blood, wine dregs, marjoram and garlic. Add enough animal fat so you can knead the mixture into small balls about an inch around. Tale these to a pond or stream. Throw them one by one into the water and wondrous illusions should appear as they disappear.

Should, maybe; will? Shakespeare has a Welsh wizard declare that he can call spirits from the deep. A skeptical Englishman counters: "But will they come?"

PROTECTIVE HERBS

These do indeed work, at least on the groundless fears of the paranoid. Noxious fumes from asafetida and other stinking plants are said to drive away evil, but so can marjoram and mullein. Anemone protects against all diseases. Balm of Gilead mends broken hearts and cyclamen in the bedroom improves the on site performances. Gladiolus has a sort of phallic suggestion about it; it is regarded as an aphrodisiac. Dill fights off spells, and blood root on the witch's doorstep reverses her spell. Henbane and rue, used in many black magic concoctions, can also protect against them. Leaves from the pepper tree are said to be able to absorb evil sent upon you: if you have been blasted with the evil eye, take the evil off each eye with the application of an egg and then place the egg on pepper tree leaves.

THE CHARGE OF THE ARTIFICER'S SON

An ancient Irish "charge of great power" from the Danes: "onions and dillisk, with ambrosia and garlic; and let the plants be broken and boiled upon beer; then add the gall of a hog's liver and a drop of wine or of doe's milk, and, when well strained, pour it into an amphora of brass, and apply the liquid to the eye, when the benefit," says Lady Wilde, "is certain." Also good for healing the eyes is Snail Drop: just stick a pin into a living snail and apply the oozing liquid to the sore eyes. I wonder if that works slowly....

WHO GETS THE MEDICINE

Magic may be present when one takes certain medicines in certain ways; it is certainly in the picture when to cure oneself one gives medicine to someone or something else! In Scandinavian folk medicine, it was a custom that to cure what they call "red sickness" (which I take to be blood in the urine rather than menstruation) in people you were supposed to take a cup of salt and in the name of Jesus give it to the cattle!

CERTAIN FOODS FOR CERTAIN OCCASIONS

This may be only tradition or merely symbolic, but sometimes it involves superstition and magic. My favorite "good luck" food is the stew of algae or seaweed and other maritime items that they boil up to bring good luck to fishing in Gallicia. Their *caldo gallego* soup is nice, but this other one is magical.

ALCOHOLICS PLEASE NOTE

You can try twelve steps or five almonds. In his *Natural History*, Pliny, who looks gullible to us but in his own time and for centuries after was regarded as completely reliable, assures us that five almonds constitute a cure for drunkenness. You must be sober enough to count to five.

URÆUS

This is the snake you see on Egyptian headdresses and other objects of the old dynasties. On the ancient amulet you see here the soul is repre-sented as an *ankh* or Egyptian cross and the serpent is spitting out a pro-tective stream of venom to protect the soul after it has left the body. The Egyptians believed that the soul might wish to come back to the body sometime and that belief is the reason for all the funerary emphasis of Egyptian art and architecture. Mummification and other preservation of the physical body was essential, in their view.

REDHEADS

Redheaded people are supposed to bring luck to oth-ers; rub their heads. Gamblers believe that rubbing dice on a red hair puts luck into them. One woman was caught in Las Vegas using this custom to put the house dice into her hairdo and substitute her own pair of loaded dice. When I commented to the per-son who brought me that information that getting caught was certainly unlucky, he replied that the woman's hair was only dyed red.

Brahmins are not permitted to marry redheaded women. Christians once looked askance at redheads because Judas Iscariot was thought to have had red hair. The stage Jew, a comic figure in Shakespeare's time, had a hooked nose and red hair, like Shylock.

AARONROOT AND CHRISTROOT

One magical book recommends you keep these on your person during conjurations to prevent demons from taking possession of you, but I am not sure what these herbs are.

RESGUARDOS

These are the protections of *Santería* and are similar to the little bags with fetish objects in them called *gris-gris* in voodoo. The *Santería* protections are an odd combination of African magic and Roman Catholic reverence for St. Barbara (a symbol of whom is attached to the *resguardo*). That is, however, basically calling not upon saints but upon the thunder god, Chango. In a little red velvet bag, sewn with red thread, you place spices and herbs, especially aloes, brown sugar, etc. It is very bad luck to open such a bag to see what is inside. The bag is best made by someone dedicated to the religion and blessed, rather like a Roman Catholic medal, like which it is worn.

RELICS

The Pardoner in Chaucer's *Canterbury Tales* was not the only one peddling false relics of saints. The Middle Ages were wild about relics and ready to believe the most marvelous stories; some of those about how relics were translated magically from one place to another I cannot really imagine anyone believing, but they did.

True, people said that if all the alleged pieces of the True Cross (supposedly found by St. Helen, mother of Constantine the Great) were assembled there would be enough wood to build a church to house the real Cross. True, some relics were hilarious: my favorite (as I have often said) was a vial containing "some of the darkness which God brought upon Egypt." I personally have seen the entire body of a certain saint in more than one Italian church. I have carefully observed the skull of St. Catherine of Siena, the arm of St. Francis Xavier, the head of more than one French saint, and so on. I have been to the great church of pilgrimage of St. John of Compostella, and some day I should like to visit in person the magnificent temple that houses a tooth of The Buddha.

But it is not impossible, however unlikely, that the crown jewels of the Austro-Hungarian empire really do include a nail from the Crucifixion. Certainly Hitler was extremely interested in getting his hands on a lance from the Hapsburg collection which was supposed to have pierced the side of Christ and have magical powers. You recall the Ark of The Covenant in one of the Indiana Jones epics. You have heard of the searches for the Holy Grail (the cup Christ used at the Last Supper), if not of the burning question one cynic uttered: "If they had found it, what would they have done with it?"

Relics of saints can do, some say, more than inspire us to emulate their holy lives. Philip II of Spain, for instance, assembled some 8,000 relics of saints and housed them in a palace he built in the shape of a gridiron, the device on which St. Lawrence was martyred. In *From Madrid to Purgatory* (1995), Carlos M. N. Eire describes how Philip, unable to walk with an ulcerated knee—dying, in fact—had brought to him in formal ritual three relics especially important to him: "the entire knee of the glorious martyr Saint Sebastian, with all its bone and skin," the rib of St. Alban (a present to His Most Catholic Majesty from His Holiness Clement VIII, which came with a plenary indulgence at the point of death and a sort of Monopoly "get out of jail" card for Purgatory), and the arm of St. Vincent Ferrer.

For venial sins, Philip daily made generous use of holy water. He prayed a lot, was very pious in an age of iconoclasts and anti-papist simplification of religion, and so arranged his palace that, sick or well, he needed only to open his bedroom door to have a view of the high altar of the church and so could attend Mass without getting out of bed.

As for cures, if psychological states can produce the stigmata, I see no reason why the inspiration derived from relics cannot produce marvelous effects too. As little old Jewish ladies say of chicken soup and other marvelous things, "It couldn't hurt." Do you denounce superstition so strongly that you would burn supposed relics, as many did in reaction to the papacy? I think all that destruction of relics was crazy, of a piece with the monsters who broke open the tombs of the kings of France at the Revolution. One of them got the heart of Henri IV—and ate it!

ADDER STONES

We may be forgiven for quoting an only slightly condensed entry in E.& M.A. Radford's fine *Encyclopædia of Superstitions* (1949) because it is harder to find than it ought to be.

Adder stones, carried in the pocket, will cure all maladies of the eyes.
—Wales.

To prevent a child having the whooping-cough, hang an adder stone round its neck.—Superstition recorded in Scotland as far back as 1699, and still extant in remote parts of the Highlands.

Adder stones are also called Serpents' Eggs and Snake Eggs. They were held in high esteem by the Druids...[because] they secured success in law-suits, and free access to kings and [other] rulers. Many adder stones are still preserved as charms in those rural areas of Britain where the Celtic population still lingers. In some parts of Wales the stones go by the name Gleini na Droedh [Wizard's Glass] or Gleini nan Druidhe [Druid's Glass].... they were believed to have been made by serpents...gathered together in a wriggling, slimy mass to generate the stones from their slaver, and shoot them into the air from their hissing jaws. It is a curious omission in superstition that such stones...were never associated with the curing of a serpent's bite. The gathering time of the snakes was held, in Cornwall, to be on Midsummer Eve; in Wales, on the eve of May Day. So recently as the early 1900s[,] the authors were told, in all seriousness, by people in the Principality [of Wales] that they had witnessed such a congress of snakes, and had seen the magic stones in the midst of froth. The stones are of various colours—green, pink, red, blue and brown. There are a number still preserved in several museums...and many of these are perforated. It was held that the perforation was caused, after the stone had been confolated by the serpents generally, by one of the serpents sticking its tail through the still viscous glass. The test of the genuineness of an Adder Stone was to throw it into a moving stream; if genuine it floated against the current, and no weight attached to it could make the stone sink.

MAKE YOUR OWN SIMPLE AMULET OR TALISMAN

Buy a pretty locket. Choose a time especially significant to yourself: the anniversary of the precise minute of your birth—this may keep you up late, because so many babies used to be born at night—or set the alarm for the stroke of midnight and when it sounds let it continue as you place in the locket the piece of paper you have earlier prepared. The alarm's noise will add excitement to the moment.

That tiny piece of paper mentioned is one on which you have written whatever words or symbols appeal to you and which you consider will protect you against harm or draw luck to you. As you don the locket, visualize with great concentration a wall of good forces that completely surround you like an aura. Never take off the locket. If it is gold, do not flaunt it in the subway.

ANTI-PIXIE

"There are varying traditions about the size, appearance and origin of the Pixies, " writes the great expert on Little Folk and Good Friends of all kinds, Katherine Briggs, in her magnificent *Encyclopedia of Fairies* (1976), " but all accounts agree about their being dressed in green, and about their habit of misleading travelers."

If you are "pixie-led," led astray and lost, just turn your coat inside out. Or to avoid the trouble in the first place, do not enter the area of the Pixies (or Pigsies or Piskies) without a "wicken-cross" or a piece of bread in your pocket.

SNAKE BALLS

Every section of this vast country has its local lore. Clifton Johnson has collected some from New England, B. A. Botkin the superstitions of The South, and so on. Jonson in *Historic Hampshire in the Connecticut Valley* (1932), for instance, tells us of snake balls, small rocks that were supposed to absorb poison. He assures us that "the common people believed in this means of cure." For a potpourri of cures from all over of one affliction, see Wheaton Phillips Webb on "The Wart" in *New York Folklore Quarterly* 2:2 (1946), 98–106, and you can spend many happy hours with the journals of the folklore of the Midwest, of Texas and the Southwest, and elsewhere. Everyone has her or his version of what we might call a "snake ball" cure, some natural object that works like a charm.

WHO IS BEWITCHING YOU?

If you are hexed or hoodooed or cursed or bewitched in any way, it certainly seems useful to know who is responsible for your misery. There are many ways, especially in American voodoo (Marie Laveau specialized in this, as well as in keeping or getting persons out of jail), for identifying a witch, but the strangest system comes from Norway, where you are supposed to take a *havrelese* (thin slab of oat bread), place it on top of a bucket of water, and pour molten lead through it. The figures that the lead forms in the water are said to give hints as to who is bothering you. These oat creations are rather similar to the cakes that King Alfred is supposed in legend to have let burn. I wonder if he was consorting with witches. In his time and place that would not have been unusual.

WHAT HAPPENED TO THE RABIES CURE

Originally it was Latin *HOC+ PO+ MO+DEUS ADIUVET* (written on a slice of apple given to the person bitten: "May by this apple God help you"). Johann Weyer wrote in sixteenth-century Germany:

> I know a gentleman of high station who is famed for a similar type of cure [to writing a magic formula on a piece of bread and eating it to cure a dog bite]. He writes *"Hax pax max Deus adimax"* upon an apple slice and then gives it to a person infected by a rabid dog. But these words are corrupted because of the ignorance of the Latin tongue and Latin literature....Thinking the crosses to be the letter x because of the similarity of form, he read *hax pax max Deus adimax* and so inscribed the apple.

Weyer fails to explain that the slice of apple was probably a substitute for a consecrated Host, which it resembles. So we have a substitute object inscribed with a substitute magical inscription but it brought in so much money (Weyer tells us) that the nobleman was able to "build a chapel next to his castle, a chapel supposedly graced by many Masses paid for by these wages of impiety."

IN BALI

The island of Bali is believed to be more infested with demons than almost anywhere else. Sir James Frazer, in the magisterial *Golden Bough*, describes how when it gets too "warm" with demons the people organize offerings for the demons at crossroads and the priest summons the demons to partake of the feast while men, lighting torches from a central fire, fan out in all directions to shoo off the evil forces: "Depart!" As these torches pass their homes, the people, who have huddled inside, make terrific noises to scare off the demons in the neighborhood. When the demons gather at their banquet, the priest curses and exorcises them. Then for two days the people observe absolute silence. Everyone stays home, stays quiet, and hopes that the formerly-resident demons will not recognize the place and will not return to their homes.

CALUSARI

These were cathartic dancers and magical healers in Romania in ancient times whose specialty was curing disease allegedly caused by the fairies. Gustav Henningsen in the anthology he edited with Bengt Ankarloo (*Early Modern European Witchcraft: Centres and Peripheries*, 1990) points out that this was odd because they claimed "their secret society is patronized by the "Queen of the Fairies," *Doamna Zinelor*—the Romanian metamorphosis of Diana, also called Irodiada (Herodias) or Arada (both names having familiar connections with western European beliefs in witchcraft and the Wild Hunt)."

Diana is now involved in American covens "drawing down the moon," and *Arada* turns up strangely as one of the powerful names of God (male) in various non-Romanian *grimoires*. The Wild Hunt was originally Scandinavian and consisted of a god and his male companions, not a goddess or witches.

BEES

In England, when someone in the family dies, you are supposed to go to the hives and tell the bees. Here is an old formula:

> Honey bees, honey bees! Hear what I say:
> Your master N. has passed away.
> His wife now begs you will freely stay
> And gather honey for many a day.

In Cornwall, when the bees swarm, go out and beat on a pot or tin can and call "Browney! Browney!" to get them back together. St. Brigit used to send bees against her enemies.

SUPERSTITIONS OF DIXIE

There has been a certain condescension in the attribution to the South, and particularly to southern African-Americans, of a very naive and superstitious cast of mind, though, as I suggest elsewhere, the black man and the white man have always been not two separate societies there as much as they have been like the two characters in a Tony Curtis movie: chained together, trying to escape. The mixture of African and European traditions has produced a unique American amalgam, nowhere more evident than in southern counter-charms and spells. B. A. Botkin in an anthology of southern superstitions (1949) writes:

> As in all counter-charms, evil smells are effective in driving away spirits, but mustard seed planted under the doorstep, or fern seed in the hollow, a sprinkling of salt, pepper, sulfur, or collard seed, a Bible or a sharp object under the pillow will keep away both "hants" [haunters] and witches, who can be killed only with a silver (sometimes brass) bullet. [Witches of course are human and can be killed in any usual way, as strangling, burning, and other violence of "the burning times" horribly testify. The writer is confusing witches and vampires, werewolves, etc.] Used against witches, a broom or hair brush across the door or a Bible or sifter under the pillow are effective because a witch has to stop to count whatever comes before her. And sharp things (forks, knives, scissors, needles, around the bed or under the pillow) catch in her skin, which she has to shed before she can ride you, and keep her from getting back into it when she is through.

Awful smells arise from burning a lock of an enemy's hair with sulfur and chanting (thirteen times!):

> Your power is gone! You are weak!
> Your tongue is stilled; you cannot speak!
> I for evermore reject thee!
> This spell for evermore protects me!

Southern superstition has many other spells and it has its own root doctors and many a *remedè* and voodoo priestesses and the zombie version of the undead and other African influences, such as the idea that if you twist your left ankle you will have good luck (and the right, bad, an African antithesis to what a European outlook might be). There is also a strong infusion of Scots-Irish demonology altered in the isolation of the mountains. There are other interesting characteristics which differentiate the South from the madness of Salem and the Spanish contributions to superstition here—though there is some of that in Louisiana and elsewhere in

The South—of The West, and the Scandinavian and German and Italian and other elements of other areas in the United States. In an overall analysis of American superstition, which has not yet been successfully attempted, cultures in contact, conflict and cooperation could be usefully studied. In a general survey the Deep South might well be found to be among the most inventively and colorfully superstitious areas.

The true magicians of the Deep South are not the publicity-seekers of New Orleans nor the devil-worshippers residing in Savannah but the rural people, off the beaten tracks, who cling without question to old ways.

BIBLICAL REFERENCES IN SPELLS

These occur even in spells so superstitious that Christians ought not to use them, and they are found in Britain, in Germany, Italy, Scandinavia. For instance, to stanch blood the Norwegian says: *Stat Blod, stil Blod, stat sas stille som Jesus stilte Jordans Flod* (Stop blood, stand still blood,/ As Jesus stemmed the Jordan's flood). There seems to be some confusion here: the sun stood still (The Bible says) to enable Joshua to fight the battle of Jericho, but when Christ was baptized in the Jordan the river did not stand still. In *Norske Trollformler og Magiske Ritualer* (Troll Formulae and Magical Rituals, 1984) Ronald Gambo even gives a spell which has The Devil standing still at the Jordan river, as if The Devil, and not The Father and The Holy Spirit, was present on that occasion.

THE WITCH'S CURSE AND THE TALKING CURE

The French writer Sabine Prokhoris (translated by G. M. Goshgarian in *The Witch's Kitchen,* 1996) advances the striking theory that the witch's curse is the origin of the talking cure of psychoanalysis. In a discussion of *Faust* and Freud, Prokhoris argues that Freud's psychoanalytic theory and cure was greatly affected by the idea of the curse, itself analytic and a product of transference.

CHRISTIAN AND PAGAN CURES

The pagans tried to cure by magic. The Jews were more interested in medicine but forbade all surgery (except circumcision) and dissection of human bodies. The low regard Jews held of medical men is reflected in passages in the scriptures such as II Chronicles XVI:12 and the gospel of Mark V:26. Christians were suspicious of this and for a long time medicine was looked down upon, though there were orders of knights hospitalers who picked up ideas from their Saracen opponents in the Crusades. Monks learned a lot about herbal medicine—think of the Friar in *Romeo and Juliet*—but were forbidden by church law to practice medicine after The Council of Clermont

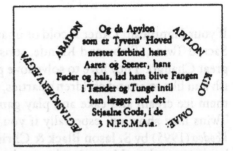

(1130). Throughout Europe, Jews were prominent in the study and practice of medicine. Among Christians, disease was regarded as a punishment for sin and ought, the church believed, to be treated with repentance, penance, prayer, and fasting. However, people did pray for relief and turned to the saints for intercession, first perhaps to the martyr St. Sebastian when in the sixth century there was a plague in the time of Justinian. Then the relics of saints came to be used in the production of miraculous cures and while the knowledge of medicine and (after Ambrose Paré in the sixteenth century) surgery made great strides, later to be followed by Christian Science and psychiatry, Christians with their relics and miracles were not far at any time from old pagan magical practices.

A pagan cure for trollfolk bothering your cattle, perhaps riding them by night so that in the morning you find them wet and exhausted, is:

Ri paa din egen husbond,
ri ikke paa min ko.
Mor og far din, reis ende
til helvedes pine!

Ride your own husband,
don't ride my cow.
Your father and mother go right to
the pains of Hell!

A spell to "bind a thief" illustrated above is extraordinary in that it adds to the pagan basis not only the "3 N" (which is "Father, Son, and Holy Spirit" names) but also names of residents of Hell such as Abbadon and Apollyon!

AMETHYST

Did you know the word means "against drunkenness"? That's the sober truth. Drop an amethyst into your glass and you won't get drunk. (Do not drive after trying this!)

It is alleged that this and indeed all violet stones if worn by children make them docile and obedient. (If this works, please let us know.)

CALL ON THE TWINS FOR HELP WITH "THE ONE"

If your Significant Other is cold or unattainable, or strays, call on the *Ibeyi*, Sacred Twins, Taebo and Kainde, sons of the Macumba thunder god, the great Chango. They love to solve love problems. But they are rather child-ish and like to attend children's parties, so get together some kids and serve them ice cream and cake and play games and have a good time and The Twins may show up, especially if you chant the formula given in *Urban Voodoo* (1995) by S. Jason Black & Christopher S. Hyatt, a well-researched book on voodoo, *Macumba* (the voodoo of Brazil), *Lucumbi* (a kind of *San-tería*), etc. They say to offer these gods a blood sacrifice "only if it is specif-ically requested." The cake and cookies may be enough—and even if the following invocation fails the kids will love the party. The invocation in a sort of Portuguese.

> *Vamos comer caruru, dois, dois,*
> *Na prata tem caruru.*
> *Vamos comer caruru, dois, dois,*
> *No bosque tem caruru.*
> *Vamos comer caruru, dois, dois,*
> *No terreiro tem caruru.*
> *Vamos charmar as criancas*
> *Pra comer munguaza.*
> *Vamos chamar as criancas*
> *Pra sarava no conga.*
> *Vamos chamar a Joaozinho*
> *Mariazbina e Cipriano.*
> *Vamos chamar o Zezinho*
> *O Manezinho e o Mariano.*

Note the presence of Christian saints. Chango himself appears on altars as St. Barbara and his spouse (Oshun, actually a version of Venus) as The Virgin of Caridád del Cobre, the patron saint of Cuba! Their twin boys appear as St. Cosmo and St. Damian! But this is African voodoo, not Chris-tian religion here! Offer The Twins crumbled cake and cookies and place some of these crumbs where the one you want to love you will come near them, preferably without noticing them. These authors, who have delved into Spanish and Portuguese sources not usually reported in English, offer "Another Spell of Attraction":

...write the name of the desired lover on a piece if [of!] paper, and place it in a dish. Cover with honey or syrup while invoking Oshun and lighting a candle in her honor. Ideally the candle should be allowed to burn completely out, but if this is a safety hazard, keep it burning while you are at home. Don't blow the candle out. Snuff it out.

I wish to add that you may be able to let it burn uninterrupted if you shield it well from wind and conceal it outdoors, where Oshun likes best to be addressed, by running water. So many candle-burners tell me that their spells do not work that I am beginning to think they must find some way to give the whole candle—as it were—a chance to strut its stuff. I realize leaving unattended candles burning is dangerous. Let me tell you what one Manhattan witch of my acquaintance does: she places lit candles to burn—while she is out of her apartment—in her shower stall and closes the door.

TAKING OFF A CANDLE SPELL

If you suspect someone is "burning candles against you," try this (in your shower or bathtub if necessary): Light two black candles at the exact moment of sunset on a Friday and let them burn out. As you light them intone:

> Beelzebub, and all ye evil spirits, in the name of Astaroth and the Light and the Dark and the gods of the Netherworld, remove thy curse and thy sting from my heart and mine, and against whomsover casts a curse at me let it be reversed upon them. Let these candles be their candles, this burning their burning, this curse a curse upon them. Let the pain they direct at me and mine fall upon them.

Some say this should be repeated every night for five nights in a row, others that five Fridays in a row is better. In any case, the candles are lit precisely at sundown and allowed to burn out completely. Do not use giant pillar candles; they burn too long.

TAKING OFF OTHER KINDS OF SPELLS

Spells can be cast on the air, with fire, water, and earth. If evil has been carried on the air, blow into the air a mixture of flour, salt, and sugar, to bring truth, clearing of the air, a sweeter report. If made with fire, spells can be reversed by lighting a candle stuck in earth and then picking it up, turning it upside down, lighting the other end, and saying something like, "As the candle has been reversed, so is the spell." For spells involving water, one source says to fill a small jar with water, add some pins, cap the jar, place on the stove, leave the room, and do not come back until the jar has exploded. Then you clean up the mess—broken glass, pins and all—and throw it into the garbage and get it out of your house and out of your life right away. The same writer, Draja Mickaharic in *A Century of Spells* (1988), says to reverse a spell placed with earth you should place a small cup half full of potting soil in a corner of your bedroom and pray over it:

> Thou art earth of which this whole world is made. Be thou my earth, and take unto thyself all that is sent against me. Bear thou that which is sent against me as Jesus Christ bore the sins of the whole world.

"Leave the dirt in the corner of the bedroom for a week and then throw it out the back door of your house" and "if you don't have a back door, use the front door." Then you wait a night and then fill the cup with cold water. Or you can repeat the regime.

The easiest cleansing is to rub an egg or a chicken over your whole body. Some magical circles do this before persons are admitted to the room where ceremonies take place.

PROTECTION AGAINST THE BUCKIES

Typical of a great many little verses (in verse for mnemonic reasons but also because verse was considered magical) known to children down the ages, this "biddy bene" or asking benediction or prayer protected Devonshire youngsters against bugbears, boggarts, bullbeggars, bogeymen, buckies, and other frightening creatures, "things that go bump in the night," lurking in the dark, products of the vivid imaginations of the young:

> Bucky, Bucky, biddy bene,
> Is the way now fair and clean?
> Is the goose ygone to nest,
> And the fox ygone to rest?
> Shall I come away?

The rhymes of childhood, not to mention the terrors of the monster in the closet or under the bed, "things that go bump in the night," prepared the adult to feel she or he needed charms and spells against all sorts of supernatural creatures.

MIDEWEWIN

In English we render that Ojibwa word as "Grand Medicine Society" and Diamond Jenness in her study of the Ojibwa Indians of Parry Island (*National Museum of Canada Bulletin* 78, 1935, 75) writes that it might quite properly be defined as a "secret medical organization garbed in the mantle of religion." From the last two surviving members of the Grand Medicine Society (both named King) still living on Parry Island in 1935 she learned of their "use of plants for curing sickness and fabricating charms" and says that

> on special occasions the *medés* united to treat a patient whose malady yielded to no other cure. They carried the sick man inside a medicine lodge, consulted over him exactly as would a group of European doctors....

The Ojibwa peoples used red and white pine tar in various concoctions, white and black spruce and larch leaves as fumigators and inhalants, ate bittersweet soup and bloodroot prepared in lye water, and burned starflower and other roots to attract deer to the hunter. Nature was their grocery and their pharmacy and the source of magical things, too. Their medicine men hid other medicaments in hemlock tea. Some natural products they just liked to eat (such as beechnuts) but others they used for stopping bleeding, hurrying along childbirth, curing diseases, etc. They used bur oak extract as an astringent and the berries of the smooth sumac ("put into boiling water and boiled one minute" and "drink one cup every hour to stop diarrhea"), the milk of white lettuce or extract of leatherwood as a diuretic tea (leatherwood was also useful for tying things together as with thongs), agrimony and bittersweet for discomforts of the urinary tract, blueberry tea as a blood purifier, gold thread as a mouthwash, waterleaf root to fatten ponies and field horsetail to make their coats glossy (the latter also cured dropsy in humans), and many more of the earth's natural medicines. However, they also used magic with their medicinal cures: the high bush huckleberry, for instance, was magical and some tribes (such as the Chippewa) burned with moose fat and deer tallow the leaves of the low bush blueberry and inhaled the smoke to cure "craziness." Some hallucinogens were used to put Amerinds in states to receive magical messages in dreams, etc.

W. J. Hoffman in a lengthy work on "The Mewiwin or Grand Medicine Society of the Ojibwa" (seventh annual report of the US Bureau of American Ethnology, 1896) says huckleberries were "one of the chief articles of trade during the summer. The berry occupies a conspicuous place in the myth of the 'Road of the Dead' referred to in connection with the 'Ghost Society'" (p. 199). Also connected to the Ghost Society rituals were other fruits, such as the scarlet strawberry, leaves, bark, etc.

Lucifuge Rofocale

The Ojibwa considered the red baneberry "male" at some seasons and "female" at others and directed when it should be administered to each. The berries are (as the name suggests) poisonous, but the roots were wrapped in basswood leaves and baked and it was from the result, not the berries, that infusions were made. For one thing, they cured (imaginary) hairs that had been swallowed. The white man picked up a number of Objiwa recipes among the "swaw remedies," of which wintergreen may be the best example, and such other useful things as wild plum (dye fixative) and the Ojibwa *kinnikinnik* (smoking mixture in lieu of tobacco), *Salix lucida* (shining willow), etc. We did not take up much of the magic, for we did not understand most of the aboriginal religions and often were frightened by the warpaint of some tribes, by the magical tattoos that Father Theodat Gabriel Sagard found among the Hurons, by the hideous magical masks of the Iroquois, by the Buffalo Dance and other magical ceremonies, and many other things.

CAT'S BLOOD

This very old recipe for curing a fever seems more magical (it's biblical) than medicinal: Cut the ear of a cat, catch the blood on a piece of bread, and eat it. You can also use the old Russian system: Tie a piece of red wool around an arm or leg.

Cats figure much in magic. Mohammed's cat is, according to the faithful of Islam, in Paradise. Although we have had a film entitled *All Dogs Go to Heaven*, there is no documentation of that comparable to that supporting the cat of The Prophet.

According to old superstition, cat's blood will not work to cure leprosy; for that, you have to bathe in human blood. The Emperor Constantine was ready to try that, but the pope of the time convinced him holy water would suffice, and it did.

To get cats to come into your garden so you can capture them for blood, plant catnip. To keep them from attacking your birds, put rue near the birds' nests.

Actually, I do not recommend using the blood of any creature, even cats, in any rites.

THE PSALTER

Tradition has in America used individual Psalms as cures or protections. For instance, the third verse of Psalm I may solve the problems of couples who cannot conceive and Psalm XX protects you on a journey. This is comparable to parts of The Koran and other scriptures being used in like manner in other cultures.

Johann Weyer, discussing curses that bring loss of virility, mentions one cure that he states he would like to see "buried in the depths of Hell" but I'll give it you anyway.

The psalm, "Deliver me from mine enemies," is read over the characters seven times, and the parchment is fastened to the man's hip.

I feel it is safe to do this because Weyer mentions "the characters written upon new 'virgin' parchment and much heralded for use" against impotence—but he does not give them! Nor can I.

KEEPING WITCHES OUT

Throw salt into your lit fireplace if and when evil is around (which you can tell by a number of signs, the easiest of which to notice is that a candle burns blue). Sprinkle fern seed or any other fine seed—the witches are kept busy counting the tiny objects—at the doorsill. Or nail up a *mezuzah*, cross, horseshoe, or other object hated by evil creatures. Or carry the plant called blow ball in a little red sachet; it is supposed to be invincible against all evil forces.

BREAKING SPELLS

There are many traditional plants for breaking spells: for breaking a love spell, for instance, lily, lotus, and pistachio. There are column candles available in your local magickal shoppe. If someone has cursed you by tying thirteen knots in a cord, get the cord and untie the knots! To unhex, try any or all of these: bamboo, chili pepper (excellent!), datura, galangal (excellent!), huckleberry, hydrangea, poke weed, squill, thistle, toadflax, vetiver (my favorite, and it smells nice), wahoo, and wintergreen. Oils for the purpose include bergamot, myrrh, rose geranium, rosemary, rue, and vetiver again.

HOW TO GET YOUR CHILD BACK WHEN A CHANGELING APPEARS

It was believed that the fairies would palm off a stick of wood (which "glamour" made seem for a while like a baby) or some inferior child of their own, stealing healthy babes from the cradle and leaving behind a sick or deformed one. This explained a lot of changes for the worse observed in infants. Autistic children were thought to be changelings.

In Lady Wilde's *Ancient Legends, Mystic Charms, and Superstitions of Ireland* (2 vols., 1887) there are typical changeling details but for once a cure for the problem is offered. When their baby is stolen and a fairy child put in its place, the parents are distraught, but then a young girl, wearing a red neckerchief, comes to their cottage and says she would rather have her own child back and tells the parents to take three sheaves to the hill where the fairies live, burn them one by one, and threaten to burn all the vegetation on the fairy hill if the fairies do not give up the human child. The threat to burn the fairy hill can also be used to get adults back who have been abducted by the fairies.

THE EVIL EYE

There are whole books on this ancient superstition. The Italians are particularly afraid of *malocchia* and say you could be born with it (like one nineteenth-century pope whom most of Rome hated to see) or get it permanently as a result of evil or temporarily, often as a result of fever. Being born in January makes you immune to it. Being born on Christmas Eve makes you almost certain to have it. It doesn't work during the period of Passover. Some Africans report witchdoctors with a killing gaze. The concept exists in many religions—or should we say superstitious cultures? The oddest belief? Maybe that the skin of a hyena's forehead repels the evil eye.

THE EASIEST BURN CHARM

Christina Hole, historian of witchcraft (*Witchcraft in England*, 1945, reprinted in 1970, highly recommended) cites a magical verse used in the East End of London and published in the *Times* for 12 April 1920: blow three times on the burn and say

> Here come I to cure a burnt sore.
> If the dead knew what the living endure,
> The burnt sore would burn no more.

I found the same sort of thing in Appalachia in our own day, and it goes back a long way. I'll be back to charms for burns later on. Another here: the Irish claim that the ends of candles burned at a wake cure burns well.

AN OLD WRINKLE

For old wrinkles the cure may be an injection or other cosmetic procedure, but to avoid new wrinkles send your lover to see the exposing of the skull of St. Valentine. This relic is exhibited in a Roman church annually, and it is believed by many that seeing it will keep new wrinkles from forming on your lover's brow for a year.

TINNITUS

To stop that ringing in your ears caused by a spell cast by an enemy, read a list of people you know. When you get to the name of the perpetrator, the ringing will stop, and you will also (African superstition translated to the Deep South assures us) have the name of the perpetrator so you can clutch your *mojo* and launch your voodoo revenge. Or you can simply untie and then retie your shoelaces and go on with your life.

QUICK CURE FOR EPILEPSY, LUNACY, AND DEMONIC POSSESSION

John of Gaddeseden (1280?–1361) in his *Rosa anglica practica medicinæ* (English Rose of Practical Medicine, Venice, 1502, 1516) cites three otherwise forgotten physicians (Constantinus, Gualterius, Bernhardus) and gives their method for curing both the medical and magical problems that "try the just and punish the unjust," as St. Augustine explains.

The patient must fast for three days and then attend Mass with his parents during Ember Day fast and the Mass of the following Saturday and Sunday. A priest should read over the patient the section of the Gospel used for the Feast of the Holy Cross, "This sort of demon is not cast out except by fasting and prayer...." Then the patient has to write that bit of the Gospel down on a paper he wears around his neck, and he will be cured.

BURNING AMBITIONS

There are sacrifices, King Lear tells Cordelia, on which "the gods themselves throw incense." And there are sacrifices of incense that are said to recruit the assistance of divine powers, or demonic ones. For love intentions, burn incense (or oils) with the pleasing scents of amber, cardamom, copal, gardenia, jasmine, lavender, musk, patchouli, rose, strawberry, vanilla, vetivert, violet, ylang-ylang. For cleansing and healing, try the astringent, clarifying scents of cedar, cinnamon, cypress, eucalyptus, myrrh, pine, rosemary, sandalwood, etc. To unhex, try cedar, honeysuckle, lemon grass, yarrow, and more. To draw evil powers, try any obnoxious or poisonous materials and especially hallucinogens, damiana, hellebore, henbane, sulfur, etc.

CLOTHES

There are special costumes for sorcery, though some witches work "sky-clad," naked. You can wear something red to keep from being bewitched. You can wear some clothes inside out to throw an evil spell back at the witch. A piece of the clothes of a saint could work miracles and a piece of some clothes the mother wore when she was pregnant could cure an infant's sickness.

DIE HELINGEN DREI KÖNIGEN

The Three Kings, or Magi (underlining the fact that they were magicians—they reached the Christ Child's birthplace by a combination of astrology and astronomy, then practically synonymous), were in the middle ages thought to be helpful in healing, and their names or pictures appear on numerous amulets from that period. H. Kehrer published at Leipzig in 1908 a detailed study of *Die heilinge drei Königen in Literatur und Kunst* (The Three Holy Kings in Literature and Art).

ALL CURES BY WITCHCRAFT ARE EVIL

Or so, refusing to make the distinction between "wise women" (or "cunning men") and those doing *maleficium* , between what some call white and black magic, thought many in olden times. For example, the clergyman William Perkins wrote *A Discourse on the Damned Art of Witchcraft* (1610) which made it clear that the conservative could not tolerate attempts to bypass either the church or the medical profession and that

> by Witches we understand not onely which kill and torment: but all Diviners, Charmers, Juglers, all Wizzards, commonly called wise men and wise women; yea, whomsoever doe any thing knowing what they doe which cannot be effected by nature or art; and in the same number we reckon all good Witches, which doe no hurt, but good, which doe not spoile and destroy, but save and deliver.

In peasant Europe, "wise men and wise women" were the physicians and pharmacists of the poor. They were sought out by everyone for their curative potions as well as their allegedly magical elixirs—and occasional poisons. It was only when villagers turned against them, or other people felt they had been injured by them, or coveted their property, that the local witches and wizards were persecuted. But, though even popes and kings with private physicians sought their aid on occasion, in time, under the prompting of such men as William Perkins, the authorities began to clamp down on

Lord Macaulay's hero Horatius dies for "the ashes of his fathers, and the altars of his gods." Romans revered *lares* and *penates* (above) as household protectors and offered them food and wine.

even those "who doe no hurt, but good" as well as those accused of doing evil, being in league with The Devil, casting spells, ruining crops, destroying livestock and livelihoods, poisoning enemies, injuring, and killing.

A significant Danish book on witchcraft (Niels Hemmingsen's *Admonitio de superstitionibus magicis vitandis)*, 1575) is typically uncompromising and defines a magical superstition as

> anything that comes from the Devil, through the medium of human beings, by whatever is imagined to be in words, signs, figures and characters [letters], whether an express agreement with the Devil occurs or not.

So it was conservative to believe that even in the absence of a diabolical pact or even malice the witches were all in league with evil. The cures the good witches had effected were forgotten and they were hunted down. They often became the scapegoats of the evils of others.

CURING WITCHCRAFT

Witches challenge the religion and the authority structures of the society. The Tzeltal of Central America have an unusual way of attacking the problem. First they kill the witch. Then they have a witchcraft trial. The trial establishes that those who killed the witch were justified in removing this threat to everyone, or it could decide that they were transgressive in that they killed an innocent person (and therefore must themselves be punished). The main thing is to avoid lawlessness in the society, of course.

THE MODERN DILEMMA REGARDING WITCHCRAFT

It is remarkable that so much interest in demonology and witchcraft remains—in fact it is increasing—as the twenty-first century dawns. At the same time, the protections and cures are regarded as empty superstitions while the existence of "entities"—as Joe Nickell calls them in *Entities: Angels, Spirits, Demons & Other Alien Beings*, 1995—is more and more believed. There is as the twentieth-century ends an astonishing percentage of Americans who are certain that angels, good and bad, exist and that they interact with humanity. Still, the "psychic" appears to have replaced sorcery, witches are looked upon as weirdos, and even herbal and other traditional medicines are pooh-poohed by a great many medical professionals. We get elaborate reference books such as the *Dictionary of Deities & Demons in The Bible* and *Deities and Demons of the Far East* (both 1995) but a book listing magical protections and cures is inevitably going to be dismissed not as scholarship but as silly superstition. Also, despite the rise of such academic disciplines now as cultural studies, ethnic studies, and popular culture, folklore (which is where superstition tends to be noticed, if at all) remains too much of a poor relation, given grudging space at the table and not much allowed into the general conversation unless it can contrive to contribute to the main interest of Academe these days, victim politics.

THE SCAPEGOAT

Sacrifices are common in almost all religions, it is said, and certainly the Judeo-Christian creeds have sacrifice as a cornerstone. The earliest Jewish religions performed animal sacrifices; only later were bread and wine offered. Christ became a human sacrifice. He was, in effect, a scapegoat on whom the sins of the people could be loaded as. In the Old Testament, the sins of the people were loaded upon a goat, and in the New Testament, upon the Savior.

In Leviticus and Isaiah we read of the Jewish scapegoat, an animal especially chosen to bear the sins of the people and distinguished by a red thread tied around its throat. The color may relate to the spilling of blood or to "though your sins be as scarlet, they shall be white as snow." Washed in the blood of The Lamb, also, left the person white with innocence.

Oddly, a red thread about the neck sometimes distinguished good medieval witches who offered to cure the ill, the bewitched, and so on, to remove the pain of sinful humanity.

GOOD KING WENCESLAUS

That is what this duke—not king—and saint (*c.* 903–935) is called in the familiar Christmas carol. He encouraged Christianity in Bohemia, despite his mother (who was rumored to be a witch) and his brother Boleslaw (who killed him because of his faith, it is said, though it was probably the fact that Wenceslaus put his duchy under German protection that was the true cause of the anger). Nonetheless, Wenceslaus was famous for his court harboring a magician named Zlito, who could perform all kinds of wonderful magical tricks. Zlito was probably most useful as a physician, offering physical rather than mystical help. In those days the nobility were likely to employ astrologers, alchemists, herbal experts, magicians, and more, but there was little any of these could do to fend off martyrdom.

EXORCISMS

We deal with demonic possession and exorcisms at some length in *The Complete Book of Devils and Demons* but perhaps here we ought at least to mention the exorcism called Baptism, which can be said to cure us of Original Sin, and the cures promised by holy water ("a mixture of exorcised salt and exorcised water," as Montague Summers puts it), the blessing of the waters, farm animals, houses, pets, and so on—anything where Satan or his minions are said to be driven out. All exorcisms are magical cures. They are not as rare as you think. Says Rick Marin in *Newsweek* (8 July 1996) of a U.S. population 48 percent of which believes in UFOs (and that the government is engaged in a massive cover-up), 29 percent of which claim to have been abducted by aliens:

> The lunatic fringe represents one end of the paranormal spectrum. At the other end are sober researchers....The interesting people are those in the middle. [(Designer) Donna Karan says that "in previous lives she was, among other things, a cowgirl and a painter in the court of the Medicis."] The guy in the next cubicle. The woman who runs your division. They have families. They can tell a joke and usually know where their car keys are. Yet they had their house exorcised before moving in....

It may seem odd to some of you that moderns have their houses exorcised, but it is true. Most Americans seem to believe in ghosts and everyone knows of some reputedly haunted place nearby. My house's top floor, alleged experts confide to me, has "a lot of energy." So far I have not seen any apparitions, nor would I be ready to move if I did. In fact, I have British relatives—Britain seems to be much more haunted than America, and tales range from the dubious Borley Rectory to the queen "with her head tucked underneath her arm" who haunts a royal palace, from theaters to my local Underground stop when I lived in London—who are proud of the family ghosts and even have made some money out of showing them off. They are harmless (the ghosts and the relatives).

Americans are leery about acquiring a property where murder, suicide, even AIDS have been known. Real estate agents conceal the bad news about such "stigmatized property," and the law says they do not have to volunteer the bad news about a house's nasty past. Says Kristin Lippet-Martin in *New York* (28 August 1995):

But people have a way of finding these things out, especially when their new neighbors start casting sideways glances at them and blood starts running out of the electrical sockets.

So be sure to ask your broker if the house is haunted. She or he will probably conceal the worst from you, but then later you can sue. Then call an exorcist. If that doesn't work, sue the exorcist. Hey, it's New York! Or you can try to make a commercial success out of your "Amityville Horror." People love even fake ghosts—in other people's houses. As Edith Wharton once remarked, it gives one a very unpleasant chill to walk into a house and get the inescapable feeling that *something is not right.* She added, scornful of those who had said that with the introduction of the electric light the ghosts all disappeared, that even a modern house "with a refrigerator" could harbor old horrors.

FECES AND URINE

I intend to omit from my recipe section a number of disgusting ways in which feces, human and otherwise, are used in magic, noting only that the greatest of Greek physicians after Hippocrates, Galen, prescribed a boy's excreta to reduce throat swelling. Medicines that taste bad are always thought to be especially salutary.

Disgusting formulae often turn up in magical texts. Remember, magic likes to increase the operator's sense of transgression, whether it be against the laws of God or man; a sense of treading down forbidden paths to perform obscene rites is conducive, some say, to the appropriate state of mind for magic. I do not want to disgust the reader with some of the revolting ways of witches. (O, go ahead! you confirmed readers of modern novels and voyeurs at modern movies say, but No!)

However, here I can mention that an old cure for bewitching is to take a "horse ball" and place one or more spoons beside it. Witches will eat the horse manure and be driven off. And animal dung is called for in some recipes both for incense and pills.

Urine is a trifle more acceptable to discuss than feces, and the subject addressed in pedantic prose is made the less offensive, I suppose, so here is the "Rev." Montague Summers (*The Werewolf*, reprinted 1966) on that subject—and I trust he will not piss you off.

In very many countries ensorcelling properties are ascribed to urine, and (under certain circumstances) to the act of urination.

...Petronius, *Si circumminxero illum, nesciet qua fugiat* (if I were to piss round him in a circle he would be unable to stir) ....[and] the Urine Dance of the Mexican Zunis, performed by one of their secret Medicine Orders, the *Nehue-Cue*, a dramatic representation of some half-forgotten wizard rite. The Shamans of Siberia brew and drink a magic potion in which human urine is the chief ingredient.... The urine of cows is used for sacred lustrations and worship among certain hill-tribes at the foot of the Himalayas, and holy images are even sprinkled with the magic stream. In Coromandel it is supposed to have supernatural healing properties so that the sick are often laved therewith. Similar beliefs and practices are found among the Huron Indians. Thiers, in his *Traité des superstitions* [1741], records an old tradition that those who first thing in the morning dip their hand in urine cannot be enscorcelled or harmed by any spell of witches during the day. Thus in some parts of Ireland urine was sprinkled on children suffering from convulsions to rescue them from the clutches of their fairy persecutors. "American boys urinate upon their legs to prevent cramp while swimming" [J. G. Bourke, *Compilation...upon the Use of Human Ordure and Human Urine in Rites of a Religious or Semi-Religious Character*, 1888]. Torquemada [*Monarquia indiana*, 1723] says that the ancient Romans had a feast [dedicated] to the mother of the gods, Berecinthia, whose idol the matrons in secret ceremony sprinkled with their urine.

WHEN A BABY IS BORN WITH A CAUL

To protect the child from witchcraft, a blood relative must enter a church by the front door, yell "The baby is an angel," and exit by a side door—three times.

PRAISE

Just as wishing an actor luck can ruin the performance—say "Break a leg!" instead—saying nice things to people is thought to bring bad luck to people. But you need not stint on praise; people need all the encouragement they can get, especially those who know they do not deserve it. So "say nice." But when someone praises you, take the corner of your coat or apron in your left hand as you listen to the kind words, and that way you cannot be gulled. When praised for beauty, take the corner of a shirt or other garment—some authorities recommend spitting on it—and rub the part praised to rub off the bad luck that may be being deposited there. Be very suspicious of anyone who does not look you directly in the eye when saying something nice, even if they are shading their eyes from the sun. Listen to no one who speaks standing by a rosebush or holds a rose in their hand, because even their seemingly good words are a curse.

ONE-ARMED BANDITS

The cure for your bad luck at the slot machines does not require the "words of power" which some offer to sell you. For the big payoff, just wait for the full moon. Then, research shows, your chances of a big payoff rise to 1 in 500. Best of all, find the machines set to pay off most; they are near the end of a row in a conspicuous place where a torrent of coins into the cup will be especially noticed. Bribe an employee to tell you which machines are set to pay off best. Think of that as an investment in a sleazy business anyhow. You need all the help you can get. There are pentacles you can carry in your pocket that claim to guarantee you'll win at the gaming tables, but I have never heard of one for the slots. I wouldn't bet on pentacles.

INVULNERABILITY

Christians are supposed to be protected by what the scriptures call "the armor of righteousness," but it never hurts to have some other defense. In addition to various holy medals—the St. Christopher medal which so long was the protection of travelers may have to be replaced now that Christopher is no longer a saint, having been discovered to be a pious allegorical figure all along—Christians have sometimes relied on magic spells not approved by their church.

For example, in the archives of The North (Lille) in France for 1608–1659 we find the case of Bénigne Morand of Burgundy. He was accused of desecrating the village church and outraging the faithful because he employed

> signs and charms, so that on Good Friday of this past year of 1634, in the church at Scey, he wrote signs on a laurel leaf during the divine service of The Passion, which many people witnessed, and confessed and said that if a hen were to eat the said leaf she could never be killed even by the bolt from an arquebus.

Writing charms on laurel leaves goes back to the ancient Egyptians and Greeks. How this magical knowledge ever reached the French peasantry is difficult to imagine. But it did. The idea of "flourishing like the green bay tree" may go far to explain the practice.

PRESCRIPTIONS FOR A SERIOUSLY ILL CHILD

Jews might change the child's name (*Ch'aim* for "Life" or some equivalent) so the Angel of Death cannot find his victim. Or name the person as if old, so the angel will be misled. Failing that, "sell" the child to another person. For more Jewish superstitions, seek other, specialized books rather than Newbell H. Puckett's collection (put together in Ohio years ago) edited by Wayland Hand et al. as *Popular Beliefs and Superstitions* (1981). That is a book to which we are particularly grateful for wonderful information.

CURE FOR LONELINESS

Witches not only made love philters but also perfumes to attract lovers. They even understood pheromones before science got around to it, and the power of musk. Among scents they recommended for attracting a woman, for instance, were bay, civet, patchouli, stephanotis, vetiver, and violet.

Today there are many perfumes for men to wear. A recent one is called Raw Vanilla. Besides vanilla, this fragrance includes the inevitable musk, bamboo, bergamot (as in Earl Grey tea), Brazilian mint, clary, dewy orchid, juniper berry, sandalwood, teak, tonka bean, and giant waterlily.

To attract women you can use musk and tonka bean but also ambergris, gardenia, ginger, jasmine, lavender, and neroli, among other scents.

You can wear the oils, burn them during magical rites, or just scatter the fresh or dried petals, barks, etc., around the place.

The list of scents "to attract love" is almost endless, but you may have around the house apple, avocado, basil, cinnamon, cloves, coriander, dill, ginger (always good to strengthen a spell), etc. Also leading off the list in alphabetical order are Adam & Eve (a natural), bachelor's buttons (probably from the name), betony, catnip (after all, it turns cats on), chamomile, copal, daffodil, damiana (which can drive you wild, like datura), etc. If you will settle for Platonic friendship, try lemon, love seed (oddly), passion flower (ditto), and sweetpea.

Love potions were among the chief goods that "wise women" had for sale—along with potions to produce abortions or kill adults. Witches always did a brisk business in all of them. Purchasers often preferred perfumes to potions; that way they were less likely, they thought, to be poisoned, for the practitioners of black magic *(maleficium)* were also feared for poisoning *(veneficium)*.

In an earlier book I discussed magician Aleister Crowley's recipe for a sexy aftershave so powerful that it made horses rear in the street as he passed by. The power of perfume, however, is not at all magical, unless you think all sexual attraction involves some sort of enchantment. In point of fact, smells that turn people on can be as odd as doughnuts, peanut butter, sweat, and shoe polish.

A CURE FOR WHAT AILS YOU

The Roman Catholic religion forbids all attempts to "talk to the dead." Nonetheless, prayers to saints are strongly encouraged. In fact, a person cannot be canonized and achieve sainthood in the church unless prayers for their intercession in human affairs have been rewarded by miracles that can pass church scrutiny.

There are patron saints for almost every condition and profession, but if your case is "hopeless" pray for a cure to St. Jude. He is "the patron of lost causes."

CURE FOR A POOR MEMORY

An ancient formula calls for wormwood, a sun opal, the heart of a bird named the hoopoe (a kind of vulture), and a "breathing stone" (?), all ground up and moistened with honey. You cleanse your mouth with a grain of frankincense gum and then apply this mixture to your lips. Or write in myrrh ink the sign *shenon* (which looks like a handwritten small L) on a leaf of cinquefoil; place it in your mouth while you sleep. These are found in the *Papyri Græcæ magicæ* translated by John Dillon & E. N. O'Neill, where you will find many old superstitious spells and formulae. There are other memory recipes, although some (especially in the essential incantations) are fragmentary. With part of them lost, of course, they are useless.

MORE MAGICAL CURES FOR BURNS

It may someday be established that the mind has greater power to cure the largest organ of the body, the skin, than the other organs. In any case, skin problems are very much discussed in the literature of magical cures.

These very interestingly often involve religion in superstition. Touch the burn with the altar cloth or other church linen. Try the Irish cure: Lay your hand over the burn, blow on it three times (a magic number, Father, Son, and Holy Spirit), and repeat each time:

> Old clod, beneath the clay,
> Burn away, burn away.
> In the name of God be thou healed.

From the West of England (and my book on superstition):

> Three angels came, from North, East and West,
> One brought fire, another brought frost,
> And the third brought the Holy Ghost.
> So out fire and in frost, In the name of the Father, Son, and
>   Holy Ghost.

"Holy Ghost" instead of "Holy Spirit" dates this; the Paraclete has fairly recently changed His name in Christian usage. This British cure I have encountered also in Appalachia, one of many cures, curses, charms and superstitions that America got from the Old Country. Americans have, in fact, many different Old Countries, so ours is a
culture rich in the superstitions of many, many nations.

A CORNY CURE

Rub a wart with corn, bore a hole in a tree, insert the corn, cover it up. The wart will disappear. Alternatively, take a mouthful of corn, spit it into any hole, cover it up.

COWS

Witches were frequently said to be responsible for blood in the milk. Only discovering the identity of the witch and forcing her to remove the spell would cure the problem, usually, but if the witch was not known some kind of sympathetic magic would have to be used, such as plunging a red-hot poker into the milk, or placing the milk in a metal container on the lid of which one put hot coals.

CUTTING OUT CURSES

Running with scissors, you must have been told as a child, brings disaster. Here's something they did not tell you: superstition is sure that scissors kept on a windowsill prevents anyone from cursing you.

A CABBAGE THAT WENT DOWN WRONG

In his *Dialogues*, Gregory the Great (*c.* 540–604), a father of the church, a man who tried to avoid the office but was unanimously elected first pope of that name, himself a miracle-working saint, tells a story which you may think of as pure superstition of the Dark Ages—but it was long believed as perfectly credible and is typical of the wonders he recorded in his extensive writings. It concerns a nun who was unwise enough to eat a cabbage in the convent garden which she did not first bless. She took in also a demon and was instantly possessed, falling down and suffering great agony. The Abbot Equitius of the province of Valeria was called and the demon complained to him that he had done no wrong. "I was sitting quietly on the cabbage," he whined, "and she came along and ate me." A simple sign of the cross would have shooed him off, and the nun had not bothered with that. The demon felt aggrieved. With a sign of the cross the abbot sent the demon on his way and the nun was cured.

The moral seems to be: Don't neglect to say grace before meals. Even snacks.

COINING A CURE

To cure bad luck, as we note elsewhere, find a penny, or get pennies in change when you shop on a Monday. Rub a penny on a wart to make it vanish soon. Put pennies on the eyes of a corpse before you bury it; Charon, the ferryman over the River Styx has to get his two cents' worth.

In the Balkans, they dig up the corpse to steal the pennies because, washed in wine, they can help a wayward wife make her husband blind to her straying. One has only to get the husband to drink the wine in which the pennies were washed. Presumably you could then return the pennies to the grave. After all, we do not want the vengeful dead to come after us. That's one reason we always speak well of them, tend their graves, and put big stones on their heads to keep them from getting up. In the Balkans you might also be well advised to drive a stake through their hearts to pin them in the grave, because vampires are much reported there.

Put a silver coin—harder to find than they used to be—in the hand of a gypsy to get your fortune told, or into a King Cake at Mardi Gras or a Christmas pudding to tell whoever finds it in his or her portion will be lucky and rich, or into the churn to make the butter come. Make a gold coin with a powerful pentacle on it and wear it. If you have a mole on the right hand, leave it alone. It is an old idea that it will bring you money. Some signs of the Zodiac are also said to promise more wealth than others, so plan your children's month of birth with care. While you are at it— if you have the money—plan to move the pregnant lady to the most propitious nearby birth site, if you insist on believing in astrology.

Above all, magic gets out there and *does* something, so (as with lawyers and other sages) hire an astrologer to advise you beforehand, not just to cast a horoscope after the baby has been born. These days, with cheap flights and drugs to control the time of delivery, there is no need whatever to be born (say) in Aspen in the daytime or in Florida under any water sign. If you are going to bring the kid up to read the daily horoscopes in the newspaper, do something to get it off to a great start. Spend money at the beginning, when it can do the most good (if any). Give the kid a break. People used to avoid marrying in May—maybe so the first child would not be born in January. The cusp of Capricorn and Aquarius is not propitious: it produces astrologers and others who are prone to irrational ideas. Even astrology admits that. Spend a little effort and money to avoid that.

Give beggars coins—always an odd number. Today they may "dis" you unless they receive folding money, but you can undo their curses. Just quietly transfer an odd number of coins from one of your pockets to another. As with a black cat crossing your path—to undo this bad luck, turn around three times and spit—magic almost always offers you a way of countering the curses and ill luck that fall upon you. What one evil person can do, a witch can almost always undo. It is comforting to believe, too, that money given in charity will always come back to you increased and that curses (especially if badly executed) will return to hurt the one who curses.

If you happen to have a silver dollar handy when you see an apparition, throw the coin through it. Carried on your person forever thereafter, it will discourage the apparition from returning to bother you. If it's an attractive or useful ghost, keep your money to yourself but hold the coin tightly as you discourse with it.

If you have no silver dollar handy when a ghost appears, do not worry. Simply ask the ghost, "What do you want? What are you doing here?" It will usually simply go away. It may just have strayed into the world of the living by accident.

WITCH BALL

People used to put witch balls in their windows to keep witches off the premises. Mine is of blue, blown glass, from eighteenth-century Virginia. It hangs in a living room window. I must say it has never kept witches (many of whom are pleasant people) from visiting me. Most witches these days are feminists (worshipping The Goddess). Many know a useful amount about alternative medicine , herbal remedies, visualization and relaxation and meditation techniques, and other salutary things. Those who deal in The Tarot can help you to get in touch (I believe) not with the Other World but with your own Inner World. That or the ancient *I Ching* is very good for you. Why be afraid of such people, or even of irrationality in general? Limit your reply to 500 words.

CURE FOR INFERTILITY

First, consult your horoscope. This may be the wrong time for you to make the effort to become a parent. Husband impotent? Check that no witches have been tying knots in cords and that no other hexes are upon him. Wife infertile? An old cure says to grind up hartshorn and cow gall and keep it on the person. If it said to take the powder, this would be a medical pre-scription. "Keep it on the person" marks it as a magical move.

MAGICAL THINKING

Some of the superstitions about cures are undoubtedly weird, but if you think about it you will realize what the thinking is behind a great many of them. Superstition itself hopes to explain the unexplained, to make con-nections that satisfy curiosity about what is going on. In the process it adds to fields as different as theology and medical science. It led Hip-pocrates four centuries before Christ to suggest willow bark as an anal-gesic, though aspirin was not synthesized until the latter part of the nineteenth century, and it led people to use digitalis for cardiac condi-tions because its leaves were heart-shaped. It also suggested that odors that repel humans would drive off demons and that if you swallowed a fish bladder you would learn more easily how to swim. It went farther off track when it traced disease to demons and a boil on the posterior to uri-nating on a path. (The cure is to say, "It's a lie/I got a sty!") and that, as in Texas, if you hang a dead snake "belly up" on a rail fence—rails, of course, must be split in the dark of the moon for best effect—it will rain.

To make rain you can dance—or wash the car. Finally, of course, if you take an umbrella with you it will not rain.

CURES FOR EVERYONE

A quick look at the shelves of an "alternate" bookshop shows me that there is a brisk trade in *Aunt Sally's Cornpone Remedies* and *Home Remedies* and *Folk Medicine Cures* and *Ayurvedic Cures* and *Chinese Herbal Cures* and more. But magical cures abound, though they are not available (as yet) from HMOs and (most) MDs. Lady Wilde (1826–1896, Oscar's mom) is back with *Irish Cures, Mystic Charms* (reprinted 1994). Though married to Sir William Wilde, surgeon and president of the Irish Academy, "Speranza," as she was called, was not above recommending superstitious cures long known in Irish peasant life . Even some of the solid folk remedies are connected with magic when numerology or astrology get involved or prayers and incantations accompany doses.

A "POTENTISED" FINAL SOLUTION

Here's a hideous story: In Trevor Ravenscroft's *The Spear of Destiny* (1973), a thorough examination of the attempts of the Nazis to put occult powers behind their dreadful work, we hear of Rudolph Steiner's homeopathic medicine and the horrible use Heinrich Himmler tried to make out it.

In the 1920s, Dr. Steiner was employed by Count Keyserlingk to rid the count's estates of rabbits. Dr. Steiner took the spleen, testicles, and a portion of skin from a rabbit, burned them, mixed the ashes with a neutral powder (sugar of milk) and with this created a "potentised solution." You add to a given amount of material nine times the amount of distilled water. The concentration is now 1 in 10. You take a tenth of that and add nine times the amount of distilled water. The concentration is now 1 in 100. And so on, until not a single molecule of the original substance is in solution—but then it works powerfully on any system into which it is introduced. Dr. Steiner sprinkled this solution around generously. The rabbits disappeared in three days, once the solution had entered their systems.

Ravenscroft alleges:
> The Nazis repeated the experiment with the "potentised" ashes of
> the testicles, spleens and portions of the skin of virile young Jews

in an attempt to drive the remnant of the Jewish population out of Germany for ever. It was the last horrible act in the final solution when the Third Reich was collapsing before the onslaught of the Allied Armies. The order to carry out this diabolical plan came from Hitler himself, but the evil genius who conceived it was Reichsführer SS Heinrich Himmler.

Is this Nazi superstition, Allied propaganda, science, magic, madness or what?

The "wise woman" could wound as well as cure by magic.

From Olaus Magnus' *Historia de gentibus septentionalis* (History of the Northern Peoples), a woodcut of a sorcerer with a magic means of transportation.

HOW TO REMOVE A BIRTHMARK

According to the superstition recorded in V. Fossel's *Volksmedicin und medicinischer Aberglaube in Seiermark* (1886), simply touch the birthmark with the hand of a dead child. Perhaps because of great emotional content, this actually has been known to work for "wine blotches" and so on.

HOW TO BREAK A PACT WITH THE DEVIL

Too bad that Dr. Faustus, dragged off to Hell by demons when fear kept him from renouncing The Devil and throwing himself on the mercy of God, didn't have the very easy method, given in Finellan's *Le triple Vocabulaire infernal*, for breaking a pact:

"If you are disposed to renounce The Devil after having entered into a compact with him, spit three times on the ground, and he will have no further power over you."

This causes A. E. Waite to add caustically in *The Book of Black Magic and Pacts*, "Black Magic with all its grim theatricals is the Art of exploiting lost Angels with impunity."

THE INTERCESSION OF THE SAINTS

I leave it to the reader to decide whether miracles attributed to the saints—and without miracles no saint can be canonized—are to be regarded as magic or not. The relics of saints are often at least thought of as magical and credited with cures. And take the case of Pierre of Luxembourg. He was a cardinal, though he died at age eighteen, and within fifteen months of his death 1,964 miraculous cures were credited to visiting his tomb. I have seen glass coffins stuffed not only with the skeletons of saints but with huge collections of wedding rings and other precious jewelry, offering to the saints for favors and cures. I thought this a great waste of valuables that might well be sold and provide money to help the poor. For some reason I cannot explain, the splendors of St. Peter's or the civic and military monuments of St. Paul's do not make me want to sell them off for the poor, but the bones wrapped with pearl and diamond necklaces, the heaps of wedding rings and so on, disturb me greatly. I am tempted to walk up to the kneeling supplicants and lie: "I am an angel. Your wish is granted. Go in peace. No charge."

The numerology of the proportions of man. From Cornelius Agrippa, *c.* 1553.

4
More Wonderful Things

MAGICAL OBJECTS

Just as the name is supposed to be a part of the individual and therefore used in magic as might be a fingernail clipping or piece of hair, just as the magical word preceded the prayer that could produce miracles, so magical objects are closely associated with mystic powers and can be used to curse or cure, to cast a spell or remove it, to perform miraculous feats. This chapter will deal with spells and charms and such objects as amulets and talismans, the paraphernalia of magical rites, the power of holy relics, and much more.

You might pick a four-leaf clover, or carry around a "lucky piece" of some kind. There also are "lucks" handed down in various families—one thinks of several cups cherished by English families, the Fairy Banner of the McLeods—and plenty of old advice, perhaps of questionable value, about what it is useful to acquire or ill-advised to hang onto. People have the strangest ideas! Some think it is lucky to own a cross-eyed cat, unlucky to live at a crossroads (where criminals and such used to be buried), to count the house before a theatrical performance, to bring a baby carriage into the home before the baby is born and home from the hospital. People say they do not but they actually do believe that this or that object carries a curse. When the tomb of King Tut was opened in 1922 and the treasures removed, the tabloids were full of stories about the allegedly strange deaths that followed the disturbing of these objects. The headlines spoke of "The Curse of The Pharaoh."

The most magical object of all? This might be the *Tabula Smaragdina*, said to have been found on the corpse of Hermes Trismegistus (Thrice-Powerful) himself and supposed to contain an inscription condensing all magic into a short inscription on a small gem.

This gem and its inscription is frequently mentioned in the more obscure books on alchemy and ritual magic. The most used in magic? Probably pentacles out of The Key of Solomon, connected to planetary influences: seven each to Sun, Saturn, Jupiter, and Mars; six to Moon; five each to Mercury and Venus. The commonest in everyday life? Probably the "lucky coin" and the rabbit's foot.

AMULETS AND TALISMANS

Some people religiously or superstitiously believe in the power of certain images and objects (because of the images they bear) have an inherent power to protect the wearer from danger or bring the wearer certain powers or luck. The distinction has to be made between the amulet and the talisman and the idol or fetish object: in the amulet and the talisman and the physical charm the power is inherent because of the image, not because some demon or divinity is resident in the object. Indeed, with the proper images, magicians believe they can with amulets and talismans and charms defy and control the powers of demons and divinities. A cult may form around such an image. The supernatural powers themselves, however, are not exactly worshipped in the image.

Some of the most famous amulets are the ancient symbol of the swastika, various symbols of the sun god, and the phylacteries of the Jews and crucifixes of the Christians and Hand of Fatima and other protections of the followers of Islam. Amulets and talismans may be worn on the person (as are blessed medals) or carried on the person (like a "lucky penny" or rabbit's foot) and may range from a bear's claw (related to the totems of the tribe) to a "magic" mathematical square, from a letter of the alphabet (the Jews use the first letter of the Hebrew word *ch'aim*, "life") to an obscure alchemical or astrological symbol. On the amulet or talisman also "magic" words and phrases can be written to be energized when seen and thought or spoken. Tibetans write prayers on scraps of paper which are placed in prayer wheels; when the wheels are turned, by hand or by the wind, the prayers are said. They also use prayer flags, fluttering in the wind.

You see amulets and talismans all over: the cross worn as a pendant, the *mezuzah* nailed to the doorpost of a Jewish home, the symbol on the cover of a book by Kipling or by W. Somerset Maugham, the bit of coral or the more vulgar symbols worn by some Italians (such as tiny images of the flying phallus, the "fig" gesture of the hand). Greeks wear blue beads—and paint a particular shade of blue around the doors and windows of their homes—to ward off vampires. There are a number of objects worn in various societies to ward off the Evil Eye, one of them the small image of a human hand making the gesture of two fingers extended that is supposed to guard against *malocchia*.

In this chapter you will learn about some amulets and talismans that are a bit different from the blessed medals and scapulas and rabbit's feet to which you may be accustomed.

And don't say you do not believe in the power of such things if you really do! Even in the modern world very ancient superstitions persist. Performers (from opera stars and actors to professional football and basketball stars) are especially superstitious. They need for their public appearances all the confidence, all the luck, they can get. So they follow elaborate procedures, from refraining from receiving good wishes before the show—rather, say "break a leg!"—to refraining from shaving, or even changing underwear, while on a "lucky streak." They have both traditional and personal lucky habits or objects which they treasure. They believe in them.

Elsewhere I have written about the CEO of a Fortune 500 company I knew who had a "lucky tie." He deprecated the superstition—but he would not have felt confident in the occasional challenging negotiation without it, so he wore it. My advice is to find all the confidence you can—rational or irrational—to meet the challenges of modern life. A positive outlook, a confident approach can seldom do you harm and may do you much good. If you feel better with a lucky penny in your pocket, carry one. Be sure to use one you have found in the street, preferably one with the date of your birth on it, ideally also slightly bent. So you then are slightly bent also. So what? As long as it works!

THE SACRED HEART OF JESUS

You may possibly be shocked to see this topic addressed here. Nonetheless, instead of discussing the relics of saints used as amulets and talismans I would like at this point to speak of a saint herself and of an image of power she created. I do this for several reasons, among them the striking aspect of the image, which would be regarded as gruesome were it not so familiar, and the connection it can help to suggest between modern religion and the superstitions of both ancient mysticism and science. The human heart used to be seriously regarded as the seat of the emotions, and it contributed

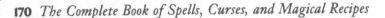

The Sacred Heart of Jesus actually drawn by St. Marguerite Marie and now in the Monastery of The Visitation at Turin.

thereby to symbolism in both art and the hermetic sciences. The image also connects to astrology—someone ought to study the exact date of its official adoption, 21 June 1675, and even cast its horoscope—and the connection to the Cabala and the alchemists, of whom more below.

I reproduce this mystic's actual 1685 drawing here (preserved by the nuns of the Visitation in Turin) of The Sacred Heart of Jesus. It is unusual to have not merely a statement but an illustration of a mystical experience from the visionary herself. Hers is an image which has led to a cult, to one of the most famous churches of Europe (*Sacre-Coeur* basilica on Montmartre in Paris), to one of the most socially-conscious orders of nuns, to works of art and novenas and the pious prayers of millions of Roman Catholics worldwide for centuries.

St. Marguerite Marie Alacocque was born in France (1647) and entered the Convent of the Visitation (1671), where she soon had that vision to create a new Roman Catholic cult. The devotion to the Sacred Heart of Jesus was officially instituted in 1675, as has been mentioned.

The French historian of witchcraft, [Émile Angelo] Grillot de Givry, was extremely learned. He was very familiar with the occult manuscripts of Paris's great libraries, especially that of The Arsenal, where nineteenth-century occultists had served as librarians and assembled a remarkable collection of documents. In his *Witchcraft, Magic & Alchemy* (1931, reprinted by Dover in 1971), Grillot de Givry proves that St. Marguerite Marie's heavenly vision owes a lot to the *Cor Chrristi in cælis erga peccatores in terris*, one of the *Opuscula* by Thomas Goodwin (1600–1688), published on the Continent, where he had been an independent clergyman, in 1658. That was the same year that Goodwin and John Owen drew up the amended Westminster Confession for the English Church. More: Grillot de Givry notes for the first time ever in print the "two exact representations of the symbolism of the Sacred Heart" occur in "a book on alchemic Cabbalism by L'Agneau, entitled *Harmonie mystique, ou accord des philosophes chymiques* dated

1636—that is, eleven years before the birth of Ste Marguerite Marie." On top of that, the memorials it notices go back to the fifteenth and sixteenth centuries. One, from the Convent of the Cordeliers, was also on the cloister wall of the Jacobins, the stained glass of the Chapel of St. Thomas Aquinas, and in four places in the Church of the Carmelites' Chapel of St. Michael. The other was at the *Charnier des Innocents*. Both derive from the hermetic philosphers, the alchemists, such as Nicholas Flamel, "who flourished at the beginning of the sixteenth century" in Paris.

These are the first inventors of the sacred heart encircled with a crown of thorns. In the occult tradition, from the heart rises a twig (symbolic of revivification); in St. Marguerite's version, it is the Cross (symbolic of how the Crucifixion brought life to sinners). In both cases, the symbol rises in divine fire. Any cabalist would recognize St. Marguerite Marie's drawing as what Grillot de Givry says it is: "a genuine hermetic design."

Note that the drawing St. Marguerite Marie herself did in 1685 (while at the Monastery of Paray-le-Monial) "must have been intended by the Saint for the official image of the Sacred Heart exactly as it ought to be shown in all churches; but her wish has not been respected, for this image is nowhere seen." This is, in sum, not exactly the Sacred Heart of the cabalists and today not the Sacred Heart image with which, Roman Catholic or not, you may be familiar. It does, however, illustrate, as does the work of Jacob Boehme, 1575–1624 (so influential on what we might call non-religious English mystics such as William Blake) how much religion owes to alchemy and the occult. *Ruach Elohim* (The Spirit of God) moves in mysterious ways and in oddly related systems of belief.

RELIGION OR SUPERSTITION?

To wear a crucifix may be regarded as religious, but to wear one of those with a double bar (such as is worn in Spain) and to stress that you must not buy this amulet but be given it is superstitious.

PROTECTIONS AGAINST DEMONS

These can be very elaborate or simply, in The Andes, a pile of flat rocks; in China, building a bridge that zigzags (because the Chinese demons move only in straight lines); in various Asian countries, large painted eyes that keep watch and ward off evil; in Pennsylvania Amish country, hex signs; in Scandinavia, crosses made with tar on a barn door; a horseshoe nailed to the wall (but with the ends up, lest the power "drain out of it."

THE POWER OF THE WORD

Parts of the scriptures of various religions are worn on the person to ward off evil. For example, Muslims often wear quotations from The Koran. Christian prayers are worn by natives in Haiti. Watch for more of this later on.

AMULETS AND TALISMANS AGAIN

Etymology (word origins) tells us that both words came to English from French, and both have ancient origins indeed: *amulet* can be traced back to the Egyptians, who used the scarab (beetle) and other amulets exten-

sively, and *talisman* describes a sacred object whose power or operation has been completed. Amulets and talismans go back further, too, to the civilizations of the Tigris and Euphrates as well as of the Nile. Later, in a section dealing with magical protections and cures, we shall have occasion to say a little about the religions of Babylon and Assyria from which the Judeo-Christian religions sprang. From the earliest times, perhaps from cavemen with "lucky" stones or animal bones, amulets and talismans have been a major feature of religion's and magic's protections.

We may also call such objects "lucky charms," or holy relics. Christians have blessed objects, and so to a great

This is a metal pin worn by some African-American women for its beauty, but in Ghana pregnant women carry wooden dolls (*akuaba*) of this design to make sure their babies will be born beautiful.

extent does Islam, pagan religions, etc. The ancient Jews also held the concept of the Holy of Holies, objects too sacred even to touch. The Ark of the Covenant, containing the Law, was so sacred that anyone touching it died on the spot. The story is told of it wobbling when carried in a procession once and a pious Jew putting forth his hand simply to steady it. He fell dead on the spot. The Hebrew God didn't bother with fine distinctions or exceptions; that came later, perhaps, with nitpicking about The Talmud.

There was no confusion or indecision, however, about the fact that a reputation for killing power can be placed upon an object (usually to protect it), just as a reputation for protecting the wearer or owner can be established. Both work well, by the power of suggestion if not by supernatural means. Negatively, a person can be destroyed by fear, hopelessness, a sense of powerlessness in the face of force; positively, a person can gain courage, confidence, optimism from feeling that an object of power is in her or his possession. Also, simply touching or just seeing a holy relic can inspire faith and impart inspiration and improvement. Science calls this psychotherapeutic process. Science recognizes the connection between mental stress and physical conditions. It classifies exotic syndromes as situation-specific (such as *folie à deux*), idiopathic (Tourette's syndrome), atypical (cycloid psychoses), and culture-bound. Among the culture-bound states we are familiar with running amok, arctic hysteria, going berserk, *koro*, voodoo death, and witico psychosis, among others. However irrational the states may be, they are real.

In pagan societies, especially those which know little and fear much, the existence of amulets and talismans is very comforting. There have been many studies of the beliefs of African tribes, such as the Asande; these reveal that so-called primitive people are not nearly so different from so-called civilized people as we might like to think.

A few recent books on the subject:

C. Andrews, *Amulets of Ancient Egypt* (1994)
Nik Douglas, *Tibetan Tantric Charms and Amulets* (1978)
Deborah Lippman, *How to Make Amulets and Charms* (1994)
J. G. Lockhart, *Curses, Luck, and Talismans* (1971)
William T. & Kate Pavitt, *The Book of Talismans, Amulets, and Zodiacal Gems* (1972)
Suzanne Eastman Sheldon, *Middle English and Latin Charms, Amulets and Talismans from Vernacular Manuscripts* (dissertation, 1979)
T. Schrire, *Hebrew Amulets* (1966)
C. Thompson, *Amulets, Talismans, and Charms* (1994)
Wm. Thomas, *The Book of Talismans, Amulets...* (1994)
Leo Vinci, *Talismans, Amulets and Charms* (1977)

ON A CHALDEAN AMULET

The evil *utukku* [spirit], the evil *namtara* [plague demon],
In the name of the Earth
May they go out of his body.
The beneficent *shedu*, the good *lamassu*, the beneficent *utukku* [all spirits]
In the name of the Earth
May they stand by him.

AMULETS OF CLASSICAL TIMES

The Greeks wore many amulets and talismans in ancient times and today still do. Many wear blue beads now to keep off the evil eye and icons are of course a significant part of their religious worship. The screen that keeps the congregation in a Greek Orthodox church from seeing the priests do their thing in a Holy of Holies is called the *iconostasis*; it is a wall of icons. I have always thought that Greek Orthodox religious ceremonies very much resemble Greek drama: something very dramatic is happening, but not here in front of your eyes, and a series of messengers is needed to keep you abreast of what is going on. At Greek Orthodox religious ceremonies, priests disappear behind the wall of icons; the singing and the incense rise up; the priests reappear.

The ancient Romans had many gods to serve, and the empire brought them more from the farthest corners of the earth. They had a god or goddess for every purpose, and each had a cult and ceremonies and special powers and cures and individual signs and symbols. Some Romans such as Ovid might look upon the deities as mere myths for poetic use; the populace looked upon them as real and of practical use. Almost all of the Romans wore some sort of seal (*bulla*) as an amulet, even in gold. And it must have bothered them to remove the good luck charm or protection even from a corpse, but the law said gold was not to be buried with people—probably to discourage grave-robbing—unless it was the gold in their teeth. Grave-robbing was for the ghoulish old women who were witches and cast spells; they cooked up the potions that might well include bits of dead bodies.

THE TALISMAN OF THE SUN

"Paul Christian" (Pitois)'s *History and Practice of Magic* (in the part translated by James Kirkup, 1963) gives instruction on making The Talisman of the Sun, a golden medal which "brings to those who wear it the goodwill and the favour of those in high positions." It also allegedly "preserves the wearer from death by syncope [stroke], aneurysm, epidemic and conflagration."

On the obverse is engraved a circle standing for eternity within the magic five-pointed star accompanied by mystic symbols. On the

Obverse   *Reverse*

The Talisman of the Sun

reverse is engraved an Egyptian head with headdress within a Star of David (or Solomon) and the mystical letters are said to spell the name of Pi-Rhé, "genius of the Sun."

ⲋ Ⲧ Ⲩ Ⲅ Ⲅ Ⲑ Ⲅ Ⲩ Ⳅ
Ⳉ Ⲉ Ⳓ Ⲡ Ṫ ' ⊥

An ancient protective charm on a silver leaf.

It must be made on a Sunday when the Moon is passing through "the first 10 degrees of the Lion [Leo] and is found in favourable aspect with Saturn and the Sun," and in the best hours for the Sun. For that you have a choice of: noon to 1 PM , 7 to 8 PM, 2 to 3 AM, and 9 to 10 AM the following morning. To consecrate the talisman you burn cinnamon, frankincense, saffron, and red sandalwood, with laurel leaves and dried heliotrope stalks [*helios* is Sun] in an earthenware vessel. "The talisman is then placed in a sachet of pale yellow silk...hung on the breast."

Shabako

THE SEAL OF SHABAKO

On the Shabako Stone was inscribed how Ptah created the world. The words on this Egyptian charm promises the wearer dominion over all things.

ICONS

The word is Greek in origin, so we may be forgiven if we look at Greek religious pictures as examples of the worldwide tendency to look to icons not only for religious inspiration but also for what the non-religious may think of as superstition. Patricia Storas, "Marble Girls of Athens," in the *New York Review of Books*, 3 October 1996:

I pass two or three icon stores in the space of six or eight blocks, hung with rows of sullen female saints, dead-eyed male saints, looking as if they are at the last moment of control before an explosion of anger. The more expensive images have ornate frames or silvered-over clothes. Women buy them and women tend them, lighting oil flames in front of them [electric lights are used by the lazy], burning incense, and misting them with holy water as if they were sacred house plants. I never actually saw a man buy one, not during the year I spent in Greece; and often remembered, as I walked by these stores, that during the two periods of fierce Byzantine iconoclasm, both times the defense of icon worship was sponsored by women, the empresses Theodora and Irene. There is something disturbing about all those blank, pent-up looking faces that demands propitiation, like a child's desperate attempts to please a remote, miserable parent. And there is something poignant, too, as if they are only so alike because they need to be rescued into individuality, they need the mercy of tending, one reason little girls play with dolls.

A GREEK AMULET

On a bit of limewood you write in vermilion this charm and wear it around your neck enclosed in a little "purple skin":

EPOCOPT KOPTO BAI BAITOKARAKO PTO KARAKO PTO
CHILOKO PTO BAI

This translates as "Guard me from every dæmon of the air, on the earth, and under the earth, and from every angel and phantom and ghostly visitation and enchantment, me NN."

BEANS

Beans have been used in many magical operations, but the most striking may be the stringing of mullaska beans to wear around the throat as an amulet. It is believed that the white beans turn black if evil strikes.

LUCKY AND UNLUCKY COINS

Gaming, as gamblers call gambling, is a major factor in American life, so it may not be amiss to give you a magic coin which promises to make you win every time at the gambling table (or at least increase the confidence with which you bluff at poker).

You start with a silver coin—a real silver coin, not the fakes we now use but, say, a silver dollar from the days when money was not alloy or "clad." You put the coin in a piece of virgin parchment on which you write:

† Lo+ Mat Nat Pat Quoat Rat Satat Nat

On a Sunday night before midnight you bury this coin at a crossroads and recite over it the (nonsense?) formula, making the nine signs of the cross as noted, three times, stamping your left (or sinister) foot three times as you do so. You walk away without looking back and return at the same hour the next day and dig up your lucky coin. Carry it on your person when you gamble. It might work—go on, "you never know!" as the lottery lout says in the ads.

An unlucky coin to receive would be the penny that a superstitious Central European used to cure his diseases. He washes with the water in which the coin is placed and then the coin is given, supposedly as charity—my source mentions "a blind beggar" as a good target—and the disease is passed on thereby.

The Complete Book of Superstition, Prophecy, and Luck mentions lucky coins, especially those with the date of your birth on them. But if people see you carry one you can't lie about your age!

THE TALISMAN

Sir Walter Scott's famous novel of this title (1825) was suggested by the Lee Penny, which has had a long history. It is a heart-shaped red pebble set in a silver groat, a coin of the time of Edward IV. It was connected with the story of Robert the Bruce and with The Douglas who was supposed to take the heart of the dead Bruce in a silver casket to the Holy Land, but did not reach there. The heart and silver casket were rescued after a battle with Saracens in Spain and taken back to Scotland by Sir Simon Locard of Lee. With the same Sir Simon the fabulous talisman was connected.

The Lee Penny, dipped in water and the water given to a sufferer, is supposed to cure the bite of a mad dog and other ills. It was used to cure cattle as well as oxen and in the seventeenth century this fourteenth-century object was still in frequent use. In that century the burghers of Newcastle borrowed it to cure a plague of the cattle, despite the fact that at least one person had been executed as a witch for using it. It was used also in the eighteenth century (when the Empress Maria Theresa gave the Lockhart family a gold casket to keep it in), and in Scott's own day and afterwards in the nineteenth century. Simon Macdonald Lockhart of Lee, of Dolphinton in Scotland, was a twentieth century owner of the Lee Penny.

INUIT AMULETS FOR DEFENSE

Eric J. Sharpe in *Man, Myth and Magic* (1985):

> Amulets are carried and worn by most Eskimo for this...purpose:
> a man's umbilical cord or afterbirth, teeth, toenails—any one of
> which might be used wrongly by sorcerers—animal bones and hair;
> carved stones and other objects. Almost anything will serve. The
> end justifies any means.

THE MAGIC SQUARE

Letters of the Hebrew and Arabic alphabets were given numbers, so we find magical squares like these in which the numbers add up perpendicularly, horizontally, and diagonally to the same sum. A is 15. B is 34. C is 36.

For *ELOHIM*, start with the *aleph* (middle letter of line 3) and read upward, downward, or sideways.

4	9	2
3	5	7
8	1	6

A

4	14	15	1
9	7	6	12
5	11	10	8
16	2	3	13

B

9	8	18	1
8	18	1	8
1	9	8	18
18	1	9	8

C

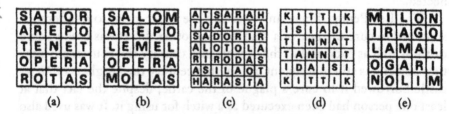

(a) (b) (c) (d) (e)

Magical squares. (a) The letters for PATER NOSTER (Our Father) plus A and O (Alpha and Omega) are made into the most famous of magical squares; TENET forms a cross. (b) This one is from *Abremelin the Mage,* an eighteenth-century book pretending to great antiquity; it is a love charm. (c) This is supposed to make you see visions of lakes and rivers. (d) This brings timber to you from the spirits (especially when you are constructing a mine). (e) Wear this under your hat to have spirits reveal all things past and future to you.

THE MAGIC CIRCLE

Egyptian magicians do not appear to have used the magic circle (a wall of protection) much, but instead wore amulets to protect themselves. This seems safer than the traditional circle, nine feet in diameter, drawn with chalk or the magic dagger, perhaps reinforced with a line of some protective substance (such as salt), and charged with the power of the Sacred Name and other symbols. Watch out, because clever demons can tempt or frighten the practitioner to step outside the circle (if it is physical) or to lose concentration and faith (if it is just visualized) where he is vulnerable. Moreover, most people do not know the Sacred Name; it is not one of the substitutes (*Adonai, Jehovah, Tetragrammaton, Ararita, Shaddai,* and so on) some grimoires recommend, and they will not work. Fortunately, they are not essential. The magic circle is conventionally nine feet in diameter; if you need a larger one (as when there are many to dance around it) increase the diameter by three feet a time. The difficulties in obtaining a magic knife (*athame,* which must be a gift, not bought, never thanked for), and then of consecrating it with ceremonies too obscure or too demanding for all but dedicated magicians, has meant that most magic circles these days are not created properly. To do it in the time-honored way, you stick the magic knife in the ground, tie a cord to it and also to another object (wand, knife, etc.) so that you have the length of the radius you need, and draw the circle with the second object. That few in so-called covens know this simply demonstrates how unprofessional, though enthusiastic, they may be.

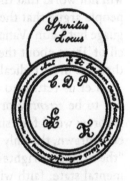

The Magic Circle of Honorius

Moreover, in magic as elsewhere in deviant behavior in America, following traditional rules is anathema to many, and "do your own thing" of the sixties has been succeeded by the "whatever" approach of the nineties, the decline of authority and the embrace of anarchy. Nonetheless, magic is a religion and religions have rules, whether the religion be (say) Christianity or a pagan one. Martin Luther *protested* about what had happened to some rules, but he himself wrote that he served "the God of the humble, the miserable, the oppressed and the desperate, and of those who are brought even to nothing"—and he set rules for religion as he saw it. The followers of The Craft think, with Friedrich Nietzsche, that Christianity is "a religion for slaves" and will have none of it. If they feel miserable, oppressed, or desperate they, very much without humility, take matters in their own hands and turn to magic, and The Adversary of God sometimes. But in their protest there is also rule. "Do what thou wilt" must have with it "so long as ye harm none," in most people's view. Even if you want to harm, there are rules for that. The ceremonies must be performed at the proper times, in the proper ways, the magical words precisely used. Most magicians assert that translations of spells, such as I give you in many cases, will not work, that the magic lies in the *sound* of the original words. Some people argue that the Consecration of the Mass will not work in any language but Latin! Vatican II, overturning the "eternal" decision of the Council of Trent about the Latin Mass, may have wrought far greater changes than the most radical Catholic desired!

Let us return to the properly drawn circle to center ourselves here, not to be *eccentric* or out of the circle, off the mark (which is what the Hebrew word for "sin" implies). However well or badly your magic circle is drawn, the only true protection, comparable to what the Epistles call "the armor of righteousness" of Christians, is the inflexible and correct mental state: faith without fear. That is invincible. That is the complete foundation of working magic, internally and externally.

THE TRIANGLE

This is created outside the magic circle in the same sort of way and is the place where the creature conjured up is confined by the conjurer, sometimes with threats, pentacles, etc. It is even more difficult to keep the figure conjured up within the triangle than it is to stay within one's circle. If the creature is malevolent and escapes, the damage can possibly be great. Oddly, the name used at the three corners is that of an archangel ("defend us in the battle," goes the prayer) broken up as *MI-CH-AEL*. The name of the archangel Michael also appears outside the magic circle, representing one of the Four Elements (fire) at the west. Raphael appears at the east on the periphery of the circle (air). Uriel appears at the north, representing earth. Gabriel 's name is written at the west, representing water. They may also be represented by candles of appropriate color, and candles may likewise mark the three angles of the angel's or demon's appearance "platform." The apex of the triangle usually points north, especially if a demon is summoned to materialize within it.

PARAPHERNALIA FOR CEREMONIAL MAGIC

Besides consecrated wands, tridents, chalices, daggers, and so on, there is also a long list of colorful hangings and candles, vestments, and so on. Just as at Mass the celebrant wears a chasuble ("little house") of a certain color that is in tune with the nature of the day (red for the feasts of martyrs, symbolic of blood shed; green for hope, drawn from the green shoots of nature reawakened in spring; etc.) and uses books, bells, holy water, incense, an altar with appropriate cloths, vessels, and the rest, so, too, the magician has to prepare elaborate tools, even to write his instructions on cards and prop them up as is done for certain standard prayers said at Mass. He must have his "bible" present for the reading of passages of power, his "grammar" of instructions, his protections, and so on.

Each day's Mass has designated readings from the Epistles and the Gospel as well as the standard *Introit* (introduction), *Credo* (creed), and so on. Each magical ceremony has its details appropriate to the intention.

EQUIPMENT FOR THE MAGIC OF THE CLAVICLE

The Clavicle (Key) is the magic attributed to King Solomon. It is an elaborate study to be undertaken only by the bravest and performed only by the most pure and dedicated. E.M. Butler's *Ritual Magic* (1949) speaks of the difficulties in the way of assembling the tools:

> The magician of the school of Solomon must...forge his own sword, knives, poniard and lancet, and fit them with handles made and engraved with the appropriate characters by himself. He must cut, fashion and inscribe his own wand and staff; make his own needles and shape his own pen. He must mix his own inks, compound his own perfumes and incense, construct his own inkwell and aspergillus [device for sprinkling liquids around]. He must mold his own candles from virgin earth dug up by his own hands, or from wax taken from bees who had never made it before. Moreover, awkward conditions are attached to all these operations. They must be performed under the right planetary aspects; the steel to be forged must be tempered in the blood of a magpie, or of a gosling, or of a mole, according to the particular instrument required, and in the juice of the fern, mercury, or pimpernel. The knife-handles must be made of box-wood cut with a new sword at one blow; the

wand of virgin hazel must be obtained in similar circumstances. The pen must be shaped from the third feather of the right wing of a male goose; and so forth and so on, almost it would seem *ad infinitum*.

You can see at a glance that Solomonic magic is not for the vast majority of Americans. We are a people who recently have gone from being traditionally suspicious of authority to downright contemptuous of it, in government, schools and universities, even religion. American Roman Catholics assert that the infallible pope is wrong on abortion, homosexuality, the refusal to ordain women as priests, and a host of other matters. American Jews make up new rules and instead of traditional straight thinking—which is what *orthodox* means—and construct new, conservative or reformed Judaism of their own, updating the Reform movement of the early nineteenth century and the Conservative reaction of the 1880s. The Nation of Islam departs significantly from the religion of The Prophet. Women activists have succeeded in some bibles of changing The Lord's Prayer! We don't take to being told what to do.

On top of that, we as a nation are overweight but cannot stick to diets (and Solomonic magic requires extensive fasting), sex-obsessed (and Solomonic magic requires chastity), and too lazy or too busy or too stupid (SAT scores continue to fall despite all attempts to falsify them rather than accept the fact of "the dumbing of America") to learn elaborate procedures and make our own tools. If one could get a package at the mall, maybe. Do it yourself and in a state of mental and physical purity—forget it!

If anyone tries to sell you the equipment for ritual magic ready-made, put a curse on them or report them to the local officials investigating consumer fraud. Even the book of instructions has to be (a) handwritten and (b) an outright gift to you.

I see nowhere, however, that the clothes one wears cannot be run up for you by Hellfinger, Ralph Omen, or DKNY (Devil Klothes New York). You will need a white crown, matching shoes, and something like the long garment worn by Mormons in The Temple or Roman Catholic priests over the cassock for Mass. That is called an alb (because it is white) and reaches the shoes; it has full long sleeves. The magical robe is made of white linen and tied at the waist, like the alb, with a white cord (cincture). On the breast of the magic robe must be embroidered in red silk ("spun by a young maiden," preferably) these characters:

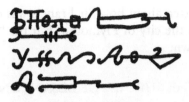

You may have seen a priest kiss the cross on the back of his stole before putting it on. All such ceremonial garments are likely to have some ritual and prayers associated with donning them. Putting on the magic robe—over nothing else—you pray. Different books give different prayers, but here is the prayer from *The Key of Solomon:*

> AMOR, AMITOR, AMIDES, IDEODANIACH, PAMOR, PLAIOR, ANITOR, by the virtue of these most holy Angelic Names I clothe myself, O Lord, in my Vestments of Power, so that I may fulfill, even to their term, all the things which I desire to effect through Thee, Most Holy ADONAY, whose kingdom and rule endure for ever and for ever. AMEN.

Some magicians prefer to wear the inscription on a medal hung from the neck by a red ribbon, which saves on cleaning bills. I cannot discover what (if anything) the inscription means or even what language it is supposed to be in—there are many such writings in magic—but I do know that the "Angelic Names" are not really names of angels.

HOW TO CREATE A NAVAL FORCE

King Alfred is supposed to have created the British Navy, but surely no Briton ever did as much in this line, or as easily, as Sir Francis Drake. That is, if the legend reported in Mrs. A. E. Bray's *Traditions, Legends, Superstitions and Sketches of Devonshire...*(1828) is true.

> One day as Sir Francis Drake was playing at Kales [bowling] on Plymouth Hoe he had news that a foreign fleet was sailing into the harbour. He finished his game and then took a hatchet and ordered a large block of wood to be brought to him. He chopped this up into small pieces and threw them into the sea with magic words. As they touched the water each one became a fire-ship and sailed against the foreign fleet so that it was utterly destroyed.

Elsewhere I have written about how Sir Francis was credited with bringing a water supply to the city of Plymouth. But the "magic words" used, if any, remain unknown.

THE SHROUD OF BESANÇON

So much has been written lately about the Shroud of Turin (carbon-dated to the Middle Ages but still believed by many to be the shroud of Christ) that is not necessary to go over all the historical, superstitious and scientific ground again here, but maybe you have not heard about another winding sheet alleged to have contained the body of the crucified Christ, the Shroud of Besançon.

This was a linen cloth taken to Besançon in France in 1206 by Otto de la Roche and placed in the cathedral there as a holy relic. The date of 11 July was set up for an annual feast day in celebration of the relic, which was supposed to have healing power.

So far as I can determine, no compelling proof for or against the shroud's authenticity has been made public. What is certain is that faith heals and such stimuli to faith are useful to believers seeking miraculous cures.

First-class relics were the bones or other parts of saints themselves, but also relics were the veil of Veronica, the stole of St. Thomas à Becket (at Sens), the chasuble of St. Regnobert (at Bayeux), some clothes of St. Scholastica (at Santa Maria Maggiore in Rome), etc. A feather from the Holy Spirit (who appears as a dove) was treasured in a European cathedral of the middle ages. The most striking story of a relic is probably not the annual liquefaction of the blood of St. Gennaro or how the skull of St. Catherine of Sienna (now to be seen in the cathedral there) lost its two front teeth—The Devil pushed her down a flight of stairs—but the story of how a mirror, supposed to have belonged to The Blessed Virgin herself, was shattered completely at the Parisian church of Ste.-Germainè-des-Près. Mabillon was carrying it in a medieval procession and dropped it.

THE LETTER OF THE LORD

The peasantry in Victorian England might well have framed on the wall of their humble cottage a letter, printed as a broadsheet, supposedly written to Argabus of Edessa by no one less than Jesus Christ Himself. Margaret Baker in *Folklore and Customs of Rural England* (1975) adds that "it was known as far afield as Newfoundland [according to George Patterson's paper to the American Folklore Society in 1894] and was particularly protective of women in childbirth."

TO FIND LOST OBJECTS

Prayers to various saints, including one St. Anthony and the Greek St. Fanourios, are recommended by some, and Spanish diabolists called *zahoris* specialized in this, but their recipes are unholy. Maybe you simply need some chemical to improve your memory; don't forget to ask your physician about this.

CURING THE CURSE OF THE SHEAF AND BLESSING THE SHEAF

The last sheaf of the harvest was, from pagan times in Britain, selected with care, prepared in accordance with old customs, and honored. It was one of many fertility superstitions. Out of straw people also made "corn dollies" and hung them up in their houses to ward off evil or bring good luck.

There was also among the witches the custom of "buying the sheaf." For this way of cursing a person, you went to the church and with your back to the altar, or visiting the Stations of the Cross in reverse order, or by some other means disrespected the house of God and made your supplications to The Devil. Then you made a straw man and stuck pins in it to bring pain upon your intended victim, whose name you gave the figure, and buried it with more incantations.

Honor and Riches

As it rotted, the victim was supposed to waste away and die. However, if the figure could be unearthed and burned before that, the spell would be broken and the victim returned to health.

The blessing of the sheaf in Cornish folklore involves the oldest reaper putting together an abundant last sheaf (for an abundant harvest next time) and saying three times, "I have it!" Each time comes the question from the others, "What do you have?" and the response, "The neck!" The sheaf is then decorated with ribbons and flowers and used to be set up as a kind of idol. Now it may appear in the decorations of the Harvest Festival, an ancient ritual revived in the nineteenth century by an Anglican clergyman. The Jews have a Harvest Festival, called *Succoth*, and so do most old traditions.

MOLES

I mean the skin blemishes, not the animals. (The blood of the animal is used in some very strange magical recipes, especially those for invisibility. The mole also makes a cute familiar.)

If you have a mole in your armpit, you may have been born a witch. If you have one on your neck, ear, back, or left hand, you may be in for money. Too many moles on the left (or sinister) side and you can expect evil. Most moles, however, are said to be marks of the favor of fortune and the ancients had a whole (pseudo)science of what they meant and "read" them. Once they were considered to be "beauty marks", and those who did not have one on the face might stick on a black patch. Today we may wonder of they might turn cancerous. We have new criteria for worrying about whether they are light or dark or changing shape over time.

CHINESE HOROSCOPES

I suppose I must mention astrology here some place, though methods of foretelling the future are enough for a whole book some other time. I have to confess I tend to agree with the learned Maimonides; he said that astrology is not a science but a disease.

Anyway, because you already know about Virgo, Pisces, Sagittarius and the rest of the Zodiac, I want to introduce you to another zoo: the twelve animals of the Chinese system, a system in which billions of people still  believe. The assertion is that there are twelve basic types of people but that their fundamental characters depend not upon the months in which they were born but the years. If you were born in late January or early February—in this period each Chinese New Year comes along, but not by any method you know to be sure of when it is—you may be a little uncertain as to which is "your" year; you'll have to investigate more deeply. Others can assume their year (say 1960) is Rat. That year actually ran 28 January 1960 to 15 February 1961.

This system is said to have begun with The Buddha, who called all the animals to a conference, but only a dozen arrived. He assigned them years in the order of their appearance before him: Rat, Ox, Tiger, Cat, Dragon, Snake, Horse, Goat, Monkey, Rooster, Dog, and Pig. The Ox has 1997 and the cycle starts over with the Rat in 2008.

I was born in a Dragon year. That makes me successful and influential, generous and healthy, clever, and scrupulous if also sentimental, domineering, irritable and malcontent, very judgmental and terrifically demanding and stubborn. Also a Sagittarian born in a Dragon year, I have to be careful not to be too enthusiastic or overly optimistic, and I must not marry anyone born in the years of the Ox or the Dog. My next especially auspicious Dragon year is 2000. My personal life involves a Snake, who is (predictably) attractive but never easy to get along with, but at least I have avoided the disaster of an Ox or a Dog. Monkeying around with a Monkey would have been ideal, but Monkeys are never as attractive as Snakes and several other groups, and as a Dragon—I have to be frank—I am so vain I want someone who looks a lot better than average.

Why not figure out what Chinese year you were born in? The Rat was 1900, 1912, etc., up to 1996. You have the 12 signs listed above. Figure it out. Many sources then, from placemats in Chinese restaurants to *Suzanne White's Original Chinese Astrology Book* (1976—a Year of the Dragon, of course), will be glad to tell you your fate.

THE THIRTEENTH

The thirteenth at table is unlucky, but not all thirteenths are. For example, you get thirteen in a baker's dozen. Actually, there is nothing superstitious involved in that old custom. It derives from the fact that short weight in bread was not uncommon and had to be drastically punished in medieval times, so the baker who sold a loaf that weighed too little or a dozen rolls that came in underweight was in great trouble. To avoid any possible prosecution, bakers took to throwing in an extra or thirteenth piece in every dozen. Like the shrewd creoles who dispensed the extras *(lagniappes* is still a common word in the vocabulary of New Orleans), a good businessman just factored this "gift" into the price. It was simply an evasion—like skipping from the twelfth to the fourteenth in the numbering of the floors in tall buildings.

BELL, BOOK, AND CANDLE

Driving out rituals, whether exorcisms or excommunications, of the Roman Catholic church involve the ringing of a bell, the shutting of The Bible, and the blowing out of a candle. These are symbols of finality. You're "closing the book on someone." However, *Bell, Book, and Candle* has, because

A Victorian Exorcism

of exorcism, become so associated with witches that it served as the title of John van Druten's light comedy about modern witchcraft (1950).

FLOWER POWER

To protect your Hawaiian retreat, plant green Ti (not the red kind, which is sacred to Pele, who might get jealous). Or you can, as people do in several other cultures, plant chrysanthemums, though the Greeks think of these as flowers of the dead. The British used to plant orderly rows of red flowers; these stood, like soldiers in their red coats, in protection. White roses placed over the gate to the cow pasture is said to prevent witches from riding the cows at night. Red rose petals scattered on the ground bring bad luck. Strawberry plants will protect your house from snakes. Pick a lily when the Sun is in Leo, mix it with the juice of laurel leaves, and put it under a pile of dung. Worms will appear. Kill them, dry them, grind them to powder, and put them in an enemy's bed. "He will not be able to sleep until the powder is removed," one authority assures us. The powder can also be put into a jug of milk and covered with a piece of cowhide and "put into a byre"; then "all the cows in the byre whose colour is the same as the piece of hide will go dry."

Flowers can be used to cast or break spells. Lucius of Patras in the old tale is turned by magic into an ass but eating a rose will reverse the metamorphosis.

PROTECTIVE HERBS

There are many magical as well as medicinal and food uses for herbs, but caraway, which the Arabs first called *karawaya* and the Romans *carvi* (Pliny's *Natural History* was sure it came from Caria, in Asia Minor), is unusual in that it was supposed to protect from theft anything that the seeds contained. It was kept in silver and gold vessels for this purpose, and added to love potions to keep a lover from straying or been stolen. It was said that caraway seeds would force a burglar to remain in the house so he would be caught. It is still given to pigeons who, if they are given caraway seeds, will never fly away permanently from home. And that's a fact. Carrying in your pocket fern seeds on St. John's Eve—which Shakespeare and Jonson and other Elizabethans talked about as conferring the gift of invisibility—doesn't work. But for pigeons, at least, caraway seeds do perform some sort of miracle. A chaplet of saffron on your head is said to prevent drunkenness, but probably because no bartender would serve you.

The Chinese herbalists use the top, middle, or root of a plant depending on whether your trouble is in the head, upper or lower body.

The great British folklorist Edward Clodd noted that Chinese practice, and also this:

> And with the practice of the Zuklu medicinemen, who takes the oldest bull or dog of the tribe, giving scrapings of these to the sick, so that their lives may be prolonged to old age, we may compare that of doctors in the seventeenth century, who with less logic, but perchance unconscious humour, gave their patients pulverized mummy to prolong their years.

Actually, the mummies may have been used because of the preservative spices and other ingredients of mummification, but the other practices are sympathetic magic.

TREES

Innumerable are the superstitions connected with the ash, the elder, the yew, the rowan, and other trees. Fairies live in oaks. Willows are said to uproot themselves and follow you through the woods at night! Magic wands should be ash wood or hazel, suitably inscribed. Like the chalice used in witchcraft, you cannot buy wands: they must be given to you. Never plant a willow, never bring mountain laurel blossoms into the house (because they used to be used to deck human sacrifices as they went to the slaughter) and

> Hawthorn bloom and elder flowers
> Fill the house with evil powers.

Following an old Central European custom, always have an odd number of stems in a bouquet—with primroses thirteen is lucky. However, watch out what tree leaves and flower leaves you mix. Never put red and white flowers together in a bouquet or arrangement. Don't bring into the house any flowering branches of peach, pear, plum, cherry, or apple. Bad luck. There's a vast lore built up about all this, as detailed as the "language of the flowers" of Victorian England which allowed you to send messages by choosing certain flowers. Greeks say avoid chrysanthemums—flowers for funerals. Others say chrysanthemums disinfect the room by driving evil off. Nasturtiums, those "nose-twisting" blooms, are disliked by demons, it is reported.

An acorn on the windowsill prevents Thor's thunderbolts from hitting. The pulls on window shades often used to be shaped like acorns. Plant barberry bushes around your house; they keep off witches and I find they also prevent passing New Yorkers from ripping off a branch of hedge for fun as they idly pass by. Early christianizers in Britain had great trouble rooting out the pagan beliefs in ash groves, oak trees, holly and mistletoe, holes in trees through which one passed a child to heal it—or give it to The Devil, some clerics thought. Laws were passed to punish such tree superstitions. Anglo-Saxon kings tried their best to keep their subjects from worshipping trees, and yet the Teutonic "Christmas toy," as Dickens calls it, the Christmas tree, has a seasonal place now in all our lives. You are bringing into your home an evergreen symbol of life in the dark of winter—but remember spirits used to dwell in the trees of the dark German forests. That's why you knock on wood.

TOBACCO

Tobacco was used by aboriginal Americans in sacred rites. The smoke was supposed to carry their prayers to the Great Manitou. The peace pipe was ritually smoked. This drug was soon noted by the earliest Europeans in America and early European settlers here had many superstitions about it. One was that you could cure an earache by blowing tobacco smoke into the sufferer's ear. The tobacco plant was used in various magical ceremonies, also.

BELLARMINE JUGS

St. Robert Bellarmine was the chief apologist for the Roman Catholic Church in the sixteenth century; he was canonized in 1911. He appears to have given his name somehow to the Bellarmine jug. You may have seen one. It has a brownish salt glaze and the face of a bearded man on it. It was the custom in the old days in England to fill such jugs with magical material and bury them to take off spells or to cast a protective charm over one's house and land.

Business Success

KNIVES

Originally iron, these always drove away the earlier, non-Iron Age people our ancestors encountered when they wandered into Europe, the strange Others whom we began to think of as ogres, giants, fairies, and elves. Many superstitions still vaunt the power of iron to drive off evil. You can put a knife under the pillow or under the bed to "cut the pain" of childbirth. You can touch iron the way you'd touch wood, for luck; there's a powerful spirit in there! You mustn't stir food with a knife; that only stirs up trouble. In ritual magic a sword or knife, consecrated in elaborate ceremonies, is essential. The Druids could not touch iron: they shaved themselves and cut mistletoe, etc., with instruments of gold. There are many superstitions about what instruments are used to cut botanicals for magic use. Everyone repeats the old story about how mandrakes were supposed to drive a person crazy with the scream they uttered if they were torn from the earth, so that they were tied to dogs' tails and people ran off and left the dogs to pull them up while vulnerable humans were well out of earshot.

MAGICAL GEMS

You have all heard of birthstones—mine, for Sagittarius, is turquoise—and maybe of so-called crystal power and the properties of gems from friendly amethyst to radioactive zircon. But here are three samples of the massive, mysterious, magical lore of precious and semi-precious stones.

CARNELIAN is a kind of red chalcedony which takes its name from Latin *carne*, "flesh." The Arabs say it fulfills desires and call it Mecca Stone. They believe that if engraved with the names of twelve *imans* and put in the mouth of a corpse a carnelian is a first-class ticket to paradise. Mohammed himself wore a carnelian ring, says Katrina Raphaell in *Crystal Enlightenment* (1985) "as a charm." Others have worn carnelian (because it is red) to stop bleeding, help with menstruation, cure blood diseases and blood poisoning, etc. The stone is said to increase the heart's strength and the heartbeat, to vitalize the whole body, to help one see into the past, etc. "As a talismanic mineral," writes Barbara G. Walker in her interesting *Book of Sacred Stones* (1989), "carnelian has much to recommend it."

MALACHITE is named from Greek *maleche*, "marrow." It is said to crack to warn of danger, to protect the young and protect against the evil eye, to stop bleeding (powder it and take in honey), to settle upset stomachs (powder it and add to milk—the milk works), to cure a range of problems (insect bites, common colds, diarrhea), to relieve a number of ills (rheumatism, vertigo, leukemia, ulcers, teething pains), and to counteract radiation from computer screens. It may be Pliny's *smaragdus medicus* (medical emerald) and people used to believe that if you drank from a goblet made of it you would, like Dr. Doolittle, be able to talk to the animals.

OPAL gets its name from the Sanskrit *upala*, "precious stone." It was long thought to protect against disease, loss of golden hair color in blonds, and myopia. It was called "the stone of thieves," who used it to become invisible. Fire opals, they say, draw money. Black opals are said to increase the powers of black magic. My grandmother wouldn't wear her opal necklace; she said the stones were very unlucky. However, she had the idea that opals were ruined if they did not get body heat now and then, so she would sometimes sit with opals in her hands as she read a book. (About pearls she had the same belief, but those she might sometimes wear to bed to keep them warm.) She gave me a book by Sir Walter Scott, *Anne of Gierstein* (1829), that had a cursed opal in it. The opal is a gem I wouldn't buy, not because I think it is unlucky but because so much fiddling can be done with inferior specimens.

BAY AND SAGE

These two will exemplify here the fascinating lore that Scott Cunningham has collected in his copious *Encyclopedia of Magical Herbs* (1993, more authoritative than the booklets that amateurs churn out). You will find more

BAY

in the encyclopedias of myth. The nymph Daphne was protected from being raped by being changed into a bay tree; bay leaves in modern Greek are still called *daphne*.

Bay was worn or chewed by the priestesses of Apollo to induce prophetic visions (you can try a crown of sage or you can drink a concoction containing bay or saffron, saffron being better because bay is so bitter). Bay occurs in recipes for clairvoyance as well as prophecy. Put it under your pillow for veridical dreams. Worn as an amulet, it gives protection as well as psychic abilities. It drives away poltergeists, exorcises demons, burned (with sandalwood) removes curses and evil spells. Share a broken twig with a lover; that will keep you together. Wear it to give you strength in athletic competitions. Hold a leaf in your mouth for good luck. Write a wish on a leaf and burn it to make your wish come true.

SAGE

Sage is another "masculine" herb. This one is of Jupiter, as bay is of the Sun. Eat sage in May. Cunningham quotes:

> He who would live for aye
> Must eat sage in May.

Carry sage to promote wisdom and to ward off the evil eye. Use it in spells for healing and to attract money. Don't plant sage in your garden, though; that's bad luck, so get someone else to do it. Don't let them plant a full bed of it; that's bad luck as well, so share the bed with some other useful herb. And feed it to your familiar: it is the catnip of toads. Cunningham concludes with this sage advice:

> If you desire to make a wish come true, write it on a sage leaf and hide it beneath your pillow. For three nights sleep upon it. If once you dream of what you desire you wish will be materialized [granted]; if not, bury the sage in the ground so that you do not come to harm.

In India sweet basil (*tulsi*) magical beads are worn to ward off evil and disease, and there are similar plant uses in all cultures known to history.

MBANJE

Some African voodoo cults use this plant to protect themselves against zombies called up from the dead by a *zwimbganana* or witch. You could burn sagebrush in America for the same purpose.

HOLY SMOKE

Certain kinds of incense are believed to attract or repel supernatural creatures and even in American Indian religions there were smudge sticks lighted to drive off evil. Occult shops offer oils to burn, "aromatherapy incense wands" (dipped in oils), all sorts of incense.

THE RING OF GYGES

This ring was cast of fixed mercury and set with a stone found in the nest of a lapwing. Around the stone (according to one French magical book) was engraved the motto: *Jesus passant † par le milieu d'eux † s'en allait.* This is from Luke IV:30, and "Jesus, passing through the midst of them, went His way" is relevant because the Ring of Gyges was supposed to grant the wearer the power to pass among people—invisibly.

You simply turned the stone inward as you wore the ring on your finger and as it "disappeared," so did you. If you turned it outward, you could be seen. But the fact that in a mirror the ring could not be seen was proof of its magical power of invisibility.

OTHER MAGICAL RINGS, AND A BRACELET

Here are pentacles of power and also the inscriptions you are supposed to engrave inside the rings worn when these pentacles are used in magic. These call up demons. That may have been what the pope called Boniface was doing, though people said his demon actually resided in his ring. *Audivit dici quod ipse Bonifacius utebatur consilio dæmonum, et habebat dæmonum inclusum in annulo.*

I shall describe several pentacles and rings of power here for you, but there are many. The rings must be metal but the talismans need not be gold or silver; embroidery on satin of the appropriate color will suffice.

First, the talisman to get treasures, understandably one of the most frequently used in magic. It is embroidered in gold on green satin. With it, and the magic words

ONAIM PERANTES RASONASTOS

it is claimed you can conjure up seven genii, each with a black-hooded bird on his shoulder but, most important, each with leather bags from which they will pour out "golden ducats" in great quantity. Unlike most conjurations intended to produce gold, this one is thought to bring the real article and not just dust or other material over which a "glamour" is thrown to deceive the magician.

Second, the talisman to win lotteries. It is embroidered in gold and silver on cherry-colored satin. You tie it on your left arm with a white ribbon and wear the ring on the little finger of the right hand. The magic words , according to A. E. Waite, "ROKES for a winning number, PILATUS for an ambes-ace, ZOTOAS for a denary, TULITAS for a quaternary, XANATINTOS for a quinary, being careful to pronounce all the words at the quine." He adds:

> At cards they should be repeated when shuffling for self or partner. Before beginning, touch your left arm with your right hand in the neighborhood of the talisman, and kiss the ring. These little contrivances, says the honest Grimoire, without exciting the notice of your opponent.

There is no instruction as to what to do should the opponent be using the same system.

Third, the talisman for sending all the hosts of demons against your enemies, including other magicians (who may be using the same talisman!), because there are often fierce struggles for power between those engaged in the black arts. This talisman is embroidered in silver on light gray satin.

It probably should be tied to the left arm with a white ribbon, but Waite says that "it may be worn in any manner." The magic words are:

OSTHARIMAN VISANTIPAROS NOCTATUR

Some magicians' rings were even more powerful. They had demons resident in them. To say so was to speak heresy, and church officials issued (and applied) stern laws to put down this sort of thing. For example, Giovanni Alberghini's handbook for the Holy Inquisition, *Manuale qualificatorum Sanctæ Inquistionis*, which first appeared in Palermo in 1642 but was still going strong in many other editions well into the eighteenth century in Venice and elsewhere, condemns the heresy of keeping a demon assistant in a ring to answer questions. This, he says, can only be done with a pact with The Devil.

Demons, of course, do not usually reside in rings the way genies reside in bottles. Demons reside in Hell and come either as disembodied voices or take on an animal's body—even a human animal's. They come to do as much evil as they can. The Gospels of Matthew IX and XII say they can make you go dumb or blind, Luke XIII says they can make you ill, Jesus drove them out, not with magic rings but with His words.

Albert Pike, author of *Morals and Dogma of the Ancient and Accepted Scottish Rite of Freemasonry* (1872), was popularly believed to own a bracelet which had the power to summon Lucifer. In fact, the public was suspicious of all secret societies such as the Masons and the Rosicrucians and the *Illuminati* and so on. Who knew what mysteries were celebrated in those temples? The public even came to be suspicious of the members of The Church of Jesus Christ of Latter Day Saints, whom "Gentiles" called Mormons, because their founder (Joseph Smith, who claimed to have translated *The Book of Mormon* with magic spectacles, from plates of gold lent to him by the Angel Moroni in Upstate New York) went so far as to borrow some Masonic ceremonies for use in the temples of his new religion. Not knowing precisely what the Masonic and Mormon paraphernalia was all about, the general public was ready to believe these secretive people might well be dealing in the black arts. They were not.

MAGICAL GEMS ONCE MORE

The crystal fad of today has a long history; precious and semiprecious stones have often been thought to be connected to astrological signs (whence "birthstones") and to be able to work magic. For the later purpose was the breastplate of the High Priest of the Jews in The Temple. He wore a breastplate with stones set in it to stand for the twelve tribes of Israel. Exodus XXVIII: 17-20 tells us how these magical stones were arranged. Reading from right to left in the top row: *BEREKETH* (emerald), *PITDAH* (topaz or peridot), *ODEHEM* (carnelian or sard). Second row, right to left: *YAHALOM* (jasper or onyx), *SAPPIR* (sapphire or lapis lazuli), *NOPEK* (ruby or carbuncle). Third row, right to left, *ALAMAH* (amethyst), *SHEBHO* (agate), *LESHEM* (jacinth). Bottom row, right to left, *YASPAR* (jasper), *SHOHAM* (crysolite), *TARSHISH* (beryl or yellow jasper).

How each gem came to be associated with the name of the tribe engraved on it is not explained. Also not explained is what the Jews were up to—because for magical purposes these gems are arranged in the wrong order! The dice secreted behind the breastplate may well have worked for fortune-telling, which is how they were used in the Holy of Holies, but the breastplate as constituted contains an unfortunate error: carnelian is in the wrong place, so of course all the rest are too. This arrangement starts off well with a green stone (hope and confidence, rain and vegetation) but eventually goes wrong. The Temple magic would not have worked!

One example of powers attributed to stones: the "Turkish stone," which the French called *turquoise*. It is a lucky color and stone of the Arabs and is used by them, as it is by other cultures, to ward off the evil eye. It has power to cleanse and to destroy evil (for which the Buddha used it). Like some other stones it is said to warn of poison (so emperors had cups made of such stones) but has the unusual extra advantage, if that is an advantage, of indicating the owner's impending death by changing color.

THE HAND OF GLORY

To make this useful device, which magicians said enabled robbers to make everyone around them stand transfixed, motionless and helpless, while they committed their crimes, all you needed was the hand—the left was preferred, but the right would do—of a hanged man. You wrapped it in a piece of his clothing or of a funeral pall and preserved it in an earthen pot with salt, niter, peppers, and (in one recipe) "zimat." That may have meant *zimar* (verdigris) or (according to David de Planis-Campy as quoted by Grillot de Givry) *zimax* (iron sulfate). The preserved hand then became the candlestick for a candle made with the fat of a gibbeted man, virgin wax, sesame, and "ponie." Grillot de Givry explains "in the dialect of Lower Normandy... *ponie* means horse-dung, and it is more than probable that this was the ingredient used by sorcerers, as it is very combustible once it

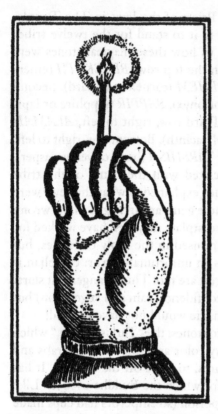

is dry." Carry this gruesome candle lit and anyone you encounter cannot stop you from doing anything you wish.

The way to prevent the use of the Hand of Glory on your premises was, according to the *Secrets merveilleux de la magie naturelle et cabalistique du Petit Albert* (The Marvelous Secrets of Natural and Cabalistic Magic of Little Albert, Cologne, 1722), to smear the threshold and other parts of your house with the powdered gall of a black cat, the fat of a white hen, and the blood of a screech owl, all compounded during the dog days of summer.

THE MAGIC CANDLE

Likewise from *Petit Albert* comes what Grillot de Givry calls a "priceless recipe" for a magical candle which works as a sort of Geiger counter to detect precious metals. In the words of his translator (J. Courtenay Locke):

> You must have a big candle composed of human tallow, and it must be fixed into a piece of hazel-wood fashioned in the manner shown in the picture. And then if this candle, being lighted in a subterranean place, sparkles brightly with a good deal of noise, it is a sign there is treasure in that place, and the nearer you approach the treasure the more will the candle sparkle, going out at length when you are quite close. You must have other candles in lanterns so as not to be left without light. When there are sound reasons for believing that treasure is watched over by the spirits of dead men it is good to have wax candles which have been blessed instead of common candles, and to conjure the spirits in the name of God to declare whether there is anything you can

do to help them to a place of untroubled rest. And you must not fail to do what they require.

You will recall that the ghost of Hamlet's father walks as a "perturbed spirit" with unfinished business, but what he wants is not some treasure to be found which he concealed in life (as Elizabethans such as Shakespeare strongly believed was one reason ghosts appeared) but an evil deed—vengeful murder—to be done. Hamlet is, of course, wrong to accede to the ghost's request.

In the view of the *Petit Albert* you are to "conjure the spirits in the name of God," but in some traditions—such as the Scandinavian—to utter a single word while treasure hunting will cause the treasure to disappear. Such treasures are guarded, however, not by "the spirits of dead men" but by evil trolls.

THE NEWBORN BABE

Of course the most important thing is to be born at the most auspicious hour, on the best day, in the right place, getting your horoscope off to a good start. If you can contrive to be born with a caul, or teeth, or the seventh son of a seventh son—which would have got you called *Doctor* in years past—all the better. You must not see yourself in a mirror and should be christened as soon as practicable, even though babies who die unbaptized apparently no longer go to Limbo for eternity. At your christening a lot depends upon whether you cry or not and who your godparents are and—remember what happened when a wicked fairy got angry at not being invited to the baptism of Sleeping Beauty!—even witches probably ought to be nicely asked to come and to cast good spells, not bad ones. But don't cut the baby's hair or nails or even wash it for as long as you can stand it because all that might provide wicked witches with material with which to enchant the child.

The Christ child was offered gold, frankincense, and myrrh. The ordinary child should get silver (for wealth), an egg (for fertility), and salt (to keep off evil), and other gifts in threes as well. Throw in a coral amulet, too. Another recommended practice was to take a live mouse and with a needle threaded in one eye and out the other put it on a cord. Then you could hang this wriggling object around the infant's neck and the life force of the mouse could be transferred into the baby to strengthen it. If you tied a knot in the sheet that covered the child, African-Americans used to think, the infant would not die until the next sunset.

GOD BLESS THIS SHIP AND ALL WHO SAIL IN HER

The beautifully carved figures on the prows of old sailing ships, so popular in modern maritime museums, have a gruesome origin: originally a victim (often a virgin) was sacrificed to the gods for a good voyage, and lashed to the front of the ship. Magic also accounts for the dragon prows of boats and eyes painted there—and what seems to be the Christian idea of christening ships by breaking a bottle of champagne on the hull before it first slides down into the water. That is not a baptism; it's a sacrifice. Blood used to be used.

One of the laws of the Vikings stipulated that one must not offend the land gods by coming to the shore "with open jaws," so the Vikings took down their dragon prows before they made for land.

Going down to the sea in ships has always been the sort of frightening enterprise that seeks solace in superstitions. Much is done in various societies to protect sailors and ships by magic. Also, the Malays cast a spell as they launch a model ship they believe they fill with the diseases and evils of the society and send off to the spirits. They chant:

Ho, elders of the upper reaches,
Elders of the lower reaches,
Elders of dry land,
Elders of the river flats!
Assemble ye, O people, lords of hill and foothill,
Lords of cavern and deep-locked basin,
Lords of deep primeval forest,
Lords of the riverbends,
Come on board this *lanchang*,
  assembling in your multitudes,
So ye may depart with the ebbing stream,
Depart on the passing breeze,
Depart in the yawning earth,
Depart in the red-dyed earth.
Go ye to the ocean which has no wave,
And the plain where no green herb grows,
And never return here.
But if ye return here
Ye shall be consumed by the curse:
At sea ye shall get no drink,

A grotesque and probably protective figure from Borneo. This is the death post of a Ngadju chieftain. In folk art, grotesque figures may represent demons or be designed to frighten off demons, serve as totems, etc.

Ashore ye shall find no food,
But gape in vain about the earth.

FAMILIARS

These are demons or imps that serve the witch in animal form. You can read more about them in *The Complete Book of Magic and Witchcraft* and in *The Complete Book of The Devil's Disciples*, of course, but I want to mention here my favorite of all. One Moll White in eighteenth-century England was widely credited with a remarkable familiar: it was a cat who spoke English with a provincial accent!

THOSE LITTLE VALENTINE CANDIES

It used to be believed that if you wrote something on a piece of paper and ate it you would in more senses than one ingest the message. So that's why we inscribe birthday cakes. The candles, by the way, are blown out to indicate that the years they represent are gone. Some people add "one to grow on," but blowing out that particular symbolic candle seems to me to be ill advised. Now, those candies. You know the little, chalky hearts with red printing on them ("Be Mine," "I Love You," "Oh, You Kid!"). Read before you eat.

A TWO-WAY STREET

From "Cross Your Fingers—Superstitions Old and New" in *Fate* (2:1, 1974):

Ironically, a bizarre two-way traffic in superstitions has evolved. Among Nigerians the photograph of Charles Atlas, the world-famous American muscle man, is now popular as a strength fetish; while in London lucky cowrie shells sell in their thousands.

MASKS

People have always used masks in some magical rites. With hideous masks they frighten away demons—or take on their characteristics. They also use masks to resemble totem animals. The wizard depicted in the prehistoric cave painting at *Les Trois Frères* near Ariège in France dances in some sort of costume, with antlers and the ears of a deer, the face and eyes of an owl, the tail of a horse (also seen in a cave painting at Lourdes in the High Pyrenees), and the beard and body of a man just like us.

When the makers of demon masks for the Guro of the *Côte d'Ivoire* even today finish making one of their artistic masterpieces, they have to make holes in the side of the face to accommodate the strings that will tie the mask on. This, they believe, hurts the resident demon, who has to be apologized to and "consoled."

THE DRUMS! THE DRUMS! THE NATIVES ARE RESTLESS!

Drumming has become a significant part of neo-pagan rituals as it has of Robert Bly's "Iron John" masculinity events, feminist ring dances, and more. It adds joy and power to rituals because of the heightening effect drumming has upon the emotions and the way it binds congregants together. Today one can buy a booklet and tape on *Drumming from Your Soul* and practice at home, tapes of several Starwood Festivals and other gatherings, recordings of the Twilight Covening at EarthSpirit, as well as *Rhythms of Santería, Sacred Earth Drums, Sacred Spirit Drums,* Native America, Voodoo, Celtic, and many other kinds of music for rituals—the list goes on and on. There are inevitably Satanist and Wicca and Neo-Pagan and New Age jazz bands, blues bands, folk groups, garage bands....It's all part of the Age of Walkman Wicca. You can buy audio tapes of DIY magic made by Selena Fox (of Circle), Isaac Bonewits (who may have been the first modern to earn a doctorate in witchcraft, at, of course the University of California), Donald Michael Kraig (*The Secret of Magical Evocation*), and many others. There are privately made tapes that convey something of the excitement or ring dances at meetings of (say) The Radical Faeries and some lesbian covens that are extraordinary. Dancing to drum music (people say) can bring rain, "raise a cone of power" (the English witches tried this against Hitler in World War II but some of the elderly ones dropped dead), cement relationships, raise Hell....

If drumbeats, strobe lights, and people's own rhythms coincide, the effects can be spectacular and dangerous to the participants psychologically. Dancing to exhaustion can also produce notable results. Dervishes do it—and club kids.

Drums and other percussion instruments are an important part of magic in a great many cultures. The most famous instruments are perhaps the rattles of Egyptian and other mystery religions and the sacred drums of the Lappish shamans. But even the steel bands—black colonials whose

African drums were banned by uneasy British governors took to beating on oil drums—can create more than music.

The word *superstition* comes from the Latin *superstites* (survivors) and drums may well be the oldest survivors of magical practices that go back to the beginning of human time.

TEMPATUNGS

These are the beautifully carved if frightening poles with the faces of demons on them that people erect in Borneo to protect themselves. The tongues of the hideous faces loll and often are depicted as snakes. There are fierce fangs in the mouths.

We have always liked to depict evil as ugly—think of gargoyles—but ugliness can also frighten off evil. Asian depictions of devils and Asian anti-demon devices often are startlingly grotesque.

Another reason for the grotesque is that qualities of animals attributed to devils and demons make them look odd, with their glaring eyes, their claws, their scales, the heads of animals or combinations of animal parts that make up the Sphinx, the griffin, the chimera, and so on. From ancient Mesopotamia we derived demons with animal and bird heads (totems, probably). Consider the motley crew of Alu, Asakku, Etimma, Gallu, Ilu Limnu, Namtar, and Utukku (this last one with a lion's head). This chorus line of nastiness, for they are all demons of disease, appears on a row on terra cotta amulets which go back into the dim and ancient past. The lion, by the way, was early associated with strength and badness. Our Satan was associated with a lion.

THE STAFF OF LIFE

Bread is a part of many spells and charms and other superstitions. People used to hang up hot cross buns for luck; it was said the cross on them kept them from ever going moldy. I know a London pub where old buns have been hung from the ceiling for generations, and this year's doesn't take long before it looks as dusty as the ancient ones. We quote folklorist Margaret Baker elsewhere. She has a lot of say about bread, and we summarize:

A cross will form on a bucket of yeast set to sponge on Good Friday.

Bread or buns baked on Good Friday will grow stale but never moldy.

Crosses are needed on bread-making equipment to prevent witches from dancing on the "leavens laid" overnight.

Do not throw bread away or burn it or cut a loaf while baking other bread.

Everywhere it was believed that turning a loaf upside down made a ship sink at sea.

For light loaves, use rainwater from Ascension Day.

Gibbet (pierce with a skewer and hang up) a defective loaf and "keep it in the cupboard as a charm to prevent the repetition of this calamity at a later baking."

And one could go right down the alphabet with folk superstitions of the sort. Witches never put bread on their tables because it is the stuff out of which, with a magical incantation, the body of Christ is created.

From Fredericks (MD) in the summer of 1899, collected by Elisabeth Cloud Seip:

If your baking fail, burn a loaf. The witch will come to you, seeking to borrow. Give her nothing at all, bite, sup, nor greeting. For, if she obtain anything from you, no counter-charm of yours will avail to lift the spell.

IMAGES

Magic often works by parallels, and the witch's doll or wax figure with pins in it or melted to destroy the victim it represents is known by everyone. The tradition is very old. Here is a medieval writer, Bernardus Guilionis (1261–1331) on the making of images:

He made and fashioned two images of wax with lead from the [weights of the] fishing nets; molded the lead; collected flies, spiders, frogs, snakeskin, and a great many other things, and placed them under the images with conjurations and invocations to the demons. Then he drew blood from some part of his own body and mixed it with the blood of the frog and offered or gave it to the demons invoked.

To undo a spell a witch puts on you with an image, you must get hold of the image and destroy its power, or you can make an image of the witch and work magic with that. Destroying anything that stands for the witch destroys her.

TIBETAN MAGIC

In demon-infested Tibet, believers hang up in front of their houses an elaborate charm that consists of a ram's skull, a variety of jewels and other precious objects, dry food for demons, and pictures or images of a man, a woman, and a house. According to L. A. Waddell, *The Buddhism of Tibet* (1895):

> The object of these figures of a man, a wife, and a house is to deceive the demons should they still come in spite of this offering, and to mislead them into the belief that the foregoing pictures are the inmates of the house, so that they may wreak their wrath on these bits of wood and so save the real human occupants.

LUCKY OBJECTS

Some British families treasure lucky objects. The Luck of Muncaster is a bowl of green glass with enamel decorations, said to have held holy water for Henry VI of England and to have been presented by him to the Pennington family in the fifteenth century. The last of the direct line of the Penningtons gave up the ghost in the eighteenth century. The Luck of Burrel Green is a shallow brass dish and the rhyme goes

> If this dish be sold or gi'en
> Farewell the Luck of Burrell Green.

The Luck of Edenhall, which may be Elizabethan or even earlier, has a similar warning attached to it:

> If this cup should break or fall
> Farewell the Luck of Edenhall.

Before dropping the subject we might mention that in 1721, while visiting Edenhall, a visitor dropped the valuable cup! But luckily a servant standing by caught it in a napkin. A poem was written about that, Wharton's *The Drinking Match*.

NAMES WRITTEN IN BLOOD

You've heard about pacts with The Devil signed in your own blood, but here is a more cheerful topic and, in fact, writing in blood that really did take place, because it used to be believed that if you wrote in your own blood your own name and the name of someone you loved and then touched them with the paper on which these names were written the person would be unable to resist you. A little Christianity was added to this pagan custom when one recited the appropriate concomitant formula:

> In the name of the supreme Savior, in the same way that our names
> are put together here in blood so may your love be forever mixed
> with my love.

In another version of the superstition in Sweden and Norway, one's blood is mixed with the blood of a mole and the two names are written and the pious prayer uttered. If you do not wish to bleed for love, just give the girl two hairs from your body: a hair from your eyebrow and a pubic hair. That's from a Scandinavian "black book" of magic dated 1670 that once belonged to Gunder Gulbrandsen Rud (1814–1891) of Brandval, Norway.

The mixing of the blood of lovers is nowhere better or more wittily discussed than in John Donne's metaphysical poem, "The Flea." The poetic conceit, or complex metaphor, is there brilliantly worked out. Look it up; you'll love it.

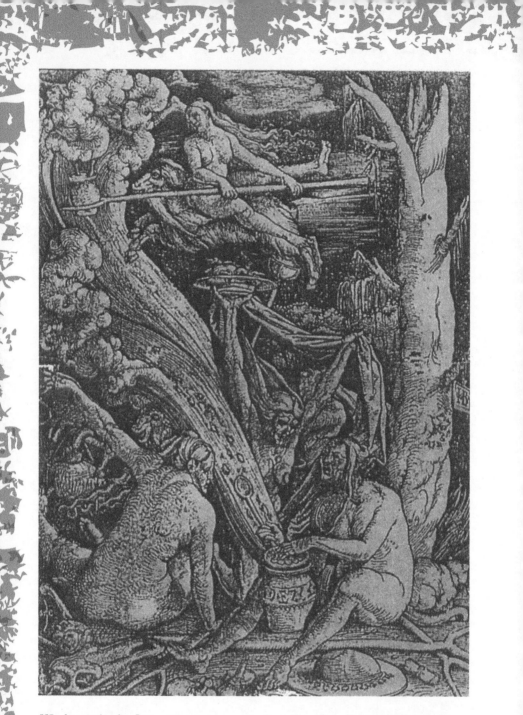

Witches make the flying ointment to get to the *sabbat*. Hans Baldung Grien, 1510.

5
More Magical Recipes

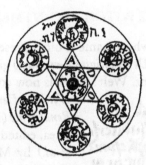

"THOSE POYS'NOUS PLANTS"

That is the phrase John Dryden used in translating a line from Virgil's *Eclogue 8*. From the very beginning, witches seem to have been making poisons as well as curative potions, and I think that the biblical injunction "Thou shalt not suffer a witch to live" would be better translated as "Thou shalt not tolerate a poisoner." In peasant life, the witches were often called upon to produce poisons and, I suspect, whenever one of their cures failed they might be blamed for worsening the patient's condition or hastening the patient's demise. Nonetheless, they knew chemistry and medicine and were scientists of a sort, though how they found their beneficial and baleful natural substances was often haphazard or governed by superstitions.

Here is John Dryden's seventeenth-century rendition of Virgil's classic Latin:

> These poys'nous Plants, for Magick use design'd,
> The noblest and the best of all the baleful Kind,
> Old Mæris brought me from the Pontick Strand;
> And cull'd the Mischief of a bounteous Land.
> Smear'd with these pow'rful Juices, on the Plain,
> He howls a Wolf among the hungry Train:
> And oft the mighty Necromancer boasts,
> With these to call from Tombs the stalking Ghosts;

And from the Roots to tear the standing Corn;
Which whirl'd aloft, to distant Fields is born.

BASIC WITCHES' OINTMENT

Johann Weir (a German whose name is often presented as Weirus because his great work is in Latin *De Præstigius dæmonum*) gives us the recipe for the famous Witches' Ointment. Weir's work is now conveniently reprinted as

A Witch on a Broomstick. This vegnette in the margin of Martin Le Franc's *Le Champion des Dames*, a manuscript of about 1440, may be the earliest depiction of a witch using this mode of travel to the *sabbat*.

Witches, Devils, and Doctors in the Renaissance (1991, translated by John Shea, edited by George Mora, MD, *et al.*) by Medieval & Renaissance Texts & Studies, a scholarly publisher (at the State University of New York at Binghamton) which also offers the like of Wayne Schumaker's editions of Dr. Dee's Conversations with Angels, Jerome Cardan's horoscope of Jesus Christ, the Abbot Trithemius on cryptography, and more, including four treatises 1590–1657 on natural magic and the beginnings of modern science: from Giordano Bruno, Tomasso Campanella, Martin del Río, and Gaspar Schott.

But you wanted that recipe. Here it is:

At the time of a waxing moon in Taurus, Gemini, Virgo, Libra, Capricorn or Aquarius, at the hour and on the day of Mercury—you see how closely astrology is involved—you mix these deadly ingredients

> *umbellifera*
> *frondes populæ balsamiferæ*
> *aqua aconiti lycotoni*
> *fuligo*

If you are not up in your Latin, that's hemlock (the stuff that killed Socrates), leaves of the poplar tree (also crushed), juice (or maybe tincture) of wolfsbane, and soot. This probably needs to be bound together with grease, but the fat of a murdered babe or a hanged man is no longer specified, though it crops up in certain other recipes. Some will accept the fat of an exhumed dead baby, and that way you could avoid a crime against another human being to start with; outrages against the dead, who basically have no legal rights, are generally unpunished. Or you could use an oil that did not involve bad cholesterol, I suppose.

Here is another noxious recipe from Weyer:

sium (cowbane)
acorum vulgare (sweet flag)
pentaphyllon (cinquefoil)
uespertitlioris sanguis (bat's blood)
solanum somniferum (deadly nightshade)
oleum (oil)

I must mention for completeness but omit for caution—and I hope nobody tries any of the recipes in my book or goes out of the way to seek recipes in other books which they then foolishly try—the awful recipe for witch's ointment in the eighteenth book of Jerome Cardan's *De Mirabilibus* (1557). Some modern monsters have actually followed that recipe. With them as with killers such as Jame Gumm in *The Silence of the Lambs*—he makes clothes out of women's skins, but not for the folklore reason, which called for the complete skin of an executed criminal to wear as a suit of invisibility—we pass beyond superstition to vicious madness.

Here is another flying ointment recipe, cited by Robert Ambelain and quoted in Maurice Bouisson's *La Magie: Ses grands rites, son histoire* (1958), translated:

human fat (or lard as a substitute)	100 grammes
first-quality hashish	5 grammes
hemp flower and poppy flower	a handful of each
powdered hellebore root and ground sunflower seed	a pinch of each

Rub it behind the ears, on the neck, in the armpits, etc. Stand naked before a statue of Baphomet after application. With all these hallucinogenics, you should fly! That's the *sabbat* preparation. For the "Satanic Electuary," the same book recommends:

aenanthol	3 grammes
extract of opium	50 grammes
extract of betel	30 grammes

extract of cinquefoil	6 grammes
extract of henbane	15 grammes
extract of belladonna	15 grammes
extract of ordinary hemlock	15 grammes
extract of Indian hemp	250 grammes
extract of cantharides	5 grammes
gum tragacanth	Q.S. [as much as you need]
powdered sugar	Q.S. [ditto]

Bouisson adds: "for external use only, extremely dangerous." I do not recommernd it it for any use at all; it would be mind-bending.

OBTAINING MATERIALS FOR MAGIC POTIONS

This is not as easy as some people might wish. You can buy herbs and dried flowers and various oils, in magickal shoppes, but eye of newt (not Newt) or bat's blood (which is dangerous, of course, if the bat is rabid) is harder to come by and, now that public executions are out of style, the hand of a hanged man is out of the question.

Johann Georg Godelman, a German with many magical recipes, in *De Magis* (Concerning Magic, 1591) defined sorcerers as those who cast evil spells, curse people and animals and crops, and generally do evil with, he says, potions which sometimes have among their foul ingredients bits of the corpses of hanged men.

In his time, hanged men were rather plentiful. In Germany the law also used the ax a lot, and burning. In England, there were a great many crimes for which hanging was prescribed, including consorting with gypsies or defacing a bridge. Public hangings were considered a sort of British spectator sport. The barbarous practice of drawing and quartering was not abandoned in Scotland until well into the nineteenth century!

BASIC WITCH'S KILLING METHOD

In an iron pot, burn chips of ironwood and throw in vervain and yarrow. To the ashes add oil and as you bottle it say the magic words:

Xapeth, Xith, Xandra, Zaped, Zapda, Zik

and when you put some of this mixture on the victim he (or she) will die. More simply, boil a black ant in oil. Put it in your enemy's food. Zap! All killing recipes require intense hateful concentration and bitter malice. Are you sure you can live with someone dying at your hand? If you desire anything besides good for everyone, you are (say those who claim to know about these things), one of the lowest spirits, trapped in a human body, and when you get to the second stage you will desire only good and in the third stage at last achieve perfection and be out of the rat race altogether. Some religions assert that you can expect to be punished after death for evil—or sent back in another incarnation of some sort to expiate your sins. If there is any truth in any of this or even if you just fear prison, then killing anyone does not seem like a wise decision. Why be stupid as well as unkind?

The basic premise of magic should be the same as the first and foremost item in medicine (in the Hippocratic Oath): "do no harm."

MAGICAL OIL NUMBER ONE

"David Conway," whose *Ritual Magic* I mention several times and whose work you will find exceptionally intelligent, gives this recipe for *oleum magicale no. 1*:

> This is a general-purpose ungent of proven efficacy. An almost indispensible accessory to magical work, it may be prepared in liquid (oily) or solid (cold-cream) base.
>
> > *Lycopodium clavatum* (devil's claw)
> > *Euphorbium* (wolf's milk)
> > *Clematis vitalba* (traveler's joy)
> > *Convolvulus arvensis* (cornbind)
> > *Sambucus nigra* (elder)
> > *Artemisia absinthium* (wormwood)
> > *Umbellifera* (poison hemlock)
> > *Atropa belladonna* (deadly nightshade)
>
> The plants called ramping fumitory and red-spur valerian may be used as alternatives to any of the first six ingredients, with henbane an alternative to either of the last two.
>
> *Clematis vitalba* and *Convolvulus arvensis* are advised for open-air work. Among other things they will, if combined with laurel leaf, assure you of good weather.

I would advise anyone to avoid all recipes with henbane, wormwood, or deadly nightshade, not to mention cantharides and cannabis and all illegal and dangerous substances, and so I omit the second recipe "Conway" gives for a magical oil, because it contains opium, cantharides, "Indian hemp," etc. Elder and elder flowers, on the other hand, have many good effects which are not dangerous and are medicinal (eye-bright, skin lotion, anti-wrinkle lotion) as well as magical (protection).

The only objection I have to the creation of magical medicines that without using any illegal substances perform wonders unapproved by the Food and Drug Administration is that while they may help the body they hurt the mind. To lose wellness (as people are starting to call health) is bad, but to lose your rational mind is worse. In my view, neither white nor black magic is victimless. Moreover, the "magical oil" that *works* deeply affects others who simply hear of that happening.

RECIPES FOR SOME OTHER MAGICAL OILS

You can buy in magickal shoppes all kinds of Success, Unhex, Power, Love, Attraction, and other oils, but really you can make your own. Here are a few recipes.

For Mistress of the House Oil, which you put on your hubby's shoes when he is not wearing them so that you can wear the pants in the family, all you need is:

> 1 oz. olive oil
> 1 teaspoon calamus
> a piece of devil's shoestring.

Shake well before using, as with all these concoctions.

For Unhexing Oil, you need:

> olive oil
> equal parts of sandalwood, myrrh, patchouli, and cinquefoil
> a pinch of salt (blessed, if you can get it).

Here's Van-Van Oil from the voodoo priestesses of NOLA (New Orleans, Louisiana): lemon grass and a pinch of salt in any oil, maybe an aromatic one. Put a little in your bath. It keeps hexes off you. Smells nice, too. Being nice, they say, means smelling nice. Think of the "odor of sanctity." That is, in fact, the odor of violets. But lemon grass is pleasant, too.

MAKING A MANDRAGORA

From "Paul Christian":

> Would you like *to make a Mandragora*, as powerful as the homunculus [little man in a bottle] so praised by Paracelsus? Then find a root of the plant called bryony. Take it out of the ground on a Monday [the day of the Moon], a little time after the vernal equinox. Cut off the ends of the root and bury it at night in some country churchyard in a dead man's grave [a bit redundant?]. For thirty days water it with cow's milk in which three bats have been drowned. When the thirty-first day arrives, take out the root in the middle of the night and dry it in an oven heated with branches of verbena; then wrap it up in a piece of a dead man's winding-sheet and carry it with you everywhere.

White Bryony
(*Bryonia dioica*)

He has a couple of other recipes for the Mandragora, one of which uses human semen (but the resulting creature then has to be fed regularly on lavender seeds and earthworms, and if it dies you are out of luck) and one of which involves bleeding a black hen at midnight at a crossroads and getting the help of the demon Berith. This last one works for only twenty years. If you want it, see pp. 402–403 in *The History and Practice of Magic* (1963), but the recipe described here is easier and does not require Berith. Berith is a duke of Hell who appears wearing a golden crown. He is handsome as a soldier in a red uniform on a red horse, but he lies a lot and his advice it is dangerous and foolish to take.

INGREDIENTS FOR CONJURING

Any part of a person (nail clippings, hair, saliva, semen, dandruff, blood), anything belonging to a person (especially underclothes), any image of a person (photograph, even from a magazine or newspaper), any pungent plant (such as cloves, cinnamon, garlic), certain plants associated with evil (devil's shoestring, jimson weed, hellebore), certain hallucinogens (including marijuana, datura, henbane), any poison, any preservative (salt, red pepper), certain juices (such as the juice of red onions), certain minerals (iron filings, lodestone, sulphur), any sharp objects (needles, pins, thorns, nails), any loath-some animals or parts of them (toads, snakes, scorpions), certain kinds of dust ("goofer" or graveyard dust, brick dust, powdered blue glass, poisonous dust of the devil's snuff puff ball), parts of certain other creatures (fur, skin, feathers). Red is good in counter-charms, perhaps because fire is cleansing; protective charms are often sewn into red flannel bags. Sometimes counter-charms are wet with whisky, smell of camphor or asafetida, etc.

TO MAKE A MAN BELIEVE HE WAS CHANGED INTO A BIRD OR BEAST

This recipe is from Giovanni Baptista Porta's *Magicæ naturalis* (in twenty books, published in his native Naples in 1589) and involves infusing man-drake, *solanum manicum*, belladonna, and henbane in a cup of wine. Porta notes that a lot of fun is to be had by making people think they have been changed in to hissing geese, fish, etc. "These, and many other most pleas-ant things," he remarks, "the curious enquirer may discover for himself; it is enough for me just to have hinted about how they are accomplished."

MEDICINE TO PROTECT YOUR CATTLE

To make your cattle immune for a year to the depridations of wolves and bears, take bones of wolves and bears and pulverize them, add salt, and feed the mixture to the cattle on a Thursday morning.

    Or you could recite this Norwegian spell:

*Jeg binder Bjørn i Grindele, Ulven grå med Bjørnen harde,
jeg binden hannom så fast i Jord som Borken på Linden gror.*

    I bind the bear to the gale, the grey wolf and the horrid bear, I bind them as fast to the earth as the bark is that grows on the linden tree.

MEDICINE TO KEEP THE CATTLE ON YOUR LAND

This, according to old Scandinavian custom, is cheaply and easily made. You just mix salt with mould taken from the underside of a stone in your pasture. As you do this you mention the names of the owners of the cat-tle. But you must then the first thing each morning spit; make sure the cows get some of this medicine before they eat anything else, and you must do this for 3 days running, saying:

Detta ska du ha   This you shall have
for at du ikkje ska trao   so that you do not stray
ifrao bø elder stø   from grazing place or pasture
og pao an manns teigemaol. and onto another man's pasture.

PAUL "CHRISTIAN'S" FLAPJACK RECIPE

This promises to get you enough money "to last to the end of the year," and among the greedyguts recipes for tons of gold and such found in so many magical handbooks it appeals by its modesty. Also, it's easy. You just have to make a dozen pancakes (flour, eggs, and milk) at home while in the church nearest your house the Mass of Candlemas is being celebrated. Candlemas is 2 February, so you'll get almost 11 months' worth of cash. How and from whom the recipe fails to specify. Maybe Ed McMahon will come to your door with a sweepstakes prize.

THE POWDER OF SYMPATHY

Today we have alleged psychics giving "readings" and advice by telephone, just as Edgar Cayce used to diagonose (and cure?) diseases by mail or by telephone. Maybe we have magic on the Internet or World Wide Web.

For curing in an odd way, however, it is hard to beat what was called the Powder of Sympathy. This strange powder convinced Sir Kenelm Digby (1603–1665), shrewd diplomat and hardheaded naval commander; Sir Kenelm was the serious scientist who discovered that plants need oxygen. In fact, Sir Kenelm is sometimes erroneously said to have been the inventor of the mysterious powder. The mysterious powder also got a boost from one of the leading physicians of the time, Thomas Sydenham, who was famous both in Britain and on the Continent but somehow was taken in by this thing which owed more to alchemy's superstition than chemistry's science.

Magic and science have long been linked. Witness Lynn Thorndike's magisterial 8 volumes of *The History of Magic and Experimental Science* (1923–1958).

Although I do not think it is worthwhile to offer you the recipe so that you can try curing wounds by rubbing a powder not on the wound but— get this!—the weapon, I think it worth noting the Powder of Sympathy here to underline the magical principle that potions and procedures (such as putting sharp objects on an enemy's footprints to wound him, as some Australian natives do) need not touch those for whom they are intended. Magic asserts that something done in one place can have notable effects far away. That's what you might call the Pin-in-Doll aspect. It is also the reason that concoctions need not be administered to the person one wishes to affect. This is also related to matters deserving more sensible investigation, such as thought transference, if not to astral projection, curses and cures.

A MORNING WISHCRAFT JAR

Put some lucky stuff in a jar (soaking in alcohol or oil) and keep the jar near your toothbrush. While you brush your teeth with the right hand, give the jar a few vigorous shakes with your left hand. Silently greet the day and wish for good things for yourself and your loved ones. Visualize yourself happy and successful all day long.

Into the jar you can place such common kitchen favorites as rosemary, thyme, nutmeg, and (if you have it) star anise. Some people keep the jar in the kitchen and shake it while the coffee is brewing. Or you can use other things besides or instead of those ingredients, such as *mojo* beans, High John the Conqueror, frankincense and myrrh, or ingredients especially suited to your current principal interests, such as love or money. For money use bayberry, lucky hand root, snakeroot, even the "money plant." We are working here to a great extent with Norman Vincent Peale's self-fulfilling optimism, which is no bad thing. If we are not attracting cheerful, helpful spirits we are at least keeping in good spirits.

TO KILL

If you are in such bad spirits you could kill, there are things nasty magicians say you can do. Mix cayenne pepper and vinegar and add to the heart of a wolf and a paper on which you have written the name of your victim, written in Dragon's Blood ink (a red dye from a tree, obtainable in *bodegas*, etc.). Seal all this in a jar with black wax. On Friday at the time of the Moon (midnight), shake the jar and curse your victim with:

N, I curse you unceasingly.
May your mind wander,
Your skin break out,
Your heart perish.

Say this ferevently and repeatedly. Then bury the jar upsdide down in a graveyard. Expect the end of your victim in thirteen days. As with all such magical operations, if it doesn't work you may have done something wrong. Trying to kill people is wrong.

You can also use an Amerind doll (as among the Ojibwa) or a voodoo doll with a pin stuck in the heart and a bit of red wool tied around the neck, and a whole lot of other little tricks. Or you could sew up a neat little *gris-gris* using valerian, a plant usually thought of as powerful because some-one—I have never been able to find out who, or on what authority—said valerian grew on the site of Golgotha, where Christ was crucified. You make that little package of evil of the powdered herb placed with a black feather and a black cat bone (or chicken bone), the left eye of a cat, the heart of a bat, and some Black Cross powder from your local occult supply house, all sewed up in a black bag. These frightening warnings of The End must be seen by the victim.

Warning: they are dangerous to try not only because there are sensible laws against cruelty to animals (humans included) but likewise because their evil may be directed back upon the sender. Maybe you have heard hippies talk of *karma*. Please note that a lot of black magic is said to bounce back on the perpetrator if she or he is not completely knowledgeable, so—once again—do not try this at home!

TO MAKE A PERSON GO AWAY

What is this? A ritual or a recipe? Anyway, in the seventies the reigning voodoo queen in New Orleans was a certain Lala. In his interesting book *Witchcraft, Mysticism and Magic* (1974) James Haskins, an expert on African-American language and folklore writes:

> Lala's charm for making a person go away is to melt a black candle and to knead the wax like dough. Write the person's name on a piece of paper four times frontward and five times backward. Roll the wax into a ball and put the paper into the middle of it. Then stick nine pins in the ball. Then get on the ferryboat and go out to the middle of the river and throw the ball in. Snap your fingers and say, "St. Expédite, make him go quick!" When the person does go away, you are to take a piece of poundcake to the statue of the saint in Our Lady of Guadalupe Church and leave it at its base. Lala says that the saying "I'm on pins and needles today" comes from the voodoo practice of sticking pins in an object representing a person.

St. Expédite is one of those saints like the (former) St. Christopher who made it to personhood and canonization though the origin was only a word or two. St. Expédite's statue stands in more than one Creole church, and if you seek one out you will see pieces of cake, fern, or other grateful offerings at his feet, just as you can see silver representations of eyes, limbs, etc., expressing thanks for cures, in Mexican churches, or thank you notices to St. Jude in the advertising columns of the daily papers. You don't have to be African-American or even Roman Catholic to turn to St. Expédite; a number of my white, Protestant, and Jewish friends in The Big Easy swear by his prompt delivery of results.

Here is another Get Out recipe from Haskins. Dry three pepper pods in an open oven. Put them in a bottle, top up with water, and place the bottle under your doorstep for three days. Then sprinkle the water around your house saying, "Leave here." People will get out and never come back. A Jewish friend of mine evicted tenants this way, so you can be Hebrew or Hoodoo; it works for anyone.

To make any little annoyance or evil go away, the Spanish have a very simple method. You extend the first and fourth fingers of each hand (as in giving the sign to ward off the Evil Eye) and you strike the table repeatedly while you say "*¡Lagarto! ¡Lagarto!*" That's "Lizard! Lizard!" Sounds silly, I know—but a lot of people do it. The kind of people who are sure that a statue of an elephant brings good luck—provided that its trunk is up.

HOW TO CREATE A ZOMBIE

The method of rendering a person practically indistinguishable from the living dead was brought from Africa long ago and now I want to give it to you, hoping of course that you will not put it to the test. The recipe calls for the *bokor* (witch doctor) not to use witchcraft but actually to poison the victim.

The horrific medicine for this consists of plants called *tremblador* and *desembre*, two kinds of stinging nettles (*maman guepes* and *mashasa*), spines of the *bwa* pine, skins of white tree frogs, crushed tarantula spiders, mashed *bouga* toads, and four species of that poisonous *fugu* fish that the Japanese like to dare to dine on (you need four different kinds of this fish whose tetrodotoxin is about 500 times more deadly than cyanide). To this you can add ground up human flesh *ad lib*. If you get too much of this bad medicine, you die. Maybe you wish you would. The desired effect is thirty to forty–five minutes of excruciating agony, inability to swallow or scream, asphyxiation, turning blue, paralysis, deathlike coma. You may or may not be able to hear people pronouncing you dead and making preparations for your funeral or you may be paralyzed and unable to complain when you find people carrying you off to the tomb to be buried alive. Not a cheerful fate.

But worse is to come. You are then revived by the *bokor* with a big dose of a foul mixture containing sweet potato and zombie's cucumber (*Datura stramonium*), sweetened with cane sugar or molasses. You are kept on a nasty diet, salt-free. Salt might wake you up out of the trance—or kill you. You live a miserable existence with backbreaking work. You drag yourself around, unable to think for yourself, a slave that can be given hard work and treated worse than a dog.

Some people believe that zombies are created by supernatural means with the help of the voodoo Baron Saturday. They say it is a magic spell and that when the body is carried past the place it used to live if it does not get up and run off it is in the grip of the magic forever. Not true. It's "worse life through chemistry." There is nothing magical about it at all.

TO IMPROVE BUSINESS

Try this: Mix together a pint of oil, half castor oil, half olive oil or corn oil. Add a binding agent such as gum arabic to make it thick, and toss in red mercuric oxide. You can add a beef heart (stuck with seven pins) to beef it up, if you wish, and a few rose petals. Some people like to put in seven packets of needles, but that seems extravagant. You burn this stuff.

FEVER

A magical cure says: Take a live pigeon, cut it in half, apply it to the body of the sufferer. I hesitate to mention anything which might lead to cruelty to creatures, but somehow people detest pigeons and yet love doves. Tom Lehrer some years back had an extremely popular song (at least in my set) called "Poisoning Pigeons in the Park."

LUCKY FEET

Wash your feet with a tea made of rattlesnake root.

HOODOO PROTECTIONS

Salt in the fire, red pepper strewn around, matches in the hair, Lucky Water, Sacred Sand, various candles—no need to have unwanted spirits around. Don't point at a grave: your finger will rot.

PHABULOUS PHARMACY

Many plants were known to the "wise women" for their medicinal powers, which were undoubted, but here are some with allegedly magical powers:

ALFALFA brings prosperity to the home in which it is stored

ALOES anoint the big toe (or phallus) of a lover with this

ANGELICA brings angelic influences, drives off evil

ANISE the odor improves consciousness

ASH TREE KEYS burn at Christmas to bring a year of prosperity

BETONY dispels depression, cures toothache

BITTERSWEET sleep on a sprig to get over a departed lover

BUCKEYE draws money to you

BUFFALO HERB worn in an amulet, it brings courage

BURNING BUSH carry a sprig for brilliant luck

CORIANDER like ASAFETIDA (but smells better!) wards off disease

DAMIANA carry some in a *gris-gris*

DILL smell it to cure hiccoughs

DOCK wash your store's doorknob with the yellow kind to bring "gold"

ELDER worn to ward off rheumatism

GALANGAL secrete some on your person when hauled into court

GINGER good for throat infections if placed under your pillow

HIGH JOHN THE CONQUEROR cures depression and brings luck

HUCKLEBERRY LEAVES cure depression (don't ingest them)

LAUREL sneak three leaves into the adored one's pocket and the person is yours

LAVENDER wear some in your jockstrap to be irresistible to women

LITTLE JOHN THE CONQUEROR carry some for luck and protection

LOVAGE attracts love, naturally

MAY APPLE carry this with your money and you'll always have money (of course!)

MAGNOLIA LEAVES placed under the mattress these improve your sex life

MOTHERWORT worn to increase nursing mother's milk

PENNYROYAL worn to counteract seasickness

PERIWINKLE powder, sprinkle under the bed, enjoy!

ROSEBUDS burn in your fireplace for luck, scatter at the roots to kill neighbors' trees

SAGE dried and held under the tongue, attracts women

SAMSON ROOT carry it in your pocket to increase virility

THYME burn it to fumigate the house of evil, put some in your bathwater to be sexier

AN ELIXIR OF POTENCY

Lady Wilde's recipe calls for steeping in a quart of brandy "and kept for use":

    2 ounces cochineal
    1 ounce gentian root
    2 drachms saffron
    2 drachms snakeroot
    2 drachms "salt of wormwood"
    rind of 10 oranges

This makes some kind of magic marmalade, presumably.

A LOVE LAMP

Cut a coconut in half and pour out the milk, then fill up one half of your *coco loco* with oil. You can add perfume or flower petals to make it aromatic or just use an aromatic oil. Drop in a couple of lodestones or magnets to "draw," and set fire to the thing.

    This is supposed to bring love to you, but you are asked to keep it burning until results are obtained and delay may be hard to cope with.

THE ELIXIR OF LIFE

Alchemists used to seek this avidly. From medieval recipes we get whisky ("water of life") and various monkish liqueurs (meant to contain many medicinal herbs), such as Chartreuse and Benedictine. Most alchemical instructions are incomplete or terribly obscure, but see what you can make out of this recipe for The Elixir. It's from Jean d'Espanet of Bordeaux. He scribbled it down in the seventeenth century.

    Take three parts of red earth, water and air, six parts altogether, mix them thoroughly and prepare a metallic paste like butter in which the earth can no longer be felt with the finger. Add one and a half parts of fire and place it into a thoroughly closed vessel and give it fire of the first degree for digestion. Then you prepare an extract of the elements according to the degrees of the fire until they are reduced to a solid earth. The matter becomes like a shining, translucent red stone and then it is ready. Put it into a pot on a moderate fire and moisten it by its oil, drop by drop, until it becomes fluent without smoke. Do not be afraid that the mercury will vaporize; the earth drinks up the humidity eagerly, because it is a part of its nature. Now you have the elixir ready. Thank God for His grace that He has granted it to you, use it for His praise, and keep the secret.

PANACEA

That means "cure-all," and witches swear by the efficacy of the following good-for-everything medicine. The ingredients, also, are not sumbul root (used to attract the opposite sex) or squill root (carried with a green lodestone to make your business prosper) or other things hard to find at the mall. You can do this with wine—red wine looks better in the final product, so choose a nice cab sauv—to which you add ground up fresh mint, honeysuckle, lily of the valley, groundsel, and heather. You cork the bottle well and let the ingredients steep a long while. Give the bottle a good shake now and then, but be patient and keep the bottle in a cool dry place, out of sunlight. It is possible to strain the liquid through a coffee filter after a few months and produce a more attractive medicine, a tablespoon of which ought to be enough at any one time.

Alternately, you can use gin instead of wine; you can even add extra juniper berries to improve the taste. Many modern witches make their tinctures with vodka. For brews, you can try using a handful of herbs to two cups of vinegar (but don't let it boil, just simmer). Vinegar substitutes for water, the result lasts much longer, and the medicine tastes bad enough to convince people it has to be good for them.

This universal medicine, like all medicines based on water, vinegar, alcohol, or oil, can do you no harm except keeping you away from early diagnosis; actually, with sufficient belief on the part of the patient, it works wonders. It is nowhere near as scary as the wine-based concoction that one Briton hit upon that was supposed to make anyone who drank it immortal. (It did not have all the poisonous snakes and other foul ingredients that the ancients used.) The fellow who devised it, an otherwise timid clergyman, for years kept it in a phial but was too afraid to drink it. Who knew what Jekyll and Hyde results it might produce? Finally, as an old man, he got up the courage to take it, but—as I tell the story elsewere which here I repeat—"it had evaporated."

VINEGAR

Just as tar water was once thought to be a very beneficial drink—they named Berkeley, CA after the fellow who touted this—so was vinegar, and in magical potions there was a lot of call for what is colorfully called Four Thieves' Vinegar. I make that out of a great many cloves of garlic and red wine vinegar, but I have also seen a recipe which asks you to put into strong cider vinegar—the white kind you can get from the supermarket, cheap— big handfuls of rosemary, lavender, sage, rue, mint, and wormwood, along with some camphor gum. You heat this up to the boiling point and when it is cooled down enough put this in a tightly-stoppered bottle and let it sit for quite a while; then you filter it and throw the herbs away.

SCRYING

There are ointments you can rub on to put you in the state to do prophecy or astral travel and so on, but you are better off with an object rather than an objectionable salve. You don't need a crystal ball. They are rare and expensive, and mere glass (which is what you usually see around) won't work well. All you need is something shiny, something to fix your attention on. Dr. John Dee (an Elizabethan occultist whose story I tell in another book) used a black basalt mirror that *conquistadores* had brought back from the Aztecs. Very romantic! But a bowl of water works equally well. Distilled water is even shinier.

Use a bronze vessel, the ancients cautioned. Nephotes advised the Pharaoh Psammetichos ("immortal king of Egypt," as he put it) to use "rainwater if you are calling up heavenly gods, seawater if gods of the earth, river water if [Egyptian deities of The Nile] Osiris or Serapis, springwater if the dead." Results with designer waters (especially from France as drunk by yuppies) have not been reported.

EGYPTIAN CHARM TO OPEN A DOOR

R. F. Hock's translation:

Take from a firstborn ram an umbilical cord that has not fallen from the ground, and after mixing in myrrh, apply to the door bolts when you want to open a door, and say this spell, and you will open it immediately. *Now this is the spell:*

"Open up for me, open up for me, door bolt; be opened, be opened door bolt, because I am Horus the Great, ARCHEPHRENEP-SOU PHIRIGX, son of Osiris and Isis. I want the goddess Typhon to flee; immediately, immediately; quickly, quickly.

This is more elaborate than what was required in *The Arabian Nights*. There, you will recall, you simply said: "Open Sesame!"

TO MAKE THE PEOPLE NEXT DOOR MOVE AWAY

Nasty neighbors? Get rid of them with urine, used in many magical recipes as a cleansing agent. Clean them right out of there with:

1 pint urine
3 tablespoons salt
3 black peppercorns
3 teaspoons powdered garlic
silver filings (file a silver dime or old spoon)
1 pint May water

Reduce this to one pint. On the night of the new moon, at midnight, sprinkle this on the neighbor's front doorstep. They will move soon.

If anyone tries this on you and you know what they are up to, you can wash your own doorsteps morning and night, twice a week for several weeks. These African-American recipes are highly regarded in the South.

FRONT DOOR PROTECTION

Here is a way to keep away practically anything annoying except salesmen and Jehovah's Witnesses. Wipe your doorstep with garlic juice on St. Lucy's Day or sprinkle it anytime with a mixture of:

salt
sugar
dirt from a baby's grave.

LIVING OR DEAD?

In ancient Egypt, before cellular phones and faxes and all the rest, it might be difficult to know if someone at a distance was alive or dead. The way you found out was this (in a papyrus translated by Morton Smith):

Make the inquirer throw this die in the bowl [which bears a magical inscription]. Let him fill this with water. Add to the [cast of the] die 612, which is [the numerical value of] the name of god, i.e., "Zeus," and subtract from the sum 353, which is [the numerical value of] "Hermes." If the number [remaining] be found divisible by two, he lives; if not, death has [him].

NECROMANCY: RAISING THE DEAD

Raising the dead was one of the most spectacular miracles attributed to Christ, and probably the major knowledge that Simon Magus was willing to buy at great cost from The Apostles. (They refused him the magical secrets and ever since the selling of church offices and powers has been called simony.)

In a French manuscript with a Latin title (*Girardius Parvi Lucii libellus de mirabilibus naturæ arcanus, Anno Domini 1730*), Grillot de Givry discovered the "necromantic bell of Girardius." On the bell you will note the *Tetragrammaton* (four letters standing for Jehovah, as if that were the sacred name, as it often is considered to be in ritual magic), the signs of seven planets (astrology entering into all this sort of magic) and the names of the tutelary spirits of each, Adonaï ("Lord," a substitute for the unspeakable name of God), and, on the ring, the name of Jesus. The manuscript says that Adonaï and Jesus must be inscribed on opposite sides of the ring.

The manuscript also shows a magician dressed in somewhat Roman fashion for the ceremony holding a chart of the same planets in his right hand and the bell in his left. This bell, the manuscript tells us, must be cast of lead, tin, iron, gold, copper, fixed mercury, and silver combined and also "at the day and hour of the birth of the person who desires to be in confluence and harmony" with it. Presumably this means the anniversary of one's birth, which (the manuscript adds) must be inscribed "between the handle and the upper circle."

Having cast the bell, you wrap it in green taffeta—the way silk protects the "power" of a pack of The Tarot, I suppose—and bury it in a grave in the cemetery for a week. This is to give the bell "emanations and confluent vibrations...mingled with the impression of the given character, this being what is needed." Later you exhume it and "ring it for your ends." Ringing it, it was said, you could call up the dead.

Once the Fox Sisters and other mediums got going, however, séances provided an easier way to talk with The Other Side, though I note that at séances the spirits have sometimes been asked to ring bells provided, or even to blow trumpets, make fingerprint impressions in soft wax, and so on—mostly with the assistance of a fraudulent medium. The dead are supposed to have spoken through trance mediums, to have dictated books and letters, to have transmitted music, and so on, but I have to be honest and say that nothing that ever has been alleged to have been spoken from The Other Side is, in my opinion, notable in content. If we can speak with the dead, there are more important questions to ask them than anyone has asked. It's about time they pitched in and were really helpful, considering they have so much free time.

Put away your Ouija boards and do not attend séances unless your religion—or lack of it—does not condemn these practices. Most western religions do, very strongly. Before you attempt to contact the dead by necromancy (as did The Witch of Endor, Dr. Dee in Elizabethan times, and even such bold associates of Lord Lytton's occult company as Éliphas Lévi in England in the nineteenth century) you had best read up on the great dangers that necromancers say they face.

Dealing with the dead can be deadly. Reading books is safer. In them the dead speak to us, and in languages we can understand and about experiences we can share.

WON'T YOU BE MY HONEY?

From a demotic magical papyrus (translated by Janet H. Johnson) how to make a woman love you (the subject of perhaps the earliest magical papyrus found, and certainly of a great many more), Egyptian style:

> A prescription to cause a woman to love a man; Fruit of acacia; grind with honey; anoint his [*sic*, your] phallus with it; and lie with the woman.

Another recipe calls for "foam from a stallion's mouth" rubbed on the phallus before insertion. Or salt, hawk's droppings, reed, *bele* plant pounded together (wet with a little wine, if necessary). Or weasel dung mixed with honey. Or you can just rub vervain on your hands and touch the person you want to attract. More elaborately, you can serve her or him tea containing the dessicated liver of a black cat, but be sure to use a black teapot. A basalt Wedgwood one from the eighteenth century would be elegant indeed. In some jurisdictions you might get in trouble with the law—over the cat. Herbal magic recommends that if your lover has walked off, she or he can be called back with archangel root (burn it and scatter the ashes to the winds), or draw another lover to you (with a conjure bag containing lavender, ash leaves, and red clover—but watch out! red clover brings pregnancy! or with vervain or vetiver perfume sprinkled around) or put some lady's thumb on a photograph of the one you want—this reportedly does not work with pictures of Tom Cruise taken from magazines—and bury the lot. To hold onto the one you have: basil leaves in the food, magnolia petals under the mattress, cumin under the bed, marjoram around the house, mistletoe hung up anywhere at any time (not just Christmas), dragon's blood and rose petals in your bathwater, orris root powder sprinkled in his socks, beth root, blacksnake root, periwinkle, queen's root, rue, rosebuds, senna, maybe henna in your hair. If you are in a hurry, you may wish to burn appropriate candles also to bring love or add the power of jasper and other supposedly powerful stones or just put ginger in all preparations to give them *oomph*.

By the way, don't make a first date on a Friday, however many herbs and other things you have going for you; say you are busy and suggest a weekday evening. Who wants to date a witch who has her (or his) weekends free anyway?

LOVE PHILTERS

Literature tells us much about the popularity of love philters, one of the best-selling items in the witch's pharmacopia. The simplest thing to do to get someone to love you, old recipes say, is to get the person in whom you are interested to swallow some of your semen or urine. Sneak it into their drink. The complex recipes are often extraordinary. From the occult manuscripts in the *Bibliothéque d'Arsenal*, where the nineteenth-century magician and historian of magic who called himself in print "Paul Christian" was librarian for a time, here is Pierre Mora's recipe from his *Zekerboni*:

> To the heart of a dove, the liver of a sparrow, the womb of a swallow, add the kidney of a hare and reduce it all to a fine powder.
> Add an equal amount of your own dried blood.

Mora assures us that "a dose of two or three drachms" will produce "marvellous success."

If you prefer a *Santería* method, try this: On the floor write with chalk the forename of the person you wish to attract left to right and his or her surname across that, up and down. (This does not work for persons you don't know but just caught sight of in the subway.) Sprinkle over this guinea pepper and ground ginger. Place a white candle over this and allow it to burn itself out. Then throw away the magical refuse into the street, and throw water on the chalk cross until it disappears.

CAN'T GET NO SATISFACTION?

Here's a magical way to attract love that does not involve the danger of swallowing some disgusting potion that could even poison you or drive you crazy. All you have to swallow is the story that this works. You can get the ingredients fairly easily, too. From my *Complete Book of Magic and Witchcraft* (1995):

> On a Friday sew into a green silk bag a mixture of vervain, southernwood, and orris root, crushed between sandstones. Wear the bag pinned to your undergarments, next to the skin.

TO ATTRACT POWER

Superstition, like religion, involves belief in the supernatural; magic undertakes to do something with these powers. To attract power, magicians can use many things. Among those things are flowers such as carnation, devil's shoestring, and gentian, and wood such as ash, ebony, and rowan.

To regain the powers of youth, people have bathed in the blood of sacrificed victims—the mad Hungarian Countess Bathóry was infamous for this—or less violently used anise, cowslip, myrtle, rosemary, vervain and other natural products.

TO GET A RAISE IN SALARY

Santería says to take roast anise seed, peanuts, and alum together, grind the result to a powder, and sprinkle this generously around your workplace.

GOLDDIGGER'S MAGIC

Another *Santería* practice: Get any single coin from the person you want to become your personal bank. Wrap the coin in threads of different colors and drop it into a jar of oil to which myrrh has been added. After a week, it will start acting as a powerful talisman for you and you can get all the money you want out of the person you have chose to be your *papi*.

INVOKING DEMONS

You can burn materials with noxious smells or hallucinogenic properties. You can use the holy name of God (anagramatized in disrespect), the names of heathen gods such as Abraxas (which is what *abracadabra* is all about), or mysterious phrases which may or may not include names (*Xilka, Xilka, Besa, Besa* is said to be powerful).

For Christians, the name of Jesus carries great weight. In His name many miracles were said to be effected. A pious tale, much repeated, concerned this holy name. Pope Sylvester I (314–335) was said to have killed an attacking bull by whispering into its ear the name of The Devil. Then the pope brought it back to life by whispering in its ear the name of Jesus. The legend was clearly designed to contrast negative and positive forces, evil and good. With an anti-Semitic twist, the story went that the bull was killed by whispering in its ear the name Jehovah and resurrected by whispering in its ear the name of Jesus, making the point that the Old Testament brought death, the New Testament eternal life.

There are also many forms of exorcism and even simple incantations to drive away devils and demons. The most obscure may be King Solomon's magic words which are said to have driven off terrifying demons that could tear the hearts out of human beings. Solomon intoned *LOFAHAM SOLOMON IYOUEL IYOSENAOUI.* No, I have no idea what that means. But in these matters you do not have to know what the magic words mean; you just have to get them absolutely right

No magic formula is needed to bring evil into someone's house. Just put salt under their rugs. Ordinarily salt drives away evil, but this is said to work. If you cannot get into the house, throw some dog grass or needles into the yard.

SOMEONE IS WALKING ON YOUR GRAVE

That's what they used to say if a person felt a sudden, unaccountable chill. The cure for this is cremation or burial at sea. Either one also foils attempts to make you into a zombie (as they say in Haiti) or a *wengwa* (as they say in Africa, whence the idea originated). Make sure your ashes are well scattered or your fish-nibbled body not recovered, however, because with leftovers sorcerers can cook up very unpleasant things.

The most unpleasant thing I have heard of following a cremation—common in Britain these days, for instance—involved a vicious widow. She had her husband's ashes made into an hourglass. "The bastard will work at last!" she vowed.

For that kind of nastiness I can think of no cure but the old custom in India of *suttee*. The widow was immolated on the funeral pyre of her hubby. Like everything in this book, I do not recommend it; I only mention it.

POPPETS

Poppets are dolls, figurines representing the victim whom the sorcerer wishes to injure. Magic is based on an principle from time immemorial "as above, so below" and often deals in two planes or attempts by some action to produce a parallel effect at a distance. So if you injure the figurine which represents your victim, with wax figure which you melt (causing the victim to weaken and die) or voodoo doll (into which you stick pins), and so on, you harm the victim by black magic.

The earliest case of witchcraft in England of which we have more than a mere mention involved the unpopular king Edward II (whose life and terrible death Christopher Marlowe memorably covered in a play). Edward of Carnavon (as he was called from his birthplace—he was made the first Prince of Wales) was born in 1284. He grew up quite unlike his robust and warlike father (Edward I, who ruled 1272–1307) and, though he accompanied his father on expeditions against the Scots, at the same time he took up with homosexual cronies such as Piers Gaveston. Edward I banished Gaveston from the kingdom, but when Edward II succeeded his father (1307) he called Gaveston back and, much to the annoyance of the feudal lords, showered him with honors. In 1308 Edward II was married to Isabella, who came to be a disappointed wife and "The She-Wolf of France." In the long run Isabella and her lover, Mortimer, had the king deposed and murdered (by having a red–hot poker thrust up his rear, which Isabella thought a suitable punishment). But even before that there were attempts to get rid of Edward II and his minions, and that is where the witchcraft came in.

Edward II made many annoying decisions and among these were some that alienated the citizens of Coventry. A few of them decided to do away with the king, two of the king's favorites (Hugh Le Despencer and another Despencer), and the prior of Coventry (whom the citizens especially disliked). They engaged the services of a sorcerer in Coventry (John of Nottingham) and his assistant (Robert Marshall, of Leicester) in 1324 to kill them all by necromancy. On 11 March John of Nottingham was given a down payment—with seven pounds of wax and a couple of yards of can-

vas—and right away, in a ruined house near
Shorteley Park (a mile or two out of Coventry),
he and his assistant starting making seven poppets. By this time the hit list comprised the king,
the two Despencers, the prior, two of the prior's
most egregious servants, and one poor fellow
called Richard de Lowe, who was going to be
the way the sorcerers test-ran their nefarious
scheme.

Around midnight on the Feast of the Holy
Cross, they stuck a large lead pin into the head
of the poppet representing Richard de Lowe. The next day the assistant
was sent to Richard's house and found him in great pain, screaming, having lost his memory and shouting "Harrow!" The sorcerers left him like
that until daybreak of Ascension Sunday, at which time they pulled the pin
out of the poppet's head and thrust it into its heart. On the following
Wednesday, Richard died. Now the conspirators were sure the magic
worked. The poppet with the crown on it might be next.

But they never got to apply it to Edward II and the other intended victims, for there was a falling out between John of Nottingham and his assistant and the latter (Robert Marshall, as we have noted) went to the
authorities and revealed the whole plot.

So much is history. But here, just as a trial would have produced a lot
of documentation, the whole matter was forgotten. Only the unfortunate
pawn in the whole business (Robert de Lowe) died. The case of intended
regicide and mass murder appears to have been dropped. It is possible that
the authorities were afraid of getting too close to John of Nottingham, who
presumably was a very dangerous man.

TO AVOID BEING HEXED

As bits of you (hair, fingernail clippings, a photograph which may contain
a piece of your soul—which is why those natives you encountered on your
holiday didn't want your camera aimed at them) can be used to hex you,
so the same burned with something the demons hate, such as sulphur—
but do this outdoors!—will keep them from bothering you. This must be
done before anyone launches a spell against you. If that has already been
done, as is the case with trying to protect your property from judgments
after a suit for money has been filed against you, you need professionals,
counter-acting witches, aggressive lawyers, etc.

WITCHES' BREW

Shakespeare's hags in *Macbeth* famously are putting together a horrid stew with such ingredients as eye of newt and bits of "birth-strangled babe." A conventional witches' brew calls for

> flesh of unbaptised babes (or hanged criminals)
> frogs (poisonous toads are sometimes called for)
> black millet (black being the color of evil)
> "magic powder" (we'd better leave that unidentified.)

SPIT

An all-purpose magical necessity. Cheap, too. Hate someone? Spit on them, or their photograph or a doll made to represent them. Spit on pins and sew them in someone's yard. Crossed by a black cat or see anything else frightening? Turn around three times, and spit. For more strength, spit on your hands. Some European spells ask you to recite them after spitting in your fist. To make someone see you in a more loving light, kiss their eyelids. To make the blind see, apply your spittle; Jesus Christ used this method. *Santería* uses spit in perfumes women apply to attract lovers. After you yawn, to avoid evil, spit three times. Threatened with the evil eye? Spit three times. Some add: on your fist.

INVISIBILITY

Haven't you heard people say, "I wish I could have been a fly on the wall when *that* was going on"? Invisibility would allow people to do many wonderful things, and many are the objects and recipes for making oneself invisible. In various concoctions for the purpose we hear that sorcerers used amaranth, chicory, eidelweiss, fern, heliotrope, mandrake root, mistletoe, poppy, and wolfsbane. Or you can carry under your right armpit "the heart of a bat, [the heart of] a black hen, or [the heart of] a frog."

SUCCESS

The superstitious burn colored candles for this purpose but also use in various ways such natural products as (lemon) balm, cinnamon, clover, ginger, High John the Conqueror (a useful herb), rowan (a tree often planted, like yew, in graveyards), wahoo, and winter's bark. With these and other herbal spells, you place a selection in a bag—having gathered them at certain rigorously appointed days and times of day—and burn or bury the bag. While you do this you visualize strongly a wished-for outcome. The ability to concentrate and to visualize is often crucial in working magic which, of course, works on yourself first of all. Or you can open the bag and strew the contents to the winds in some appropriate (often high) place. You must do that in this order: north, east, south, west. Or you can call upon water sprites and such by throwing the herbs into streams, lakes, the ocean, all the while concentrating on your intention.

WEATHER WISE

In my extensive section on witchcraft in Scandanavia in *The Complete Book of The Devil's Disciples*, I mention a number of recipes. Here I'll repeat the fact that sorcerers used to sell to Vikings and other sailors bits of rope with three knots in them. Unloose one knot for a little wind, a second for more, and a third for quite a lot. It was also possible to stay onshore, of course, and harry sailing ships with tempests. In *Macbeth*, the witches say that their power along these lines, however, is limited. The sailor on whom they seek revenge cannot have his ship lost, merely "tempest–toss'd." The Scottish monarch (James I of England by then) for whom Shakespeare wrote the "royal play" of *Macbeth* was a firm believer that Scottish witches were quite capable of creating disastrous storms at sea. He would have told you he knew that from personal experience as well as hearing it from the mouths of witches themselves at whose trials he personally presided. When James wrote his *Demonologie*—the other book with which his name is forever connected was The Bible—he had no doubts whatever about the powers of witches.

HIGHLY INCENSED DEMONS

One cure for devils and demons domestically is burning sweet-smelling incense. The inhabitants of the underworld like stinks: sulphur, asafetida, stinkling gladdon, and such. They detest sweet smells which rise, like prayers, to The Almighty.

Ritual magic makes much of incense to attract or repel spirits, and the smoke of incense gives apparitions something with which to make an appearance. At fake ceremonies, I have noted, smoke and mirrors are as useful as in politics. For one thing, burning hallucinogenic substances, such as datura or henbane, gets the observers all confused. They are a compelling reason to stay away from such rites. For another, I have seen very clever slides projected on columns of thick smoke, and movies are even more impressive.

Before smoking was banned in theatres, I sometimes used to see the show through a pall of tobacco smoke. At séances and rituals, though, I strongly object to tacky muslin "ectoplasm" and deplore figures projected on smoke. Whatever can be done in the dark ought to be possible in the light, and if the medium or the magician insists on the cover of darkness, be rightfully suspicious. Smoke out the frauds.

BATHING

To get the beneficial powers of various herbs, believers in the occult add them to bathwater. There are a number of magical cleansers to remove bad spirits, bad influences, etc., the simplest of which may be basil among herbs and vinegar (in which uncooked cloves of garlic have been steeped for a long time) among liquids. Anything you add to your bath that you truly believe makes you smell sexy will increase your confidence with the opposite sex—or the same sex, if your tastes run that way. You can add coarse salt to the herbs and put in some food color—the color chosen for the appropriate intention, such as blue for calm, green for hope, etc. You can use the herb and salt mixture as bath salts. Here is a New York recipe for a *Santería* bath additive in the words of Migene Gonzalez-Wippler, the leading expert:

> A bath is made with five bunches of parsley, five sticks of cinnamon, imo macho, rosura de venao, anis seed, amanza guapo, a bit of quicksilver, and honey. The bath is taken once a week for best results.

I wouldn't use any preparation containing mercury (quicksilver) if I were you. If some of the other ingredients sound strange to you, they will be familiar to your local *bodega*. In lieu of mercury, how about iron filings that have been magnetized? Magnets are part of many charms to attract, naturally.

A simple magical water can be created by "solarizing" it: just put it in a bottle in the sun. Better still, add some ordinary water to a bottle at the first full moon each month; in twelve months you will have a bottle of water that some magicians are convinced is very powerful. They "charge" it with intentions and invocations as they use it in small quantities. To bathe in water prepared like this requires too much preparation and storage. There are many baths you can take with this or that oil or this or that herb (or combination of herbs) added to the bathwater. There are little booklets on this kind of thing at your local witches' supply house or you can order by mail from various publishers.

I do not think it worthwhile to take up space here with lists of oils and herbs to use (most often to become more sexually attractive or to wash off evil influences). Just put a little vervain in your bathwater and see what happens. Or float a few leaves of bay or basil on top of the bathwater. Or periwinkle—but do not pick it from a grave because superstition says that will cause the dead to haunt you for a year. Moreover, periwinkle must be gathered only on the first, ninth, eleventh, or thirteenth day of the moon; in fact, there are elaborate rules for gathering many plants for magical uses. Pine can be obtained any way, any time, and is a good scent for purifying. Really spectacular effects have been reported for the use of attar of roses (which is very expensve) and likewise not bathing at all and letting natural musk and other sex-attractors do their work.

What works best is, of course, whatever "flavor" gives you the most confidence that your wishes will be granted.

HOW TO MAKE AMULETS, CHARMS AND TALISMANS

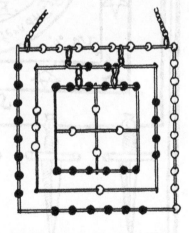

That is the title of a practical, well illustrated book by Deborah Lippman and Paul Colin (1974). In it you will find precise instructions on how to make the Chinese *ho tu* diagram made into a pendant of red and white beads: "The red beads will help to keep away demons, and the white will protect the wearer from the Evil Eye."

These authors also give detailed instructions on how to make other protective amulets (including Ashanti stakes to put in your garden to protect your plants), objects to attract love (such as the Runic Love Charm) and ward off hate, Buddhist charms, Egyptian talismans, the Benkert Bean Charm, pillows with Amish hex signs on them, the famous wooden cross with colored yarns on it (the *ojo de dios* or "Eye of God," even a Martian Amulet (but that's for the astrological influence of Mars, not to keep you safe from UFO abductions!), and much more in all sorts of materials.

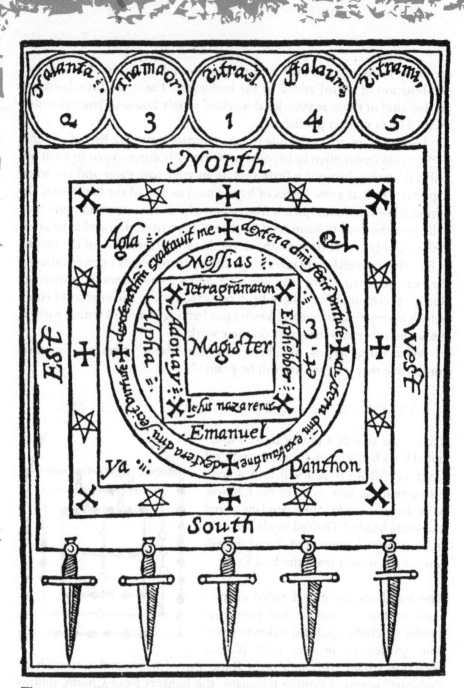

The conjuror (*Magister*) stands in the center to summon the Five Kings of the North (whose names are inscribed at the North).

6

Rituals and Ceremonies

MAGICAL RITUALS TODAY

There's a distinction to be made between Ritual Magic and magic rituals. The latter are usually, in America, mostly of recent and imaginative—if occasionally learned and synchretic—origin. These last serve the needs of small and somewhat independent groups of practitioners of Goddess worship, Wicca, and other neo-pagan beliefs. In this chapter I shall put a greater emphasis on the traditional (and complex) Ritual Magic. I do that because if you want a neo-pagan ritual you can pretty much make up your own, although I shall cite a few examples on which you can pattern your creations. As the old Andy Hardy movies used to say, we have the barn so let's put on a show—a musical, with dances and striking costumes.

The bibliography of neo-pagan rituals in America is easily assembled. It offers something for catholic (not just Catholic) tastes. Rituals are not often described as they are denounced by those who, for instance, are frightened by *The Organization of Paganism...* (1994), a little insight into networking in West Central Florida; or Loretta Lee Orion's *Revival of Western Paganism in the Contemporary United States* (1993); or by those who are writing scary books about Satanism rampant or who are handing out religious tracts. Carl A. Raschke's *Painted Black* (1990) and other sensational surveys of "how Satanism is terrorizing our communities," however, are seldom or never written by anyone who knows much if anything about ceremonies conducted. They do not attend them. It's like trying to write the history of the Ku Klux Klan (those whites in knight satin, as someone says) from the movies.

239

T. Newton's *The Demonic Connection* (1987) goes well beyond Satanism in Britain to warn of an "international black magic conspiracy"—but he and his informants have not attended local or foreign rituals nor published full descriptions. In Costa Mesa, California, occult books and tapes pour from Walter Ralston Martin; his press publishes the One Way Library. We might say that each side in the controversy is creating a One Way Library, misunderstanding, even misrepresenting, the other side—and nowhere spelling out the rituals, giving the text and choreography. Except for the earth-loving, gentle souls in gay and feminist Wicca. They publish their made-up chants and circle jerks, often as sweetly homebred and half-baked as the marriage vows and commitment rituals we used to see in the summers of love in the sixties.

We note this elsewhere, but it is worth repeating here: Wiccan rituals have no great historical provenance. Don't believe me? (I know there will be great opposition to the statement from some quarters.) Here's Eamon Duffy reviewing Ronald Hutton's standard new history of the ritual year in Britain, *The Stations of the Sun*. Duffy in the prestigious *Times Literary Supplement* for 11 October 1996, writes of

> the invention by one of the more dubious early twentieth-century members of the [British] Folklore Society, of an entirely bogus "ancient" pagan religion, "Wicca," which now has many modern practitioners.

Of course there is nothing wrong with a pagan religion being created at any time—unless you are a Christian, a Jew, or a follower of Islam and are therefore the enemy of infidels—but the "Old Religion" is really a New Religion, and the fact might as well be admitted.

One thing that you cannot ever expect to be confessed publicly is Satanism (which is not at all the same thing as nature worship but does set up another god, as does The Goddess religions). You cannot expect real Satanists to surface with directions for sacrificing a baby. Some San Francisco "Church of Satan" devotees might titillate with pseudo–posturings, a hint of sadomasochistic orgies, but not murder and mayhem. I won't quote from F. T. Rhodes's rituals in *The Satanic Mass* (1960). If you want them, go there yourself—and not to anything by Anton LaVey. But even play-Satanists are "healthy to stay away from," as a wise woman I know has said to me, and I believe her.

You can find, if you look hard enough, real rituals that at least lay claim to tradition and to serious power, and some of these I shall print for you here. Remember, I do not advise any reader to perform these rituals. *Don't try this at home*.

If you are in fact seriously interested in Ritual Magic and really want to be a Merlin, a Faustus, or a Gandulf, you will have a difficult road to follow. You can begin with something like Tanya M. Luhrmann's reportage in *Persuasions of the Witch's Craft* (reprinted 1991) and "David Conway"'s excellent primer *Ritual Magic* (reprinted 1978) and then try to locate Israel Regardie's exposure of the ceremonies of The Order of the Golden Dawn, the works of A. E. Waite (who was a leader in that movement), the works of the greatest ritual magician of the nineteenth century, who called himself "Éliphas Lévi," and more. In this corner of the arcane you will encounter more and more obscure and fraudulent, more and more difficult and difficult even to find, works of the sorcerers. They are chiefly in English, French, and German. They derive much from dead (Rosicrucian) and living (Freemasonry) ceremonies and they were written down, and very likely thought up, in the last couple of hundred years. No matter how patently idiotic they seem, many pretend to great antiquity and power. All magical ceremonies reflect the fundamental fact about magic: magic is an attempt to advance or protect the self by what Daniel Lawrence O'Keefe calls "counterattacking the moral order."

A magical ritual may be as simple as crossing your fingers or holding the thumb of each hand in the hand of the other. It may be as complex as one of the ceremonies, with astrology, incantations, and elaborate paraphernalia, described in "David Conway"'s *Ritual Magic* or Donald Tyson's *Ritual Magic* or one of the other traditional and arcane magical rituals. Even the leading experts on magic have seldom, some never, conducted or attended one of these ceremonies. The longest-running and most widely attended magical rituals are connected with the leading religions, the Roman Catholic Mass, with transubstantiation being possibly the commonest miracle performed.

Some ceremonies even derive from a personage whom I think never ever existed: King Solomon. That's right, the biblical hero, for whose existence there is absolutely no archeological evidence whatever. I think he's a literary invention in The Bible, like Ruth, not an historical person, like King David or Jesus. But the fact that magic was attributed to him and magic was attempted in his name is very significant. I think the same is true of many of the black magic rituals that we are asked to believe were wrested from and can command the evil power. Jesus commanded them. Can a man? Or a woman? I think as well that in considering performing high magic we are perhaps succumbing to the temptation that Satan offered

Jesus: great reward. But do not cast yourself down from the heights. Even Jesus wouldn't do it. Do not in pride presume on the mercy of God if you play with The Adversary.

Think again about what happened to Dr. Faustus. "A sound magician is a mighty god"—but how did he end? What is it you *really* want?

ASMODEUS

Asmodeus is a terrible demon derived from the Persian *A_shma daêva*, meaning "demon of lust," said in the *Avesta* to rank second only to the demon king Angromainyus. In Sebastien Michaëlis's *Histoire admirable de la possession et conversion d'une pénitente séduite par un magicien* (1612) Asmodeus is reported at his evil habit of leading nuns astray. Father Michaëlis assures us that Asmodeus tempts through luxury, Beelezebub through pride, Astaroth through vanity and sloth, and so on.

Asmodeus figures largely in Jewish tradition; there he is credited with breaking up marriages and leading people into debauchery. Later he is said to appeal principally to the *magas,* or pleasure-seeking women engaged in witchcraft.

In The Bible, Tobias is guided by the Archangel Raphael to use the liver and the heart of a great fish (which attacks him in the Tigris) to drive off Asmodeus. Then the archangel took Asmodeus "and bound him in the desert of Upper Egypt."

The ritual of burning a heart and a liver occurs in various religions.

HOW TO MAKE A PACT WITH THE DEVIL

Like all the information in this book, this information is not provided in the hope that you will attempt to use it. "For entertainment only," as the psychics say on TV.

There are many ways of making a pact with Satan, and there are whole books about the practice. All you really need to do is to renounce your Christian baptism, the Christians say. If you want to hear about something a little more elaborate—and I do not want to venture into describing foul rites, deeds signed in blood, human sacrifices, and so on—hear this:

Go to a churchyard at midnight and in a place where you will not be disturbed draw a magic circle. Traditionally, this is nine feet in diameter. If you do not have a consecrated magical sword, use a birch branch. Within the circle draw elaborate anagrammatized names of God, etc., or simply two large Xs, which are quite sufficient. Take a handful of wormwood in each hand—you must also be holding The Bible in your left hand—and toss the left handful down, the right handful up. Say the Lord's Prayer backward. (You can read it out of The Bible; it's in Matthew 6.) You now have sold your soul to Satan. On your way home, leave your Bible on the steps of an church. You will not be needing it for seven years—or after that.

STATE OF MIND

Certain ceremonies can put us in an elevated state of mind, give a feeling of wholeness, or holiness. Some rituals are performed in states of great excitement, or trance. At least one scholar said that the shamans of the Lapps actually lapse into what he described as "northern hysteria." It is well known that some rituals in Tibet put the practitioners into extraordinary states of consciousness, with unusual powers over mind and body. It was alleged that St. Ignatius Loyola had to be held down by tugging at his chasuble when he offered Mass: at the consecration, he tended to levitate. I have seen incontrovertible proof of people who claim to be able to contact The Beyond in which, though I beg leave doubt they really do contact any such thing, most certainly do drop their body temperatures by four or five degrees while everyone around them stays at 98.6, normal, and they do it in seconds.

The most interesting aspect of magic ritual to me is still not seriously studied, and that is not the physical changes but the harder to measure alterations in the state of mind of people who are—or think they are—performing magic, and the effect of that state of mind upon the spectators.

A wonderful *curandero* ("witch doctor" does not seem to be the best translation of the term in this case) whom I have seen work in Mexico, does indeed produce apparently miraculous cures in a lot of his patients. I have observed, however, that he sometimes cheats. He produces a pebble or a thorn or even a tumor from the patient for all to see, but these are things which he has in his preparation secreted on his own person and brings forth by sleight of hinad. I've confronted him privately about that.

"Why do you do that?" I asked him.

"It is necessary for the patient, and sometimes the bystanders, who have an effect inevitably upon the patient by their very presence and reactions," he tells me, "to see something palpable. Something they can hold. I give it to them. It is not part of the cure. It is, you might say, part of the operations. When you do not operate on the body but on the mind, these things are necessary. I do not think I could operate on an anaesthetized patient, the way surgeons do. I could not even approach such a patient in my necessary state of mind, nor connect to his or hers. I am the facilitator of the patient curing themselves. We must be in appropriate states of mind and consciously cooperate."

IT'S DIFFICULT TO GET GOOD HELP

Here is an ancient Greek procedure for getting a demon to help you with your magic, live in, and "eat and sleep with you."

You take "two of your own fingernails"—I hope clippings only—and "all the hairs from your head" and a "Circaean" falcon. Even E. N. O'Neil, who translated this from a Greek magical papyrus, isn't sure what that means, so just use an ordinary falcon. You drown the falcon to "deify" in a mixture of honey and the milk of a black cow. You wrap the falcon, the fingernails, and the hair in an undyed piece of cloth. You write on a papyrus the following:

A	OOOOOOO
EE	YYYYYY
EEE	OOOOO
I I I I	I I I I
OOOOO	EEE
Y Y Y Y Y Y	EE
OOOOOOO	A

To the papyrus strip add uncut frankincense and old wine. Drink the honey and milk before sunrise "and there will be something divine in your heart." Make a shrine of juniper wood and install the falcon as a statue. Crown the shrine and make an offering of non-animal foods and old wine. Before you go to bed, make a sacrifice to the bird and recite the spell:

A EE EEE OOOOO YYYYYY OOOOOOO, come to me, Good Husbandman, Good Daimon. HARPON KNOUPI BRINTANTEN SIPHRI BRISKYLMA AROUAZAR [RAMESEN] KRIPHI NIPOUMICHMOUMAOPH. Come to me, O holy Orion, you who lie to the north, who cause the currents of the Nile to roll down and mingle with the sea, transforming them with life, as it does man's seed in sexual intercourse, you who have established the world on an indestructible foundation, who are young in the morning and old in the evening, who journey through the subterranean sphere and rise breathing fire, you who have parted the seas in the first month, who ejaculate seeds into the sacred figtree of Heliopolis continually. This is your authoritative name: ARBATH ABAOTH BAKCHABRE.

When you are dismissed, walk backwards and shoeless and eat the prescribed food after you come face to face with your new companion, the god. This rite requires complete purity. "Conceal, conceal the [procedure and] for [seven] days [refrain] from having intercourse with a woman."

It is worth remarking that purity, achieved by fasting and cleansing oneself and abstaining from women, is often demanded of magicians. Sometimes they must go for long periods of preparation with only tiny meals once a day and no meat, no sex, sleeping on the ground, no connection with the everyday world.

THE DIVINIG DISC FROM PERGAMON

The ancient city of Pergamon gave us parchment, but no written instructions, unfortunately, are available anywhere for the ritual the magicians of Pergamon used with this bronze object here illustrated, now in a Berlin museum. We know only that it dates from about the third century, that Greek letters and magical symbols abound on it, and that there is even an Egyptian letter and astrological symbols (for sun and moon). It and other magical objects found with it in 1899 are described in T. Hopfner's study  of Greek and Egyptian magic, *Greichische-Ägyptischer Offenbarungszauber* (1924, p. 146). In this case, what the ritual was we do not know, and this bronze disc can stand for many other magical objects that have been discovered whose ritual use is unknown.

RITUALS IN EVERYDAY LIFE

The commonest in our culture are probably the Sign of the Cross, crossing one's fingers, and throwing spilt salt over the left (that is, sinister) shoulder. The commonest rituals of avoidance may be turning around (usually three times) in place, turning one's coat inside out, or being careful not to step on the cracks in the sidewalk ("break your mother's back"). Every culture has its superstitions and its rituals of these types and often hardly notices them while, at the same time, there are extremely important and elaborate ceremonies used for various magical purposes. A thorough study of Sir James Frazer's magnificent *The Golden Bough* convinces one that there are interesting examples both of uniqueness and of cultural parallels or transmissions.

WHERE THE FISH ARE BITING

Right into modern times, in Scandinavia very ancient methods of magic are used to determine where the fishing will be best. Superstition has always been rife, in every culture, in connection with occupations that are dangerous or subject to chance. In pagan times the names of crews would be written around the edges of a plate filled with sea water and bubbles might indicate which would do best out fishing. In the eighteenth century, on the first night of Christmas, a manuscript says, you are to fill a dish with sea water. From the bubbles, etc., on the surface next morning you will be able to tell about the best fishing places after Yule; it is a sort of magical map. Or you can trace a little map on the bottom of the plate before adding the sea water and see things even more clearly.

"IT'S ALIIIIVE!"

It may be difficult for some people to believe that other people have through history fully believed that devils and demons can be summoned and manipulated by magic, that some rituals actually work. Some people still, in the modern world, are quite certain that rituals do work; some claim to have proved this by personal experience. Others treat this as they treat reports of abduction by UFOs; that people believe is undoubted, that they are utterly deluded is assumed.

Let us look at an alleged expert of a little while back, Johann Joseph von Görres (1776–1848), author of four large German volumes 1836–1842, short title *Mystik*. These received wider attention in French translation by Charles Ste.-Foi. The first French edition was 1854, the second 1862, and looking at those dates you may find it incredible that Görres believed implicitly in demons, and human intercourse with them, in vampires and the evil eye, in diabolical possession and exorcism, in familiars, *sabbats* and black masses. As for rituals:

> Why should they [demons] be deaf to conjurations, to the entreaties of magic, to the charms of its mysterious words or even to its threats? The moment we suppose that spirits cannot resist these things, theurgy springs up as of itself and develops into all its forms.

He admits that charlatanism and delusion exist and the invocations often fail, but he is sure some succeed. He admits that a lot is pure human invention, but he adds that many effective invocations may have been learned from demons. He believes that there are actual ways you can summon The Devil. One way is to paint his picture on the wall, and he may come. He comes, says, Christopher Marlowe in *Dr. Faustus, per accidens*, not because we have any power to command him but because he sees an opportunity to damn another human soul. "Misery loves company," says the devil Lucifer sends to Faustus; The Devil is always ready to "enlarge his kingdom."

RITUAL TO BRING THE SPIRITS OF THE AIR

Well, you do not have to bring them. Many of the doctors of the church, not to say the writers on demonology, have assured us that the universe is jam-packed with invisible spirits, as I detail in *The Complete Book of Devils and Demons*. However, if you "fear nothing" and are crazy, you may wish to see some spirits in person. Here is how that is accomplished, according to the mysterious *grimoire* of *The Count of Gabalais*.

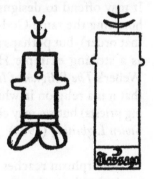

Retired to a quiet place where you will not be disturbed, to the brain of a (black) rooster add dirt from nearest the coffin in a grave, oil of almonds, and virgin (bees)wax. Knead these materials together and wrap the result in a piece of virgin parchment on which you have written the magic words *GOMERT* and *KAILORETH* and added "the character of Khil." Light this object and you will (the grimoire assures us) see prodigious if unspecified effects, "the vision of the spirits in the air."

A. E. Waite calls this "Black Magic in a nutshell, a combination in equal proportions of the disgusting and the imbecile." He adds that it has been "exceedingly popular, and is to be found in most of the Grimoires."

The demon Vassago is said to declare "things past, present, and future" and is invoked by these signs in the *Lesser Key of Solomon* both in black magic (left) and white magic (right).

To save the curious the trouble of summoning spirits, the Pseudo-Agrippa (ripping off the reputation of the great Cornelius Agrippa von Nettesheim, 1486–1535, reputed a magician) tells us that the Spirits of Saturn are tall and thin and angry, those of Jupiter are not so tall but choleric and horrible, those of Mars tall and choleric and also horrible, and on and on. Who wants to deal with this lot?

THE *KIVA* ON THE INTERNET

The Chetl Ketl Great *Kiva*, a subterranean ritual chamber of the Caco Anasazi Indians (who lived in New Mexico from about A.D. 500 to A.D. 1150), was guarded against unbelievers, but now you can visit a modern approximation on hhtp://www.sscf.ucsb.edu/anth/projects/great.kiva/, thanks to a web site set up by John Kantner of the University of California at Santa Barbara. He admits it does not have the "atmosphere" of dark and smoke, earth and leather and human smells, and such things can probably never capture the awe of holy places or the excitement of expecting magic to occur. However, it's right up to date, like the High Holy Days services on the web from Temple Emmanu-el—or drive-through places to view the corpse at some California undertakers' establishments.

HINDUISM

It may offend to designate rituals of Christianity, Judaism, or Islam—all honoring the same God—as having magical rituals (probably the most in that order), but perhaps among infidels (all other religions) we may notice as a striking example Hinduism. The best book on the subject is Max Weber's *The Religion of India* (which regards Hinduism as extraordinary in that it is a religion in which the magicians attained power without becoming priests) but we may cite an apt passage from Daniel Lawrence O'Keefe's *Stolen Lightning* (1982):

> Amorphism reaches a kind of limit in Hinduism, where even the main "denominations" like Saivism and Vaishnavism are themselves collections of sects with little organizational structure, no churches, etc. And the whole thing is organized around a caste of magicians, rather than priests, and rationalized by magical theosophies rather than religious theologies. Hinduism thus resembles totemic systems of individual caste and family cults (it is called "Arya Dharma" or "Aryan Duty" by its members) supplemented

by magical sects, with no formal organization, no theology, magicians rather than priests at the center, and the only overarching cognitive unity provided by a succession of magical theosophies (Vedanta, the Upanishads, etc.) rather than religious theology. These magical theosophies, working like archetypes, in turn program the magical protest movements that spring up endlessly around them, so Hinduism looks less like a solid house than an arena in which this is staged.

It can be argued that any ritual of Hinduism is magic, whatever the Brahmins think of it.

THE MOST SECRET CEREMONY OF THE FREEMASONS

There are encyclopedias of Freemasonry—A. E. Waite edited one—and remainder tables at bookshops sport handbooks such as *The Lodge and the Craft* (Rollin C. Blackmer) and exposés such as *The Deadly Deception* (by Jim Shaw and Tom McKenny). In the latter, a former Mason reveals—he claims for the first time ever—the initiation to the Thirty–third Degree. I was urged to include it here, but I contend it is not a magical ritual. Masonic ceremonies derive from a few old religious practices and have influenced the ceremonies of new religions (such as the Temple rites of The Church of Jesus Christ of Latter Day Saints) and some magical groups, but they are essentially not magical.

There has been almost as much foolishness written about the Masons as about the less interesting more or less secret societies such as the revivals of Rosicrucianism, the Order of the Templars, etc. We need none of that here.

CHANGO MACHO

From the *Libero de los sueños...Chango Macho* (no known publisher, or date) you can get your dream interpretations, your horoscope and lucky numbers (mine "for Brooklyn: 623, 670, 759, 974, 080, 201," because I am a Sagittarius and resident in that borough—Manhattan, naturally, is in a different area code!), and various prayers, etc. Here is one to the god Chango, with my translation:

Baba Changó mi	Father Chango on me
wo mi...dabobo mi.	look... protect me.
Daraya on idaraya wa	Keep off evil spirits and bring happiness

siele on fún no obi	to me and those I love
omo-ilé emi ranti	remember that I am your son and you are
Alalia, onile	the master of my house.
A dupe, Olawa.	Thank you, glorious god.

In the service of Chango, Christian elements are characteristically mixed with the African paganism. Here is a prayer to Chango as spirit of good luck, in Spanish:

En nombre del Padre, del Hijo, del Espiritu Santo, yo te invoco, Ponderoso Guerrero, para que a traves de tí, se cumpla la voluntad de Nuestro Señor. Solo reclamo tu gracia para que mi fe se me fortifique y haya paz, amor y justicia en mis actos y pensaminentos. Postrado ante tu ímagen, pido tan solo suerte para cubrir mis necesidades, para llevar alegría y regocijo a mi hogar y a mis semejantes, para ...

at this point, prostrate before the statue of Chango, you make your petition and conclude with:

Juro que no hay egoismo en mi petición, sino solo confianza en la Divina Providencia.

DANCING IN A RING

Not enough guides to witchcraft practices explain how to enter into the magic circle and conduct ceremonies. I suggest as a simple book *Witchcraft: A Tradition Renewed* (1990), put together by Evan Jones and Doreen Valiente after Robert Cochrane, a figure in California Craft, committed suicide by eating belladonna plants. It has some nice rituals and explains how the participants form up, enter the circle through the gates of the north (jumping over the besom, or witch's broom), and what they then do and say for various rites. As with almost every book on magic, some things are held back, but not much in this case, and the information (too detailed to quote here) is very helpful. Today many covens are same-sex; for them this book is "too breeder."

MAGIC IN HUNTING

Once a way of life and famously a sport—kings and nobles once had great hunting estates—hunting, like every other human activity into which luck enters, has always been surrounded by superstitions. A saint once saw a crucifix of light between the antlers of a stag in the darkness of the Black

Forest; ordinary people claim to have seen supernatural creatures in the woods, giant animals, half-human sometimes. The forest has always been a place of mystery, and the New Forest in England is only one such place where magic is still supposed to be especially active.

In Teutonic superstition we hear of what Germans call *Die Freischütz*, a hunter connected with The Devil. There are many tales of pacts with The Devil to succeed at hunting.

One tradition says that if you encounter three animals you must not kill more than two, and if there is only one you must throw a piece cut from the left forefoot (or the left foot, if a bird) of it toward the north, a sort of sacrifice to evil powers. Other traditions tell you what to do when hunting bears and wolves, what magical formulae to recite so that the spirits of dead animals will not return to harm you, and so on. When you recite the curse on all fanged and clawed creatures, be sure to except the hunting dog! You begin the whole magical business by setting out to hunt by walking backwards out of your house.

Prehistoric man's cave paintings were essentially magical. This one, from *Les Trois Frères* (The Three Brothers) in Ariège, France, shows a paleolithic man in the skin and antlers of the beasts the hunters hoped to kill. Disguising oneself in the hides of animals was also a magicians' practice in cultures as different as these of the aborigines of American and the natives of Africa.

The aborigines of America greatly respected the animals they hunted and had various rituals to make sure that the herds of bison and other animals upon which they depended for food and clothing and even housing—they made tipis from animal skins, of course—were appeased and encouraged to come again to serve mankind. The Plains Indians' belief was that all living creatures were put here, to live together, by the Great Manitou and that a balance of nature, of which man himself was a part, not the master, was essential.

A RITUAL TO SEE THE MAN YOU WILL MARRY

Back when marriage was just about the only career open to women outside the nunnery, rituals to learn about whom you would marry were often practiced by young maidens. These could be as simple as cutting an apple into nine pieces while looking into a mirror or more elaborate: consider what the maiden does in John Keats's great poem, "The Eve of St. Agnes."

(By the way, never call a child Agnes; superstition is sure that anyone named Agnes will go crazy.)

One simple ceremony involves finding an "even" ash twig—that is one with an even number of fronds. Ash trees are good for lots of magical things, the commonest of which is carrying ash keys in your pocket (or your shoe) to be sure you cannot be attacked by devils and demons. In this case the curious young lady puts the ash twig under her pillow with a request that she see her future husband

> Not in his vest, not in his best,
> But in the clothes of every day.

He will come to her in her dreams. As with so much that happens in the night, whether this is magic or imagination at work is hard to say. "Do I wake or dream?" is always an apt question when you see something like the guy who is going to have future visiting rights to your children, or a ghost, in the wee and weird hours of the night.

RELIGION OF THE WHITE CLOTH

Nigeria has more than 750 different languages and a great number of different tribes and religions, of which the worship of Obatala (Chief of The White Cloth, the fabric which binds the universe together and weaves together the strands of man and nature) is among the most interesting. Its *awa* (rituals) have made their way to America with other aspects of the Yoruba culture. To this spiritual being devotees pray and offer water, sweet potato, corn mush, eggs, and rice. They keep a shrine in their homes and burn a candle before it and pray before it every day, with special ceremonies at the beginning of every week. (The African week in this instance has five days.) In trance or at least altered states of consciousness, worshippers gain wisdom and power; we might say they are possessed, but they would say they have got in touch with their inner spark of divine fire, which they call their *ori*.

A number of pamphlets on the *Ifá* religion of West Africa are published in New York (where the religions are practiced by many) and are available conveniently from Original Publications, 2486-88 Webster Avenue, The Bronx, NY 10458.

Here is the ceremony by which the worshipper becomes one with the spirit (often called an *orisha*). He stands before the shrine with his *orisha* pot and a container of pure water. He places these beside the image's lit candle. He says his *oriki* or invocation (with I shall try to translate accurately):

Ibà se Obatala o rin n'eru ojikutu s'eru.
Oba n'lé Ifon alabalase oba patapat n'ile iranje.
Otabatala, Oba igbo oluwaiye re e o kebi ow la.
Otabatala, o pe o. (said three times)
Otabatala, o pele o.
Otabatala, ro.
Osun l'ala o fi koko ala rumo.
Ase!

I show respect to the Chief of The White Cloth who does not fear death.
The Father of the Realm of my Ancestors is the ruler of all generations
    to come.
Chief of The White Cloth, Chief of the Sacred Grove, Possessor of all
    Blessings, increase my wisdom.
Chief of the White Cloth, I summon thee.
Chief of The White Cloth, I greet thee (said three times).
Chief of The White Cloth, descend.
Protector of the fabric of the universe, I salute thee.
[May I have] the Power!

When the ceremony is complete, the worshipper breathes the spirit into
the container of water and says *Tò!* (Enough!)

Here follows the *Orin Obatala* or Hymn to Obatala, sung antiphonally:

Baba, Oba i to ase to'mole ase, to'mole ase.
Response: *Oba i to ase to'mole, ase to'mole.*
Oba i to ase tomole, Obatala to'mole.
Response: *Oba i too ase to'mole, ase to'molo.*

Father, The Chief has the power to bring the light, to bring the light.
Response: The Chief has the power to bring the light, to bring the light.
The Chief has the power to bring the light, The Chief of The White Cloth
    brings the light.
Response: The Chief has the power to bring the light, the power to bring
    the light.

See Awo Fatunmbi's *Yemoja/Olokun*, J.O. Awolalu's *Yoruba Beliefs & Sacrificial Rites*, Baba Ifa Karade's *Ojise*, El Obatala's *Creative Ritual*, C.O. Ibie's *Ifism*, and John Mason's *Four New World Yoruba Rituals*.

AMERINIDIAN RITUALS

Each of the hundreds of aboriginal groups, from the Inuit to the people eventually called the Seminoles of Florida, every nation and tribe from Maine to California, had its own religion and its own ceremonies, some of them magical. It is difficult for us now to separate religion from magic in (say) the Bluejay Dance (or, better, Midwinter Spirit Dance) of the Salish. Some of the intention was to praise their god, some to honor departed souls, some was festive dancing, and some shaman activities and magical rituals.

The Indians, as everyone knows, dance to the sound of drums, gourd rattles, whistles, rasp sticks, and other percussion instruments. Among the dances we might mention half a dozen as samples:

CHEROKEE BEAR DANCE—there are dances honoring the bear as totem and as food, just as there are those involved with the buffalo, the black-tailed deer, the snake, the rabbit, and so on, in many Indian cultures

IROQUOIS EAGLE DANCE—the image of an Indian dancer imitating an eagle in an energetic dance is not one soon to be forgotten, and the Iroquois dance was paralleled in other Indian societies just as was the Eagle Society of warriors

MEXICAN FOLKDANCES—as performed by the *Ballet Folklórico de México* for tourists in Guadalajara, and elsewhere among the *índios*, feature a graceful Deer Dance in which a young male impersonates the animal

OGALA HORSE DANCE—horses introduced by the Europeans changed the lives of nomadic peoples such as the dwellers on the Great Plains—their huge feathered headdresses made the Plains Indians *the* Indians in the mind of many Americans and almost all foreigners—and led to new ceremonies relevant to these important animals

TEWA PUEBLO CLOUD DANCE OR DANCE OF THE CORN MAIDENS—clouds, women, rain—all symbols of fertility—are involved in these ceremonies with their symbolic costumes for men and women and their emphasis on good weather and good crops, prosperity and propagation

YAQUI DEER DANCE—dancers and singer cement "relationships between the people" but the dancer with the deer headdress is performing some kind of magic rite related to hunting the deer

There are many other ceremonies combining religion with magic. Well known and colorful are (for instance) the Quileute Wolf Dance, the Blackfoot Grass Dance, the Lakota Sioux Sun Dance, the *Hulkilal wok* or Dance of the Dead, the Hupa Dance of the White Deerskin, the Ojibwa Drum Dance, the Pawnee Whistle Dance, the Hoop Dance of the Plains Indians, war dances and rain dances, dances to honor the animal world as well as divinities and to call the animals (as in the Buffalo Dance of the Mandan) or the spirits, dances for fertility and death, etc. In addition, there are drumming and other non-dance ceremonies and, of course, the fascinating rituals by which young people see visions that define them and direct their lives. Amerindians' directions in life were bloody: moderns may recall the depiction in the cinema of the piercing and torturing of the pectoral muscles and may even have heard in a television series or a popular book on the West of the sacrifice of Sitting Bull. He offered for his vision from Wakan Tanka (Great Holy that is everywhere and in everything) before what we whites call the Battle of the Little Big Horn and the redmen call the Battle of the Greasy Grass a "scarlet blanket" of fifty pieces of his flesh dug out of his arms. Like early Christian mystics, men subjected themselves to hunger and torture to put the mind in a state to receive visions.

Quite apart from rituals and mystic visions are magic objects, such as *kachinka* dolls, and supernatural creatures of folklore such as *yais*. The *yai* is a small black personage of the Nootka peoples of the Pacific Northwest. The *yai* can breed with human women but is so fragile that when touched turns into foam! See E. A. Saper and M. Swadesh, *Nootka Texts* (1939). Naturally there are similar items of interest in the folklore of all the other Amerind peoples, from the Ghost Dance to the grotesque characters represented on masks.

THE GREEN CORN DANCE

Here, from Sam D. Gill and Irene E. Sullivan's *Dictionary of Native American Mythology* (1992), is one Amerind ritual summarized fully. It is the Green Corn Dance of the Seminole, Creek, and southeastern Iroquoian tribes, also known as the *busk* or *posketa* dance. It greets the New Year— the fire and the medicine bundles are renewed at this time—and is celebrated in July or August when the crops have matured.

The Seminole medicine bundle is renewed by the *Es-te fas-ta* lest the tribe die. The Oklahoma Seminoles have an established square ground used year after year; other groups set a couple of young men to clear a dancing place when needed, moving (as with the Florida Seminoles) to guarantee privacy each time. The Iroquoian tribes perform the dance in the space ringed by log sheds (open to the center) where the participants prepare by purging themselves with emetics and with prayer.

For the dance, the whole village cleans homes, extinguishes fires and cleans the hearths, and fasts for three days (in most groups), the fast ending when the "breath master" new fire is lit by a friction drill at the point where four logs (representing North, South, East, and West) meet in the center. The Seminoles and some others burn in this fire all worn out clothes and utensils, while the Creek and Iroquois medicinal herbs and offerings of green corn. From the central fire, the women take coals to bring fire to their individual dwellings.

There is a feast to end the ceremonies, a time of making peace with all and forgiving enemies, and ritual cleansing with emetics, putting on and washing off ashes from the fire. Ballgames, mock battles, and dancing in costumes welcomes in the New Year and marks the rejuvenation, re-energizing of the tribe. Is this religion, custom, magical ceremony, or what? A mixture of many things, very likely, including tradition, like the famous War Dance, the Rain Dance, or the Ghost Dance.

SYMBOLISM IN A MAGIC DANCE

The Spirit World (1992) is a typically carefully researched and richly illustrated study of Amerind beliefs and customs. It describes many rituals, including this one:

> In some Indian communities, dancers would act out the arrival of the animals. Anthropologist Ruth Underhill [author of *Red Man's Religion* 1965, and *Papago Indian Religion*, 1969] described a Pueblo deer-calling ceremony she observed in the 1940s at which costumed men played the part of the prey—a ritual that is still performed at a number of Pueblos today. "It was almost dawn when we heard the hunter's call from the hillside....Then shadowy forms came bounding down through the piñon trees. At first we could barely see the shaking horns and dappled hides. Then the sun's rays picked out men on all fours, with deerskins over their backs and painted staves in their hands to simulate forelegs. They leapt and

gamboled before the people while around them pranced little boys who seemed actually to have the spirit of fawns." The sprightly Deer Dancers were escorted by their Owner, the Mother of Game, a beautiful woman with long black hair. "She led the animals where they would be good targets for the hunters, and, one by one, they were symbolically killed."

Magic from the very beginning has always been about the magician getting his desire. Magicians from the first were relied upon to give the people what they needed, whether it be the game on which they lived, the crops they planted and harvested, or the guidance they needed while wandering for years in the desert.

THE GHOST DANCE

From James Mooney's authoritative *The Ghost Dance Religion* (1896):

> The dance commonly begins about the middle of the afternoon or later, after sundown....the leaders walk out to the dance place, [form a circle] and facing inward, join hands so as to form a small circle. Then, without moving from their places they sing the opening song...in a soft undertone. Having sung it through once, they raise their voices to their full strength and repeat it, this time slowly circling [deosil, clockwise] around in the dance....As the song rises and swells the people come singly and in groups from several tipis, and one after another join the circle until any number from fifty to five hundred men, women, and children are in the dance....At intervals between the songs, more especially after the trances have begun, the dancers unclasp hands and sit down to smoke or talk for a few minutes. At such times the leaders sometimes deliver short addresses or sermons, or relate the recent trance experience of the dancer....Dogs are driven off from the neighborhood of the circle lest they should run against any of those who have fallen into a trance and thus awaken them. The dancers themselves are careful not to disturb the trance subjects while they are in the spirit world....

It is only fair to say that Amerind rituals are or were regarded as religion by Native Americans, if we can in fact say they had anything resembling our religions (which separate—as the beliefs of the Amerindians did not—

God from nature and the spiritual from the profane), and that we all have a habit of referring to the religions of others whom we do not understand as superstitious. I include these and other rituals because they deal in magic as well as religion, and I do not judge them or compare them to religious ceremonies which most people would say involve no magic (such as a Quaker meeting) or religious ceremonies that undoubtedly do involve magic (such as the transubstantiation in the Roman Catholic Mass). Are the cures of Christian Science magical? The séances of Spiritualism? Marriage rites in Mormon temples? The little verses from Deuteronomy inside the *mezuzahs* that some Jews nail to their doors?

RITUALS OF THE FOLK FESTIVALS

A good deal of the Old Religion and surviving superstition is found in historical and still current folk festivities. This is not the place to examine them all, but as a single example I offer a few comments on British and Irish May Days.

On the first of May you can see old ceremonies such as the Hobby Horse at Padstow (in Cornwall), the renewal of the May Garland at the church at Charlton-in-Otmoor (in Oxfordshire), the carol singing (formerly from the top of the Bargate) at Southampton, and the maypoles all around the country. The people dance around these phallic symbols for potency or just fun. May Day is the time for all sorts of celebrations (including the enthronement of the Queen of the May and sometimes a May King, called Jack-i'-the-Green), the most important pastoral celebration of the old rural year.

At Temple Sowerby (Westmorland) May Day was the time for the old liar's contest. The person who told the biggest lie won a grindstone, and other prizes were offered. Once, a passing bishop of Carlisle, traveling the road between Penwith and Appleby and going through Temple Sowerby as the contest was in progress, denounced this pagan celebration and said, "I have never told a lie in my life." He was instantly awarded a razor honing stone, one of the minor prizes. He refused it, but it was tossed into his carriage as he left with the taunt that he might well use it to sharpen his wits!

In Oxfordshire and elsewhere children carry May Garlands or decorated staffs, religious objects from some almost forgotten celebrations of Spring and rebirth. Some sing:

> Good morning, missus and master,
> I wish you a happy day.

> Please to smell my garland
> Because it's the first of May.

Margaret Baker (*The Folklore and Customs of Rural England*, 1974) advises us to see Flora Thompson's *Lark Rise to Candelford* (1954) and writes of

> children about 1880 dressed as king and queen, lord and lady, maids of honour, carrying willow wands topped with a flamboyant yellow crown imperial and garlands of leaves, wallflowers, bluebells, yellow cowslips, from the mowing grass, pink and white ladysmocks, cuckoo-flowers or milkmaids, red flowering-currant, daisies and sweet briar, fixed to a wooden framework, with a doll—'the lady'—within. Muslin draped over the garland was removed only after a donation, and the procession moved off, to walk many miles round farms, cottages, and rectory and "big house."

Just as children cadging pennies for the Old Guy on Guy Fawkes' Day (like the American Halloween trick or treat, in a way) are representatives of the returning dead, and these "remember the garland" children dimly recalled ancient ceremonies of Celtic Spring.

In Ireland (Lady Wilde writes):

> As a preservative against fairy malice and darts [which wounded cattle], which at this season wound and kill, it is the custom on May morning, at sunrise, to bleed the cattle and taste of the blood mingled with milk. Men and women [in ancient times] were also bled and their blood was sprinkled on the ground. The practice, however, has died out [late nineteenth century], even in the remote West [of Ireland]; but the children are still lifted through the [bon]fire when it has burned low, and the cattle are driven through the hot embers—as in ancient times both children and cattle were "passed through the fire to Moloch"—and the young men still leap through the flames after the dance round the burning bush is over, and they carry home a lighted branch of the sacred tree to give good luck to the family during the coming year.

The folk customs and rituals often tell us a lot about the pre-Christian faiths and facts, just as "Athena Starwoman" and Deborah Gray's *How to Turn Your Ex-Boyfriend into a Toad and Other Spells* bespeaks modern feminist rage.

ORDINATION OF THE PRIESTHOOD

The Roman Catholics held to the tradition of the laying on of hands which conveyed magically the powers given to the first apostles to the prelates and priests of the modern church. The Reformation changed things in Protestant denominations, and Martin Luther altered the rites of ordination in accordance with his belief that priests are to offer spiritual sacrifices, pray for the congregations, and preach to them. "He who can do this is a priest," said Luther. "If shaving the head [the tonsure] and anointing made one a priest," Luther scoffed, " I could even oil and anoint the hoofs of a jackass and make him a priest too." See Ralph E. Smith's *Luther, Ministry, and Ordination Rites in the Early Reformation Church* (1996) to understand why and how the ordination rites which gave Roman Catholic priests magical powers were altered to confirm Protestant ministers in their offices.

Ordination to the priesthood conveys, some Christians believe, magical powers, and these are retained even if the priest falls from grace and leaves the ministry.

WASHED IN THE BLOOD OF THE LAMB

That is a Christian expression meaning saved, redeemed by the sacrifice of Christ on the cross, Christ seen as the human, blood sacrifice to an angry god in the old tradition of the Jews. It occurs in hymns of the sort used by the Salvation Army (motto: "Blood and Fire") and parodied as

> Wash me in the water
> That you washed the colonel's daughter
> And I shall be whiter than
> The whitewash on the wall.

Vaguely behind all this seems to be nearly forgotten ceremonies in which the blood of sacrifices was wiped on worshippers, transferring some kind of power to them. In the *criobolium* and *taurobolium* of the worship of Cybele, to cite one example of the use of blood in baptism, the blood of sacrificed rams and bulls was applied to the heads of those being inducted into the mysteries. Christian baptism uses water, in our symbolism linked with blood to represent the mixture of divinity and humanity in Christ, and so remembered in the Mass.

Without stretching too much one might say that the vampire drinking the blood of victims is engaged not so much in a meal as in a ritual, for "the blood is the life," as The Bible says. Blood represents the vital force that vampires need to continue, the soul power that they must drain from others because they have lost their own. (The fact that they have no soul is represented in the superstition that a vampire cannot be seen in a mirror. Some folklore connects selling one's soul to The Devil, as is recorded in my book on the subject, by selling one's shadow.) Also, in effect this ritual of taking the blood of the victim is a baptism of the victim into the ghastly company of the vampires; it is a ritual of induction. Losing the blood, one loses one's soul to the vampire as in signing a pact with The Devil in blood one loses one's soul to evil.

We are born in blood, of the products of blood. In our blood—or so we were told well before anyone had ever heard of DNA or genes—our nature, our characters, our souls are given to us. Thus, blood is a feature of many consecrations and reconsecrations as well as desecrations of the human body. It is basic to a number of magical rituals. Satanism is drenched in it—though those obscene rites may involve other bodily fluids as well.

EXECRATIONS IN THE DIABOLICAL CHURCH

David H. Darst in *Proceedings of the American Philological Society* 123: 5 (October 1979), introduced and translated Martín de Casteñega's *Tratado...de las supersticiones hatcheríes* of 1529, eleven chapters on diabolism, thirteen on sorcery. Casteñega writes:

> As in the Catholic church there are sacraments ordained and established by Christ who is true man and God, so in the diabolical church there are execrations ordained and fixed by the devil and his ministers. Although circumcision was a sacrament God gave a long time ago to Abraham (Genesis 17), one can't say now that the circumcision the Jews use is or was ordained by God, since the way Abraham did it has ceased. What the Jews now have is like the Muslim rite, which isn't ordained by God but by the deceit of the devil and his ministers. Such ceremonies are called execrations because the sacraments are vessels of grace by the virtue of which those who take them receive grace; and those who take the execrations receive neither virtue nor grace, but rather incur the sin of heresy, which is the worst of all sins. Besides the circumcision that the Jews now use and is similar only in appearance to the matter, manner, and ceremony of of the true

circumcision that God gave to Abraham, the diabolical church has other ceremonies and execrations of the sacraments of the Catholic church, and we popularly call them superstitions and witchcrafts.

In our time of rainbow coalitions, celebrated diversity, fuzzy definitions and feel-good ecumenism, it is refreshing to read of a sixteenth-century thinker who is convinced that his religion is right and Judaism and Islam are *wrong*.

The symbol of The Devil is the five-pointed star upside down. He represents, as Satan (The Adversary) all good reversed, but some say the 2 points upward represent his horns. Christianity represented The Devil as having horns after identifying him with the pre-Christian Horned God of Western Europe. The nimbus or halo in Christian art represents an actuality (the aura of the blessed), but the horns of The Devil, like the wings of angels, are merely symbolic: The Devil is bestial, angels are swift.

He goes on to distinguish witchcraft from all these religions and to describe the "diabolical church" in great detail, being credulous in some matters (such as the existence of witch cults), skeptical in others (such as witches flying), and shrewd in psychological discussion (why do some people turn to witchcraft?). He makes an essential point which needs even now to be underlined: *no one interested in witchcraft needs to be or should be at all concerned with the rituals of other religions.* When you see heresy, blasphemy, parody you are dealing in political reaction to established churches, the New Religion, not the Old Religion at all. The true rituals of The Craft should and do pay no attention whatever to the rituals of Catholicism, Protestantism, Judaism, Islam, Buddhism, or what have you. Those religions are totally irrelevant to the follower of Wicca, The Goddess, The Horned God, and so on.

In constructing your rituals of a modern Druidism (in the absence of any details about the past) or reviving some Old Religion of which some details are known, always act as if Judaism and its "improvements," Christianity and Islam, do not exist and never were. Anything else is too like Satanism, a rebellion of angry, disappointed, perverted believers, too bound to what it opposes, as flawed and foolish as the dogmatisms that irked it into existence.

PSEUDO-SATANIST RITUALS

Real Black Mass goings-on would make snuff films, but the Black Mass (which is a parody of the Roman Catholic Mass) is basically itself parodied in the annoying, maybe blasphemous, but not murderous rituals seen in the film shown in San Francisco to potential recruits for The Church of Satan. In that film there are numerous nasty remarks about God but no sacrificed babies, nudity but not homicide. Thank God.

SATANIC CHILD ABUSE

Real Satanists do indeed "abuse" children: they murder them as a condition of initiation into the cult and sacrifice them in their diabolical ceremonies. But by "ritual child abuse" something else is generally meant—sexual abuse. Susan J. Kelley in an article in *Nursing Research* 39: 1 (January/February 1990), defines "ritualistic abuse" better than is usually the case, though not entirely grammatically or absolutely precisely:

> Ritualistic abuse refers to the systematic and repetitive sexual, physical, and psychological abuse of children by adults engaged in cult worship. The purpose of ritualistic abuse is to induce a religious or mystical experience for adult participants. Perpetrators of ritualistic abuse involve children in group religious practices and ceremonies that often include the ingestion of human excrement, semen, or blood; witnessing the mutilation of animals; threats with supernatural or magical powers; ingestion of drugs; and use of songs or chants. The child victims are threatened with supernatural powers and physical harm to prevent disclosure of the ritualistic activities. For example, children may be threatened that the devil or demons may harm them.

The so-called "Satanic Panic," dealt with at some length in *The Complete Book of Devils and Demons* (1996), in a book by Jeffrey S. Victor called *Satanic Panic: The Creation of a Contemporary Legend* (1993), and other publications, especially from the Religious Right, could, of course, have adults as victims as well as children. However, child abuse and supposed Multiple Personality Disorder deriving from child abuse are much more popular as topics in the sensational press. The alleged rituals are seldom described in detail in the press. Many of them appear to be imaginary.

AN EVEN EASIER PROTEST RELIGION

Americans seek simplicity, and sometimes simple-mindedness. How about a really simple religion, or quick-acting religious substitute? Plop, plop, fizz, fizz—results!

A whole new religion offers the temptation to novelty we find it so hard to resist but it also challenges with many complexities and duties; even being born again in your former religion faces more interaction with other congregants and the larger community and thereby helps to cure the lack of connection that is one of the worst modern malaises. What is offered to those who are more anti-social, but equally long for fulfillment? What about those who, in Durkheim's postmodern society, with its abnormal "division of labor," have to do the work of the weirdo sector and by that very fact do not fit in with religion, which means rituals that tie individuals not only to a higher power but likewise to other people? What about the true Outsider?

How about a bit of some exotic religion that you know and care little or nothing about but which can make you feel Differentiated from the unenlightened, inexpensively both financially and emotionally, without having to do good deeds, be nice to other people, or get out of your little self or your apartment?

Meditate. Or buy a Vedic *mantra* and sit around all alone chanting it to yourself. This is truly turning on (alpha waves) and dropping out (better than *OM, OM, OM* would be *ME, ME, ME*). If you have to have friends, hang with those who do the same thing and dress weirdly and feel deviant and thereby superior to everyone else. This is a ritual that will give you what so many Americans need, an Identity. This is cheaper than buying brand-name sneakers, easier than getting publicity as a performer, serial killer, etc., and alters whatever little bit of mind you have to something like *Atman* (higher states) without drugs. Combined with (say) macrobiotic diet, pretentious jargon, and odd clothes it can be a whole way of life.

Want a simple ritual that will make you feel special? Just say the word! And it works like magic, inside, where magic works best.

THE BLACK MASS

First of all, the Black Mass can only be said by a renegade, ordained Roman Catholic priest, so most of the so-called Black Masses are not what they say they are. Also, the *Grimoire of Honorius* and other sources make it clear that the short attention span of so many modern Americans makes it highly unlikely that they will, after going to the trouble of getting a priest and all the paraphernalia for these obscene rites, want to fulfill all the requirements. The sin of Pride tempts us to many outrages, but the sin of Sloth prevents many would-be villains from doing anything really evil.

Black-massing is a complicated and demanding business. First you have to wait until the first Monday of a month and celebrate a Mass of the Holy Spirit, asking for divine help and inspiration. At sunrise on the Tuesday following, the priest-magician sacrifices a black cock, saves a feather, dries the eyes, tongue, and heart and grinds them to a powder, and buries the rest. On Wednesday he celebrates the Mass of the Angels and uses the feather to dip in the consecrated wine and write certain magical symbols on a parchment for protection, also calling on St. Michael the Archangel to protect him against the dangerous demons he proposes to summon. He reserves a piece of the consecrated Host in a piece of violet silk. On Friday following he prays (with a cruciform candle of yellow wax and Psalm 78) and celebrates the Requiem Mass, asking God for help in calling up demons. At sunrise he sacrifices a male lamb. He buries the lamb (symbolic of Christ, the *Agnus Dei*) with funeral prayers, and rubs the powdered black cock remains on the lamb skin to make parchment. On the parchment he writes magical symbols as he chants psalms and then he says a second Mass for the dead using the "seventy-two great names of power"— a more recent take on the Hebrew seventy–two-letter secret name of God— and by sorcery he invokes demons as desired.

The whole thing also involves, as we see in *The Complete Book of the Devil's Disciples* (where J.-K. Huysmans's description of the climax of a Black Mass is quoted at length), obscenities and blasphemies, the power being derived from a deep sense of transgression, the hateful perversion of the priestly powers which exist even in fallen priests, for once ordained, one is "a priest forever." This energizing sense of outrageousness is simply not available to the layman of Catholicism or to adherents of any other faith, certainly not pagans, to whom the rituals of the Roman church must be matters of utter indifference. The rituals of the Church of Satan are ineffectual imitations of real Black Masses, and, as far as I can ascertain, real Black Masses are extremely rare these days, performed only by a few lapsed Roman Catholic and one or two remarkably eccentric Old Catholic lapsed clergymen.

Moreover, though I can appreciate the argument that these rituals offend God as well as true believers, and can involve at the extreme Satanic human sacrifice and other horrors, I cannot get much exercised about them nor do I see any clear road to eliminating them easily. Fortunately, in addition to those opinions I cannot subscribe to the belief that Black Masses succeed in raising demons from Hell. Rather Black Masses are (I believe) simply pathological instances, proof that evil and destruction and hatred of the good are not in some Hell of burning brimstone but resident in the darkest corners of the human heart and mind. For Original Sin I can offer no original solutions.

Having noted in this present book many practices which, I repeat, I do not recommend, it is hardly necessary for me to say this here, but I shall: If invited to a Black Mass, do not go. Curiosity, they say, killed the cat.

THE MASS OF ST.-SÉCAIRE

In France the Mass of St.-Sécaire was a Roman Catholic Mass said backwards by a renegade priest to kill somebody. There are a few undoubted records of this having been done and some less reliable assertions that it was effective.

Those who could not persuade a priest to this blasphemy, or who could not afford the exorbitant prices charged for the service, simply went to any church, lit a candle, and recited the Lord's Prayer, the *Ave Maria*, and the *Credo* backwards. Or, in Brittany, they could appeal to St.-Yves. You went fasting on three Mondays to the chapel of St.-Yves (near Trégunier), terror of the dishonest, upholder of truth, and prayed against an enemy: "If right is on his side, condemn me. But if I am in the right, make him die within the time limit dictated." You then left a small payment, a coin, for the saint and walked around the chapel three times, reciting your prayers backwards. Some few people made a business of performing these rites for others, and were paid a small sum for the work, but anyone could do it for themselves if they could get to the chapel.

The important French historian of sorcery, Jules Michelet, was at pains to make the point that the *sabbat*, black or other blasphemous masses, and similar manifestations of outlawry were expectable rebellions by the peasantry ground down by feudal lords and the church, the law, and the other institutions that favored themselves over the average person.

THE MASS OF THE HOLY SPIRIT

The *Messe du Saint Ésprit* was likewise blasphemous. Its purpose was to compel God to grant whatever intention, good or bad, the Mass was said for. It is considered pious to have Mass said for an intention but it is black magic to attempt to compel rather than supplicate. Prayers (as we have noted before) request; magic demands.

RITUALS FOR DIVINATION

About some things, humanity remains extremely curious. Perhaps, in the minds of most people, the great questions of where we come from are less significant than those concerning what will happen to us personally. Peering into the future, as I show with a long list of methods in *The Complete Book of Superstition, Prophecy, and Luck*, has always been popular, if not possible. Nobody stops to ask what good it might be to know the future if the future is knowable, fixed, and therefore unalterable.

If you knew,
What would you do?

People go on casting horoscopes, consulting with the *I Ching*, reading The Tarot or tea leaves or palms of the hands, and so on. In his famed books on the occult, Michael Scot (*c.* 1175– *c.* 1230) "condemned magic, but he enjoyed writing about it," says Will Durant. Scot "listed twenty-eight methods of divination, and seems to have believed in all of them." You can seek the rituals there.

If you need one to get started on, I recommend The Tarot. That fascinating tool will put you in touch with yourself (not demons). I believe that genethlialogy (casting the horoscope of the precise second and place of your birth as a way of predicting your entire life) is almost never done exactly and is a waste of time to try in any case. If you must be superstitious and want to play at prediction, why not get the very best book on palmistry, by "Cheiro"? Accept no substitutes. The book by this ingenious Englishman on a "science" of reading palms that went back to the earliest civilizations of India and was mentioned in The Bible—"What evil is in my hand?" I Samuel XXVI: 18; " Length of days is in her right hand, riches and honor are in her left,"Proverbs III: 16—had been through thirty–three reprintings by the time I came across it in paperback in 1968.

That popularity tells you something in itself. As to whether palmistry itself can tell you anything useful, I suggest you keep an open but highly critical, skeptical mind.

A *SANTERÍA* RITUAL FOR DIVINATION

Migene Gonzalez-Wippler's *Rituals and Spells of* Santería (1984) is essential to the student of this widely-practiced religion. The author describes the four systems of divination: *diloggun* (casting cowrie shells), casting coconut pieces, the *opon Ifa* (Table of Ifa, consulted for serious problems), and the *okuele* (for less serious ones). I shall summarize the coconut system because the cowrie one is too complicated.

The religion believes that Olofi (God) put some of his *aché* or divine power into flat stones which became spirits called *orishas*. There are hundreds of these, but Elegguá, their messenger to humanity, is perhaps the most accessible. Another is Obatala the "first created" of the *orishas*, identified with Jesus Christ.

The ritual of fortune telling by coconut bits (brown on one side, white on the other) somewhat resembles the reading of the *I Ching* and begins with three drops of water put in front of the statue of the *orisha* to be consulted. The *santero* (priest) says:

Omi tutu, ana tutu, tutu Laroye, tutu ile.

Then he proceeds to *moyubar* (remember) all the dead elders of the religion, despite the fact that in divinations one wants to contact not the dead but the divine powers, whose assistance he implores, saying:

Oloddumare ayuba. Bogwo iku olowo embelese Oloddumare ayuba. Igbae baye tonu.

Then he drives off evil forces:

Cosi iku, cosi ano, cosi eyo, cosi ofo, ariku babagwa.

He asks the saints for their blessing on himself and his followers:

Kinkamache Iyaremi. Kinkamache Oyu Bbonami.

He greets the other *santeros* present:

Aché bogwo igworo Afache semilenu.

The divination can now begin. The *santero* prays and then tears off pieces from each of the four pieces of the rind of a coconut (*obinu*) to be cast and drops them on the stones of the *orisha* consulted. The number of these little sacrificial pieces varies. For Elegguá three pieces are torn off each rind. As he does this, he says:

Obinu iku, Obinu ano, Obinu eyo, Obino ofo, ariku babagwa.

Then he transfers the coconut rind pieces from his left to his right hand, and thrice says, as he touches the floor and the *orisha* with his left hand:

Ike moueo, mokueo, Acueye.

Then he says to the congregation:

Akueye omo, akue oma, ariku babagwa.

They respond: *Apkwana.*

He brings his hands together on his chest and tosses the coconut rinds on the floor. They are, of course, going to fall white side or brown side up, which produces five possible answers to the question the oracle is supposed to answer. They are:

Eliffe (2 white, 2 brown), the strongest Yes. Elegguá and some other *orishas* "speak in this pattern."

Alafia (4 white), not quite as strong a Yes, but the *santero* kisses the floor to thank Changó or Orunla for this reply.

Itagua (3 white, 1 brown), uncertain—the *santero* must throw again (if this comes up again, the ceremony is flawed). Changó and some other *orishas* "speak in this pattern," but not Elegguá.

Okana Sode (3 brown, one white), No, but it can also mean Death. Changó, some other *orishas*, and the dead all can speak in this manner.

Oyekun (4 brown), a definite No, and Death, an evil pattern which demands that *orishas* be consulted immediately to remove *ossogbo*, bad luck.

It is *iré* which is to say good luck, if any piece falls on another in *Alafia*. When this happens, to get the good luck to the questioner, water is put on top of the top coconut and the questioner drinks it.

SÉANCES

The séance as usually practised is pretty much an American invention, despite the French name for it. It derives principally from the (faked) table-rapping of the Fox Sisters in the mid-nineteenth century. It most often involves a medium (today "channeling" is a popular term), sometimes assisted by a spirit guide (Indians or Red Indians used to be popular, along with little girls) who gets through The Veil and contacts the dead. Maybe you won't believe this, but a Chicago national polling institute swears it's true: four out of ten Americans believe we can contact the dead—and well over 60 percent of widows are sure they have had after-death contact with their dead husbands.

There may be ghostly voices as well as raps, trumpets and other instruments sounded, manifestations of ectoplasm (too often discovered to be gauze to be much credited now). All this is aided by darkness, sometimes accompanied by music on a gramophone. This writer had great difficulty concentrating when *Somewhere a Voice is Calling* was played; that piece produces giggles, I confess, in me. The audience is often asked to sit around a table in the dark, their arms outstretched to the sides, their fingers touching those of the people on either side of them. This has led a lot of fake mediums to work with their toes, etc.

There can apart from all this hardly be said to be a ritual for the magic at a séance—which is, after all, an attempt at forbidden necromancy, raising the dead in a sense—and here I shall describe one unusual séance that I wish I had had the opportunity of attending. It featured Daniel Dunglas Home.

Daniel Dunglas Home (1833–1886) was born in Scotland. Later he was a sensation in England, but he first noted his exceptional powers when a child in America; his best friend appeared as an apparition at the bottom of Daniel's bed one night and with one hand made three little circles in the air. The next day thirteen-year-old Daniel told his family that his friend Edwin had died three days before. Eventually this was discovered to be true.

Picking up on the Spiritualist vogue in America and later on the Continent and in England, Home became, for my money, the greatest in this line in his time: he could perform wonders in a trance state, he could produce prodigious table rappings and ghostly hands, he could teleport objects, he could float up to the ceiling.... He did this in London to the titled audience British snobbery required and he was a sensation. On top of all this, he was never caught in any deception, and people truly believed in his amazing powers.

Here is a brief description of a typical Home séance. It took place at the home of Madame Jauvin d'Attainville and *tout le monde* was there, including the Prince and Princess Metternich. Fifteen lucky guests were seated around a large table in a magnificent drawing room ablaze with light. No darkness to cover foolery here! Home sat some distance away from the group. He went into a trance, called his spirit guide (named Bryan), and produced moving furniture, loud table raps, a bunch of violets that went across the room on its own and landed in Princess Metternich's lap, a spirit who played a selection on the accordion, and more. On this occasion Home did not levitate or fly out one window and in another, as he did on another famous occasion, but this was all done with the lights on!

COMMUNING WITH THE DEPARTED

There are many rituals involving candles—and many books about those rituals, by Raymond Buckland and others—but here is a very simple one for getting in touch with the dear departed.

Place two light blue candles in simple holders on a table covered with a clean white cloth. On the cloth, between the candles, place a photograph of the dead person, face down, some possession of theirs (clothing is best), and a little mound of salt. You may burn incense if you think it creates the right mood. You may have music playing.

Light the candle, think for a while about being with the person in life. Wet a finger, touch it to the salt, touch it to your tongue, and turn the photograph face up. Stare at it and think of talking with the person. Be patient. Take more salt. Silently form a question to the person. Concentrate. More salt. Visualize the person answering you. Wait for a response to come into your mind.

Repeat this process for twenty minutes or half an hour at the least every night at the same hour until you are satisfied you are in touch with the person. Just attempt to establish contact; do not attempt to get the person to do anything for you.

A METHOD OF KILLING SOMEONE AT A DISTANCE

This horrible procedure starts with a killing—the murder of a newborn baby—and promises another—the death of an enemy. An American of northern European ancestry in Cleveland in 1961 told Newbell Puckett, the collector of superstitions, this:

> If you kill a newborn baby, take some parts from the body and make a stew with herbs at full moon on a midsummer night evening. Eat some of the parts, walk around the fire. When you stop, the first person you name will be dead.

Bloodthirsty types who read this ought to be warned that cannibalism produces pirons, or chemicals in the blood, that destroy the brain and lead to the ghastly "laughing death" reported in Africa. As Flanders and Swan used to sing, "Eating people is wrong."

VOODOO INITIATION

Representative here of all the various rites of initiation—into the tribe, into manhood, into a secret society, into a coven, and so on—we select an often quoted passage from Francis Huxley's study of voodoo, *The Invisibles*:

> The novices were brought in. There was a turmoil at the door of the seclusion hut [where they had been kept] but as the hounsis [voodoo priests] struggled to get through the crowd—for each novice is hidden under a white sheet and has to be carried on the back of a hounsi, as limp as a corpse....
>
> Idem attended to them in turn. She smeared her hands with cold oil, took the novice's left hand from beneath the sheet and smeared that too. Scooping a handful of the now seething mixture from the zin [pot] she pressed it into the novice's hand and closed the fingers over it, for four or five seconds. The père ["wise father"] peered anxiously over Idem's shoulder, his candle still alight. This is the central moment of initiation, when the novice is made to grasp heat without flinching—a heat which will sear the flesh only if the loa [spirits] are displeased through some lapse on the novice's part. For the nature of the loa themselves is fire, and it requires much courage and preparation to support them.
>
> From one to another of these crouching figures Idem moved, lit by the small fires till all was finished and the novices were

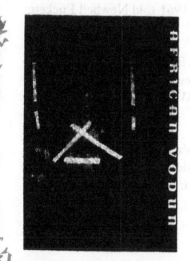

> humped back through the crowd like unwilling dragons. The pots were now emptied and a mixture of rum and oil brushed onto them, inside and out. Oil was poured into the fires below till ribbons of flame towered into the air, each pot a crucible for some gros-bon-ange ["great good angel," a soul]. Back the novices were called, still carried by the hounsis, their arms and legs seized and passed through the blaze....
>
> A hounsi...became possessed. Sobgwe, a thunder loa, took her, and she whirled, radiantly good-natured, about the centre post. Idem became possessed:

now peering round with staring eyes and nostrils, as Ogoun; now with eyes shut and eyebrows raised, one hand touched the thatch above, as Louis André, the spirit of her grandfather, now as Brave Tonnere Crasé, with hunched shoulders and a lengthened jaw working lugubriously under a hollowed face; or as the Baron [Samedi], an intimate self-satisfied death.

THE RITUAL OF THE *OUANGA* (VOODOO DOLL)

On a clean white cloth between two black candles place a doll, preferably one with some piece of the body (hair, fingernail clippings, blood) or possession or picture of the intended victim. Place a red stone at the feet of the doll, a piece of iron at the head. Touch the iron. Light the candles. Say:

> Be you gone and may you, N, rot in the grave. Damballah. I curse him as I curse the doll. I hurt him as I hurt the doll. By the fire at night, by the dead black hen, by the bloody throat, by the [sacrificed] goat, by the rum [poured] on the ground, this *ouanga* be upon him! May he not have rest in bed, nor joy at his food, nor may he be able to run and hide. Waste him and wear him and tear him and rot him as this [doll] rots.

Then in Haitian Creole call three times for the Great Zombie to come and make magic:

> *L'Appi vini, le Grand Zombi!*
> *L'Appi vini pour fe le gris-gris!*

If nothing personal to the victim is part of the doll, a further chant is needed, summoning the god of the crossroads and three lit matches are waved over the doll as you say:

> *Carrefour, Carrefour! Conga Noune De Le!*

Then you call on the god of the cemetery as you sprinkly graveyard dirt on the doll:

> *Baron Cimitière, Baron Cimitière! Conga Bafo Te!*

Then you call on Ghede, god of the dead, and sprinkle water on the doll as you say:

> *Aia Bombaia Bomba, Ghede, Ghede, Conga Do Ki Le!* Your suffering shall be that of N.

Now stick pins, nails, etc., into the doll. You mean by sympathetic magic to injure the victim as you injure the doll. A similar magic obtains when you bury a doll representing the victim, when you place a piece of paper with the victim's name on it in a sealed bottle and let it be carried away by the current of a stream, or when you stage a miniature funeral for the victim on his or her doorstep with a little doll in a little coffin, ends of black candles, etc.

If you just want power over a person buy some Controlling Oil, put a little on the person, put a little on a candle (red or pink is best for white folks, brown for persons of color), and burn the candle with visualization for a half an hour or so a day until it is all used up. Put the juice of doe's tongue (a plant) on the soles of another's shoes and the person cannot speak against you. Put Money Drawing Oil on your heels before you go to the al parts of frankincense, myrrh, and sandal wood in any oil, say olive oil. A bit of barberry gives the mixture extra power.

FOR YOUR DAY IN COURT

One of Marie Laveau's biggest lines in voodoo was getting New Orleaneans off the hook when tried in court or out of jail after being found guilty. She may have made use of this potent mixture, which you have to make three days before your trial and keep in a cool, dark place until the morning of your day in court. All you need is water, a little snake head, a bit of jalop powder, and a pinch of salt. Shake well before using (perhaps with concentrating on getting off). Pour the mixture on your stoop and walk through it on your way to court. If you feel you need backup, there are books with pentagrams to carry on your person into court, but this oil is often enough.

In *Original Black and White Magic*, ascribed on what evidence I know not to the famous Marie Laveau, there are other fascinating things such as prayers "For the Man whose Wife Has Left Him" and "For the Lady who Cannot Hold onto Her Men." Now, prayers are best if sincere and spontaneous, I suppose, but these published prayers were as useful to the uneducated as the model letters which were so popular in the eighteenth century and which contributed so much to the epistolary novel of the sort written by the greatest of all "women writers" in English, Samuel Richardson, author of the giant tomes of *Clarissa* and *Pamela*.

RITUAL TO STRAIGHTEN OUT A JUVENILE DELINQUENT

Ray Malborough in *Charms, Spells and Formulas* has a seven-day ritual, involving a poppet and a lot of candles (white, red, pink, light blue) rubbed with various oils (Courage, Success, Power, Love, Attraction) and allowed to burn out after the chanting of some dreadful doggerel, but I won't bother to give you this way of setting your teenager on the right path. For one thing, you have to say:

> The parents have done all they could
> To teach the child what's bad and good,

but I presume what is meant is not exactly what this says—parents do indeed teach their kids both bad things and good things—but that the parents have taught the kids the *difference* between right and wrong and set them a good example. Were that true, you very likely would not have a bad seed around the house turning into a blooming nuisance.

Malborough's ceremony seems to blame neither the parents nor the children for being rotten. It shifts the responsibility to peers leading the kids astray by their influence. Bad kids come from bad homes; bad companions are not the whole explanation at all.

THE INVOCATION OF ORION

K. Preisendanz's *Papyri Graecæ Magicæ* (Greek Magical Papyri, 1928–1931) gives us in its first volume (p. 118) the incantation of *The All-Puissant Power of the Constellation of The Great Bear* translated into English something like this:

> I invoke you, Holy Ones, mighty, majestic, glorious Splendors,
> sacred, born of the earth, powerful arch-dæmons; peers of the Great
> God; citizens of Chaos, of Erebus and the unfathomable deep;
> dwellers in the earth, haunters of the depths of the skies, infesting
> nooks, wrapped in clouds; scanning the mysteries, guarding the
> secrets, captains of the hosts of Hell; rulers of the infinite space,
> lords of the earth, shakers of the world, firm in foundation, cre-

ators of earthquakes; strangling by terror, striking panic, turning the spindle; scatterers of snow, carriers of rain, spirits of the air; fire tongues of the summer sun, tempest-tossing lords of fate; dark figures of Erebus, senders of fate; fanners of the flames of darting fires; commanders of snow, lords of dew; raisers of the gales, sounders of the abyss, aerial spirits bestriding the calm; dauntless in courage, despots who crush hearts; leapers of chasms, overwhelming iron-nerved dæmons; wild-raging, unfettered; watchers of Tartarus; delusive phantoms of fate; all-seeing, all-hearing, all-conquering, wanderers of the skyey heavens; inspiring of life, destructive of life, primal movers of the pole; happy-hearted dealers of death; revealers of angelic powers, judges of mortal beings, sunless revealers, masters of dæmons, rovers of the air, omnipotent, sacred, invincible [here the magic names are to be inserted], perform what I ask.

INVOKING INFERNAL SPIRITS

Probably the most famous invocation is in Christopher Marlowe's play of *The Tragical History of Dr. Faustus* (1589). Marlowe took the Latin formula out of some book of black magic. The Puritan William Prynne in *Histriomastix* (The Player Whipped, 1633), a fierce attack on the stage in all its aspects, soberly announces that The Devil himself "appeared on the stage at the *Belsavage* Playhouse in Queen *Elizabeth*'s days" because the conjuration Marlowe used was correct in every detail. Prynne adds that "the truth of which I have heard from many now alive who well remember it." Why

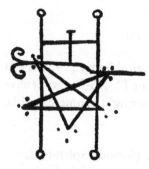

this would not work at each and every performance goes unexplained by this biased scandal-monger. The tale can stand as an example of many unsupported but popular rumors that this or that ceremony actually did produce The Devil. In Marlowe's play, by the way, The Devil does not appear in response to the call; he sends an assistant, Mephistophilis, and Mephistophilis is at pains to make it clear to the ambitious doctor that it was not the power of his conjuration that compelled demons to come from Hell but only the fact that by conjuring he was marking himself as a likely addition to the legions of the damned. Magic says that demons must come when called. Marlowe says they come when Lucifer sends them because he sees an opportunity to damn another soul, spitefully.

Another of Marlowe's heterodox ideas is that Hell is not a place but a state of mind, alienation from God, being without hope and "deprived of everlasting bliss." "Why, this is Hell, nor am I out of it," says Mephistophilis as he stands before a Faustus who says that "Hell's a fable."

Indulging in blasphemous rites to raise Hell may in that sense be said to work: it can produce in the long run the alienation from God that is the sinner's dire punishment and puts him in a mental Hell of his own, inhabited not by devils and demons but his own lost soul.

It is worth remembering that The Devil and Hell do not need to exist for you to suffer from choosing to be an opponent, a Satan, of God. Just as evil is that which partakes of the negative which God had not organized, so joining The Adversary is simply detaching yourself from the Good. In our language, the emphasis is on the relationship of Good and God, not on His power to rule over us as an *adonai*, a *deus*, a lord. Alienated from the good, from peace, from hope, you are in Hell here and now, whatever—if anything—comes after this life of yours. Choosing to rebel against God is not really a way to seek mastery; it is a form of suffering masochism. Any ritual in which you think you have abandoned God and good is self-delusion. Why would an omnipotent God permit you to do that if not in still another way to serve His purposes?

Even Satan is just another servant of the Most High, and one whose final retirement is not going to be marked by a golden parachute. If you want to Succeed in Business, find out how the Organization works and place your bets with the guaranteed winners, not the losers.

HOW TO PRODUCE MAGICAL DWARFS

Paracelsus and other German occultists spoke a great deal of little creatures who are supposed to live in the bowels of the earth. We encounter a couple in the first volume of J. Grimm's *Deutsche Sagen* (German Sayings, 1816):

> There was a man in Nuremberg named Paul Creuz who used a marvelous conjuration. He placed a quite new little table at a certain spot, with a white tablecloth and two small bowls of milk on it, two little saucers of honey, two small plates and nine small knives. Then he took a black pullet and killed it in such a way over a brazier [burning incense] that the blood mingled with the food. Then he threw half [of the pullet] to the east and half to the west. After that he went and hid himself behind a big tree and he saw two tiny dwarfs that came up out of the ground and sat down at

the table and ate beside the precious incense burner he had likewise placed there. Then he asked them questions, to which they replied, and after several such occasions they got so friendly with him that they moved as guests into his house.

IN THE APPLE ORCHARD

In Cornwall, pretty much cut off from the rest of the British Isles until the great bridge over the Tamar was built in the nineteenth century, ancient customs remained. Some are followed to this day. It is apple-growing country, not to mention cider and scrumpy country, and here is information about magical ceremonies of the apple orchards.

Take a jar of cider, an empty bottle, and a loaded gun and go out into the orchard. Take a twig from the principal apple tree, put it in the bottle, and chant:

> Here's to thee, old apple tree!
> Hats full, sacks full, great bushel bags full!
> Hurrah!

Then fire the gun in the air. That will help the harvest. In Devonshire, in the West Country, they do this: Put some cider in a bowl and float some pieces of toast on top and go into the orchard in procession to put toast in the clefts of some apple trees and throw cider on the roots of some trees as you chant:

> Health to thee, good apple tree!
> Well to bear pockets full, hats full,
> Pecks full, bushel bags full!

In some other places in Britain the apple trees are not treated so well. They are beaten to make them bear fruitfully.

HOW TO GET A SPIRIT OUT OF A TREE

From Colin Wilson's *The Mammoth Book of the Supernatural* (1991):

In a book called *Ju-Ju in My Life*, James H. Neal, former Chief Investigations Officer for the Government of Ghana....[reports he]

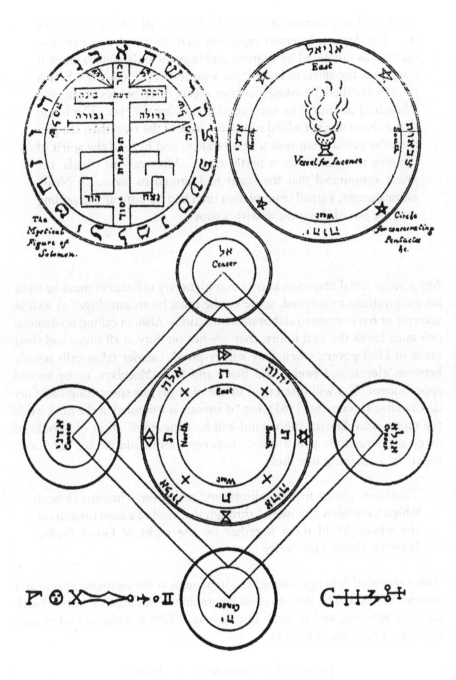

Figures for Solomonic conjurations.

was told that a certain small tree had defied all efforts to remove it.... The African foreman explained that the tree was a Fetich—that it was inhabited by a spirit, and that the only way to move it was to ask the spirit to leave it for another tree. Finally the Fetich priest was called; he asked for three sheep, three bottles of gin, and a hundred pounds if he succeeded in moving the tree. The blood of the sheep was sprinkled round the base of the tree, then the gin; then the priest went into a semi-trance, and begged the spirit of the tree to vacate it for a better tree.... After various rituals, the priest announced that the spirit had agreed to leave. To Neal's astonishment, a small team of men then had no difficulty in pulling the tree out of the ground with a rope.

THE IMPORTANCE OF TIMING

Any serious ritual magician knows that planetary influences must be right for conjurations to succeed, so he or she must be an astrologer as well as sorcerer or have access to elaborate instructions. Also, in calling up demons one must know the best hours; they are not on duty at all times and their ranks in Hell govern when they will respond. Lucifer takes calls mostly between eleven and twelve and three and four, Mondays, or by special appointment. You will often read in old manuscripts something like Guy de Chauliac's comment (1363) that "if anyone is wounded in the neck while the moon is in Taurus, the wound will be dangerous" or in old books of magical instructions you will see "between eleven and twelve" or "midnight" in something like this:

Take three chains from a gallows, and nails from a [torture] wheel which have been hammered through the head of a man broken on the wheel. Weld them together on the night of Good Friday between eleven and twelve....

There is special "energy" thought to be around at the solstices. Spring and summer are said to be the two most favorable seasons for conjuration (with some exceptions), and in some Hindu magic Tattvic Tides are taken into account. These are as follows:

Prithivi: 23 December to 21 March
Taijas: 21 March to 21 June

Vayu: 21 June to 23 September
Apas: 23 September to 23 December

Of these, *Taijas* may be the most propitious. Few non-Hindus pay any attention to this, but astrologically propitious times connected to the zoo of The Zodiac greatly influences the West.

THE EARLY RITE OF EXORCISM OF THE CHRISTIAN CHURCH

I print in full in another volume the exorcism ceremonies from the *Ritualum Romanum* which are still in (limited) use, and they are too extensive to be repeated although relevant here. Instead, I shall quote from the Pseudo-Clement's *De Constitutione apostolica*, Book 7, the rite as it existed in the early church. The catechumens in the early Christian church were novitiates, not yet admitted to full membership and mysteries, and in the modern services the first part of the Mass is still called "The Mass of the Catechcumens." After that part, and before the supreme magic of transubstantiation, the catechcumens had to leave the church; the initiates remained. The author, who pretended to be Pope Clement (but was not), wrote:

After the cathecumens have left, let the deacon say: "Pray, you who are possessed, you who are vexed by unclean spirits. Pray intently for them, all of you here present, that a kindly God, through [the intercession of] Christ, may rebuke the unclean spirits and snatch His servants from the grasp of the enemy. He Who rebuked a legion of devils and The Devil himself, the Prince of Evil, let Him now rebuke these foes of piety and let Him deliver His creatures from the vexations of The Devil and purify them He has created in His mighty wisdom. Let us also pray attentively, saying, Save them, O God, in Your power, and raise them up! Bow down, you who are possessed, to receive the blessing." Then let the bishop pray in these words: "You who have bound the mighty adversary and Who have torn asunder all his possessions, Who have given us the power to tread [with impunity] on scorpions and serpents and overcome all the power of the enemy, Who has delivered the murderous serpent to us in bondage, as though giving a sparrow to little children [as a harmless toy], the serpent before whom all things tremble in fear when without the face of Your power, You Who have cast him down like a lightning bolt from heaven to earth, not in a fall through space but in a fall from honor to disgrace because of his depraved obstinacy, You Whose glance dries up the abyss and Whose threats cause mountains to melt—the truth of The Lord remains forever; babes praise him; infants at the breast bless Him; angels celebrate and adore Him; He looks upon the earth and causes it to tremble; He touches the mountains and smoke issues forth; He extends His power over the ocean and it dries up and makes barren waste of all the rivers; clouds are the dust of His feet and He walks upon the waters as upon pavement. Only-begotten God, Son of a mighty Father, rebuke these vile spirits, and deliver the creations of Your hands from vexation by a hostile demon, because Yours is the glory, honor and adoration, and through You Your Father's, and the Holy Ghost's, forever and ever. AMEN."

LETTING THE SOUL ESCAPE

In Switzerland, as I have written in another book, they have tiny windows in the bedrooms of old chalets. These windows are opened only when a person dies in the room, to let the soul out. Here I add that in Britain and in some parts of America still, where old customs prevail, it is a ritual to open all windows and doors, and to unlock all locks when a person is about to die, so that the passing will be easy.

Many of the theories about ghosts relate to the spirit being unable or unwilling to move from familiar earthly surroundings. Even people who do not believe in ghosts sometimes visit the graves of the dead to talk to them. Jews pray at the tombs of relatives and annually place pebbles on the tombstone. This looks to us non-Jews as the survival of a rite in which more stones were placed annually on the dead to prevent them from getting up, but the pebbles may just be a token of tending the grave, a proof that the annual visit was made. In orthodoxy, the dead are quickly buried and are then dead, surviving only in the genes and memories of their descendants. There can be, therefore, no orthodox Jewish ghosts. Yet spirits of the dead are spoken of in the Old Testament and resurrection figures in the New Testament.

AFRICAN INFLUENCES ON THE ART OF THE AMERICAS

Quite apart from the African masks that so influenced Picasso and also American artists, there are the African elements that came to the Americas in connection with the voodoo of Haiti and the United States, the *obeah* of Brazil (also exported), and the peculiar and striking combination of African and Christian elements that is *Santería*. In an earlier book, *The Complete Book of the Devil's Disciples*, I remarked on the contribution of voodoo to the popular arts. Here I should mention the first book to explore the Afro-Caribbean, Cuban-American religion of *Santería* and its effect upon art. Arturo Lindsay collects eleven essays of importance in *Santería Aesthetics in Contemporary Latin American Art* (1996) and I hope that some of my friends who have documented the colorful *bodegas* and even some of the cult ceremonies of New York City may soon produce a volume or two of photographs.

VOODOO IN NEW ORLEANS A CENTURY AGO

American witchcraft activity today may be more common in the off-the-grid communes and even the cities of the Middle West than in The Big Easy, but New Orleans has always had a reputation as the voodoo capital of the United States. Now Anne Rice has brought New Orleans to even wider national prominence, because she is the most publicized figure in the occult world of Louisiana since Marie Laveau.

Politically incorrect now to a dangerous degree, nonethless this is what *Almanach de la Louisiane* published (in French) in 1886 about the *brulé zin* voodoo ceremonies in NOLA, contributing mightily to racial conflict and misunderstanding:

New Orleans presents the curious spectacle of this sombre cult brought from barbarism into the middle of our enlightened religious practices.

The black race, like all inferior and ignorant races, is naturally superstitious. In Africa it cultivates the most stupid fetishism. The most simple natural or scientific occurrences are beyond their intelligence and are attributed to a malignant force. The slaves brought from the banks of the Niger introduced and developed voodooism in Louisiana. Their ceremony consists of invoking, by incantations, the force (or spirit) of witchcraft and sorcery. This force or spirit is called *Grisgris*. To obtain his favors, they gather in a secret place, make themselves absolutely nude, and light a large fire on which bubbles a pot full of ingredients. Giving themselves up to dancing around the pot like the sorcerers of *Macbeth*, they throw into it various animals and snakes and unclean things, while mystically muttering sacramental words.

After a time of cooking, during which the Voodoos work themselves into an ecstatic state, the High Priest gives the signal for communion. Then each one of the faithful in turn dips his fingers into the horrible and nauseating food and puts it into his mouth after having made cabalistic signs on his forehead, his chest and shoulders. Once a year they have a ceremony in each congregation with human sacrifices. The rite calls for a child to be sacrificed in fire to the divine Voodoo. One of the small unfortunates condemned by fate to be sacrificed succeeded one day in escaping the sacrificial knife. He ran away and placed himself under the protection of the police. Although the authorities have made the greatest efforts for a long time to break up the Voodoos, they have never been able to prevent them from gathering for the mysteries of the night.

The original French document is reprinted in Jay K. Ditchy's *Les Acadiens Louisianais et Leur Parler* (Louisian Acadians and their Speech, 1932) and the English translation is in B. A. Botkin's *A Treasury of Afro-American Folklore* (1947). Add from "Creole Slave Songs" by George Washington Cable in *Century Magazine* 31: 6 (April, 1886):

To what extent the Voodoo worship still obtains here [Louisiana] would be difficult to say with certainty. The affair of June, 1884, as described by Messrs. Augustin and Whitney, eye-witnesses, was an orgy already grown horrid enough when they turned their backs upon it. It took place at a wild and lonely spot where the dismal cypress swamp behind New Orleans meets the waters of Lake Ponchartrain in a wilderness of cypress stumps and rushes. It would be hard to find in nature a more painfully desolate region. Here in a fisherman's cabin sat the Voodoo worshippers cross-legged on the floor about an Indian basket of herbs and some beans, some bits of bone, some oddly-wrought bunches of feathers, and some saucers of small cakes. The queen presided, sitting on the only chair in the room. There was no king, no snake [elsewhere: "The worship of Voodoo is paid to a snake kept in a box"]—at least none visible to the onlookers. Two drummers beat with their thumbs on gourds covered with sheepskin, and a white-wooled old man scraped that hideous combination of banjo and violin, whose head is covered with rattlesnake skin, and of which the Chinese are the makers and masters. There was singing—*"M'allé couri dans désir"* ["I am going into the   wilderness"], a chant and refrain not worth the room they would take [to report here]—and there was frenzy, and a circling march, wild shouts, delirious gesticulations and posturings, drinking, and amongst other frightful nonsense the old trick of making fire blaze from the mouth by spraying alcohol from it upon the flame of a candle....

White prejudice has even to our day stood in the way of a balanced appreciation of voodoo as a religion rather than as a some peculiar black aberration such as eating starch out of the box, composing rap lyrics, or shouting back at the preacher in church. The tourist-trap interest in voodoo has completely distorted what it is about. There is a great deal more to it than the admixture of black to white elements which produced American jazz and other features of American popular culture, a lot more to it than Mardi Gras costumes and flags, a lot more than voodoo dolls for a dollar to take home as souvenirs. In my view, it is a lot more colorful an American religion than Shakers, Unitarians, and Mormons combined. Though I must say that if you get beyond *The Book of Mormon* and don the white garments and participate in the secrets of The Temple, the rituals in Salt Lake City do rank among American sights to see—if you can get to see them.

THE DEGRADING OF A VOODOO WORSHIPPER AT DEATH

In Haiti, it is believed that persons of talent, wisdom, or psychic abilities are possessed of a spirit or *loa* and that after death, ceremonies must be performed to free the *loa*, perhaps so it can enter another member of the community. That exceptional ability comes from the inspiring ("breathing into") of a person by a spirit—the word *genius* has that meaning, as in *genius loci* for the tutelary spirit of a place—is believed in many cultures. Haitian voodoo is rather exceptional in that it greets the death of the adept with an office for releasing not only the soul of the dear departed but the spirits whom he used to advantage in this life.

At the voodoo worshipper's wake, Roman Catholic prayers and traditions have added to them certain African-derived pagan customs. For one, there is a *canari* or large pot into which various people place all kinds of food for the dead, and they stand around waving flags and green branches while voodoo *hougans* conduct prayers. The chants are translated by George Eaton Simpson in *American Folklore* for April–June 1946, and I present them with a few improvements in spelling and punctuation. Simpson reports that following prayers and hymns, amid loud lamentations the leader of the degradation ceremony says over the body, covered with a white sheet:

> Innocent! A good man has left us!
> Mother of children, weep!
> Weep, console yourselves.
> Accelon lived among us.
> He is dead!
> Master Pierre Jean-Baptiste lived among us.
> He is dead!
> General Baptiste lived among us.
> He is dead!
> Marius, who survived them,
> He is dead!
> But Brother Joseph is still with us.
> We weep, but we console ourselves because of him!

In the next room a *père-savanne* (wise man) intones:

> I have only one soul
> That is necessary to save.
> By the eternal flame,
> I must preserve it.

Simpson quotes the *houngan*'s next words, addressed directly to the corpse to lay the ghost:

> Boss Marius, here is a *canari* that your heirs have especially pre-
> pared for you so that in the future you will not have any trouble
> and demand other sacrifices of them. You others, the dead, you are
> always unreasonable. Because you have peace you forget that the
> times are hard and that on this earth we unfortunate [living] men
> are crushed by suffering. Leave your family to peace after this ser-
> vice, Boss Marius. Do not torment them, and do not send illnesses
> to their children or misery to their older people. You were always
> a good father when you were living. Continue to protect your fam-

ily after death. If you need other services give abundantly to your heirs in order to obtain satisfaction. Ohy, good father, good servant, good parent, good friend! Good-bye! Do not forget us as we shall not forget you.

Then, striking the *canari*, "three times with a piece of palm bark," he chants:

> I advise all the *loas*.
> *Legba-qui-Sous-Miroi,*
> *La oué! La oué!*
> In the "capital of the *loas*"
> A great event has occurred!
> Let us pray to God Who is in Heaven.
> Let us pray to the *loas* below.
> There is God, our Good Father,
> Who protects us!

Thje chief mourners dance in their places and wave their green branches, as do the rest. The *hougan* chants:

> Mother in heaven and mother below,
> *Hé lou-hé! Hé lou-hé!*
> None, no matter how great he may be, is superior to God!

"After all sorts of variations the couplet [there are three lines] is discontinued" and the ceremony of The Twins (a special category of the dead) begins.

> Twins, here is the food
> That we give you.
> Twins, you are accustomed,
> After you have recieved food from us,
> To say you have not eaten!

Another *hougan* adds:

> Twins, *Marassa*, the devil cries.
> *Dossi! Dossi-dossa!* the devil cries!
> *Credo*, Mother of Twins,
> The devil cries!

The song is repeated over and over, the dancing becomes more animated, and then a *badjican* (acolyte to a *hougan*) chants:

> I say, Mother of Twins,
> Please leave this room!
> *Marassa*, Twins,
> Please leave this room!

The *hougans* present, who may have been rivals of the dead in local magic and may still be rivals of each other, nonetheless combine to offer prayers and hymns to God and to *loas*, to Roman Catholic saints and tribal gods, to angels and to *zanges* "of the woods...known and unknown," imploring all powers to admit the dead man into paradise and peace. As throughout, I could improve the translation ("Saint Mary" would probably be better as "Holy Mary," and so on) but I quote Simpson's translation:

> Saint Mary, Mother of God,
> Pray for all the children.
> Aradas, our friend, has departed!
> Pardon for all of the children!
> Say good evening to me, Haitians!
> Say good evening to me, Haitians!
> It is a mistake to have too much confidence.
> Say good evening to me, Haitians!
> It is a mistake to have too much confidence.
> Laoka, prepare the charms.
> Laoka, good dancer,
> Prepare the charms, Laoka!

At this point all the spirits with whom the dead man dealt in his life, all the *loas* of Arada and the Congo, return to the assembly and one by one possess the frenzied dancers. Each of these acts in the character of the particular *loa* who has entered them and each in tears approach the corpse to discover how he died, what his last wishes are, what is to be done, and shouts the messages to the dancing and mourning assembly. The magic shells used by the dead *hougan* are brought out, and, having been muttered over and charged by the officiating priest, are placed on the floor, three times doused with *tafia* (homemade rum), and, a candle lighted beside them, consulted for messages. This is done three times, in the course of which the officiating *hougan* announces: "three indifferent me, four *loas* demanding offerings" as well as "two enemies plotting against the family, three children of the dead *hougan*, two curious men, a thunder stone, and a relative seeking protection because he is in danger [of witchcraft]." A *vévé* is drawn on the ground by the *hougan* with symbols of the crossroads, the four cardinal points of the compass, the four family *loas*, liberty and peace.

The praying family declares itself ready to make "any sacrifices" as they plead for mercy and grace to the *zanges* "of our fathers" and the *loas* of the family. The officiating *hougan* declares solemnly that the dead *hougan* has gone to *Ville au Camp*, the resting place of the spirits "under the water" and from there will continue to protect his family members so long as they show themselves pious and worthy. The *hougan* then breaks into an improvised chant with this "dolorous rhythm" [Simpson means "refrain"]:

> *Bassin* [basin], *canari* [jar],
> I am going to seek a new charm.

This refrain is repeated by the assembly, dancing with their green branches, and then the *hougan* sings
> *Canari* of the *houmfort! Canari* of the *houmfort!*
> I am going to take a wife
> In a balance, *canari* of the *houmfort!*

Whatever that means! Then:

> *Loas Bolodjoré*, seek some leaves
> To cover the *canari*!

and, with " appropriate gestures,"

> Ah! *Legba* San-Yan San-Yan!
> We shall break the *canari*
> To serve all the living!

"All the children"—*hougans, badjicans, petites feuilles* (literally "little leaves, but actually people who have been helped by the dead man's magic during his life) then "pretend to cover the *canari*," a hymn of adoration is sung, and relatives and friends pile offerings of money on top of the jar. Then the officiating *hougan* draws a cross with a pencil on it and the pencil is given in turn to everyone present, each of whom also makes a cross. Whether this is a Christian symbol or the signatures of the illiterate is uncertain. This constitutes a kind of document, in any case, which can be adduced against the dead should he later demand more offerings and sacrifices. The *bougan* strikes the jar lightly three times, and so does everyone else included in the bargain. Then they all march around the jar, with the strut familiar from the people "second lining" in jazz funerals, first in one direction, then in the other.

By this time it is four o'clock in the morning and the participants are hoarse from singing, tired from dancing, and hungry, so food is served—even to the *loas* (for whom it is placed under the trees outside and the dead man.

Now the *loas* of the dead man can be sent on their way.

St. Barbara has been co-opted for voodoo worship.

> Everything is vanity,
> Lies, fragility.

and

> Come back, sinner,
> It is God who calls you

and other songs to send the *loas* off.

> Spirits of Guinea,
> Today we renounce you.
> Seek again a rock
> Which is suitable for you,
> Where you may put your *garde*.

The *guardes* (amulets, charms) are no longer of use to this corpse. The officiating *bougan* leads off a procession, followed by two *badjicans* carrying the *canari*, followed by a member of the deceased's family, carrying two elements of the food already in the *canari* (cornmeal and water), and the rest. The group in the other room joins in and all sing:

> Let us send away *papa-loi*
> To seek the place he must find.

The chant continues until the procession reaches the crossroads. "After an impressive silence, all sorts of gestures to the four cardinal points, invocations, and genuflexions" follow. You, dear reader, cannot conduct such a ceremony because neither Simpson nor I offer full details, needed magical words, etc.

This may be a good point to stress something which applies to each and every ritual, recipe, instruction, etc., in this present book. No book can be on sound legal ground—as this one certainly intends to be—which, as publishers' contracts often say, contains "instruction, recipe or formula...injurious to the reader" if the reader is foolish enough to follow it. I must insist that if you do attempt anything injurious to yourself you do so without my permission or encouragement; you are on your own. Remember that, and act accordingly. Releasing *loas* may, in fact, be far less dangerous to anyone's bodily or mental health than some of the things described in this present book, but nothing in this book at all are you urged to try, nor are any guarantees offered or responsibilty taken by the author. Quite the opposite. Now back to the ceremonies, which have been long, but I do want at least one very long ritual in this collection, to stand for many others.

At the crossroads, always a place of power in ceremonies, the *hougan* chants:

> Congo, open paradise,
> That paradise,
> For us to enter!
> We send away all *loas*.
> [*Loas*] If you continue to [be] disturb[ed],
> You must tell us what you desire.
> We have no further relations with you,
> On earth,
> Until we come before God.
> Good courage, friends!
> Peace for the living and the dead!

New cries and lamentations follow and when the *hougan* has restored silence:

> Now we shall dance!
> We shall dance around the broken *canari*.

They all dance around the *hougan* who, lifting the *canari* on high with all the solemnity of the elevation of the Host at Mass, sings a hymn, "Where shall I find refuge?", and shatters the *canari*.

"The food is scattered, the loas are satisfied, and the crowd breaks into disorderly flight," adds Simpson. No one dares to look back, much less take any of the scattered food or money (the property now of the *loas*) on pain of death within the year.

Simpson concludes with a few paragraphs we for once shall quote with just a few cuts for the sake of brevity:

> Several hours later the body is placed in its coffin, and the scene ... in the house almost defies description. All the loas [persons possessed by them] ...jump and whirl...not sad in their mourning. Roasted corn, chopped coconut, bread, and cake cut into small pieces [similar to the contents of the *canari*] are thrown like confetti. The flags [of *loas*, not the nation] salute the body, the coffin is covered again, and the crying is intensified. Four badjicans hoist the coffin to their shoulders. Then the procession forms itself again and starts off toward the mysterious spring whose waters have cured many sicknesses which the physicians had pronounced incurable.
>
> > Oh, Congo! Congo loas!
> > Oh, loas Arada! All you loas,
> > Open the door, open the road,
> > Open the road for us to pass.
>
> But first the coffin is taken to the trees of the loas, and to all of the sacred places. Finally they arrive at the last station. The bearers of the coffin [with it] circle the spring several times. The coffin is swung for each of the four cardinal points. The rain of roasted corn is repeated. The houngan has performed the complicated rite and the cortegè returns to the house. The pèresavanne now takes charge of the participants, and in the midst of piercing cries leads the funeral procession to the village. Those who remain in the house throw water to the left, to the front, and to the right at all the entrances. Everything has been done properly and the [deceased] houngan may be proud of his last ceremonies. Nothing can prevent him from enjoying happiness in Ville-au-Camp, the residence of the loas.

Nothing except perhaps the magic of another *hougan* who, with the assistance of the dreaded Baron Saturday, turns the dead man into a zombie! The participants, even the onlookers—who must not count funeral carriages unless they want to die within the year!—and those who had no connection with the dead man, all are diminished and threatened by any death in the community. "Ask not for whom the bell tolls...."

BURIAL OF THE DEAD

Some magic is involved in the Christian rites for the burial of the dead, most noticeably the asperging of the corpse before it is brought into the church lest demons come in with it. On top of that, Christian rites of baptism and burial are among sacraments deriving from the earliest days of the religion, while marriage was not so sacred a rite for more than a thousand years. Some people begin to date the humanity of man from the time, lost in the mists of prehistory, when a bouquet of flowers or an offering of useful grave goods was buried beside a body, when love and tenderness—and some belief in a life after this life—entered into the thought of men and women.

The Christian burial rites are too familiar to be repeated here. We may, however, say something of the less familiar but traditional burial of Jews. Even when superstition was rife in medieval Jewish communities and the cabalists were very active, nevertheless Jewish burial was notably practical and unsuperstitious. From the will of Eleazar of Mainz (*c.* 1337):

> Wash me clean, comb my hair, trim my nails, as I was wont to do
> in my lifetime, so that I may go clean to my eternal resting place,
> just as I used to go on every Sabbath to the synagogue. Put me in
> the ground at the right hand of my father....

He was to be buried without much delay or ceremony to "lie with his fathers," anointed with pleasant unguents but not embalmed like an Egyptian with chemicals, and wrapped in a linen shroud. Shrouds rather than clothes were common for Christians at one time, too, but we had the superstition that all strings attached to the shroud had to be undone before the burial; the idea was not to put obstacles in the way of the escape of the soul. It was the custom for Jewish mourners to tear their clothes in sorrow, for the pallbearers to walk barefoot, for the women to walk chanting a dirge before the bier (perhaps with one with a drum beating it slowly), and for any Jew who saw the procession pass to join it and follow the body to the grave. Later the bereaved would sit in mourning and be visited and consoled by faithful friends. This is called today "sitting *shiva*" and is practiced even by "non-observant" Jews, because it is a very sensible way of working out grief, honoring the dead, and letting go. Quite a while after the Jewish burial a marker would be placed on the grave and after that it was supposed to be visited yearly on the anniversary by relatives of the deceased.

While Christians looked to a continuation in hell, purgatory, or paradise and to "the same bodies" which they had in this life resurrected at the Last Judgment—"the trumpet shall sound and the dead shall arise, incorruptible"—the Jews once dead would never rise again but in their descendants the Seed of Israel would last until the Messiah and the end of the world. For Jews, death was the natural end of life. For Christians, death was the supernatural beginning of eternity.

The Jews used to use the ashes of a red heifer burned near The Temple to take away the pollution caused by the dead, but later their scriptures announced "we are all polluted by the dead" and purification rights fell into disuse, although there were certain taboos still clinging to the dead body. Certainly Jews even more than Christians believe that the dead should be left alone and that necromancy or grave desecration is terribly wrong. The horrendous burning of dead Jews in the Holocaust (along with gays, gypsies, and other "unwanted" persons) was the final insult to those whose faith required them to be returned to the earth from which they had sprung, "ashes to ashes, dust to dust," but by the methods of nature, not the efficient horrors of technology and ovens.

The Chinese, to cite another culture, also consigned the dead to the earth instead of burning them or putting the corpses out to be devoured by scavengers, chiefly birds (both methods still used in India in some faiths). The Chinese gave the corpse a going-away ceremony. They put "hell money" into the coffin to help the departed in the next life. Traditionally the Chinese wore white for mourning, and so did we in the West until black became the color of choice. I notice now that the Roman Catholic Requiem Mass seldom or never calls for black vestments anymore; white is now thought to be more upbeat. When my mother, a Catholic, died more than 20 years ago I found it very difficult to get the burial Mass said in black vestments—and in Latin. Customs change.

An interesting Chinese custom is that mourners are given candies to eat as they depart from a funeral "to bring sweetness back into their lives." They remember their ancestors, bring food and money to their graves, honor them, try never to disgrace them, and send off with the relatives lists from which the names of future descendants will be selected so that, in this way, the departed will be able to intercede with the gods for their descendants for generation after generation. The dead to the Chinese are always watching the behavior of their descendants.

In Africa the dead may be kept in the house and on occasion taken down from their resting places and treated to parties. Skulls or complete corpses may be part of everyday households. Or in other ways the spirits of the departed may be kept near, sometimes honored, even feared.

In some Asian religions, monks and such are not given permanent names until after they are dead. It is those names that are inscribed on burial tablets. Some Asian religions look upon death as a transition, not an end, and in a sense there are no dead members of the group, only reincarnated ones or those released from the whole cycle of life and death.

Improper burial or improper lives are said in many societies to lead to unquiet graves. In many societies ghosts stalk. In Greece and other countries, most famously Transylvania, vampires and other revenants rise. In Bermuda, there are tales of restless coffins. In many cultures there are stories about the reanimation of the dead.

In some other groups, Martians and other creatures from outer space have taken over in popular imagination from spectral skeletons and the undead. Most people do not want to think much about death, and some wrote to tell me that a book I had recommended for those who wanted a physician to explain to them precisely what happens to the body at the point of death and afterwards shocked and disturbed them mightily. One person said she wished she had never read it, although she admitted she eagerly sought it out and couldn't put it down. She severely censured me for giving her the title of the book. Most people hate to face the final fact of life. They do not want "gory details," as one put it. A less horrific book, if you must have one, is by a journalist and not a physician. It takes you through the shutdown of the body but only as far as the "first spadeful." It is Robert T. Hatch's *What Happens When You Die.* Post-"spadeful" is too grisly for most people. They are satisfied that, as Mike Nichols and Elaine May put it in a skit on American funerals years ago, "two men come and pick up the body and do God knows what with it."

NECROMANTIC RITE

The Witch of Endor in The Bible raised a spirit from the dead. Edward Kelley and an assistant in a Lancashire graveyard are likewise said to have done so. Éliphas Lévi claimed to have raised Apollonius of Tyana (but he did not say much). Throughout history, in other cultures as well as our own, through necromancy and other black arts and through spiritualism (which somehow has not been greeted with the usual opprobrium for trying to contact the dead), people have sought messages from The Other

Side, or at least the comforting assurance that there is not "mere oblivion" on the far side of physical death.

In his *Transcendental Magic*, as translated by A. E. Waite, Éliphas Lévi, ritual magician, writes with some horror of one ritual for raising the dead:

There are also necromantic processes, comprising the tearing up of earth from grave with the [finger]nails, dragging out bones, placing them crossways on the breast, then assisting at midnight mass on Christmas Eve, and flying out of the church at the moment of consecration, crying: "Let the dead rise from their tombs!" Thereafter the procedure involves returning to the grave-

yard, taking a handful of earth nearest to the coffin, running to the door of the church, [the congregation of] which has been alarmed by the clamour, depositing the two bones crosswise and again shouting: "Let the dead rise from their tombs!" If the operator escapes being seized and shut up in a madhouse, he must retire at a slow pace, and count four thousand five hundred steps in a straight line, which means following a broad road or scaling walls. Having traversed this space, he lies down upon the earth, as if in a coffin, and repeats in lugubrious tones: "Let the dead rise from their tombs!" Finally, he calls thrice the person whose apparition is desired. No doubt anyone who is mad enough and wicked enough to abandon himself to such operations is predisposed to all chimeras and all phantoms. Hence the recipe of the GRAND GRIMOIRE [a guide to rites of magic] is most efficacious, but we advise none of our readers to test it.

THE NECROMANTIC RITUAL BOOK

Leilia Wendell of New Orleans has produced a pamphlet of this title (1995) "to align one's soul with the Death Energy." She offers "rites of twilight" she considers neither white nor black magic. She advises the practitioner to get used to death by spending the night in a tomb—alone, in pitch blackness, beside the "exposed" corpse. She stresses "no TVs, no radios, etc." She is not adverse to using the corpse as a "catalyst," but regards necrophilia as the height of "irreverence" toward the dead. She recommends you get a hexagonal key from the hardware store to open caskets.

I begin to understand why, though cremation is strictly forbidden by some mainline religions, it is rapidly gaining in popularity in the US: in 1996 it is preferred by 43 percent, up from 37 percent in 1990. Who wants to be disturbed, even desecrated, when they have gone to supposed "eternal rest"?

We used to worry about resurrectionists who robbed graves and sold corpses to anatomists. (In Britain, Burke and Hare created their own supplies for the business.) Now we must worry about drop-in visitors. You can decapitate corpses. You can nail them to (not just into) the coffin, bury the heart elsewhere, or put certain terrible charms in the coffin with the body or under the slab that covers the tomb. Those are protections against necromancers. Against romancers of necrology, one is almost tempted to put a bomb in the coffin which will teach the tamperer a lesson. Legal exhumations could bring along the Bomb Squad.

If ghouls like death so much, one is tempted to help them along. I think "necromantic rituals" are no better than housebreaking. True, the laws are such that if a burglar breaks into your home and injures himself on some unsafe thing you have permitted—or even simply breaks a leg falling downstairs because he couldn't see over the top of your big TV set he's stealing—he can sue you. Let the ghouls try to sue the dead for unsafe conditions of grave molesting.

So ghouls are, as someone said of biography, "one of the new terrors of death!" For the necromancers, try burying the body with a knife; the corpse can fight back (voodoo worshippers believe) if anyone tries to raise it from the dead. As for creepy curiosity seekers, it seems too bad it is so hard to catch them and get them psychiatric help.

Communion with the dark angel Azrael, Ms. Wendell warns, can make one lose one's sense of perspective. Do not become too morbid or caught up in "workings" like this with corpses! She writes:

> The Death Energy is meant to be savored slowly like a fine wine, not guzzled like a six-pack of Bud.

Some kinds of intoxication I don't approve of at all. Send her off to the Mummy Museum in Mexico, but keep her and her associates away from graveyards. Let the dead rest in peace. If I were dead and anyone broke into my tomb for a bit of her kind of meddling meditation, I'd haunt the hell out of them, if I could. And if the dead don't mind, some of the living definitely do. Many of the living are still very emotionally attached to their dead. In earlier times they wore locks of the hair of their departed loved ones in lockets, or bracelets or rings woven of the hair. Today they are being offered jewelry which can hold a pinch of the ashes of cremation!

If you think that turning the product of the crematorium into a memorial or a *momento mori* that you wear as jewelry is sick, I think breaking into coffins to commune with corpses is sicker. I for one look with disgust and horror on the fact that Ms. Wendell's little pamphlet has gone through several printings already. That is evidence that she is far from alone in her strange obsession.

HOW FIRM A FOUNDATION

We now have ceremonies of laying cornerstones but ancient peoples had rituals to guarantee a firm foundation. They built upon a skull or sacrificed body, they fortified mortar with blood of humans or animals, they built a shadow of a person into a wall, they added water in a bottle to the foundation, they used bread and salt to make the basis firm, and they believed that faith was the firmest foundation of all and that he who was without faith built upon sand.

BLACK MAGIC CONJURATION WITH A TALISMAN

I, NN, a servant of God, desire, call upon thee, and conjure thee, Tehor, by all the holy angels and archangels, by St. Michael, Sts.

Seal of Fortune

Gabriel, Raphael, Uriel, Thrones, Dominions, Principalities, Virtues, Cherubim and Seraphim, and with unceasing voice I cry: Holy, Holy, Holy is the Lord God of Sabbath and by the most terrible words [I conjure]: Soab, Sother, Emmanuel, Edon, Amathon, Mathay, Adonai, El, Eli, Eloy, Zoag, Dios, Anath[anatos], Tafa, Uabo, Tertragrammaton, Aglay, Joshua, Jonas, Caplie, Caiphas. Appear before me, NN, [Tehor] in a mild and human form and do what I desire!

This spell ought to be directed at a member of that order of angels called Thrones and you need the name of one to do so. Try Aha, Roah, Habu, Aromicha, Lemar, or Hamaya.

MAGIC OF THE CONGO

Much of the infusion of African beliefs into the religions of African-Americans (and sometimes through them to other Americans) can be traced back to The Congo. There there are two kinds of dealers in magic. The bad ones are wicked wizards, called *mlozi*. The good ones are what we might call witchdoctors and the natives call *mufumu* or *mganga*; these are root doctors, counselors and psychologists and social workers, sages and prophets and exorcists and trance mediums. Belief in their powers does much to assist the medicines to work and the advice to be heeded. They may wear bones and skulls instead of white coats but their doctoring works most of the time, and when it fails it is assumed that they are being bested by a still more powerful witchdoctor.

IF YOU'VE GOT THE MONEY, HONEY, I'VE GOT THE THYME

Here is one of many rituals that promise to make you rich. It takes time, and thyme. Cut pieces of paper the size of dollar bills. Put them one by one in a box, sprinkling thyme on each before adding the next, twelve in all (for the months of a year). Tie up the box with green string using thirty–one pieces (one for each day of a regular month). Bury the box seven inches deep (one inch for each day of the week), preferably at the Feast of All Saints. Dig it up exactly a year later. You ought to find twelve real bills. They may be dollar bills or hundred dollar bills.

It is faster to put into a conjure bag a cent, a nickle, a dime, a quarter, a half dollar, and dollar- and five-dollar, even ten-dollar and twenty-dollar bills. Do not open for a week, and carry this conjure bag everywhere with you. When you finally open the bag, you hope to find in it your money increased seven-fold—or seven times seven, if you are really lucky. Meanwhile, at least you have never been broke, for a whole week.

TO CAUSE A GIRL TO SEEK YOU OUT, HOWEVER PRUDENT SHE MAY BE

Whether in the increase or the wane of the Moon, a star must be observed between eleven o'clock and midnight. But before beginning do as follows.

Take a virgin parchment. Write thereon her name whose presence you desire. The parchment must be represented as in the, below, left.

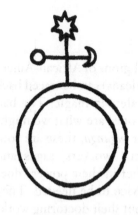

On the other side inscribe these words: *Melchiael, Bareschas.* Then place your parchment on the earth, with the person's name against the ground. Place your right foot above it, while your left knee is best [*bent* is meant] to the earth. In this position observe the brightest star in the firmament, holding in the right hand a taper of white wax large enough to last for an hour, and recite the following

CONTURATION [CONJURATION]

I salute and conjure you, O beautiful Moon, O beautiful star, O bright light which I hold in my hand! By the air which I breathe, by the breath which is within me, by the earth which I touch, I conjure you, and by all the names of the spirits who are princes residing in you; by the ineffable Name N, which hath created all; by thee, O resplendent Angel Gabriel, together with the Prince Mercury, Michiael, and Melchidael! I conjure you again by all the divine Names of God, that you send down to obsess, torment, and harass the body, spirit, soul, and five senses of the nature of N., whose name is written here below, in such a way that she shall come unto me and accomplish my will, having no friendship for any one in the world, but especially for N., so long as she shall be indifferent to me. So shall she endure not, so shall she be obsessed, so suffer, so be tormented. Go then promptly; go, Melchidael, Baresces, Zazel, Firiel, Malcha, and all those who are without you [*sic*]. I conjure you by the great living God to accomplish my will, and I, N., do promise to satisfy you duly. Having thrice pronounced this conjuration, place the paper on the parchment and let it burn. Take the parchment on the morrow, put it in your left shoe, and there leave it until the person for whom you have operated shall have come to seek you out. You must specify in the Conjuration the day you desire her to come, and she will not fail.

This conjuration is criticized by Arthur Edward Waite where he gives it in *The Book of Black Magic and of Pacts* (fifth printing, 1984). Nonetheless, if you really have trouble getting a date you may think of going to such extremes, silly as it seems.

THE LOVE OF MONEY IS THE ROOT OF ALL EVIL

Legends are plentiful about supernatural creatures—trolls in Scandinavia, dwarfs in Germany, elves in England, terrifying gods in Mexico and Asia guarding hoards of silver, gold, and gems—and then there are the treasures which have been hidden by men who, having died, come back or have to be drawn back by necromancy to reveal hoards to the living. It is striking that, having summoned the dead, people seem to want to know not so much What is it like after death? as Where can I get some gold while I am alive? The history of magic is the history of the search for power, and treasure is always a part of the appeal. Magicians want instructions on where to dig. Alchemists seek the Philosopher's Stone, which can change base metal into gold. Astrologers want to know when to try to make money. Palmists and other fortune-tellers are consulted to say if and when one is going to be rich.

Here is one "very powerful conjuration...for treasures hidden by men or spirits, that the same [he means the treasures] may be possessed and transported." True, the magician needs to perform the usual preparations, which ideally involve three weeks of vegetarian dieting and one week of a tiny meal (salt-free!) each evening, of black bread and beans, for a week, and elaborate prayers and ablutions and costume and fumigation and incensing and preparing the circle and magical instruments. The one thing you need most here is the Pentacle of Solomon which I have conveniently placed on the title page of the book you hold, so aren't you glad you purchased (or borrowed) it and read this far? Now here is the conjuration:

> I command you, O all you demons dwelling in these parts, or in
> what part of the world soever ye may be, by whatsoever power may
> have been given you and our holy Angels over this place, and by
> the powerful Principality of the infernal abysses, as also by all your
> brethren, both general and special demons, whether dwelling in
> the East, West, South, or North, or in any side of the earth, and,
> in like manner, by the power of God the Father, by the wisdom of
> God the Son, by the virtue of the Holy Ghost, and by the author-
> ity I derive from our Saviour Jesus Christ, the only Son of the
> Almighty and the Creator, who made us and all creatures from
> nothing, who also ordains that you do hereby abdicate all power

to guard, habit, and abide in this place; by whom further I constrain and command you, *nolens volens*, without guile and deception to declare me your names, and to leave me in peaceable possession and rule over this place, of whatsoever legion ye be and of whatsover part of the world; by order of the Most Holy Trinity, and by the merits of the Most Holy and Blessed Virgin, as also of all the saints, I unbind you all, spirits who abide in this place, and I drive you to the deepest infernal abysses. Thus: Go, all spirits accursed, who are condemned to the flame eternal which is prepared for you and your companions, if ye be rebellious and disobedient. I conjure you by the same authority, I exhort and call you, by all the powers of your superior demons, to come, obey, and reply positively to what I direct you in the name of Jesus Christ. Whence, if you or they do not obey promptly and without tarrying, I will shortly increase your torments for a thousand years in hell. I constrain you therefore to appear here in comely human shape, by the Most High Names of God, HAIN, LON, HILAY, SABOATH, HELIM, RADISHA, LEDIEHA, ADONAY, JEHOVA, YAH, TETRAGRAMMATON, SADAI, MESSIAS, AGIOS, ISCHYROS, EMMANUEL, AGLA, Jesus who is ALPHA and OMEGA, the beginning and the end, that you be justly established in the fire, having no power to reside, habit, or abide in this place henceforth; and I require your doom by the virtue of the said names, to wit, that St. Michael drive you to the uttermost of the infernal abyss, in the name of the Father, and of the Son, and of the Holy Ghost. So be it.

I conjure thee, Acham, or whomsoever thou mayest be, by the Most Holy Names of God, by MALHAME, JAE, MAY, MARRON, JACOB, DASMEDIAS, ELOY, ATERESTIN, JANASTARDY, FINIS, AGIOS, ISCHYROS, OTHEOS, ATHANATOS, AGLA, JEHOVA, HOMOSION, AGA, MESSIAS, SOTHER, CHRISTUS VINCIT, CHRISTUS IMPERAT, INCREATUS SPIRITUS SANCTUS.

I conjure thee, Cassiel, or whomsoever thou mayest be, by all the said names, with power and with exorcism! I warn thee by the other sacred names of the most great Creator, which are or shall hereafter be communicated to thee; harken forthwith and immediately harken to my words, and observe them inviolably, as sentences of the last dreadful day of judgment, which thou must obey inviolately, nor think to repulse me because I am a sinner, for therein shalt thou repulse the commands of the Most High God. Knowest thou not that thou art bereft of thy powers before thy Creator and ours? Think therefore what thou refusest, and pledge therefore thine obedience, swearing by the said last dreadful day of judgment, and by Him who hath created all things by His word, whom all creatures obey. *Per sedem Baldarey et per gratiam et diligentiam tuam habuisti ab eo hanc nalatimanamilam*, as I command thee.

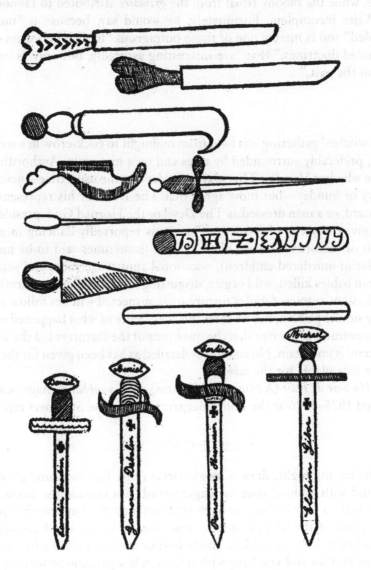

This does sound like a lawyer after money, but the "boilerplate" language doesn't mention "lead me to the treasure" and at least some of the Most High Names of God just aren't, nor is it explained just how the user of these names of power derives the authority to employ them like this. Waite gives this conjuration without explanation. At least it does not involve the "bloody sacrifice, characterised by details of a monstrous kind" that Waite gives in the same *Book of Black Magic and of Pacts* (Chapter 7) and is complete, while the bloody ritual from the *grimoire* attributed to Honorius is in Waite incomplete. Fortunately, he would say, because it "must be avoided" and is merely one of those outrageous "foolish mysteries of old exploded doctrines," that "are interesting assuredly, but only as curiosities of the past."

SABBAT

The witches' gathering was held from midnight to cock-crow in a secluded spot, preferably surrounded by trees and on a mountain. Authorities disagree whether Monday, Thursday or Friday was the usual time—never Saturday or Sunday—but most agree that The Devil or his representative, Leonard, or a man dressed as The Devil or the Horned God, presided and was given obscene obeisances. There was reportedly dancing in a ring, harsh or discordant music, black candles (sometimes said to be made of the fat of murdered children), occasional animal sacrifices and some say human babies killed, wild orgies, disgusting food and plenty to drink. The confessions extracted under torture from suspected witches follow a strikingly similar pattern, but whether this is evidence of what happened or simply repetition of a script that the questions of the torturers led the witches to recite is uncertain. No routine as detailed as has been given for the Black Mass is available for the *sabbat*.

Un Soir de Folie (A Night of Madness), with a *sabbat* onstage, was presented 1925–1926 at the Folies Bergères, Montague Summers reports.

RAISING LUCIFER

Thursday midnight, draw a magic circle (nine feet in diameter) on the ground with a bloodstone or magic sword. Just outside the circle at the East, make a triangle large enough for Lucifer to stand in when he appears. The point of the triangle is away from the circle, the two base angles of it marked by lit black candles. You hold your magic wand (of ash) and handfuls of vervain and you have within the circle a parchment with a powerful pentacle drawn on it a single silver coin, no other metal within the circle. Your incantation (thrice):

> O Lucifer, appear before me!
> I give you my heart!
> I give you my soul!
> I give you my body!
> My desires and my service are yours!
> Look favorably upon me!

Or without anything but two handfuls of wormwood, one thrown up (left) and one thrown down (right), and reciting the Lord's Prayer *backwards* you can make a pact with The Devil, who will appear (or send a representative).

RITES OF THE ORDER OF THE GOLDEN DAWN

The rituals of this mystic order were allegedly dictated by astral spirits to S. L. Magregor Mathers, which is even less credible than the angel Moroni delivering golden plates to be magically translated from "Reformed Egyptian"to Joseph Smith in Upstate New York. The poet William Butler Years took time out from trying to raise the ghost of a rose from its ashes to tinker with the rituals, too, and in the long run, after various battles within the organization, A. E. Waite revised the rituals. You will find them, if you need them, in renegade Israel Regardie's *The Golden Dawn* (2 vols., reprinted 1938) and perhaps better in R. Torrens's *Secret Rituals of the Golden Dawn* (1973), and you might have a look at Yeats's pamphlet called *Is the Order of the Golden Dawn to Remain a Magical Order?* (1901). New Falcon Publications of Tempe (AZ) offers Regardie on three tapes and *The Complete Golden Dawn System of Magic* and other books. The rite for invisibility in the new, sixth edition of *The Golden Dawn*, by Regardie *et al.*,for instance, is interesting but too long to reproduce here. You could seek it out.

The problem with the magical order's magical rituals to accomplish The Great Work is that they don't work.

A RITUAL FROM ST. HILDEGARD OF BINGEN

This famous German saint (1098–1179) recorded her mystical visions in *Scivia* along with many medical and magical recipes and rituals. Here is one:

Take a wheaten loaf and mark a cross on top of it. Draw a jacinth through one arm of the cross and say: May God Who cast away all the preciousness of gems from The Devil when he transgressed His precepts remove from you, NN, all phantoms and magical spells and free you henceforth from the malady of this madness.

Then draw a jacinth through the other cross of the loaf and say: As the splendor with which The Devil once was possessed departed from him as a result of his transgression, so may this madness which haunts NN by various phantasmagorias and magical arts be removed from you. Let it depart from you!

The patient then eats the bread around the cross and will be cured.

A RITUAL FROM NAROPA

Naropa is the name Tibeta lamas give to a learned adept from Kashmir who learned what Buddhists call the "Short Path" whereby his black magic would be forgiven and in a single life he might attain buddhahood. Naropa put a great deal of effort into learning from his master, one Tilopa, but became enlightened one day in a flash when Tilopa took off his shoe and hit Naropa once with it in the face, very hard.

Ascribed to Naropa, the tenth-century miracle worker, is *Chös drug bsdus pahi zin bris* (A Treatise of Six Doctrnes). From that an Englishwoman, Alaxandra David-Neel in *Magic and Mystery in Tibet* (reprinted 1958), draws an abbreviated account of Naropa's method of *tumo* to be used, of course, by monks well trained in breathing exercises.

The posture of the body is described as follows:
Squat with the legs crossed, the hands passing under the thighs and then clasped together.

In that posture one must (1) turn the stomach from right to left thrice and from left to right thrice ; (2) churn the stomach as hard as possible; (3) shake the body in the way "a restive horse shakes imself," and perform a short leap while keeping the legs in the same crossed position. These three exercises must be repeated thrice successively and concluded with a leap, jumping as high as possible.

It does not seem to me very wonderful that a man should feel warm after performing this feat. The exercise is borrowed from

Indian *hatha yoga* practices, but in *hatha yoga* treatises it is not connected with the kind of *tumo* [briefly, control of such things as bodily temperature in trance state] known to Tibetans.

The process continues by holding in the breath, until the abdomen becomes "the shape of a pot."

Next comes the visualization of Dorjee Naljorma....

We interrupt to explain that in a state of relaxed calm Dorjee Naljorma, a feminine deity, is called up in the mind by imagining a golden lotus existing in your body at the level of the navel and in it, shining like the sun, is the syllable or "seed" *ram* and above it the one called *ma*. The goddess arises from *ma*, from the "fire." As soon as one visualizes the goddess rising from this fire, one identifies oneself with her. When one has done this, one imagines the letter *A* in one's navel and another Tibetan letter, *Ha*, at the top of one's head. Breathing correctly stokes the fire, the *Ha* as it were drips oil down to the *A* to feed the fire which gradually fills the body, taking it over entirely.

To return now to the exercise or ritual being described:

Then a sun is imagined in the palm of each hand, on the sole of each foot and below the navel. By rubbing together the suns placed in the hands and in the feet, fire flows up and strikes the sun below the navel, which flares up in its turn and fills the whole body with fire. The exercise ends by twenty-one big leaps.

I wonder if this ought really to be included here among magical rituals, because although the effect achieved is a marvel any Tibetan would say it is unusual but not unnatural, a perfectly ordinary and natural result of the power of the mind to create by suggestion. But wouldn't we call that magic? There are many more magical rituals and more spectacular results, or delusions, achieved in the vast corpus of Tibetan "magic and mystery," and if you read this book by Davis-Neel or any of the other first-person accounts of Westerners amng the Tibetans you will be amazed. Tibetan belief has reached our shores, too. As I write the reincarnation of a Tibetan lama is thought to be a young boy living in one of our western states. He is on the verge of adolescence now and for some years has been deeply educated in Tibetan mysteries. Coming from an American schoolchild, they seem even more strange to us, but they really are no more strange than the sight of housewives and office-workers, "sky-clad" or not, dancing around in Wiccan circles, or Tantric yoga in Hollywood.

THE SPIRAL DANCE

This is the title of a book about the resurgence of the worship of The Goddess, much connected to the modern Women's Movement but claiming great antiquity. "Starhawk," as the woman who wrote *The Spiral Dance: Rebirth of the Ancient Religion of the Goddess* (1979) calls herself, presents a number of rituals. Over the years these have been somewhat modified in the innovative spirit of modern covens, or entirely replaced by further new ceremonies. "Starhawk" remains the one, at least, to consult for the basic rituals, the dance in a ring (widdershins or against the movement of the sun) being the most common feature of all Wicca. The cabalistic tradition is in modern witchcraft generally ignored, the hermetic practices of The Renaissance forgotten, Transcendental Magic almost entirely abandoned—even A. E. Waite thought it was too foolish for moderns to contemplate—and ritual magic too complex for all but a very few devotées.

RITES OF THE GODDESS

"Many women today," writes Barbara G. Walker in her *Women's Rituals: A Source Book* (1990), feel that the old rituals, invented by men to serve their own purposes are not satisfying the spiritual needs of women." Also, women cannot officiate in the traditional churches, orthodox synogogues, and mosques; they are relegated to second-class status. They can agitate for ordination in some denominations, but the orthodox usually will not countenance this. They can start their own religions in which women take a more than usual part, among them Spiritualism, Theosophy, Christian Science, or some homemade worship of Kali (which one observer has described as Satan with Pre–Menstrual Syndrome). Women can become priestesses in religions where women are central, such as Voodoo. Or they can worship The Goddess. "Women need to reclaim their own spiritual history and practice their own ceremonies, recognizing their own priorities," says Ms. Walker.

I digress for a moment to reiterate that Wicca may be an imitation of the Old Religion but it is a very new religion, and one that women appear to have originated in this century—perhaps it all goes back to a witch in the New Forest who got Gerald Gardner into her coven—and in which they are most prominent. While not wishing to annoy all of those readers of mine (especially in college towns all around the country, my mail suggests) who are active in Wicca, I must say it is part of the modern Women's Liberation Movement to a much greater extent than it is any kind of continuation of the practices of The Burning Time. Though it does not have the ancient roots it sometimes pretends to, I think Wicca is a perfectly satisfactory religion for women who feel they are outside of traditional denominations. In my experience, Wiccans are Good People and more aware than most Americans of the crying need for some kind of ritual in one's life, even if it is not historic ritual.

Ms. Walker cleverly creates rituals, often on the basis of her own wide observation of rituals other women have recently put together. Ms. Walker offers a number of games, show-and-tell adventures, and ceremonies for the solstices, etc. She tells you how to make a robe, how to control conversation with a talking stick to be handed to the person who has the floor—or the circle—and she confects a number of chants that soar well above the usual drivel. Here is an impressive script for antiphonal chanting at Samhain, the autumn equinox we call Halloween or The Feast of All Souls.

N[orth]: What is this night?

S[outh]: It is the night of Samhain.

E[ast]: What is the meaning of this night?

W[est]: It is the feast of the dead.

N: What do we honor on this night?

S: We honor those who have gone before us into the dark, and who left us the legacies of their existence.

E: After this feast of the dead, what will we do?

W: We will learn from the shadows, and prepare for our own night.

N: How do we recognize ourselves on this night?

S: We clothe ourselves in darkness. We study the deep secrets. We become wise.

E: Who helps us?

W: Our Goddess helps us.

N: What is our Goddess?

S: She is the future's hidden void, the great black matrix, the beginning and the end of all things.

E: Who is our Goddess?

W: She is the Virgin of Light, the Crone of Darkness, the Mother of Time.

N: Where is our Goddess?

S: She is in our hearts in all seasons of the turning year.

E: Who is our Goddess?

W: Behold, she is ourselves.

This is rather typical of such new ceremonies. It borrows from Judaism ("How is this night different from all other nights?") and Christianity ("the beginning and the end," *alpha* and *omega*), strives for a bit of poetry (but wisely avoids doggerel), and most especially gives all participants a chance to say something, something more than simply responding to a priest. In this age of the widespread rejection of authority figures, even in the university I noted that the most promising students prefered to engage in class discussion rather than be lectured at. (The vast majority of my students were content to be college potatoes—they passively sat back and watched the classroom discussion as they would watch a television talk show.)

All these new religions are hands-on; women are tired of sitting in pews and want to get up and dance. Finally, God is Us is a basic principle of those who seek divinity in self-realization, divinity inside themselves, and not so much to worship as to self-improve.

Watch out, men! Women are getting together (like the witch/bitch combo in *The First Wives' Club* which gleefully sings *You Don't Own Me*) and playing by the new book, *The Rules*, which the authors recommend you do not show to anyone grownup and principled. The authors rightly feel—people *feel* these days rather than *think*—that the ethical may tell you these rules are "dishonest and manipulative." Womyn have "come a long way, baby" since they were called "baby" and after all these years they do not want to hear you being the worst thing any American of today can be. That's *discriminating*. That's *judgmental*.

A PAGAN RITUAL FOR BELTANE

Margot Adler's *Drawing Down the Moon* (revised 1986) is a major work that ought to be read by anyone who is interested in pagan or Craft ceremonies of the feminist-ecologist persuasion. She quotes several rituals, though she says, rightly, that people engaged in these practices prefer to make up their own. Here's my entry, much different than the one cited as the Beltane ceremony performed in Central Park in 1978 by a (now defunct?) New York City group calling themselves the Manhattan Pagan Way. They drew two or three dozen; I would hope this would involve more.

I

Spiral dance around a simple altar of a large rock or a cairn you construct around which branches of (preferably flowering) trees are stuck in the ground and pulled together at the top to be tied with a white ribbon. The dancers come in single file from the right of the circle. They dance with the sun. They are led by Priestess I carrying a giant armful of spring flowers.

When the dance ends, the dancers holding hands raise them to heaven and sway them back and forth until the seven priestesses in II have done their dance.

II

Priestess I casts the circle and says:

> Come, Gentle Spring! Ethereal mildness come!

Music (pipes and tabors might be best, live is preferable to a recording being played) begins and continues under:

> The ever-returning spring warms our earth and our hearts. We salute as women the promise of fecundity. We revel in the new green of hope and joy. Come, Spring! Come celebrate the Spring!

Priestess I gives most of her flowers to Priestess II, who says:

> As these flowers have sprung from the earth, so have we, the daughters of earth. May we be as beautiful and as varied.

Priestess II gives most of her flowers to Priestess III, who says:

> As all nature reawakens in the Spring, so may we reawaken to the best that lies within ourselves!

Priestess III gives most of her flowers to Priestess IV, who says:

> As the rains of Spring bring new life from the earth, so may the tears we have shed in the winters of our lives make new things blossom now.

Priestess IV gives most of her flowers to Priestess V, who says:

> As the warmth of Spring brings forth new buds, so may we grow as we bask in the sun of happiness.

Priestess V gives most of her flowers to Priestess VI, who says:

> This is the time of creativity bursting from the womb of our mother earth. May all our creative juices flow.

Priestess VI gives most of her flowers to Priestess VII, who says:

> Let us all celebrate a new birth in the Spring, a reawakening, a renewal. Let us flourish and rejoice.

All the priestesses dance in a ring as the music mounts and end the dance by distributing flowers to the other participants. Then all dance in a ring and pass flowers from one to the other until all the flowers are in the arms of Priestess I, who places them all in a mound in the center of the circle. There a fire is lit near the flowers. All dance around the fire holding hands crossed.

III

Guardian of the Fire steps to the altar and says: At this season, the women of old extinguished all household fires and relit them, signifying a new beginning from the sacred fire. Let us each take from the fire our bit of that tradition. May it light our way and warm our hearts.

Guardian of the fire lights the fire that has been laid on the rock(s) of the altar. A cup of oil or alcohol can be used instead of tinder, if desired. From the fire, the Guardian takes a light for a candle (stored with others near the altar, one for each participant) and the Priestesses come forward to get candles and have them lit one from the other in order, the Guardian passing light to Priestess I to begin.

The Priestesses circle the altar. Optional hymn to the fire here. With their lights, they dance around the altar briefly. Then their circle breaks and they move to the larger circle. The Guardian of the Fire's assistant moves around the circle and distributes a candle to each participant. The Priestesses then light from their candles the candle of the person to their left. Each of those persons hands on the light to the candle at their left. When all candles are lit, the whole circle dances to the left and chants together:

> For winter's rains and ruins are over,
> And all the season of snows and sins;

The days dividing lover and lover,
    The light that loses, the night that wins;
And time remember'd is grief forgotten,
And frosts are slain and flowers begotten,
And in green underwood and cover
    Blossom by blossom the Spring begins.

More music and joyful dancing with the repeated refrain "Blossom by blossom the Spring begins!"

IV

The seven Priestesses take May Wine from the flower-decked central altar and serve it to all the participants. (If you can put woodruff into the May Wine, so much the better.) All the participants raise their cups on high and drain their cups all at once, with a high, shrill, sustained ululation to follow. They conclude the ritual with tossing paper cups into the fire, running from the circle each in her own time and rejoining it quickly at a new place at random. They do this to create a kind of confusion of individual movement which resolves into a unified, sisterly cooperation of a single, regular circle again. The dance they perform is a Cauldron Dance "She Will Bring the Buds of Spring" (words and music in *Songs of the Old Religion*).

At the end of the ceremony, the circle dance can be repeated, if desired, with participants breaking from the circle to invite spectators one by one to join in. For this, a simple hop to the left movement, holding hands with dancers on either side or another simple step is best. Some people might produce tambourines at this point.

If the Swinburne verse is not enough for you, various participants can each contribute before that a verse of her own selection on the subject of Spring. None should be much longer than the Swinburne verse. Instead of an armful of flowers, a great garland long enough to stretch all around the circle can be played out in stages, in which case the final dance finds the garland on the ground, as the circle, and the dance consists in stepping back and forth over it as the dancers move to the left. All dancing begins on the left foot. The main things about this or any such ritual is that it have some simple symbolism; that it involve everyone actively; that it not rely on priestess and acolyte but stress sisterhood and equality and selected individuals acting for all; and that it give vent to genuine joy in being and moving together.

There need be no elaborate costumes; everyone in something white and barefoot would be fine. No jewelry at all should be worn. Chaplets of leaves or flowers are not necessary, though they would be pretty. If you want to go to the trouble, light flowing muslin robes with large sleeves, tied with a cord that passes behind the neck, crosses the breasts, goes behind, and is brought to be tied in the front at the waist with some length hanging down, are impressive; these can be of any one color or of various pastel colors symbolic of the various functions of the participants. Each participant should bring flowers of her own to be used in the ceremony, and should take home a flower or two as a reminder of the ritual. When souvenirs fade, they are to be burned, not just thrown away. In the variety of flowers used, the variety of the participants is reflected; therefore, no planning as to who should bring which flowers should be done. If a garland is to be used, it can be constructed of leaves wired together and brought to the ceremony, the flowers added to it by each participant before the ritual begins. A piece of rope (dyed green?) would do to attach flowers to if something more elaborate is not feasible. The ritual should put the emphasis on energy, not elaboration. It must be conducted with happiness rather than solemnity. It is a ritual for *enthusiasts*—those (according to the ancient Greek) who have the god (or goddess!) in them!

FAERIE RITUALS

There are notable rituals of the Radical Faeries available in homosexual publications, and for heterosexuals there are two Faerie unification ceremonies in Kisma K. Stepanich's *Faerie Wicca: Book II* (1996): one is for trial marriage (aka shacking up) and the other is for "Handfasting" (a more serious sort of relationship, like marriage). Most people into Faerie rituals, however, like to make up their own. These, however, offer patterns.

LOVE RITUAL FOR TEENAGE LUST

From Darius H. James, "Way Down Under New Orleans," in *New York Press* for 25 September–1 October 1996, p. 36:

> "T.O.P.Y. [Temple ov Psychick Youth] draws on Austin Osman Spare, [Aleister] Crowley and William Burroughs," Weirdsli explains. "One of the first requirements is making a sigill. A sigill can be anything, but basically it's something that works on a sub-

conscious level. You write down whatever desire you might have and then make the sigill as elaborate as possible. You do whatever you want to it that you think will give it power. Then you wait till the 23rd hour of the 23rd day. Twenty-three is the number for Joy/Life/Party/Bread [money]. It comes from Burroughs. You think of this desire and bring yourself to a state of sexual frenzy. You cum. You take this cum or "ov" and put it on the sigill. Then you cut yourself and bleed on the sigill.

"It was funny the first time I did it," Weirdsli goes on, "because I masturbated so hard I tore the skin on my penis. I thought, 'Wow! Blood and cum at the same time! This has got to work!'"

WHAT DOES MAGIC DO?

Nothing unnatural, except in terms of speed. Even The Devil cannot break the fundamental laws of nature. Only God can, when He performs miracles. Albertus Magnus makes a clear distinction between a miracle and magic. When Christ raised Lazarus from the dead, that was a miracle. It was only magic when the wands of the Egyptian magicians were turned by Moses and his brother Aaron into snakes. That was simply, if marvelously, speeding up the process of nature by which dead wood breeds worms. Science ought to investigate more deeply what magic does, or claims to be able to do, within, not against, the laws of nature. As science discovers more and more, events and powers which are now regarded as magical may well come to be seen as perfectly natural—even clairvoyance and other kinds of mental sensitivity, even telekinesis and teleportation, and demonology and even theology may have to be redefined or fully or partly abandoned as were theories of phlogiston.

My learned friend the late D. P. Walker, author of *Unclean Spirits* (1981), described demonic possession as "an aspect of early modern science that has not yet...been investigated." There are many aspects of magic that fall into that same category. Magic remains almost as shadowy as the question of whether so-called Unidentified Flying Objects are actually appearing in increasing numbers in (in this order) Washington State, California, Oregon, Michigan, and Florida. The scientists and the others continue their investigations, and their battles. The scientists claim to be objective and open minded; the faithful say with the German bishop of the sixteenth century called Peter Binsfeld that science is stubbornly wrongheaded: "Physicians may say what they like, but we who believe in the Gospel believe that demons cause lunacy...."

MAGICAL TEXTS

I would steer clear of the *Grimoire of Honorius* and the works of Israel Regardie, Sandor S. LaVey, and any people similar to those described by Arthur Lyons (1970, i.e. Satanists), but scholars will find much as specific as it is startling in such works as the following:

Sefer Yezriah (Book of Creation, after Sixth Century)

Sefer ha-Babir (Book of Light, actually Isaac the Blind and perhaps Azriel, c.1190)

Sefer ha-Zohar (Book of Splendor, Thirteenth Century, brought to Spain by Moses Shem Tob de Léon but ascribed by him to Simon ben Yohai, Second Century)

The Book of Abramelin the Mage (date uncertain)

Plaingière (probably a false attribution), *Grimorium verum* (True Magical Handbook, date uncertain)

Raymond Lull (1235?–1315), *Ars magna* (The Great Art, date uncertain)

Levinius Lemnius, *Occulta naturæ magica* (1561, translated as *The Secret Miracles of Nature*, 1656)

"Arbatel," *De Magia veterum* (Concerning Old Magic, 1575)

Niels Hemmingsen, *Admonitio de superstitionibus magicis...* (Warning against the Superstitions of Magic..., 1575)

Francisco Victoria, *Reflectiones theologicæ* (Theological Reflections, 1587)

Reginald Scot, *The Discoverie of Witchcraft* (3rd ed. 1665 has more rites than 1584)

Antonio Venetiana del Rabina, *Grand Grimoire* (Great Magical Handbook, date uncertain)

Francesco Maria Guazzo, *Compendium maleficarum* (use the translation by Montague Summers, 1929, of the sixteenth-century writer)

François Perrault, *Demonologie...* (1656)

Legemeton or Clavicula Salomonus Rex or the Little Key of Solomon (c. 1700)

Francis Barrett, *The Magus; or, Celestial Intelligencer* (1801)

Le Véritable Dragon Rouge, plus la Poule Noir...(The True Red Dragon, plus the Black Pullet, 1821, falsely said be much older)

J. C. Horst, *Zauberbibliothek* (Library of Magic, 6 vols., 1821–1826)

J. Scheible, *Das Kloster* (The Cloister, 12 vols., 1846)

"Papus," *Traité élémentaire de magie practique* (1893)

A. E. Waite, *The Book of Black Magic and Pacts* (1898)

———, trans., "Éliphas Lévi," *Transcendental Magic* (n.d.)

S. L. Macgregor Mathers, ed., *The Key of Solomon* (1899)

Sepher Maphtheah Shelomo (Book of the Key of Solomon, 1914)

Idres Shah, *The Secret Lore of Magic* (1970)

"David Conway," *Ritual Magic* (1972)

E. M. Butler, *Ritual Magic* (1979)

MERRY MET! MERRY PART!

In *La Lozana Andaluza* (The Andalusian Lozana), a picaresque novel by Francisco Delicado (the Spanish book appeared sometime between 1528 and 1530) the lusty heroine has many sensational occupations. She is seen here as a wise woman or healer. The title page boasts *muchas más cosas que la Celestina*—many more things than Rojas' *La Celestina*!

7
Literature and Folklore

HUGVENDING

That eye-catcher is a Norwegian word that means "turning the soul." I begin this section with it to catch your attention but also because this concept of magically altering the outlook of another person is common in legend, especially in connection with making someone love you.

The old sagas tell of Harold *Harfågne* falling in love with a Lappish girl of great beauty. Her name was Snøfrid, which means "beautiful as snow." She was, however, a witch. Harold was so enchanted that he could not tear himself away from her, even after she died. Then he discovered that he had been enchanted and was so angry that he rejected the sons he had with her and chased them from him, never wanting to see them anymore, according to the chronicler Snorri Sturlasson. One of those sons, Ragnvold Rettelbeini, studied magic and began to imitate his mother in witchcraft deceptions. Harold ordered him killed.

The sagas are full of magic, for legend is there inextricably mixed with history.

WHY ONE WOMAN BECAME A WITCH

In the tragicomedy of *The Witch of Edmonton* (written about 1631 but not published until years later), Thomas Dekker seems to be the author of the scenes in this multi-plotted play—which also engaged the writing talents of William Rowley and John Ford—in which Elizabeth Sawyer, an old woman, is so taunted by the townsfolk and so often called a witch that she is ready to become one. When a demon appears (in the shape of a black dog) she is more than ready to sell her soul. First, Old "Mother Sawyer" complains:

> Some call me witch,
> And being ignorant of myself, they go
> About to teach me how to be one; urging,
> That my bad tongue (by their bad usage made so)
> Forespeaks their cattle, doth bewitch their corn,
> Themselves, their servants, and their babes at nurse.
> This they enforce upon me....

So the script was written by popular superstition for the witch, just as her testimony under torture later might be led by tradition and the questions of her interrogators. At around this point in Elizabeth Sawyer's story a group of country people come along and insult her some more. She reflects:

> I am shunn'd
> And hated like a sickness: made a scorn
> To all degrees and sexes. I have heard old beldames
> Talk of familiars in the shape of mice,
> Rats, ferrets, weasels, and I wot not what,
> That have appeared, and suck'd, some say, their blood;
> But by what means they came acquainted with them,
> I am now ignorant. Would some power, good or bad,
> Instruct me which way I might be revenged
> Upon this churl, I'd go out of myself,
> And give this fury leave to dwell within
> This ruin'd cottage, ready to fall with age;
> Abjure all goodness; be at hate with prayer;
> And study curses, imprecations,
> Blasphemous speeches, oaths, detested oaths,
> Or anything that's ill; so I might work
> Revenge upon this miser, this black cur,
> That barks, and bites, and sucks the very blood
> Of me, and of my credit. 'Tis all one,
> To be a witch as to be counted one.

RECIPE "TO HOUSE THE HAG"

To house the Hag, you must doe this:
Commix with Meale a little Pisse
Of him bewitcht: then forthwith make
A little Wafer or a Cake;
And this rawly bak't will bring
The old Hag in. No surer thing.
—Robert Herrick (1591–1674)

A SORCERER AND HIS APPRENTICE

The crucial importance of knowing the right magic words to stop a spell, as well as to start one, is shown in this story which the Rev. Sabine Baring-Gould contributed to William Henderson's *Notes on the Folk-Lore of the Northern Counties* (1866). You may recall Mickey Mouse in this plight in Walt Disney's *Fantasia*. The tale:

There was once a very learned man in the north country who knew all the languages under the sun and who was acquainted with all the mysteries of creation. He had one big book bound in black calf and clasped with iron, and with iron corners, and chained to a table which was made fast to the floor; and when he read out of this book, he unlocked it with an iron key, and none but he read from it, for it contained all the secrets of the spiritual world. It told how many angels there were in heaven, and how they marched in their ranks, and sang in the choirs, and what were their several functions, and what was the name of each great angel of might. And it told of the devils of hell, how many of them there were, and what were their several powers, and their labours, and their names, and how they might be summoned, and how tasks might be imposed on them, and how they might be chained to be as slaves to man.

Now the master had a pupil who was but a foolish lad, and acted as servant to the great master, but never was he suffered to look into the black book, hardly to enter the private room.

One day the master was out, and then the lad, impelled by curiosity, hurried to the chamber where his master kept his wondrous apparatus for changing copper into gold, and lead into silver, and where was his mirror in which he could see all that was passing in the world, and where was the shell which when held to the ear whispered all the words which were spoken by anyone the master desired to know about. The lad tried in vain with the crucibles to turn copper and lead into gold and silver; he looked long and vainly into the mirror—smoke and clouds fleeted over it, but he saw nothing plain; and the shell to his ear produced only indistinct murmurings, like the breaking of distant seas on an unknown shore. "I can do nothing," he said, "as I don't know the right words to utter, and they are locked up in this book." He looked round, and see! the book was unfastened; the master had forgotten to lock it before he went out. The boy rushed to it and unclosed the volume. It was written with red and black ink, and much that was in it he could not understand; but he put his finger on a line and spelled it through.

At once the room was darkened and the house trembled; a clap of thunder rolled through the passage of the old mansion, and there stood before the terrified youth a horrible form, breathing fire, and with eyes like burning lamps. It was the Evil One, Beelzebub, whom he had called up to serve him.

"Set me a task!" he said with a voice like the roaring of an iron furnace.

The boy only trembled and his hair stood up.

"Set me a task, or I shall strangle you!"

But the lad could not speak. Then the evil spirit stepped toward him and, putting forth his hands, touched his throat. The fingers burned his flesh.

St. John's Wort (*Hypericum*) in the Middle Ages was called *Fuga Dæmonum* or Scare-Devil. Folklore also knows it under many other names, including Goat Weed, Klamath Weed, Tipton Weed, and *Sol terrestris* (Sun of the Earth). It makes warriors invincible, wards off disease, attracts love. To cure melancholy or madness, collect it at Midsummer's Day or on any Friday and stick it in your hatband or pin it to your clothes.

"Set me a task."

"Water that flower," cried the boy in despair, pointing to a geranium which stood in a pot on the floor.

Instantly the spirit left the room, but in another instant he returned with a barrel on his back and poured its contents over the flower; and again and again he went and came, and poured more and more water, till the floor of the room was ankle-deep.

"Enough, enough!" gasped the lad, but the Evil One heeded him not; the lad didn't know the words by which to dismiss him, and still he fetched water.

It rose to the boy's knees, and still more water was poured. It mounted to his waist, and still Beelzebub kept on bringing barrels full. It rose to his armpits, and he scrambled to the table-top. And now the water in the room stood up to the window and washed against the glass and swirled around his feet on the table. It still rose; it reached his breast. In vain he cried; the evil spirit would not be dismissed. And to this day he would have been pouring water, and would have drowned all Yorkshire, but the master remembered on his journey that he had not locked his book, and therefore returned, and at the moment when the water was bubbling about the pupil's chin rushed into the room and spoke the words which cast Beelzebub back into his fiery home.

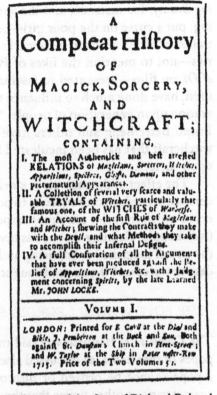

A

Compleat History

OF

MAGICK, SORCERY,

AND

WITCHCRAFT;

CONTAINING,

I. The most Authentick and best attested RELATIONS of *Magicians, Sorcerers, Witches, Apparitions, Spectres, Ghosts, Demons,* and other preternatural Appearances.

II. A Collection of several very scarce and valuable TRYALS of *Witches,* particularly that famous one, of the WITCHES of *Warboyse.*

III. An Account of the first Rise of *Magicians* and *Witches;* shewing the Contracts they make with the *Devil,* and what Methods they take to accomplish their Infernal Designs.

IV. A full Confutation of all the Arguments that have ever been produced against the Belief of *Apparitions, Witches,* &c. with a Judgment concerning *Spirits,* by the late Learned Mr. JOHN LOCKE.

VOLUME I.

LONDON: Printed for *E. Curll* at the *Dial* and *Bible, J. Pemberton* at the *Buck* and *Sun,* both against St. *Dunstan's* Church in *Fleet-Street;* and *W. Taylor* at the *Ship* in *Pater noster-Row* 1715. Price of the Two Volumes 5 s.

Titlepage of the first of Richard Bolton's two volumes (1715–1716) on *Magick, Socery, and Witchcraft.*

FAIRYTALES AND FOLKTALES

These are perhaps the richest, most easily accessible source of stories about the subjects of this book, spells, curses, magical recipes, rituals, and the rest. There is no need here to recount the familiar story of *The Sleeping Beauty*, for instance, and the witch who, not invited to the christening, put a curse on the poor girl—or the Prince Charming who was able to take it off. It needs to be remarked, however, that this and similar stories—not to mention the likes of *Peter Pan* on the stage or *The Wizard of Oz* on film—presented to fascinated and sometimes frightened children, have done much to influence the minds and adult behavior of generation upon generation of people. "As the twig is bent, so shall it grow." Bruno Bettelheim and others have shown that the belief in magic and witchcraft that has been inculcated in this way has had a profound effect upon society.

The effect of the marvelous stories in *The Arabian Nights*, where wonders are everyday occurences, is to produce a mindset for millions of readers in which miracles are almost expected. In one of the 1001 tales, a thief (for example) claiming that he has been for years trapped in a donkey's body (by an evil magician) is implicitly and instantly believed. In real life, "wonders never cease" if you are brought up on such tales.

THE POPE WHO ALLEGEDLY SOLD HIS SOUL TO THE DEVIL

The *Grimoire of Honorius* was said to be written by one or another of the popes of that name, as discussed elsewhere, but whether it was written by a pope cannot be proved or disproved. Neither can the charges made against various other popes that they attained the papacy, or held onto it, by acts of black magic. There were many rumors of popes with demon familiars, magic rings, obscene ceremonies of the black arts, murder of rivals by spells, dabbling in necromancy and sorcery. One rumor will be enough to give you an idea of legends of the sort. It concerns Sextus V (1521–1590).

Legend had it that Sextus V sold his soul to The Devil so that he could be pope for six years. But after five years The Devil called in his chips. The pope objected: he had signed up for six years, not five. The Devil replied that once, somewhat earlier, a woman had been condemned to death but was not quite old enough to suffer the punishment. "Take a year of my life," the pope was supposed to have said, and the woman went to the stake. So, said The Devil, the pope's time was up a year early—and he dragged the pope off to Hell.

J.-A. de Thou in his *Histoire universelle* (1754) repeated this slander and called it "a rumor spread by the Spanish, and I should be sorry to guarantee its truth."

THE BRAZEN HEAD

A head made of brass—a head that speaks!—was a sensation on the Elizabethan stage in Robert Greene's comedy of *Friar Bacon and Friar Bungay* (1584). Like much of Greene's work, it had a literary source, in this case a prose pamphlet about two famous magicians, Friar Roger Bacon and Friar Thomas Bungay. The two magicians with the help of The Devil contrive a brazen head that will speak some time in the ensuing month but the magicians must be there before the speech ends. They watch and wait and after a few weeks they give the job over to a servant, Miles, who hears the head say "Time is" and "Time was" and "Time is past." That's all, and Miles is roundly cursed when Friar Bacon wakes up and realizes he has missed the performance. The story is reprised in Michael Swanwick's dark fantasy novel *The Iron Dragon's Daughter*.

Legend has it that Albertus Magnus actually made a whole man out of brass; he worked on it for thirty years. Isaac D'Israeli in *Curiosities of Literature* (1866) writes:

This man of brass, when he reached his maturity, was so loquacious, that Albert's master, the great scholastic Thomas Aquinas, one day, tired of his babble, and declaring it was a devil, or devilish, with his staff knocked the head off....

That time a disconnected head ceased to speak! In the modern world we have some decapitated heads, frozen in liquid nitrogen, awaiting a scientific breakthrough that will enable them to live again, which sounds both magical and impossible indeed to us now. There have been a few science-fiction movies with decapitated heads in lively operation.

STORIES OF THE BIG BLACK DOG

In British folklore there is the Black Shuck, a huge black dog with eyes like burning coals, eyes which are there even when the dog is (as he apparently sometimes likes to be) headless. The "Shuck" bit shows how old this superstition is, for *sceocca* is Anglo-Saxon for "devil." Various other countries have their Devil Dogs, too.

The best British stories come from the more desolate parts of the island, the windswept moors of Yorkshire and the West Country, because this Hellhound, also called the Galleytrot or Hell Beast, likes to appear out of the midst and howl over the noise of the storm.

I have caught frightening (or frightened) beasts in my headlights in Britain and even in America and can understand how these stories get started, but dogs as large as the folklore Black Shuck, which is supposedly even bigger than an Irish Wolfhound, do seem to belong to the imaginative world of the Wendigo, Bigfoot, and other such creatures.

ALCHEMY

Magic deals in transformations; so does alchemy, a pseudo-science from which chemistry sprang just as astrology connects to astronomy. Alchemy may have arisen in China centuries before Christ, but it reached Western Europe after Mohammed, as you can see by the word *alchemy* (which is Arabic, like *algebra*, *Algiers*, even *admiral*). The literature of the occult is full of alchemical matters, and alchemy, mixed with magic as well as with science and philosophy, enters into English and other literatures. We do not have room for a sample here but want to mention a fine survey of alchemy in literature from Chaucer to The Restoration (mid-seventeenth century): *Darke Hieroglyphics* (1996) by Stanton J. Linden. For the connections of alchemy with magic and medicine see Lynn Thorndike's *History of Magic and Experimental Science* (8 vols., 1923–1958), with philosophy A. J. Hopkins's *Alchemy* (1943), and with chemistry John Read's *Through Alchemy to Chemistry* (1957).

The best play on alchemy, and one of the greatest comedies of all time, is Ben Jonson's *The Alchemist* (1610). In its realistic London setting, two of Jonson's most delightful villains (Subtle and Face) fleece the man about town Dapper (who wants to see the Queen of the Fairies). Marchette Chute in her biography *Ben Jonson of Westminster* (1953) gives us this almost incredible news:

> A short time after Jonson wrote his play, John and Alice West were arraigned in Old Bailey [London criminal court] for dressing up as the King and Queen of the Fairies and promising fairy gold in exchange for coin of the realm; and four years earlier a young gentleman from Dorset paid six pounds to a crook who had promised him an introduction to the same Queen.

Jonson's con men also tell the tobacconist Able Drugger which way his shelves ought to face (think of modern New York decorators and Chinese *shui feng*) and which days are best for him, a Libra, to do business (think of Linda Goodman's *Sun Signs* and all the horoscopes in the daily newspapers). The play also includes the magnificent gull Sir Epicure Mammon (still a US stereotype today) and a couple of sleazy and money-hungry clergymen who look disturbingly like Renaissance equivalents of televangelists and certain ambitious puritanical politicians in modern America.

A TRUE STORY FROM THE INQUISITION

There is a suspicious similarity in many of the so-called confessions, chiefly obtained under hideous torture, made to the Holy Inquisition by witches; it suggests to me that confessions were often part of a genre of fiction. On

Death, the Alchemist, transforms everything. From T. Stimmer's *Alterstuffen des Weibes* series, woodcuts illustrating old wives' superstitions, etc.

the other hand, there are many stories of real events that came to light in the papers of that terrible institution, stories which had their undoubted impact upon the art of fiction for a long time thereafter and yet must be regarded as history.

Here is a tale we find in *De sortilegiis* (1533), a report on sorcery by Paulus Grillandus (as the Latin title page calls this Florentine inquisitor of the 1520s at Arezzo).

In addition to the *sabbat* which was sometimes actually attended by thousands of witches, according to the Holy Inquisition, there was what the French historian Jules Michelet calls "an imaginary *Sabbath*, which many terrified individuals believed themselves to attend, especially women somnambulists, who would get up in the night and scour the country."

In one case Grillandus recounts, a young man crossing the fields at daybreak meets a young neighbor of his, a woman hiding in the bushes and softly calling his name. She is practically naked. The young man asks what she is doing out at this hour and she says she has lost her donkey. When he refuses to believe that transparent falsehood, she breaks into tears and confesses that she was in bed asleep when The Devil came to take her to a *sabbat*, just as she was, in scant nightclothes. As he flew along with her he suddenly heard a church bell, dropped her, and disappeared. Now she found herself awake and shivering in the cold in the bushes. She wanted help to get back home and, most of all, the young man's silence about her dreadful secret.

Though she bribed the young man with a cap, a pair of boots, and three cheeses, he couldn't keep so good a story to himself. People in those days thrilled to recount and to hear startling tales of witchcraft and sorcery. The young man tattled all over town. The poor woman was apprehended, tried by the Holy Inquisition, and burned at the stake as a witch. Grillandus was not present but he goes so far as to suggest that she burned well, because of fat: "she was a fine woman and plump."

THE WISDOME OF DOCTOR DODYPOLL

I shall quote a little from *The Wisdome of Doctor Dodypoll* (1600) because it is much harder to come by than *The Alchemist*. *Dodypoll* is an anonymous play (1600) attributed to George Peele (1556–1596), a minor writer about whom I happen to have written two books. It is one of the dozens of anonymous plays of his time attributed to this author, and I discussed the authorship of it in my book *Authorship and Evidence in Renaissance Drama* (1968). I mention it here because it has, as one of its threads of plot, a husband

and wife taken into the fairyland under the hill by a wizard who enchants them, puts the husband into a deep sleep, and tries to convince the wife that he is her lover. The Enchanter is speaking:

ENCHANTER: Come, sit downe faire Nimphe
And taste the sweetnesse of these heavenly cates,
Whilst from the hollow crain[ni]es of this rocke,
Musicke shall sound to recreate my love.
But tell me, had you ever lover yet?

LUCILLA: I had a lover I thinke, but who it was,
Or where, or how long since, aye me, I know not:
Yet beat my timerous thoughts on such a thing,
I feele a passionate heate, but finde no flame:
Thinke what I know not, nor know what I thinke.

ENCHANTER: Hast thou forgot me then? I am thy love,
Whom sweetly thou wert wont to entertaine,
With lookes, with vowes of love, with amorous kisses.
Look'st thou so strange? doost thou not know me yet?

LUCILLA: Sure I should know you.

ENCHANTER: Why love, doubt you that?
'Twas I that led you through the painted meades,
Where the light Fairies daunst upon the flowers,
Hanging on every leafe an orient pearle,
Which [,] strooke together with the silken winde,
Of their loose mantles made a silver chime.
'Twas I that winding my shrill bugle horne,
Made a guilt pallace breake out of the hill,
Filled suddenly with troopes of knights and dames,
Who daunst and reveld whilst we sweetly slept,
Upon a bed of Roses wrapt all in goulde,
Dost thou not know me yet?

LUCILLA: Yes, now I know you.

ENCHANTER: Come then confirme thy knowledge with a kiss.

LUCILLA: Nay stay, you are not he, how strange is this.

ENCHANTER: Thou art growne passing strange my love,
To him that made thee so long since his bride.

LUCILLA: O was it you? Come then, O stay a while,
I know not where I am, nor what I am,
Nor you, nor these I know, nor any thing.

The Devil with witches and monsters
in an eighteenth-century chapbook.

The seduction fails, because Lucilla's father, at this juncture equipped with a magic gem, gets into the hill and breaks the enchantment. Had Lucilla kissed the Enchanter (or eaten anything of the fairy banquet) she would have been caught, like Persephone.

A LEGEND OF TARA, A TIBETAN GODDESS

There was once a farmer who was exceedingly poor and experienced insurmountable hardship. He beseeched Tara to help him, and suddenly a girl, whose clothing was the leaves of trees placed over her body, instructed him to go eastward and lie down upon a rock. The farmer accordingly went eastward and lay down upon a rock, when all at once he heard the sound of small horse bells and saw a green-colored horse digging in the ground with its hoof. He waited until it had left, then he got up and dug into the hole it had made; and in the middle of it there appeared a silver door set with the seven precious stones. He entered in, and it was the palace of the serpent-kings and demons. The farmer thus stayed there, and by the time he got out again the king[ship] of his country had changed three times. When he inquired about his family, [he learned that] they had all been dead for a long time. He thus entered a monastery and became a monk. He saw that men and women made offerings to Tara with incense and flowers; he bought some flowers, scattered them about, and returned [to his monastery]. Later, the king of the country heard about these wonders, and he married the farmer to his daughter. When the king died, the farmer ruled the country, and he repaired the 108 buildings of the Tara temple.

This is from the Chinese No-na Hutukhtu, *Er-shih-i tsun tu-mi mu-chou kung-té lu...* and quoted from a Hong Kong edition by Stephan Beyer in *The Cult of Tara: Magic and Ritual in Tibet* (1973). That has many tales of how the mere mention of this divinity's name, or carving her mantra on stone to be seen by passersby, works wonders.

Tibetans believe that if for six months one will devote all one's waking hours to contemplating the wheel in the heart of Tara—for sleep one checks into Emptiness—thereby one will gain "all the magical attainments and one is undefiled by the stain of death." One priest, Drubch'en *rinpoche*, is reported to have believed: "It is said that if one recites the ten-syllable mantra ten–million times, one's qualities will equal those of the noble Tara herself."

Though Dr. Faustus in Marlowe's famous play said "a sound magician is a mighty god," there surely can be few magical rituals, however demanding, that offer the mortal man the powers and status of divinity.

TAKE AWAY THAT HEAD!

The following story is reported as fact by Jean Bodin in his *Démonomania* (1587) but may be legend, not history.

Catherine de' Medici was much involved in magic and brought to France not only the cooks that gave that nation its culinary reputation but also the occultists who gave it a tradition of demonology. One day she gave the order that at the Château de Vincennes a special Mass be said for the recovery of her son, Charles IX, from the mysterious disease that seemed to be killing him. The idea was to call up the dead and get the diagnosis and some idea about a remedy. It was a Black Mass.

At midnight the rite began in front of a statue of Satan, at whose feet an inverted cross was placed. (An inverted cross was later to be reported on the chasubles or copes of priests saying Black Masses.) The priest consecrated two Hosts, one white and one black. The white Host was given in communion to a little girl and immediately her throat was slit. In fact, her head was cut off and placed on top of the black Host, which was then fumigated with incense. It appears that the idea was that with the help of a demon the severed head would speak. The head was supposed to have said "*Vim patior.*" ("I am subjected to violence.")

That was very apt for the head, you will agree; but it did the sick king no good whatever. On his deathbed he had some kind of terrifying vision and died screaming "Take away that head!"

THE FARMER MAKES A PACT WITH THE DEVIL

A pact with The Devil is a major feature of one of the major masterpieces of German literature, Goethe's *Faust*. Such a pact also is mentioned in a great many stories of German folklore, and here is one I offer my retelling of the tale from the German (with the assistance of Ola J. Holten, who remembers reading it in a schoolbook in Norway when he was a boy). The folktale is typical of those in which The Devil is outwitted. In Scandinavia, too, The Devil often appears as a comic and not very bright individual.

Once upon a time there was a clever farmer, and many stories have been told about him.

The busy farmer spent the day readying his large field to sow his crop. In the evening he went home, only to discover a heap of glowing coals [on his hearth]. Moving closer he saw that a little black devil was sitting on top of the coals.

"I suppose you are sitting on top of your treasure," said the farmer.

"Oh, yes," The Devil replied. "In fact I am sitting on a very great treasure, and it consists of more gold and silver than you have ever seen in your whole life."

"If there is treasure in my field," said the farmer, "it belongs to me."

"It can belong to you if for two years you will give me half the yield that your field brings," replied The Devil. "I have plenty of money. I just want the products of the beautiful earth."

The clever farmer agreed to that, but he added: "I want to make sure that there will be no quarrel between us when the time comes to share the crop. Therefore, let's decide now that you shall have that part which lies above the earth and I shall have what lies below it."

And The Devil agreed.

But the farmer sowed turnips, and when The Devil came to get his share of the crop the farmer had taken the root vegetables and left him only the leaves.

"Well," said The Devil, "this time you may have won, but that will never happen again. Now you shall have that which is above the earth and I shall have that which lies below."

"That's all right with me," said the farmer.

And he sowed wheat. When harvest time came, he reaped the wheat and there was nothing useful left for The Devil. The Devil in anger retreated to his underground den.

"This is the way you have to be, wiser than the foxes," said the farmer, who, now that The Devil was gone away, also got the gold and silver under his property.

HALF A DOZEN RECENT ADDITIONS
TO THE LITERATURE OF CURSES

Jeffrey Louis Falco, *The Malediction in Indo-European Tradition* (UCLA dissertation, 1992)

Padráic O'Farrell *"Before the Devil Knows You're Dead:" Irish Blessings, Toasts and Curses* (1993)

Geoffrey Grigson, *Blessings, Kicks, and Curses: A Critical Collection* (1982)

Patrick Power, *The Book of Irish Curses* (1995)

Marc Urogin, *Anathema: Medieval Scribes and the History of Book Curses* (1993)

John Vornholt, *"Break a Leg!" Famous Curses* (1995)

AMERICAN PROVERBIAL WISDOM

Curses never put men in hearses, but lying tongues dig men graves.
A light purse is a heavy curse.
Curses, like chickens, come home to roost.
Cursing the weather is mighty poor farming.
A curse won't strike out an eye unless a fist goes with it.
Curses are The Devil's language.

SOME YIDDISH REMARKS ON LUCK

If you are lucky you don't have to be wise.
If you are lucky, your ox calves.
If luck comes your way, offer him a chair.
It is better that luck seek the man than that the man seek luck.
It is better not to be born at all if you can't be born lucky.
Lucky for you!
He's so unlucky, if he bought a suit with two pairs of pants he would
burn a hole in the jacket.

CURSES! FILMED AGAIN!

No one can deny that the literature of today must include the dramas of
the big and small screens. At the movies, which have an immense impact
on the popular imagination, the curse of this or that monster has often been
the subject of a scary film. Witness these select examples:

Curse of the Cat People (1944)
The Mummy's Curse (1944)
Curse of the Undead (1959)
Curse of the Werewolf (1961)
Curse of the Living Corpse (1964)
Curse of the Golem (1966)
Curse of the Swamp Creature (1966)
Curse of the Fiend (1989)

Foreign films of the same sort come from The Philippines and Europe,
South America and Asia. Some foreign shockers are

La Chambre ardente (1961)
Der Fluch der goldener Schlange (The Curse of the Golden Snake, 1963)

El Retorno de Walpurgis (Walpurgis Night *Sabbat*, Spain, 1973)
Yotsuya kaidan (The Curse of the Ghost, Japanese, 1969)

Pop audiences have also rejoiced in films on witchcraft from Scandinavia (*Háxan* 1921 and *Tro, håb og trolldom*, Faith, Hope and Witchcraft, 1960) and Italy, Britain, Germany and specifically the likes of

Pharaoh's Curse (1956)
Curse of the Mummy's Tomb (1964)
The Legendary Curse of the Hope Diamond (1975)

THE FLYING DUTCHMAN

In German Romantic literature in the early nineteenth century appeared the sailors' legend of The Flying Dutchman. As a result of an intemperate remark during a terrible storm—the captain of a ship refused to pull in to more sheltered waters and swore that he would rather sail, doomed, forever than seek safety—a ghostly ship is said to appear near The Cape of Good Hope with none of its crew alive. Sometimes the ship puts out a small boat with mail that is delivered to passing ships, but these letters are magical. Addressed to people long dead at addresses that have long since vanished, the letters grow heavier and heavier each day until the unfortunate passing ship which took them on sinks with the weight of them.

This story of a curse is known best from the writings of the poet Heinrich Heine and as a result of the opera *Die fliegende Holländer* by Richard Wagner, which was not well received when it appeared about the middle of the last century but now is in the standard repertoire. The legend is a striking one, and often reappeared. A ghost ship with all the crew dead occurs in many stories such as that by Wilhelm Hauff (1826), and there is such a ship in Bram Stoker's *Dracula*.

DRAMAS ABOUT CURSES

From the Greek tragedies about the great curse on the House of Atreus on, the use of the curse as a plot device seems to have gone downhill, until in modern times there is precious little that is really good, with the exception of a dramatization of stories such as W. W. Jacobs' "The Monkey's Paw" and Montague Rhodes James' "Casting the Runes." In the melodrama the family curse or stolen cursed jewel (*The Idol's Eye* type of thing) was frequently a feature, and popular. Practically no one has ever heard of such modern curse plays and playlets as Jephson's *The Count of Narbonne*, Kelly's *Who Walks in the Dark?*, Miller's *The Curse of Hag Hollow*, Palin and Jones's *The Curse of the Claw*, Silverman's *The Curse of McNamara's Castle*, Sodaro's *The Curse of the Cobra's Kiss*, etc. There are, naturally, many other plays that use a curse or curses (not cussing!) as a major part of the play. How many can you think of?

SUPERNATURAL FICTION

There is, even excepting science fiction, far more fiction of this sort than you would expect. You need:

Lynn Andrews, *Dark Sister* (1997)
Neil Barron, *Horror Literature: A Reader's Guide* (1990)
Everett F. Bleiler, *The Guide to Supernatural Fiction* (1983)
Peter Penzholdt, *The Supernatural in Fiction* (1952)
Fred Siemon, *Ghost Story Index* (1967)
Jack Sullivan, *Elegant Nightmares: The English Ghost Story from [James Sheridan] LeFanu to [Algernon] Blackwood* (1978)
Ann B. Tracy, *The Gothic Novel 1790–1830* (1981)
James B. Twitchell, *Dreadful Pleasures: An Anatomy of Modern Horror* (1987)

44 NOVELS AND SHORT STORIES ABOUT CURSES

Anatoli Afanasyev, *Love's Curse*
"F. Anstey," *The Curse of the Catafalques*
Paul D. Augsburg, *Curse*
Charles Barker, *How Spoilers Bleed*
Jonathan Baumbach, *The Curse*
Algernon Blackwood, *Tongues of Fire*
Robert Bloch, *Beetles*
Taylor Caldwell, *Captains and Kings*
G. K. Chesterton, *The Curse of the Golden Cross*
C. W. Chestnutt, *The Gray Wolf's Ha'nt*
Dame Agatha Christie, *The Lemesurier Inheritance*
August W. Derleth, *Here, Dæmos!*
Edward, Lord Dunsany, *Witch Wood*
Elizabeth Gaskell, *Poor Clare*
W. F. Harvey, *The Arm of Mrs. Egan*
Victoria Holt, *Bride of Pendoric*

John Jakes, *Storm in a Bottle*
E. von Keyserling, *The Curse of the Tarneffs*
Stephen King, *Salem's Lot*
Hector Lee, *The Mink Creek Ghost*
Eric Linklater, *The Abominable Imprecation*
H. P. Lovecraft, *The Hound*
P. Lovesey, *The Odstock Curse*
B. Lumley, *The Viking's Stone*
George Moore, *Julia Cahill's Curse*
Nugugi Wa Thiong'o, *The Black Bird*
I. L. Peretz, *Devotion without End*
Eden Phillpotts, *The Curse*
Luigi Pirandello, *The Benediction*
Salman Rushdie, *The Prophet's Hair*
Rod Serling, *The Curse of Seven Towers*
B. A. Smith, *The Scallion Stone*
Lee Smith, *Oral History*
D. Stansbury, *Story for the Removal of a Curse*
J. R. R. Tolkein, *Quenta Silmarillion: Of Túrin Turambar*
P. Tremayne, *The Pooka*
H. R. Wakefield, *The Nurse's Tale*
Elizabeth Walter, *The Tibetan Box*
M. W. Wellman, *Nine Yards of Other Cloth*
W. A. P. White, *Sriberdigibit*
H. S. Whitehead, *The Lips*
C. Williamson, *The Cairnwell Horror*
Barbara Wood, *The Dreaming*
Patricia C. Wrede, *Stronger than Time*

THE ORPHAN BOY

One of the clichés of nineteenth-century British literature, though not unknown before and after that and in many other cultures, was the orphaned heir who fell into the clutches of a ruthless guardian. This villain tried (as in R. L. Stevenson) and succeeded (as in Charles Dickens in at least some instances) to do away with the rightful heir and seize the fortune for himself.

In Dickens' "A Christmas Tree" we find the story of the little ghost coming back to exact revenge. The house was once "held in trust by the guardian of a young boy, who was himself the next heir, and who killed the young boy by harsh and cruel treatment." In the story Dickens tells,

Charlotte asks her maid one morning, "Who is the pretty, forlorn-looking child who has been peeping out of that closet all night?" The maid flees in terror, for this was The Orphan Boy, a ghost. He had, in fact, already appeared to three of Charlotte's brothers' sons, "in succession, who all died young." Dickens continues:

> On the occasion of each child being taken ill, he came home in a heat, twelve hours before, and said, O mama, he had been playing under a particular oak-tree, in a certain meadow, with a strange boy—a pretty, forlorn-looking boy, who was very timid, and made signs! From fatal experience the parents came to know that this was the Orphan Boy, and that the course of that child whom he chose for his little playmate was surely run.

THE LOVE PHILTRE

Love potions figure in many stories from ancient epics and old romances to Shakespeare and Gilbert & Sullivan (whose J. Wellington Wells causes comic consternation with one). Sullivan, in fact, grew so tired of what he used to denigrate as "the lozenge plot"—one takes a pill or draught and everything is different—that he almost broke up the collaboration with Gilbert. Gilbert sat down to write something more serious—but then a samurai sword fell off the wall. The result was without a "lozenge plot" but hardly a serious libretto: it was *The Mikado*.

From one of the greatest of all love stories, that of Tristan and Isolde, here is a kind of "lozenge plot." It is by Gottfried von Strassburg, who around the year 1200 wrote the German version of the tale (also the subject of a great German opera, by Wagner), which makes love sound like a disease that only a few days in bed could cure. Note that while most love philtres were supposed to make lovers fall into each other's arms immediately, this tragic affair begins with doubt and deception and hesitation. This is my translation; A. T. Hatto (1960) does better.

> Now, when the young woman and the man, Isolde and Tristan, drank the potion, instantly that arch-disturber of tranquility, Love, was present, the waylayer of all hearts, and had stolen into [their hearts]. Before they were aware of it she had planted her victorious standard in their two hearts and subjected them to her yoke. They, who had been two and separate, now became one and united.

No longer were they at variance. Isolde's hatred was vanquished. Love, the reconciler, had purged their hearts of enmity, and so joined them in affection that each reflected the other like a mirror. They shared a single heart. Her anguish was his pain; her pain, his anguish. The two were one in both joy and sorrow, but they hid their feelings from each other. This was because of doubt and shame. She was ashamed, and so was he. However blindingly the craving in their hearts was centered on a single desire, their anxiety was how they might begin. This concealed their desire from each other.

DON DEMONIO

Here is a Spanish folktale I have heard told. It's about a curse, and The Devil himself.

Once upon a time in the village of La Zubia there lived a widow who was famous for her long tongue and her short temper. She was a terrible termagant. She was never content or quiet.

Tia Pía, as she was called, had a daughter who was pretty but lazy, named Panfila, and who did practically nothing but dress up and sit in the window, waiting for her true love to come along. But not one of the likely village lads was at all interested in getting involved, however beautiful Panfila was, with Tia Pía as a mother-in-law.

One day Tia Pía did manage to get Panfila to do something around the house for a change, which was to help her with a pot of hot lye cooking on the fire. But, uninterested, distracted, with her mind running only on possible lovers, Panfila managed to spill some of the hot lye on Tia Pía's foot. Then there was a temper tantrum worth seeing!

"You lazy good-for-nothing," screamed Tia Pía in pain. "You never think of anything but lovers. May you marry The Devil himself!"

And—guess what?—soon after that there appeared in the village a tall, dark, and handsome young stranger, elegant in a cape of red silk and a hat which, oddly, he never was seen without. Did he have horns under there, or what? He said he had come from somewhere far off and certainly he made friends easily with the other young men, generously buying them wine at the inn. But the old men of the village were slower to take to him.

"There is something decidedly odd about this fellow," they said as they drank the wine they had bought for themselves. "You know, he has been carefully avoiding the church and hides when the priest goes by."

THE DEVIL

But the stranger, who said his name was Don Demonio, in practically no time began to court Panfila and didn't appear to be in the least frightened by old Tía Pía. Soon he had asked Tía Pía if he could marry Panfila and she agreed. The date for the wedding was set, much to everyone's surprise in the village.

Now, Tía Pía may have been shrewish but she also was shrewd. She by no means had forgotten the curse she had flung at Panfila when the careless girl had splashed her with lye, and she had her suspicions of the suave stranger. She was sure there were horns under that hat.

"The first thing you are to do," she told her daughter, "when you are alone with your husband, is to make sure the room you are in is complely sealed, doors, windows, even the chimney. Then you must take a branch that the priest will give you, that he has blessed, and thrash the young man with it. It is important that he understand from the beginning who is going to be boss in the house!"

Well, the wedding was celebrated with much feast and folderol and the bride and groom repaired to their new, neat little house, on the highroad to Granada, just outside the village. And so, secretly, did Tía Pía, having equipped herself with the oddest little empty bottle. Maybe you can guess what she was going to do!

After Don Demonio and his new bride had entered the house, Panfila made haste to seal it up tightly, every nook and cranny, and then she attacked Don Demonio with the blessed branch. He was in a terrible panic and ran to and fro but there was no escape—except through the keyhole of the door. So he gave up all pretense, assumed the shape of the devil he had been all along, and, making himself tinier and tinier, he made his way out—through the keyhole, right into Tía Pía's little bottle, into which she, with a hoot of victory, firmly stuck the stopper.

It's true what they say, isn't it? There are times when The Devil himself is no match for a woman!

So Panfila went back to Tía Pía's house and took up her place in the window again, waiting for another young fellow to happen by. And Tía Pía rode off on her donkey to the heights of the Sierra Nevada. There, deep in a snowdrift, she buried the bottle with The Devil inside of it. Then she rode back in triumph to her village, a good day's work well done.

Well, The Devil having been laid to rest, the village and all its inhabitants became wonderful, happy in every respect, and in this blissful state they all remained for many long years.

And then Panfila finally caught some young fellow and they got married and she moved away, leaving the little house in La Zubia to Tía Pía, who one day met as he came through the village a dashing young fellow called Ricardo. He said he was going to cross the Sierra Nevada, come hell or high water. So off he went, and when he got to the heights what should happen but that, as he stopped to rest, his eye fell upon that little bottle that Tía Pía had put up there in the deep snow so many years before.

From the bottle Don Demonio said to Ricardo, "If it were not for that damn mother-in-law of mine I'd be a happy person. If you will let me out of this bottle into which the ugly old crone put me, I'll grant any wish you like!"

It so happened that Ricardo did have a wish, though it was a startling one. He would like to marry the king's daughter.

"*No problema,*" said Don Demonio from inside the bottle. "Simply let me out of this cursed bottle and I'll arrange the whole thing for you. I will have my freedom and you will have your princess."

"Not so fast," said Ricardo. "Just how do you plan to get the princess for me?"

"*No problema,*" replied The Devil. "I shall make the princess fall ill with a mysterious disease. The king will be distraught and he will call all the most learned physicians to come and cure her. But none shall succeed until you, Ricardo, appear as a physician and quickly rid her of her sickness. Surely in gratitude the king will give the princess's hand to the most wonderful doctor in all of Spain, you. Now, let me out of this bottle and let us go to the king."

"Oh, I think you had better stay in the bottle for a while longer," replied Ricardo, "until I present myself as a physician and work my wonderful cure. There will be time enough when the king gives me my reward for me to give you your freedom."

So Ricardo went to the king and, though all the physicians had tried and failed, he promised to cure the princess right off.

"Right off is right," thundered the king. "I am sick and tired of watching these bumblers try and fail. You do it—and by sunset, or I shall have you hanged from the highest tree in the royal gardens!"

So Ricardo took the princess into a private room and said to Don Demonio in the bottle, "Well, let's do it."

"Not so fast," replied the sly devil. "Let's see you suffer for a while."

But Ricardo had another idea. Rushing out of the chamber, he said to the king and the courtiers, "The cure is almost completed. The princess is going to be fine. Give the order that all the church bells be rung to celebrate this happy day!"

Then Ricardo rushed back to the chamber and said to Don Demonio, "You hear those bells? The city is rejoicing because Tia Pía, your very own mother-in-law, is about to arrive."

"Let me out of here," screamed Don Demonio, and as Ricardo removed the cork The Devil resumed his full size and hurriedly flew off. He was not going to face the terrible Tia Pía again. Hell, no!

So it all ended happily, with Ricardo marrying the princess and—best of all—it was The Devil and not Ricardo who was stuck with Tia Pía for a mother-in-law. And they all (except The Devil, of course) lived happily ever after.

LA CELESTINA AND LAZARILLO DE TORMES

La Celestina—the title is the name of a procuror involved in the affair between Calisto and Melibea, which is the main action—is an early and master work of Spanish drama, by a writer of Jewish descent, Fernando de Rojas (*c.* 1465–1541). He may have brought something of Jewish magic into the play. An old woman in Act 7 of this very long work remarks to Pármeno that his mother had the reputation of being a *bruja* (witch) because she was observed with candles at a crossroads (which suggests the cult of Hecate) in the dead of night digging up earth with her hands (presumably to use in spells and charms). There is something in the play that can be seen as commentary on Spain's forcible conversion of the Jews, and Jewish magic may be one of the old traditions that *conversos* secretly held onto. It is certainly true that in Spain especially the Jews were considered to be expert in the occult and the inheritors of Chaldean and other ancient magical traditions. Some guides to magic supposedly written in the Middle Ages were actually written as late as the nineteenth century. It was sometimes pretended that writings were much more ancient than they were to give them a boost by being falsely attributed to Jewish authorship.

It might be added that another great contribution to the early development of the novel is the prose work of *Lazarillo de Tormes*, which was written before 1539. Its authorship is disputed but if it happens to be (as some say) from the pen of Fray Juan de Ortega it is worth noting that he was an Jeronymite and that many of the members of that order were, though militantly Christian, of Jewish origin and interested in Jewish magic.

MARTIN LUTHER TELLS A TALE

Martin Luther really believed in the supernatural. He once threw an inkwell at The Devil. But that is another story. Here's one from Luther's *Table Talk:*

> The Emperor Frederick, the father of Maximillian, invited a sorcerer to dinner and, because he was well versed in magic himself, he turned his guest's hands into the claws of a griffin [talons]. Then he invited him to eat, but the sorcerer was ashamed and would not take his hands from under the table. He got his revenge, however, for the trick that had been played on him. He caused it to appear that a loud altercation was taking place in the courtyard, and when the emperor stuck his head out the window to see what was the matter the sorcerer magically clapped on his head a huge pair of stag's horns, so the emperor could not pull his head back into the room again until he had removed his own spell from the sorcerer. It pleases me a lot when one sorcerer plagues another. They are not always, however, equally matched.

THE CURSE OF A FINNISH WITCH

The story is told of a man who threw a stone at a Finnish witch. She said, "This stone you shall search for for the rest of your life!" The man went mad. Whenever he saw a heap of stones he would compulsively fill his pockets with them, but then when he came upon more stones he would throw away those he had already collected and fill his pockets with the new stones. Thus he lived his life, and people said the witch had "stolen him," meaning she had cursed him.

THE MAGIC OF THE FINNS AND LAPPLANDERS

The Lapps, who were said to have learned their magic ages past from Zoroaster the Persian, were far famed for magic. They were said to be able to send out *Hexenschusse* (which in English we might call "fairy shot"), what the peope to the south call *nordskott* (shots from the north), magical arrowheads to wound people or animals. It was believed that the bleak northland was the origin of all evil and that the people who lived there could change themselves into bears, could make wolves leave their territory and go elsewhere ("Here we have clothed you," said one witch, throwing some of her clothing on the snow. "Farther north they will feed you.

Now you must go!"), knew all about love magic, had the Evil Eye, could level terrible curses, could make weapons useless, could in trance leave their bodies and journey to distant places, and could foretell the future. In Sweden, twelfth century laws were passed forbidding all Swedes to visit the Lapps and the Finns to seek knowledge of the future. Even earlier it had been written,"No one should believe in the Lapps or anyone being able to perform magic, nor in the magic of herbs, nor in any heathen way of improving one's health." But people did so believe, and the people of the far north were greatly feared for their wise women and magicians, their shamans and sorcerers. About 1730 in Olof Broman's *Glygisvallur* it is written that the farhter north one went the more terrible the magicians, the Lapps being worse than the Finns as "instruments of The Devil." The Lapps had only to throw their gloves up into the air to bring on terrific thunderstorms.

In 1644, a court record shows a Finn with the Swedish name of Per Nilsson, from Långskog, which was a village of Finns in Attmar Parish, Medelpad, was tried for having killed the wife of Anders Pålsson was himself a Finn and no mean magician, known for making love potions and being able to find lost or stolen objects. In this case Anders bested Per, Per retaliated, and Per was found guilty of murder by witchcraft and was decapitated.

In 1647 the court at Ramsele tried a Finn for making idols and worshipping them and using them to make neighbors with whom he had fallen out fall sick or even die. To make them ill he drove a nail halfway into an idol. When he drove a nail all the way in the victim died.

The Finns, being closer to the Swedes, were better known to them and to the Finns the Swedes attributed a lot of magic they claimed the Finns learned from the Lapplanders. Swedish soldiers returning from the Finnish War (1808–1809) brought back many tales of the magicians of the Finnish territory. These magicians could read minds, bring storms, and perform many other wonders.

In the work of the distinguished Swedish folklorist Carl–Herman Tillhagen, from whose work I take details here, is the story of a man in Västergötland who said that

> a Finn had come to his grandmother to ask for money. "I have no money," his grandmother replied. The Finn retorted, "Oh yes you have. You have two crowns in your dresser." The grandmother (who did indeed have two crowns there—but how would he know that?) said, "Would you be satisfied with one?" And he was.

Occasionally a shrewd Finn cold be beaten by a clever Swede. The story is told of a Swedish officer who had an affair with a local girl when he was stationed in the *Finnmark* and when he was leaving her, to return to Sweden, she asked him for two hairs of his head. He fobbed off on her two hairs from his fur coat. Soon after he got back home, his fur coat disappeared; the girl had tried to bring him back with a magic spell and had got only the coat!

A SPELL TO STOP BLEEDING

Ditt blod skall stå uti ditt liv
Som vatten in Röda havet stod
När Israels barn över floden drog.
I namn fadrens och Sonens och den Helge Andes.

You, blood, stand in your life
As the water of the Red Sea stood
When the children of Israel passed over the flood.
In the name of The Father and of The Son and of The Holy Ghost.

A SWEDISH SPELL FROM A SWEDISH–SPEAKING AREA OF FINLAND

Din blod skall stå
Som Nordisstjärna
Står på himmelen
Och som stjänan stod
I Österlandet
Då Maria födde Frätsaran
Och såsom vattnet stod
I Jordons flod
Dä Israels barn gingo över
Och Farao fördränktes
Så skall ock din blod stå
I den treenige Gudens
Fadrens, Sonens och den Helge andres namn!

Your blood shall stand firm
As the North Star

Stands in the firmament
And as the star stood
In the East
When Mary bore The Savior
And as the water stood
In Jordan's flood
When the children of Israel passed over
And Pharoah was drowned
Like that also shall your blood stay
As in the Trinity
In the name of The Father and of The Son and of The Holy Ghost!

AND ANOTHER SPELL, THIS ONE IN FINNISH

Seiso sinä veri kuin seinä
Asa kuin aita
Älä vuora äläkä juokse
Niinkuin Jortanin virta
Jossa Jeesus Kristus kastetiin
Nimeen Isän ja Pojan ja Pyhän hengen.

Stand you, blood, like a wall
Be firm as a fence of stone
Do not float, do not flow
Just like Jordan's stream
In which Jesus Christ was baptized
In the name of The Father and of The Son and of The Holy Ghost.

THE LITERATURE OF OMENS

There always have been writers ready to point to omens, most often after the event. Just an an example, when William the Conqueror was handed at his coronation the white lance that signified the Duchy of Normandy, he rudely pushed it aside. Later in his reign he lost the duchy. That great gossip, John Aubrey, in his *Brief Lives* tells us about personally attending the coronation of James II. He says that the crown nearly fell off the king's head during the receiving of the oaths of allegiance of the peers and that, though there was no wind at all, the canopy of cloth of gold, that was held over James's head as he came to Westminster Abbey to be crowned, was torn. Aubrey himself saw it happen and noted it as a bad omen, perhaps related to the Cinque Ports, whose wardens were supporting the canopy.

Of course you know of many bad omens. For instance, it is a bad omen indeed to trip upon entering a building, which is why brides are carried over the threshold of their new homes.

The literature of omens is vast and could be the subject of a whole book. Mankind has been looking for omens ever since we first looked at strange comets and other spectacles in the skies, ever since we tore open animals to see if we could read the future in their vitals.

The Magic of Specters and Spiritual Apparitions by Cronius (after Hackius), the Hague, 1656.

A "POISONOUS BOOK"

This is what Oscar Wilde calls whatever volume it was that Lord Henry gave the decadent young protagonist in Wilde's *The Picture of Dorian Gray*. I believe the book must have been *À rebours* (Against Nature, 1884) by Georges-Charles Huysmans (1848–1907, who preferred to stress his Dutch background by being known as Joris-Karl Huysmans). In *The Complete Book of The Devil's Disciples* I quote Huysmans's personal and horrifying account of attendance at a Black Mass celebrated in Paris by a mad priest, the Abbé Boullan, who was at the center of a very decadent and dangerous group deeply involved in the black arts. The Parisian occult community in the latter part of the nineteenth century generated a great deal of *fin-de-siècle* literature which lies somewhere between pornography and blasphemy.

A MASTERPIECE OF A BOOK

Probably the greatest work of the leading figure in all German literature, Johann Wolfgang von Goethe (1749–1832), is the story of Faust, who epitomizes the Romantic hero in the unquenchable thirst for knowledge and adventure that causes Faust to sell his soul to The Devil. Published in two parts, the vast drama of *Faust* shows us both the Romantic concerns of the young Goethe and the wisdom of his later life. "They come and ask me what idea I tried to embody in my *Faust*," Goethe said to his friend Eckerman, "as if I myself knew and could say!... It was not in my nature to attempt, as a poet, to make a concrete formulation out of something abstract." But he did add:

Witch of the Woodlands;

OR, THE

COBLERS NEW TRANSLATION.

Here Robin the Cobler for his former Evils,
Is punish'd bad as Faustus with his Devils.

PRINTED AND SOLD IN ALDERMARY CHURCH YARD,
BOW LANE, LONDON.

Here the old Witches dance, and then agree,
How to fit Robin for his Lechery;
First he is made a Fox and hunted on,
Till he becomes an Horse, an Owl, a Swan.

At length their Spells of Witchcraft they withdrew,
But Robin still more hardships must go through;
For e'er he is transform'd into a Man,
They make him kiss their bums and glad he can.

That The Devil loses his wager [with Faust, with God], and that a man continually fighting his way through dire confusion towards something better may be redeemable—this is of course an effective thought that explains a lot.

"Men err as long as they strive," Mepistopheles tells Faust, but in the end Faust is saved because he persists in struggling, because he is driven by an undying love (the most powerful of all human emotions) and "a bold, untrammeled spirit." He encounters the messenger of The Devil,

Kin to that power, little understood,
Which always wills Evil, but which works the Good.

He is given a love potion by a witch and drinks it. He makes a pact with the Evil One, urged on by Mepistopheles. Get *Faust* and read it, in German if you can, in a poetic Victorian translation into English (such as Bayard Taylor's), or in one of the more modern translations. I regret there is no room to quote a long pasage here, for Goethe at his best requires a lot of time to work up to his greatest moments.

Goethe's story ought to be compared with the odd mixture of tragedy and farce in Christopher Marlowe's *Dr. Faustus*. For that, you can even rent a videotape of the film starring Richard Burton with Elizabeth Taylor as Helen of Troy, "the face that launched a thousand ships."

THE WEATHERMAN OF THE KENNEBEC

Emma Huntington Naso of Maine is but one of the many writers who have created our American heritage of local legends which have no less intrinsic value than the legend of Faust and, as Faust's story reflects its time and place, tell a great deal of American life in the old days. Here, from Mrs. Naso's rather obscure but interesting book on *Old Hallowell on the Kennebec* (1909) is the tale of a local wizard, "Uncle Kaler."

One of these earlier local characters, whose story borders on the marvelous, was an old man, called "Uncle Kaler," who lived on Loudon Hill. Uncle Kaler had Finnish blood in his veins and was reputed to be a "wizard" [the Lapps long having had that reputation]. By his magical art, Uncle Kaler could make amulets that would bring good luck to the sailor, love philtres for despairing swains and forlorn damsels, and efficacious potions to cure the cattle who were bewitched. This weird enchanter could also make good weather or bad weather to order, although he sometimes overdid the matter, as the following tradition shows. Uncle Kaler lived in an old house just below the millbrook, and the road from Cobbossee to the Hook ran close by his door. One warm misty evening in May, Uncle Kaler heard some horses speeding up the hill and stopping at his door. He opened it, and a man's voice came in from the darkness: "Is this Mr. Kaler?"

"It is, at your service."

"Well, my name is——, and this lady with me is Miss——of Pownalboro.

"We are on our way to Hallowell to be married. Her relatives don't like the match and are after us hot foot. Listen!"

Away down the river could be heard the long-drawn bay of hounds.

"You hear, old man! Now our horses are about used up, and if something isn't done they will overtake us; then there will be murder. You have the reputation of being a windjammer and a wizard. Here are a hundred Spanish milled dollars for the worst weather you have got, and if it does the business, [I'll give you] another hundred when I come back."

The old man made no reply, but went to a chest and taking out a small leather bag gave it to the stranger, saying, "Go back a little on the road, cut open the bag, squeeze out its contents, throw the bag away, then come back and resume your journey." The man did as he was told, and returning in a short time said: "If you have played us false, something will happen to you."

"Rest easy," said Uncle Kaler. "Hark!" and away in the southwest was heard a low grumbling like distant thunder. It increased and deepened momentarily till it seemed as if a cyclone was tearing through the forest.

"What is it?" asked the stranger.

"A cloudburst in the hills. It will be a sharp hound who follows your track in five minutes. Go in peace, and good luck go with you, from a man who can make good luck."

Away they dashed through the gathering storm and darkness, speeding to happiness, or the contrary, as the case may be with married people. Under the roaring thunder, and nearly deafened by the roar and crash of the raging torrent he had conjured, the old man went into the house saying to himself: "I am afraid I made that bagful too strong, but I don't know as I am sorry, as it would never do to have the young people caught."

The next morning the day broke clear and beautiful; but where, the day before, a peaceful little brook had flowed through a green pasture, and the little mill had clattered merrily grinding the few grists the neighbors brought, there was now a fearful gorge gullied down to the bedrock and choked up with uprooted trees and brush; the mill was gone and the big boulder that formed a part of its foundation had been swept away far out into the river, and now forms that impediment to navigation known as Mill Rock. If anyone will take notice at low tide they will see quite a large point stretching out into the river from the mouth of the brook; it is the debris of the cloudburst.

Many such folktales are told to explain extraordinary natural features, and American maps are dotted with such named for The Devil or magical acts in the distant past.

A SELECT LIBRARY OF RELEVANT AMERICAN FOLKLORE

Gillian Bennett & Paul Smith, eds., *Monsters with Iron Teeth* (1988)

Jan H. Brunvand, *The Vanishing Hitchhiker* (1982)

John Camp, *Magic, Myth and Medicine* (1974)

Tristram P. Coffin, *Indian Tales of North America* (1961)

Harold Courlander, *A Treasury of African Folklore* (1975)

J. Frank Dobie, *Legends of Texas* (2 vols., reprinted 1975)

Richard M. Dorson, *Jonathan Draws the Long Bow* (reprinted 1970)

Patrick W. Gainer, *Witches, Ghosts, and Signs* (1975)

Wayland D. Hand, *Magical Medicine* (1984)

John Harden, *Tar Heel Ghosts* (1980)

Mike Helm, *Oregon's Ghosts and Monsters* (1983)

Louis C. Jones, *Things that Go Bump in the Night* (1959)

George Lyman Kittredge, *Witchcraft in Old and New England* (reprinted 1972)

William E. Koch, *Folklore from Kansas* (1980)

Hector Lee, *Heroes, Villains, and Ghosts* (1984)

Mary A. Owen, *Voodoo Tales, as Told among the Negroes of the Southwest* (1893, reprinted n.d.)

Louise Pound, *Nebraska Folklore* (reprinted 1976)

Michael P. Smith, *Spirit World...of Afro-American New Orleans* (1984)

This illustration from a Christmas story called "[An] Toinette and the Elves" shows the heroine serving fern-seed broth to ther little friends. Peascod the Elf gave her the recipe: "It is very simple...only seed and honey dew, stirred from left to right with a sprig of fennel.... Be sure and stir from the left; if you don't it curdles, and the flavour will be spoiled." The tale was by "Susan Coolidge" [Sarah Chauncey Woolsey], whose *What Katy Did* (1872) and other children's books made her famous in her day. She always pointed a moral. As elf Thistle says at the end of this story: "Be lucky, house...for you have received and entertained the luck-bringers. And be lucky, Toinette. Good temper *is* good luck, and sweet words and kind looks and peace in the heart are the fairest of fortunes. See that you never lose them again, my girl."

Harold Thompson, *Body, Boots, and Britches* (2nd edn., 1970)

Newman I. White, ed., *The Frank C. Brown Collection of North Carolina Folklore* (7 vols., 1952–1964)

Marion Wood, *Spirits, Heroes and Hunters from North American Indian Mythology* (1982)

SAMPLE DISCUSSIONS OF VOODOO IN LITERATURE

Asselin, Charles. "Voodoo Myths in Haitian Literature," *Comparative Literature Studies* 17 (1980), 391–398

Giordano, Fedora. *"Cent'anni di esotismo: Il voodoo de G[eorge] W[ashington] Cable a Ismael Reed,"* pp. 173 - 197 in *L'esotismo nella letteratura anglo-americana* (Exoticism in Anglo-American Literature, ed. Elemire Zolla, 1979)

Southerland, Ellease. "The Influence of Voodoo on the Fiction of Zora Neale Hurston," pp. 172–183 in *Sturdy Black Bridges...* (ed. Roseann P. Bell et al., 1979)

THE RELIGION OF THE GODDESS

The roots go deeper, but the late 1970s and 1980s was the heyday of Goddess movements, part of the feminist identity and women's liberation movements. Here are nine leading books on the Mother's Religion from that period. The political writings on the subject have proliferated in the nineties. Lesbian magic has eclipsed a brief period of "gay" magic of the time of Leo Martello and other sixties writers. Some say the hippies have turned harridans, others that women are gaining greater recognition that they "hold up half the sky."

Margot Adler, *Drawing Down the Moon* (1987)

Christina Downing, *The Goddess* ...(1984)

Naomi R. Goldenberg, *The Changing of the Gods...* (1979)

M. Esther Harding, *Women's Mysteries* (1976)

Hallie Iglehart, *Womanspirit...* (1983)

Carl Olson, ed., *The Book of the Goddess...* (1976)

Billie Potts, *Witches Heal: Lesbian Herbal Self-Sufficiency* (1981)

Charlene Spretnak, *The Politics of Women's Spirituality* (1981)

"Starhawk," *The Spiral Dance* (1979)

THE SUMMONED

I suppose that a very minor department of literature is the creation of little legends which give, or explain, a nickname. My example is drawn from a king of Spain, Ferdinand IV (1286?–1312). Spanish history knows him by the equivalent of "The Summoned." The story is that he rejected the pleas of Peter and John de Carvajal and sent them to their deaths on circumstantial evidence. Before they died they cursed him, saying that he would be summoned within a month before God to defend his action. Thirty days thereafter the king was discovered in his bed, dead.

MEPHISTOPHILIS SIEGEL ODER CHARACTEUR

ZUM   ZWANG

UND GEHORSAM

CASTING A FATAL SPELL

Rather than being responsible for giving instructions here, I give you M.R. James's story of "Casting the Runes," with the note on the author I appended when I anthologized the story in my book, *Tales of Mystery and Melodrama* (1977).

M[ontague] R[hodes] James (1862–1936) was an authority on Christian art; a medievalist who discovered important psalters and pseudoepigraphia; provost of King's College, Cambridge (1905–1918) and of Eton (1918–1936); an expert on stained glass; and a fine writer of horror stories. James Sandow wrote of James in *Poetry Magazine* (1946):

Only a very few of the writers who have conjured up supernatural horrors can, in the end, be relied upon to horrify us at all. And the older masters, while we may bow in theory to their enterprise, seem often more laborious than effective. Of the acknowledged masters of the more conventional story of the supernatural, I find few as steadily palatable as M. R. James, the Cambridge don who found horrid, possessive creatures in cloistered studies, in Canon Alberic's scrapbook, in an old mezzotint.

James's stories were collected in books such as *Ghost Stories of an Antiquary* (1910), *More Ghost Stories* (1912), *A Thin Ghost and Others* (1919), and *Twelve Medieval Ghost Stories* (1922). James bridges the gap between early, sensational works such as the anonymous *The Iron Shroud* (1832) and modern works by writers in the genre such as John Collier and Algernon Blackwood.

We had considered selecting the lesser-known story "TheMezzotint," whose haunting qualities linger disturbingly in the mind; but we finally decided upon his masterpiece "Casting the Runes." The story first appeared in 1904. Its frantic action and thrilling conclusion are unforgettable.

CASTING THE RUNES

April 15th, 190—

Dear Sir,

I am requested by the Council of the——Association to return to you the draft of a paper on *The Truth of Alchemy*, which you have been good enough to offer to read at our forthcoming meeting, and to inform you that the Council do not see their way to including it in the programme.

I am,
Yours faithfully,
—*Secretary*

April 18th

Dear Sir,

I am sorry to say that my engagements do not permit of my affording you an interview on the subject of your proposed paper. Nor do our laws allow of your discussing the matter with a Committee of our Council, as you suggest. Please allow me to assure you that the fullest consideration was given to the draft which you submitted, and that it was not declined without having been referred to the judgement of a most competent authority. No personal question (it can hardly be necessary for me to add) can have had the slightest influence on the decision of the council.

Believe me (*ut supra*).

April 20th

The Secretary of the ——begs respectfully to inform Mr. Karswell that it is impossible for him to communicate the name of any person or persons to whom the draft of Mr. Karswell's paper may have been submitted; and further desires to intimate that he cannot undertake to reply to any further letters on this subject.

"And who *is* Mr. Karswell?" inquired the Secretary's wife. She had called at his office, and (perhaps unwarrantably) had picked up the last of these three letters, which the typist had just brought in.

"Why, my dear, just at present Mr. Karswell is a very angry man. But I don't know much about him otherwise, except that he is a person of wealth, his address is Lufford Abbey, Warwickshire, and he's an alchemist, apparently, and wants to tell us all about it; and that's about all—except that I don't want to meet him for the next week or two. Now, if you're ready to leave this place, I am."

"What have you been doing to make him angry?" asked Mrs. Secretary.

"The ususal thing, my dear, the ususal thing: he sent in a draft of a paper he wanted to read at the next meeting, and we referred it to Edward Dunning—almost the only man in England who knows about these things—and he said it was perfectly hopeless, so we declined it. So Karswell has been pelting me with letters ever since. The last thing he wanted was the name of the man we referred his nonsense to; you saw my answer to that. But don't you say anything about it, for goodness' sake."

"I should think not, indeed. Did I ever do such a thing? I do hope, though, he won't get to know that it was poor Mr. Dunning."

"Poor Mr. Dunning? I don't know why you call him that; he's a very happy man, is Dunning. Lots of hobbies and a comfortable home, and all his time to himself."

"I only meant I should be sorry for him if this man got hold of his name, and came and bothered him."

"Oh, ah! yes. I dare say he would be poor Mr. Dunning then."

The Secretary and his wife were lunching out, and the friends to whose house they were bound were Warwickshire people. So Mrs. Secretary had already settled it in her own mind that she would question them judiciously about Mr. Karswell. But she was saved the trouble of leading up to the subject, for the hostess said to the host, before many minutes had passed, "I saw the Abbot of Lufford this morning." The host whistled. "*Did* you? What in the world brings him up to town?" "Goodness knows; he was coming out of the British Museum gate as I drove past." It was not unnatural that Mrs. Secretary should inquire whether this was a real Abbot who was being spoken of. "Oh no, my dear: only a neighbor of ours in the country who bought out Lufford Abbey a few years ago. His real name is Karswell." "Is he a friend of yours?" asked Mr. Secretary, with a private wink to his wife. The question let loose a torrent of declamation. There was really nothing to be said for Mr. Karswell. Nobody knew what he did with himself: his servants were a horrible set of people; he had invented a new religion for himself, and practised no one could tell what appalling rites; he was very easily offended, and never forgave anybody; he had a dreadful face (so the lady insisted, her husband somewhat demurring); he never did a kind action, and whatever influence he did exert was mischievous. "Do the poor man justice, dear," the husband interrupted. "You forget the treat he gave the school children." "Forget it, indeed! But I'm glad you mentioned it, because it gives an idea of the man. Now Florence, listen to this. The first winter he was at Lufford this delightful neighbour of ours wrote to the clergyman of his parish (he's not ours, but we know him very well) and offered to show the school children some magic–lantern slides. He said he had some new kinds, which he thought would interest them. Well, the clergyman was rather surprised, because Mr. Karswell had shown himself inclined to be unpleasant to the children—complaining of their trespassing, or something of the sort; but of course he accepted, and the evening was fixed, and our friend went himself to see that everything went right. He said he never had been thankful for anything as that his own children were all prevented from being there—they were at a children's party at our house, as a matter of fact. Because this Mr. Karswell had evidently set out with the intention of frightening these poor village children out of their wits, and I do believe, if he had been allowed to go on, he would actually have done so. He began with some comparatively mild things. Red Riding Hood was one, and even then, Mr. Farrer said, the wolf was so dreadful that several of the smaller children had to be taken out: and he said Mr. Karswell began the story by producing a nose like a wolf howling in the distance, which was the most gruesome thing he had ever heard. All the slides he showed, Mr. Ferrer said, were most clever; they were absolutely realistic, and where he had got them or how he worked them he could not imagine. Well, the show went on, and the stories kept on becoming a little more terrifying each time, and the children were mesmerized into complete silence. At last he produced a series which represented a little boy passing through his own park—Lufford, I mean—in the evening. Every child in the room could recognize the place from the pictures. And this poor boy was followed, and at last pursued and overtaken, and either torn to pieces or somehow made away with, by a horrible hopping creature in white, which you saw first dodging about among the trees, and gradually it appeared more and more plainly. Mr. Farrer said it gave him one of the worst nightmares he ever remembered, and what it must have meant to the children doesn't bear thinking of. Of course this was too much, and he spoke very sharply indeed to Mr. Karswell, and said it couldn't go on. All *he* said was: "Oh, you think it's time to bring our little show to an end and send them home to their beds? *Very* well!" And then, if you please, he switched on another slide, which showed a great mass of snakes, centipedes, and disgusting creatures with wings, and somehow or other he made it seem as if they were climbing out of the picture and getting in amongst the audience; and this was accompanied by a sort of dry rustling noise which sent the children nearly mad, and of course they stampeded. A good many of them were rather hurt in getting out of the room, and I don't suppose one of them closed an eye that night. There was the most dreadful trouble in the village afterwards. Of course the mothers threw a good part of the blame on poor Mr. Ferrer, and, if they could have got past the gates, I believe the fathers would have broken every window in the Abbey. Well, now, that's Mr. Karswell: that's the Abbot of Lufford, my dear, and you can imagine how we covet *his* society."

"Yes, I think he has all the possibilities of a distinguished criminal, has Karswell," said the host. "I should be sorry for anyone who got into his bad books."

"Is he the man, or am I mixing him up with someone else?" asked the Secretary (who for some minutes had been wearing the frown of the man who is trying to recollect something). "Is he the man who brought out a *History of Witchcraft* some time back—ten years or more?"

"That's the man; do you remember the reviews of it?"

"Certainly I do; and what's equally to the point, I knew the author of the most incisive of the lot. So did you: you must remember John Harrington; he was at John's in our time."

"Oh, very well indeed, though I don't think I saw or heard anything of him between the time I went down and the day I read the account of the inquest on him."

"Inquest?" said one of the ladies. "What has happened to him?"

"Why, what happened was that he fell out of a tree and broke his neck. But the puzzle was, what could have induced him to get up there. It was a mysterious business, I must say. Here was this man—not an athletic fellow, was he? and with no eccentric twist about him that was noticed—walking home along a country road late in the evening—no tramps—well known and liked in the place—and he suddenly begins to run like mad, loses his hat and stick, and finally shins up a tree—quite a difficult tree—growing in the hedgerow: a dead branch gives way, and he comes down with it and breaks his neck, and there he's found next morning with the most dreadful face of fear on him that could be imagined. It was pretty evident, of course, that he had been chased by something, and people talked of savage dogs, and beasts escaped out of menageries; but there was nothing to be made of that. That was in '89, and I believe his brother Henry (whom I remember as well at Cambridge, but *you* probably don't) has been trying to get on the track of an explanation ever since. He, of course, insists there was malice in it, but I don't know. It's difficult to see how it could have come in."

After a time the talk reverted to the *History of Witchcraft*. "Did you ever look into it?" asked the host.

"Yes, I did," said the Secretary. "I went so far as to read it."

"Was it as bad as it was made out to be?"

"Oh, in point of style and form, quite hopeless. It deserved all the pulverizing it got. But, besides that, it was an evil book. The man believed every word of what he was saying, and I'm very much mistaken if he hadn't tried the greater part of his receipts."

"Well, I only remember Harrington's review of it, and I must say if I'd been the author it would have quenched my literary ambition for good. I should never have held up my head again."

"It hasn't had that effect in the present case. But come, it's half–past three; I must be off."

On the way home the Secretary's wife said, "I do hope that horrible man won't find out that Mr. Dunning had anything to do with the rejection of his paper." "I don't think there's much chance of that," said the Secretary. "Dunning won't mention it himself, for these matters are confidential, and none of us will for the same reason. Karswell won't know his name, for Dunning hasn't published anything on the same subject yet. The only danger is that Karswell might find out, if he was to ask the British Museum people who was in the habit of consulting alchemical manuscripts: I can't very well tell them not to mention Dunning, can I? It would set them talking at once. Let's hope it won't occur to him."

However, Mr. Karswell was an astute man.

This much is in the way of prologue. On an evening rather later in the same week, Mr. Edward Dunning was returning from the British Museum, where he had been engaged in research, to the comfortable house in a suburb where he lived alone, tended by two excellent women who had been long with him. There is nothing to be added by way of description of him to what we have heard already. Let us follow him as he takes his sober course homewards.

A train took him to within a mile of two of his house, and an electric tram a stage farther. The line ended at a point some three hundred yards from his front door. He had had enough of reading when he got into the car, and indeed the light was not such as to allow him to do more than study the advertisements on the panes of glass that faced him as he sat. As was not unnatural, the advertisements in this particular line of cars were objects of his frequent contemplation, and, with the possible exception of the brilliant and convincing dialogue between Mr. Lamplough and an eminent K.C. on the subject of Pyretic Saline, none of them afforded much scope to his imagination. I am wrong: there was one at the corner of the car farthest from him which did not seem familiar. It was in blue letters on a yellow ground, and all that he could read of it was a name—John Harrington—and something like a date. It could be of no interest to him to know more; but for all that, as the car emptied, he was just curious enough to move along the seat until he could read it well. He felt to a slight extent repaid for his trouble; the advertisement was *not* of the usual type. It ran thus: "In memory of John Harrington, F.S.A., of The Laurels, Ashbrooke. Died Sept. 18th, 1889. Three months were allowed."

The car stopped. Mr. Dunning, still contemplating the blue letters on the yellow ground, had to be stimulated to rise by a word from the conductor. "I beg your pardon," he said, "I was looking at that advertisement; it's a very odd one, isn't it?" The conductor read it slowly. "Well, my word," he said, "I never see that one before. Well, that is a cure, ain't it? Someone bin up to their jokes 'ere, I should think." He got out a duster and applied it, not without saliva, to the pane and then to the outside. "No," he said, returning, "that ain't no transfer; seems to me as if it was a reg'lar *in* the glass, what I mean in the substance, as you may say. Don't you think so, sir?" Mr. Dunning examined it and rubbed it with his glove, and agreed. "Who looks after these advertisements, and gives leave for them to be put up? I wish you would inquire. I will just take a note of the words." At this moment there came to call from the driver: "Look alive George, time's up." "All right, all right; there's something else what's come up at this end. You come and look at this 'ere glass." "What's gorn with the glass?" said the driver, approaching. "Well, and oo's 'Arrington? What's it all about?" "I was just asking who was responsible for putting the advertisements up in your cars, and saying it would be as well to make some inquiry about this one." "Well, sir, that's all done at the Company's office, that work is: it's our Mr. Timms, I believe, looks into that. When we put up tonight I'll leave word, and per'aps I'll be able to tell you tomorrow if you 'appen to be coming this way."

This was all that passed that evening. Mr. Dunning did just go to the trouble of looking up Ashbrooke, and found it was in Warwickshire.

Next day he went to town again. The car (it was the same car) was too full in the morning to allow of his getting a word with the conductor: he could only be sure that the curious advertisement had been made away with. The close of the day brought a further element of mystery into the transaction. He had missed the tram, or else preferred walking home, but at a rather late hour, while he was at work in his study, one of the maids came to say that two men from the tramways were very anxious to speak to him. This was a reminder of the advertisement, which he had, he says, nearly forgotten. He had the men in—they were the conductor and driver of the car—and when the matter of refreshment had been attended to, asked what Mr. Timms had had to say about the advertisement. "Well, sir, that's what we took the liberty to step round about," said the conductor. "Mr. Timms 'e give William 'ere the rough side of his tongue about that: 'cordin to 'im there warn't no advertisement of that description sent in, nor ordered, nor paid for, nor put up, nor nothink, let alone not bein' there, and we was playing the fool takin' up his time. 'Well,' I says, 'if that's the case, all I ask of you, Mr. Timms,' I says, 'is to take and look at it for yourself,' I says. 'Of course if it ain't there,' I says, 'you may take and call me what you like.' 'Right,' he says, 'I will': and we went straight off. Now I leave it to you, sir, if that ad., as we term 'em, with 'Arrington on it warn't as plain as ever you see anythink—blue letters on yeller glass, and as I says at the time, and you borne me out, reg'lar *in* the glass, because, if you remember, you recollect of me swabbing it with my duster." "To be sure I do, quite clearly—well?" "You may say well, I don't think. Mr. Timms he gets in that car with a light—no, he telled William to 'old the light outside. 'Now,' he says, 'where's your precious ad. what we've 'eard so much about?' ''Ere it is,' I says, 'Mr. Timms,' and I laid my 'and on it." The conductor paused.

"Well," said Mr. Dunning, "it was gone, I suppose. Broken?"

"Broke!—not it. There warn't, if you'll believe me, no more trace of them letters—blue letters they was—on that piece o' glass, than—well, it's no good *me* talkin'. *I* never see such a thing. I leave it to William here if—but there, as I says, where's the benefit in me going on about it?"

"And what did Mr. Timms say?"

"Why 'e did what I give 'im leave to—called us pretty much anythink he liked, and I don't know as I blame him so much neither. But what we thought, William and me did, was as we seen you take down a bit of a note about that—well, that letterin'—"

"I certainly did that, and I have it now. Did you wish me to speak to Mr. Timms myself, and show it to him? Was that what you came in about?"

"There, didn't I say as much?" said William. "Deal with a gent if you can get on the track of one, that's my word. Now perhaps, George, you'll allow as I ain't took you very far wrong tonight."

"Very well, William, very well; no need for you to fo on as if you'd 'ad to frog's-march me 'ere. I come quiet, didn't I? All the same for that, we 'and't ought to take up your time this way, sir; but if it so 'appened you could find time to step round to the Company orfice in the morning and tell Mr. Timms what you seen for yourself, we should lay under a very 'igh obligation to you for the trouble. You see it ain't bein' called—well, one thing and another, as we mind, but if they got it into their 'ead at the orfice as we seen things as warn't there, why, one thing leads to another, and where we should be a twelve–munce, 'ence—well, you can understand what I mean."

Amid further elucidations of their proposition, George, conducted by William, left the room.

The incredulity of Mr. Timms (who had a nodding acquaintance with Mr. Dunning) was greatly modified on the following day by what the latter could tell and show him; and any bad mark that might have been attached to the names of William and George was not suffered to remain on the Company's books; but explanation there was none.

Mr. Dunning's interest in the matter was kept alive by an incident of the following afternoon. He was walking from his club to the train, and he noticed some way ahead a man with a handful of leaflets such as are distributed to passersby by agents of enterprising firms. This agent had not chosen a very crowded streeet for his operations: in fact, Mr. Dunning did not see him get rid of a single leaflet before he himself reached the spot. One was thrust into his hand as he passed: the hand that gave it touched his, and he experienced a sort of little shock as it did so. It seemed unnaturally rough and hot. He looked in passing at the giver, but the impression he got was so unclear that, however much he tried to reckon it up subsequently, nothing would come. He was walking quickly, and as he went on glanced at the paper. It was a blue one. The name of Harrington in large capitals caught his eye. He stopped, startled, and felt for his glasses. The next instant the leaflet was twitched out of his hand by a man who hurried past, and was irrecoverably gone. He ran back a few paces, but where was the passerby? and where the distributor?

It was in a somewhat pensive frame of mind that Mr. Dunning passed on the following day into the Select Manuscript Room of the British Museum, and filled up tickets for Harley 3586, and some other volumes. After a few minutes they were brought to him, and he was settling the one he wanted first upon the desk, when he thought he heard his own name whispered behind him. He turned round hastily, and in doing so, brushed his little portfolio of loose papers on to the floor. He saw no one he recognized except one of the staff in charge of the room, who nodded to him, and he proceeded to pick up his papers. He thought he had them all, and was turning to begin work, when a stout gentleman at the table behind him, who was just rising to leave, and had collected his own belongings, touched him on the shoulder, saying, "May I give you this? I think it should be yours," and handed him a missing quire. "It is mine, thank you," said Mr. Dunning. In another moment the man had left the room. Upon finishing his work for the afternoon, Mr. Dunning had some conversation with the assistant in charge, and took occasion to ask who the stout gentleman was. "Oh, he's a man named Karswell," said the assistant, "he was asking me a week ago who were the great authorities on alchemy, and of course I told him you were the only one in the country. I'll see if I can catch him: he'd like to meet you, I'm sure."

"For heaven's sake don't dream of it!" said Mr. Dunning. "I'm particularly anxious to avoid him."

"Oh, very well," said the assistant, "he doesn't come here often: I dare say you won't meet him."

More than once on the way home that day Mr. Dunning confessed to himself that he did not look forward with his usual cheerfulness to a solitary evening. It seemed to him that something ill–defined and impalpable had stepped in between him and his fellow–men—had taken him in charge, as it were. He wanted to sit close up to his neighbours in the train and in the tram, but as luck would have it both train and car were markedly empty. The conductor George was thoughtful, and appeared to be absorbed in calculations as to the number of passengers. On arriving at his house he found Dr. Watson, his medical man, on his doorstep. "I've had to upset your household arrangements, I'm sorry to say, Dunning. Both your servants *hors de combat*. In fact, I've had to send them to the Nursing Home."

"Good heavens! what's the matter?"

"It's something like ptomaine poisoning, I should think; you've not suffered yourself, I can see, or you wouldn't be walking about. I think they'll pull through all right."

"Dear, dear! Have you any idea what brought it on?"

"Well, they tell me they bought some shell–fish from a hawker at their dinner time. It's odd. I've made inquiries, but I can't find that any hawker has been to other houses in the street. I couldn't send word to you; they won't be back for a bit yet. You come and dine with me tonight, anyhow, and we can make arrangements for going on. Eight o' clock. Don't be too anxious."

The solitary evening was thus obviated; at the expense of some distress and inconvenience, it is true. Mr. Dunning spent the time pleasantly enough with the doctor (a rather recent settler), and returned to his lonely home at about 11:30. The night he passed is not one on which he looks back with any satisfaction. He was in bed and the light was out. He was wondering if the charwoman would come early enough to get him hot water next morning, when he heard the unmistakable sound of his study door opening. No step followed it on the passage floor, but the sound must mean mischief, for he knew that he had shut the door that evening after putting his papers away in his desk. It was rather shame than courage that induced him to slip out into the passage and lean over the banister in his nightgown, listening. No light was visible; no further sound came: only a gust of warm, or even hot air played for an instant round his shins. He went back and decided to lock himself into his room. There was more unpleasantness, however. Either an economical suburban company had decided that their light would not be required in the small hours, and had stopped working, or else something was wrong with the meter; the effect was in any case that the electric light was off. The obvious course was to find a match, and also to consult his watch: he might as well know how many hours of discomfort awaited him. So he put his hand into the well–known nook under the pillow: only, it did not get so far. What he touched was, according to his account, a mouth, with teeth, and with hair about it, and, he declares, not the mouth of a human being. I do not think it is any use to guess what he said or did; but he was in a spare room with the door locked and his ear to it before he was clearly conscious again. And there he spent the rest of a most miserable night, looking every moment for some fumbling at the door: but nothing came.

The venturing back to his own room in the morning was attended with many listenings and quiverings. The door stood open, fortunately, and the blinds were up (the servants had been out of the house before the hour of drawing them down); there was, to be short, no trace of an inhabitant. The watch, too, was in its usual place; nothing was disturbed, only the wardrobe door had swung open, in accordance with its confirmed habit. A ring at the back door now announced the charwoman, who had been ordered the night before, and nerved Mr. Dunning, after letting her in, to continue his search in other parts of the house. It was equally fruitless.

The day thus begun went on dismally enough. He dared not go to the Museum: in spite of what the assistant had said, Karswell might turn up there, and Dunning felt he could not cope with a probably hostile stranger. His own house was odious; he hated sponging on the doctor. He spent some little time in a call at the Nursing Home, where he was slightly cheered by a good report of his housekeeper and maid. Towards lunch–time he betook himself to his club, again experiencing a gleam of satisfaction at seeing the Secretary of the Association. At luncheon Dunning told his friend the more material of his woes, but could not bring himself to speak of those that weighed most heavily on his spirits. "My poor dear man," said the Secretary, "what an upset! Look here: we're alone at home, absolutely. You must put up with us. Yes! no excuse: send your things in this afternoon." Dunning was unable to stand out: he was, in truth, becoming acutely anxious, as the hours went on, as to what that night might have waiting for him. He was almost happy as he hurried home to pack up.

His friends, when they had time to take stock of him, were rather shocked at his lorn appearance, and did their best to keep him up to the mark. Not altogether without success: but, when the two men were smoking alone later, Dunning became dull again. Suddenly he said, "Gayton, I believe that alchemist man knows it was I who got his paper rejected." Gayton whistled. "What makes you think that?" he said. Dunning told of his conversation with the Museum assistant, and Gayton could only agree that the guess seemed likely to be correct. "Not that I care much," Dunning went on, "only it might be a nuisance if we were to meet. He's a bad–tempered party, I imagine." Conversation dropped again; Gayton became more and more strongly impressed with the desolateness that came over Dunning's face and bearing, and finally—though with a considerable effort—he asked him point–blank whether something serious was not bothering him. Dunning gave an exclamation of relief. "I was perishing to get it off my mind," he said. "Do you know anything about a man named John Harrington?" Gayton was thoroughly startled, and at the moment could only ask why. Then the complete story of Dunning's experiences came out—what had happened in the tramcar, in his own house, and in the street, the troubling of spirit that had crept over him, and still held him; and he ended with the question he had begun with. Gayton was at a loss how to answer him. To tell the story of Harrington's end would perhaps be right; only, Dunning was in a nervous state, the story was a grim one, and he could not help asking himself whether there were not a connecting link between these two cases, in the person of Karswell. It was a difficult concession for a scientific man, but it could be eased by the phrase "hypnotic suggestion." In the end he decided that his answer tonight should be guarded; he would talk the situation over with his wife. So he said that he had known Harrington at Cambridge, and believed he had died suddenly in 1889, adding a few details about the man and his published work. He did talk over the matter with Mrs. Gayton, and, as he anticipated, she leapt at once to the conclusion which had been hovering before him. It was she who reminded him of the surviving brother, Henry Harrington, and she also who suggested that he might be got hold of by means of their hosts of the day before. "He might be a hopeless crank," objected Gayton. "That could be ascertained from the Bennetts, who knew him," Mrs. Gayton retorted; and she undertook to see the Bennetts the very next day.

It is not necessary to tell in further detail the steps by which Henry Harrington and Dunning were brought together.

The next scene that does require to be narrated is a conversation that took place between the two. Dunning had told Harrington of the strange ways in which the dead man's name had been brought before him, and had said something, besides, of his own subsequent experiences. Then he had asked if Harrington was disposed, in return, to recall any of the circumstances connected with his brother's death. Harrington's surprise at what he heard can be imagined: but his reply was readily given.

"John," he said, "was in a very odd state, undeniably, from time to time, during some weeks before, though not immediately before, the catastrophe. There were several things; the principal notion he had was that he thought he was being followed. No doubt he was an impressionable man, but he never had had such fancies as this before. I cannot get it out of my mind that there was ill will at work, and what you tell me about yourself reminds me very much of my brother. Can you think of any possible connecting link?"

"There is just one that has been taking shape vaguely in my mind. I've been told that your brother reviewed a book very severely not long before he died, and just lately I have happened to cross the path of the man who wrote that book in a way he would resent."

"Don't tell me the man was called Karswell."

"Why not? that is exactly his name."

Henry Harrington leant back. "That is final to my mind. Now I must explain further. From something he said, I feel sure that my brother John was beginning to believe—very much against his will—that Karswell was at the bottom of his trouble. I want to tell you what seems to me to have a bearing on the situation. My brother was a great musician, and used to run up to concerts in town. He came back, three months before he died, from one of these, and gave me his programme: he always kept them. 'I nearly missed this one,' he said. 'I suppose I must have dropped it: anyhow, I was looking for it under my seat and in my pockets and so on, and my neighbour offered me his, said "might he give it me, he had no further use for it," and he went away just afterwards. I don't know who he was—a stout, clean-shaven man. I should have been sorry to miss it; of course I could have bought another, but this cost me nothing.' At another time he told me that he had been very uncomfortable both on the way to his hotel and during the night. I piece things together now in thinking it over. Then, not very long after, he was going over these programmes, putting them in order to have them bound up, and in this particular one (which by the way I had hardly glanced at), he found quite near the beginnnig a strip of paper with some very odd writing on it in red and black—most carefully done—it looked to me more like Runic lietters than anything else. 'Why,' he said, 'this must belong to my fat neighbour. It looks as if it might be worth returning to him; it may be a copy of something; evidently someone has taken trouble over it. How can I find his address?' We talked it over for a little and agreed that it wasn't worth advertising about, and that my brother had better look out for the man at the next concert, to which he was going very soon. The paper was lying on the book and we were both by the fire; it was a cold, windy summer evening. I suppose the door blew open, though I didn't notice it: at any rate—a warm gust it was—came quite suddenly between us, took the paper and blew it straight into the fire: it was light, thin paper, and flared and went up the chimney in a single ash. 'Well,' I said, 'you can't give it back now.' He said nothing for a minute: then rather crossly, 'No, I can't; but why you should keep on saying so I don't know.' I remarked that I didn't say it more than once. 'Not more than four times, you mean,' was all he said. I remember all that very clearly, without any good reason; and now to come to the point. I don't know if you looked at that book of Karswell's which my unfortunate brother reviewed. It's not likely that you should: but I did, both before his death and after it. The first time we made game of it together. It was written in no style at all—split infinitives, and every sort of thing that makes an Oxford gorge rise. Then there was nothing that the man didn't swallow: mixing up classical myths, and stories out of the *Golden Legend* with reports of savage customs of today—all very proper, no doubt, if you know how to use them, but he didn't: he seemed to put the *Golden Legend* and the *Goden Bough* exactly on a par, and to believe both: a pitiable exhibition, in short. Well, after the misfortune, I looked over the book again. It was no better than before, but the impression which it left this time on my mind was different. I suspected—as I told you—that Karswell had borne ill will to my brother, even that he was in some way responsible for what had happened; and now his book seemed to me to be a very sinister performance indeed. One chapter in particular struck me, in which he spoke of 'casting the Runes' on people, either for the purpose of gaining their affection or of getting them out of the way—perhaps more especially the latter: he spoke of all this in a way that really seemed to me to imply actual knowledge. I've not time to go into details, but the upshot is that I am pretty sure from information received that the civil man at the concert was Karswell: I suspect—I more than suspect—that the paper was of importance: and I do believe that if my brother had been able to give it back, he might have been alive now. Therefore, it occurs to me to ask you whether you have anything to put beside what I have told you."

By way of answer, Dunning had the episode in the Manuscript Room at the British Museum to relate. "Then he did actually hand you some papers; have you examined them? No? because we must, if you'll allow it, look at them at once, and very carefully."

They went to the still empty house—empty, for the two servants were not yet able to return to work. Dunning's portfolio of papers was gathering dust on the writing-table. In it were the quires of small-sized scribbling paper which he used for his transcripts: and from one of these, as he took it up, there slipped and fluttered out into the room with uncanny quickness, a strip of thin, light paper. The window was open, but Harrington slammed it to, just in time to intercept the paper, which he caught. "I thought so," he said; "it might be the identical thing that was given to my brother. You'll have to look out, Dunning; this may mean something quite serious for you."

A long consultation took place. The paper was narrowly examined. As Harrington had said, the characters on it were more like Runes than anything else, but not decipherable by either man, and both hesitated to copy them, for fear, as they confessed, of perpetuating whatever evil purpose they might conceal. So it has remained impossible (if I may anticipate a little) to ascertain what was conveyed in this curious message or commission. Both Dunning and Harrington are firmly convinced that it had the effect of bringing its possessors into very undesirable company. That it must be returned to the source whence it came they were agreed, and further, that the only safe and certain way was that of personal service; and here contrivance would be necessary, for Dunning was known by sight to Karswell. He must, for one thing, alter his appearance by shaving his beard. But then might not the blow fall first? Harrington thought they could time it. He knew the date of the concert at which the "black spot" had been put on his brother; it was June 18th. The death had followed on September 18th. Dunning reminded him that three months had been mentioned on the inscription on the car window. "Perhaps," he added, with a cheerless laugh, "mine will be a bill at three months too. I believe I can fix it in my diary. Yes, April 23rd was the day at the Museum; that brings us to July 23rd. Now, you know, it becomes extremely important to me to know anything you will tell me about the progress of your brother's trouble, if it is possible for you to speak of it." "Of course. Well, the sense of being watched whenever he was alone was the most distressing thing to him. After a time I took to sleeping in his room, and he was the better for that: still, he talked a great deal in his sleep. What about? Is it wise to dwell on that, at least before things ar straightened out? I think not, but I can tell you this: two things came for him by post during those weeks, both with a London postmark, and addressed in a commercial hand. One was a woodcut of Bewick's, roughly torn out of the page: one which shows a moonlit road and a man walking along it, followed by an awful demon creature. Under it were written the lines out of the 'Ancient Mariner' (which I suppose the cut illustrates) about one who, having once looked round—

> *walks on,*
> *And turns no more his head,*
> *Because he knows a frightful fiend*
> *Doth close behind him tread.*

The other was a calendar, such as the tradesmen often send. My brother paid no attention to this, but I looked at it after his death, and found that everything after Sept. 18th had been torn out. You may be surprised at his having gone out alone the evening he was killed, but the fact is that during the last ten days or so of his life he had been quite free from the sense of being followed or watched."

The end of the consultation was this. Harrington, who knew a neighbour of Karswell's, thought he saw a way of keeping a watch on his movements. It would be Dunning's part to be in readiness to try to cross Karswell's path at any moment, to keep the paper safe and in a place of ready access.

They parted. The next weeks were no doubt a severe strain upon Dunning's nerves: the intangible barrier which had seemeed to rise about him on the day when he received the paper, gradually developed into a brooding blackness that cut him off from the means of escape to which one might have thought he might resort. No one was at hand who was likely to suggest them to him, and he seemed robbed of all initiative. He waited with inexpressible anxiety as May, June, and early July passed on for a mandate from Harrington. But all this time Karswell remained immovable at Lufford.

At last, in less than a week before the date he had come to look upon as the end of his earthly activities, came a telegram: "Leaves Victoria by boat train Thursday night. Do not miss. I come to you tonight. Harrington."

He arrived accordingly, and they concocted plans. The train left Victoria at nine and its last stop before Dover was Croydon West. Harrington would mark down Karswell at Victoria, and look our for Dunning at Croydon, calling to him if need were by a name agreed upon. Dunning, disguised as far as might be, was to have no label or initials on any hand luggage, and must at all costs have the paper with him.

Dunning's suspense as he waited on the Croydon platform I need not attempt to describe. His sense of danger during the last days had only been sharpened by the fact that the cloud about him had perceptibly been lighter; but relief was an ominous symptom, and, if Karswell eluded him now, hope was gone: and there were so many chances of that. The rumour of the journey might be itself a device. The twenty minutes in which he paced the platform and persecuted every porter with inquiries as to the boat train were as bitter as any he had spent. Still, the train came, and Harrington was at the window. It was important, of course, that there should be no recognition: so Dunning got in at the farther end of the corridor carriage, and only gradually made his way to the compartment where Harrington and Karswell were. He was pleased, on the whole, to see that the train was far from full.

Karswell was on the alert, but gave no sign of recognition. Dunning took the seat not immediately facing him, and attempted, vainly at first, then with increasing command of his faculties, to reckon the possibilities of making the desired transfer. Opposite to Karswell, and next to Dunning, was a heap of Karswell's coats on the seat. It would be of no use to slip the paper into these—he would not be safe, or would not feel so, unless in some way it could be proffered by him and accepted by the other. There was a handbag, open, with papers in it. Could he manage to conceal this (so that Karswell might leave the carriage without it), and then find and give it to him? This was the plan that suggested itself. If he could only have counselled with Harrington! but that could not be. The minutes went on. More than once Karswell rose and went out into the corridor. The second time Dunning was on the point of attempting to make the bag fall off the seat, but he caught Harrington's eye, and read in it a warning. Karswell, from the corridor, was watching: probably to see if the two men recognized each other. He returned, but was evidently restless: and, when he rose the third time, hope dawned, for something did slip off his seat and fall with hardly a sound to the floor. Karswell went out once more, and passed out of range of the corridor window. Dunning picked up what had fallen, and saw that the key was in his hands in the form of one of Cook's ticket–cases, with tickets in it. These cases have a pocket in the cover, and within very few seconds the paper of which we have heard was in the pocket of this one. To make the operation more secure, Harrington stood in the doorway of the compartment and fiddled with the blind. It was done, and done at the right time, for the train was now slowing down towards Dover.

372

In a moment more Karswell re–entered the compartment. As he did so, Dunning, managing, he knew not how, to suppress the tremble in his voice, handed him the ticket–case, saying, "May I give you this, sir? I believe it is yours." After a brief glance at the ticket inside, Karswell uttered the hoped–for response, "Yes, it is; much obliged to you, sir," and he placed it in his breast pocket.

Even in the few moments that remained—moments of tense anxiety, for they knew not to what a premature finding of the paper might lead—both men noticed that the carriage seemed to darken about them and to grow warmer; that Karswell was fidgety and oppressed; that he drew the heap of loose coats near to him and cast it back as if it repelled him; and that he then sat upright and glanced anxiously at both. They, with sickening anxiety, busied themselves in collecting their belongings; but they both thought that Karswell was on the point of speaking when the train stopped at Dover Town. It was natural that in the short space between town and pier they should both go into the corridor.

At the pier they got out, but so empty was the train that they were forced to linger on the platform until Karswell should have passed ahead of them with his porter on the way to the boat, and only then was it safe for them to exchange a pressure of the hand and a word of concentrated congratulation. The effect upon Dunning was to make him almost faint. Harrington made him lean up against the wall, while he himself went forward a few yards within sight of the gangway to the boat, at which Karswell had now arrived. The man at the head of it examined his ticket, and, laden with coats he passed down into the boat. Suddenly the official called after him, "You sir, beg pardon, did the other gentleman show his ticket?" "What the devil do you mean by the other gentleman?" Karswell's snarling voice called back from the deck. The man bent over and looked at him. "The devil? Well, I don't know, I'm sure," Harrington heard him say to himself, and then aloud, "My mistake, sir; must have been your rugs! ask your pardon." And then, to a subordinate near him, "'Ad he got a dog with him, or what? Funny thing, I could 'a' swore 'e wasn't alone. Well, whatever it was, they'll 'ave to see to it aboard. She's off now. Another week and we shall be gettin' the 'oliday customers." In five minutes more there was nothing but the lessening lights of the boat, the long line of the Dover lamps, the night breeze, and the moon.

Long and long the two sat in their room at the "Lord War-den." In spite of the removal of their greatest anxiety, they were oppressed with a doubt, not of the lightest. Had they been justi-fied in sending a man to his death, as they believed they had? Ought they not to warn him, at least? "No," said Harrington; "if he is the murderer I think him, we have done no more than is just. Still, if you think it better—but how and where can you warn him?" "He was booked to Abbeville only," said Dunning. "I saw that. If I wired to the hotels there in Joanne's guide, 'Examine your ticket–case, Dunning,' I should feel happier. This is the 21st: he will have a day. But I am afraid he has gone into the dark." So telegrams were left at the hotel office.

It is not clear whether these reached their destination, or whether, if they did, they were understood. All that is known is that, on the afternoon of the 23rd, an English traveller, examin-ing the front of St. Wulfram's Church at Abbeville, then under extensive repair, was struck on the head and instantly killed by a stone falling from the scaffold erected round the northwestern tower, there being, as was clearly proved, no workman on the scaf-fold at that moment; and the traveller's papers identified him as Mr. Karswell.

Only one detail shall be added. At Karswell's sale a set of Bewick, sold with all faults, was acquired by Harrington. The page with the woodcut of the traveller and the demon was, as he had expected, mutilated. Also, after a judicious interval, Harrington repeated something of what he had heard his brother say in his sleep: but it was not long before Dunning stopped him.

Magicians have known all along that people's religious needs and expectations provide the greatest opportunity for the most effec-tive of all deceptions. But instead of turning against religion, as the skeptics among the Greek and Roman philosophers did, the magicians made use of it. After all, magic is nothing but the art of making people believe that something is being done about those things in life about which we all know that we ourselves can do nothing. Magic is the art that makes people who practice it feel better rather than worse, that provides the illusion of security to the insecure, and the comfort of hope to the hopeless.

GERMAN–AMERICAN SPELLS, MAGICAL REMEDIES, *UND SO WEITER*

We cannot think of even touching here on all the many ethnic aspects of our topics here. America is too large and various. But we can suggest you look into the colorful journals *Pennsylvania Folklife*, *Pennsylvania Dutchman*, *Pennsylvania Dutch News and Views*, *Der Reggeboge*, and *Keystone Folklore Quarterly*, Amish country and similar newspaper files from Pennsylvania, Texas, and elsewhere, and list some readings about the Germans who, very early, were numerous in America, and whose powwowing and *Hexenemiesteren* (witch doctors) and peculiar folk medicine, "measuring" for ailments, preaching in trance, dunking, dowsing, and dosing, etc., are extremely interesting. Who doesn't know about the hex signs of the Pennsylvania Dutch (really *Deutsch*)? Here are ten books on German-American folklore to get you started. Check also general books on US folklore, *American Folklore* and other standard journals, Adolf Bach's basic *Deutsche Volkskunde* (several editions), and your local reference librarian. To get started in a field of ethnic studies in folklore may be the beginning of a lifelong love affair with learning.

A. Monroe Arand, Jr. *Popular Home Remedies and Superstitions of the Pennsylvania Germans* (1941).

———. *The Realness of Witchcraft in America* (1942). "With Special Reference to the Pennsylvania Germans...."

"Junghans Buschbauer" (Francis Arnold Hoffman). *Der Familienschatz...* (1888). Family recipes, etc.

Lee R. Gandee. *Strange Experience* (1975). "The Autobiography of a *Hexenmeister.*"

Wayland D. Hand, ed. *American Folk Medicine* (1976). A symposium from the UCLA Center for the Study of Comparative Folklore and Mythology.

Abraham Reeser Horne. *'M Horn sei Pennsylvawnisch Deitsch Buch* (1910). Moon phases in folk medicine, etc.

Isaac Lieb. *Wohlerfahrner Pferde–Artz* (1842). Nineteenth–century folk medicine in Lebanon, PA.

Kenneth Roberts. *Henry Gross and His Dowsing Rod* (1951).

Frank G. Speck et al. *Rappahannock Herbals...*(1942). "Folklore and Science of Cures."

Harry B. Weiss and Howard R. Kemble. *The Great American Water–Cure Craze* (1967). "A History of Hydrotherapy in the United States."

I admire the practicality of the Pennsylvania Dutch. Riddle: *Was fer Stee hots es mencsht im Wasser?* What kind of stones does one ususally find in the water? Answer: *Nasse.* Wet stones.

FROM GERMANY

Heile, heile, Segen
morgen gibt es Regen,
und übermorgen Schnee,
dann tut es nicht nehr weh.

Healing, healing, blessing,
Tomorrow will bring rain,
The day after will bring snow,
And nothing will hurt any more.

NUNC DIMITIS

In concluding, I turn to a kind of literature often ignored, little scraps of papyri on which in very ancient days very sincere people wrote magical texts. *The Greek Magical Papyri in Translation* (edited by Hans Dieter Betz, 1986, its publication by a distinguished university press supported by a grant from the National Endowment for the Humanities) is a very specialized and erudite book, but in its introduction it says something that we can all understand and appreciate, something with which I should like to end this present book:

MERRY MET! MERRY PART!

Index

adder stones, 132
alchemy, 326
Amerindian rituals, 254
Amerindian healing plants, 128
Amethyst, 139
amulets, 168
    of classical times, 174
    disgusting, 114
    Hebrew, 115
    how to make, 237
    from nature, 114
    and talismans, homemade, 133
art, African influences on, 282
Asmodeus, 242
Assyrian and Babylonian religion, 120
Babylonian Talmud, 15
Babylonian devil trap, 115
Balaam, 105
Bali, 135
bathing, 236
bees, 136
Bell, Book, and Candle, 187

Bible, 64
    references in spells to, 138
birthmark, removal of, 164
Black Mass, 264
bleeding, a spell to stop, 345
blood, 46
    names written in, 206
brazen head, 325
breaking spells, 146
Buddhist protection, 117
burn charm, 147
burns, cures for, 157
butter, 36
cálusari, 136
candle spell, removal of, 141
candles, and prayers and spells, 25
"Casting the Runes," (James, M.R.), 354
casting spells, 54
cat's blood, 144
caul, 154
changelings, prevention of
    kidnapping by, 146

Chango Macho, 249
Christian prayer, 23
Clavicle, equipment for the magic
    of, 181
clothes, 148
coins, lucky and unlucky, 176
Congo, magic of, 299
conjuration, 93
cows, 158
    medicine for, 216
crops, blasting of, 55
cursed kiss, 98
curses, dramas about, 335
dead (people), 119
    burial of, 293
Della Mirandola, Pico, 104
demon invocation, 35
demons, incense and, 235
    invocation of, 231
    protection against, 171
devil, breaking pacts with, 164
    making a pact with, 242, 332
disease, demons of, 126
dispelling spells, 55
divination, rituals for, of Santería,
    268
divinidae, 95
Dixie (Southern U.S.), supersti-
    tions of, 136
Don Demonio, 339
drums, 202
dwarfs, magical, production of,
    277
elixir of life, 223
elves, 36
enemies, beating by magic, 71
enemy, how to bring evil upon, 87
    how to drive away, 60
    injuring an, 43

evil eye, 146
    spell against, 27
exorcisms, 152
    early rite of Christian church,
    281
faerie rituals, 314
"fairy–struck", 125
fairytales and folktales, 323
fever, Irish spell for, 28
fingernails, 121
Finns, magic of, 343
Flying Dutchman, 335
folk festivals, rituals of, 258
folkore, American, 351
four-leaf clover, praying over, 26
Freemasons, secret ceremony of,
    249
Friday, and luck ("Thank God
    It's")
frostbite, prevention of, 47
future, fortelling of, 51
garlic, slayer of monsters, 128
gems, magical, 191, 196
German–American spells, 374
Ghost Dance, 257
ghosts, banishment of, 59
ghouls, curse on, 107
goddess, religion of, 352
    rites of, 308
Golden Dawn, rites of the order
    of, 305
Gordons, 87
Halloween spells, 53
hands, how to make someone's
    burn, 92
hare, turning oneself into, 42
hatred, witchcraft spell of, 32
herbs, 129
Hinduism, 248

Hispanic magic, 82
Holy Spirit, Mass of, 266
honey, 228
horoscopes, Chinese, 186
horse whisperer, 37
horseshoes, 86
houses, curses of, 102
hugvending, 319
hunting, magic in, 15, 250
hypnotism, protection from, 48
I benandanti, 103
impotence, 88
incantations, ancient, 19
infertility, cure for, 123, 161
inquisition, true story from, 327
intercession of saints, 165
Internet *see* Kiva, 248
invisibility, 234
    recipe for, 59
invulnerability, 155
Irish cures, 122
Jannes, 104
Jesus, Sacred Heart of, 170
juvenile delinquency, ritual to
    straighten out, 275
kapu, 90
karma, 90
killing, (recipe for), 218
knocking on wood, 126
La Celestina, 342
Lapplanders, magic of, 343
lipstick, 122
loneliness, cure for, 156
love spells, Celtic, 39
love philtres, 229, 338
love–making, 37
Lucifer, 304
Lull, Raymond, 78
madness, Irish spell for, 29

magic candle, 198
magic circle, 179
magical environment, 24
magic rituals, current day, 239
magic square, 178
magical thinking, 161
making passes, 17
Mambres, 104
Mandragora, 215
marriage, 27
masks, 201
memory, cure for poor, 157
Midewewin, 143
moonlight, 49
Mylor, Saint, 73
Naropa, ritual from, 306
nawales, 104
necromancy, 227, 295
    ritual book of, 296
Ninevah, incantation recorded at,
    19
Norwegian peasants, spells of, 29
oils, magical, 213, 214
omens, literature of, 346
Orion, invocation of, 275
Ouanga (voodoo doll), ritual of,
    273
pagan ritual for Beltane, 310
Paracelsus, 58
Pergamon, diving disc from,
    245
pointing the finger, 18
poppets, 232
potions, obtaining materials for,
    212
Powder of Sympathy, 217
power in objects, 97
prayers, 20
    oldest in the world, 21

prescriptions, written for diseases, 118
priesthood, ordination of, 260
protective herbs, 189
psalter, 145
pygmy spell to protect against a fallen elephant, 16
rabies, cure for, 135
rain, 26
redheads, 130
relics, 131
religion of the White Cloth, 252
removing a curse, 102
resguardos, 131
Ring of Gyges, 194
rings, magical, 194
Roman Empire, laws of, 16
rusalkas, 49
sabbat, 304
sage, 118
Sagensprecher, 45
satanic child abuse, 263
scapegoat, 151
scrying, 225
Seal of Shabako, 175
séances, 269
Sephiroth, 30
Shroud of Besançon, 184
snake balls, 134
soul, escape of, 282
spells, removal of, 141
spiral dance, 308
spit, 234
St.-Sécare, Mass of, 266
success, 234
suitor, casting a spell on, 18
symbolism in a magic dance, 256
taboo, undoing punishment for breaking, 15
Talisman of the Sun, 174

Talisman, the, 177
talismans, 168
black magic conjuration with, 298
Tara, legend of, 330
teenage lust, love ritual for, 314
tempatungs, 203
Tibetan magic, 205
tinnitus, 147
tobacco, 190
toothache, cure for, 116
two-dollar bill, 69
vinegar, 225
voodoo, degradation at death of a worshipper of, 285
in literature, 352
initiation, 272
in New Orleans, 283
priestesses of, 58
walking on water, 43
Wandering Jew, 73
war, declaration of, 104
protection in, 121
Wenceslaus, King, 151
white magic, 60
wine, 118
Wisdome of Doctor Dodypoll, The, 328
witch ball, 161
witch's killing method, 212
witchcraft, cures by cures of, 149
witchcraft, Elizabethan law against, 66
witches, flying, 24
witches, identification of, 109
witches ointment, 210
wounds, Irish spells for, 28
Yiddish remarks on luck, 334
zombie, creation of, 220